SOMETHING ABOUT THE AUTHOR

ISSN 0276-816X

SOMETHING ABOUT THE AUTHOR

Facts and Pictures about Authors
and Illustrators of Books for Young People

EDITED BY
ANNE COMMIRE

VOLUME 41

GALE RESEARCH COMPANY
BOOK TOWER
DETROIT, MICHIGAN
48226

Editor: Anne Commire

Associate Editors: Agnes Garrett, Helga P. McCue

Senior Assistant Editor: Joyce Nakamura

Assistant Editors: Dianne H. Anderson, Linda Shedd, Cynthia J. Walker

Sketchwriters: Rachel Koenig, Eunice L. Petrini

Researcher: Kathleen Betsko

Editorial Assistants: Lisa Bryon, Carolyn Kline, Elisa Ann Sawchuk

Permissions Assistant: Susan Pfanner

Production Director: Carol Blanchard

External Senior Production Associate: Mary Beth Trimper

External Production Associate: Dorothy Kalleberg

Internal Production Associate: Louise Gagné

Internal Senior Production Assistant: Sandy Rock

Layout Artist: Elizabeth Lewis Patryjak

Art Director: Arthur Chartow

Special acknowledgment is due to the members of the *Contemporary Authors* staff
who assisted in the preparation of this volume.

Publisher: Frederick G. Ruffner

Executive Vice-President/Editorial: James M. Ethridge

Editorial Director: Dedria Bryfonski

Director, Literature Division: Christine Nasso

Senior Editor, Something about the Author: Adele Sarkissian

Library of Congress Catalog Card Number 72-27107

ISBN 0-8103-2251-X

ISSN 0276-816X

Computerized photocomposition by
Typographics, Incorporated
Kansas City, Missouri

Printed in the United States

Contents

Contents

Introduction

As the only ongoing reference series that deals with the lives and works of authors and illustrators of children's books, *Something about the Author (SATA)* is a unique source of information. The *SATA* series includes not only well-known authors and illustrators whose books are most widely read, but also those less prominent people whose works are just coming to be recognized. *SATA* is often the only readily available information source for less well-known writers or artists. You'll find *SATA* informative and entertaining whether you are:

—a student in junior high school (or perhaps one to two grades higher or lower) who needs information for a book report or some other assignment for an English class;

—a children's librarian who is searching for the answer to yet another question from a young reader or collecting background material to use for a story hour;

—an English teacher who is drawing up an assignment for your students or gathering information for a book talk;

—a student in a college of education or library science who is studying children's literature and reference sources in the field;

—a parent who is looking for a new way to interest your child in reading something more than the school curriculum prescribes;

—an adult who enjoys children's literature for its own sake, knowing that a good children's book has no age limits.

Scope

In *SATA* you will find detailed information about authors and illustrators who span the full time range of children's literature, from early figures like John Newbery and L. Frank Baum to contemporary figures like Judy Blume and Richard Peck. Authors in the series represent primarily English-speaking countries, particularly the United States, Canada, and the United Kingdom. Also included, however, are authors from around the world whose works are available in English translation, for example: from France, Jean and Laurent De Brunhoff; from Italy, Emanuele Luzzati; from the Netherlands, Jaap ter Haar; from Germany, James Krüss; from Norway, Babbis Friis-Baastad; from Japan, Toshiko Kanzawa; from the Soviet Union, Kornei Chukovsky; from Switzerland, Alois Carigiet, to name only a few. Also appearing in *SATA* are Newbery medalists from Hendrik Van Loon (1922) to Robin McKinley (1985). The writings represented in *SATA* include those created intentionally for children and young adults as well as those written for a general audience and known to interest younger readers. These writings cover the spectrum from picture books, humor, folk and fairy tales, animal stories, mystery and adventure, science fiction and fantasy, historical fiction, poetry and nonsense verse, to drama, biography, and nonfiction.

Information Features

In *SATA* you will find full-length entries that are being presented in the series for the first time. This volume, for example, marks the first full-length appearance of Nicola Bayley, Phyllis Rose Eisenberg, Fred Gwynne, Winsor McCay, Walter Dean Myers, Jerry Pinkney, Reynold Ruffins, Ruth Sanderson, and Sue Tarsky, among others. Since Volume 25, each *SATA* volume also includes newly revised and updated biographies for a selection of early *SATA* listees who remain of interest to today's readers and who have been active enough to require extensive revision of their earlier entries. The entry for a given biographee may be revised as often as there is substantial new information to provide. In Volume 41 you'll find revised entries for Gyozo Ambrus, Clyde Robert Bulla, Crescent Dragonwagon, Tove Jansson, William Bartlett Peet, and Jay Williams.

Brief Entries, first introduced in Volume 27, are another regular feature of *SATA*. Brief Entries present essentially the same types of information found in a full entry but do so in a capsule form and without illustration. These entries are intended to give you useful and timely information while the more time-consuming process of compiling a full-length biography is in progress. In this volume you'll find Brief Entries for Tom Batey, Caroline B. Cooney, Shirley Gordon, Nancy Jewell, Deborah Ann Kent, Claudia Mills, Stephen Roos, Patti Stren, and Don Arthur Torgersen, among others.

Obituaries have been included in *SATA* since Volume 20. An Obituary is intended not only as a death notice but also as a concise view of a person's life and work. Obituaries may appear for persons who have entries in earlier *SATA* volumes, as well as for people who have not yet appeared in the series. In this volume Obituaries mark the recent deaths of Wyatt Rainey Blassingame, David H. Dietz, Maxwell Nurnberg, Elizabeth Rider Montgomery, Amabel Williams-Ellis, and others.

Each *SATA* volume provides a cumulative index in two parts: first, the Illustrations Index, arranged by the name of the illustrator, gives the number of the volume and page where the illustrator's work appears in the current volume as well as all preceding volumes in the series; second, the Author Index gives the number of the volume in which a person's biographical sketch, Brief Entry, or Obituary appears in the current volume as well as all preceding volumes in the series. These indexes also include references to authors and illustrators who appear in *Yesterday's Authors of Books for Children*. Beginning with Volume 36, the *SATA* Author Index provides cross-references to authors who are included in *Children's Literature Review*.

Illustrations

While the textual information in *SATA* is its primary reason for existing, photographs and illustrations not only enliven the text but are an integral part of the information that *SATA* provides. Illustrations and text are wedded in such a special way in children's literature that artists and their works naturally occupy a prominent place among *SATA*'s listees. The illustrators that you'll find in the series include such past masters of children's book illustration as Randolph Caldecott, Kate Greenaway, Walter Crane, Arthur Rackham, and Ernest L. Shepard, as well as such noted contemporary artists as Maurice Sendak, Edward Gorey, Tomie de Paola, and Margot Zemach. There are Caldecott medalists from Dorothy Lathrop (the first recipient in 1938) to Trina Schart Hyman (the latest winner in 1985); cartoonists like Charles Schulz, ("Peanuts"), Walt Kelly ("Pogo"), Hank Ketcham ("Dennis the Menace"), and Georges Rémi ("Tintin"); photographers like Jill Krementz, Tana Hoban, Bruce McMillan, and Bruce Curtis; and filmmakers like Walt Disney, Alfred Hitchcock, and Steven Spielberg.

In more than a dozen years of recording the metamorphosis of children's literature from the printed page to other media, *SATA* has become something of a repository of photographs that are unique in themselves and exist nowhere else as a group, particularly many of the classics of motion picture and stage history and photographs that have been specially loaned to us from private collections.

What a *SATA* Entry Provides

Whether you're already familiar with the *SATA* series or just getting acquainted, you will want to be aware of the kind of information that an entry provides. In every *SATA* entry the editors attempt to give as complete a picture of the person's life and work as possible. In some cases that full range of information may simply be unavailable, or a biographee may choose not to reveal complete personal details. The information that the editors attempt to provide in every entry is arranged in the following categories:

1. The "head" of the entry gives

—the most complete form of the name,
—any part of the name not commonly used, included in parentheses,
—birth and death dates, if known; a (?) indicates a discrepancy in published sources,
—pseudonyms or name variants under which the person has had books published or is publicly known, in parentheses in the second line.

2. "Personal" section gives

—date and place of birth and death,
—parents' names and occupations,

　　　　—name of spouse, date of marriage, and names of children,
　　　　—educational institutions attended, degrees received, and dates,
　　　　—religious and political affiliations,
　　　　—agent's name and address,
　　　　—home and/or office address.

3. "Career" section gives

　　　　—name of employer, position, and dates for each career post,
　　　　—military service,
　　　　—memberships,
　　　　—awards and honors.

4. "Writings" section gives

　　　　—title, first publisher and date of publication, and illustration information for each book written; revised editions and other significant editions for books with particularly long publishing histories; genre, when known.

5. "Adaptations" section gives

　　　　—title, major performers, producer, and date of all known reworkings of an author's material in another medium, like movies, filmstrips, television, recordings, plays, etc.

6. "Sidelights" section gives

　　　　—commentary on the life or work of the biographee either directly from the person (and often written specifically for the *SATA* entry), or gathered from biographies, diaries, letters, interviews, or other published sources.

7. "For More Information See" section gives

　　　　—books, feature articles, films, plays, and reviews in which the biographee's life or work has been treated.

How a *SATA* Entry Is Compiled

A *SATA* entry progresses through a series of steps. If the biographee is living, the *SATA* editors try to secure information directly from him or her through a questionnaire. From the information that the biographee supplies, the editors prepare an entry, filling in any essential missing details with research. The author or illustrator is then sent a copy of the entry to check for accuracy and completeness.

If the biographee is deceased or cannot be reached by questionnaire, the *SATA* editors examine a wide variety of published sources to gather information for an entry. Biographical sources are searched with the aid of Gale's *Biography and Genealogy Master Index*. Bibliographic sources like the *National Union Catalog*, the *Cumulative Book Index*, *American Book Publishing Record*, and the *British Museum Catalogue* are consulted, as are book reviews, feature articles, published interviews, and material sometimes obtained from the biographee's family, publishers, agent, or other associates.

For each entry presented in *SATA*, the editors also attempt to locate a photograph of the biographee as well as representative illustrations from his or her books. After surveying the available books which the biographee has written and/or illustrated, and then making a selection of appropriate photographs and illustrations, the editors request permission of the current copyright holders to reprint the material. In the case of older books for which the copyright may have passed through several hands, even locating the current copyright holder is often a long and involved process.

We invite you to examine the entire *SATA* series, starting with this volume. Described below are some of the people in Volume 41 that you may find particularly interesting.

Highlights of This Volume

EDGAR RICE BURROUGHS......author and creator of "Tarzan." Since the publication of *Tarzan of the*

Apes in 1914, Burroughs's legendary ape-man has swung his way through more than twenty adventures, as well as countless movie adaptations. Although Burroughs contended that *Tarzan of the Apes* was not written primarily for children," he added, "possibly the greatest pleasure...has come through the knowledge...that I have given them a character, however improbable he may seem, that will set for them a higher standard of manliness, integrity and sportsmanship." In addition to Tarzan stories like *The Son of Tarzan* and *Tarzan and the Lost Empire,* Burroughs wrote nearly fifty books of science fiction and adventure, including *The People That Time Forgot, A Princess of Mars,* and *At the Earth's Core.*

TOVE JANSSON......Finnish artist, author, and illustrator. Jansson is known for her "Moomintroll" books featuring gentle, hippopotamus-like creatures born out of her childhood memories. "I let the trolls experience my own happy summers," she reflects, "or maybe I experience theirs, take it how you will." Jansson has won many awards for her books, including the Hans Christian Andersen Medal. To her, writing and illustrating are *not* means to the same end: "When I illustrate my stories I never get this feeling I have when I write, of walking in a strange world that was my own long ago.... Illustrations are simply an attempt at explaining what I have perhaps failed to express in words." Her special Moomintroll world is revealed to children in titles like *The Happy Moomins, Moominland Midwinter, Tales from Moomin-valley,* and *Moominpappa at Sea.*

GEORGE MENDOZA......an author who remembers spending many childhood days alone at sea on his rebuilt sloop. "I had to find my own strengths," he recalls. "I was able to discover them through the sea, through the days of sea songs, seagulls, tides and stars." Not surprisingly, Mendoza's first book, *And Amadeo Asked, How Does One Become a Man?,* was written about a boy's sea-going adventure. Through the years, Mendoza has produced over sixty children's stories and poems, like *The Puma and the Pearl, And I Must Hurry for the Sea Is Coming In, The Hunter I Might Have Been, Lost Pony,* and *Need a House? Call Ms. Mouse!* He admits to being a compulsive writer: "I feel that I *must* write...or else be punished. It will be more painful *not* to write than to write.... Through writing, I find the *juste milieu."*

FREDERIC REMINGTON......American painter, illustrator, sculptor, and writer whose first-hand observations of life in the Old West have made his name synonymous with that era. Remington traveled West in 1881 at the age of nineteen, making his way as a cowboy, scout, sheep rancher, and stockman. Through paintings, illustrations, and bronze sculptures, he forever preserved images of a lifestyle that was disappearing even as he recorded it. "I knew the railroad was coming...," he wrote. "I knew the wild riders and the vacant land were about to vanish forever.... I saw the living, breathing end of three American centuries of smoke and dust and sweat...." Remington's undying fascination with the last vestiges of the American frontier is evident in books like his *Pony Tracks, Crooked Trails,* and *The Way of an Indian.*

ANN TAYLOR and JANE TAYLOR......who jointly wrote children's verse that has endured for more than a century. The Taylor sisters belonged to an artistic and literary family known as "The Taylors of Ongar." Educated at home, Ann and Jane began writing poetry when they were very young. Their first published volume appeared under the title *Original Poems for Infant Minds.* Their second volume, *Rhymes for the Nursery,* contained Jane's most famous poem, "The Star," which begins: "Twinkle, twinkle, little star...." The Taylor sisters' poetical collaboration spanned more than twelve years. During that time they produced nearly a dozen volumes of verse, including *Rural Scences; or, A Peep into the Country, Limed Twigs to Catch Young Birds,* and *Signor Topsy-Turvy's Wonderful Magic Lantern; or, The World Turned Upside Down.*

These are only a few of the authors and illustrators that you'll find in this volume. We hope you find all the entries in *SATA* both interesting and useful. Please write and tell us if we can make *SATA* even more helpful for you.

Forthcoming Authors

A Partial List of Authors and Illustrators Who Will Appear in Forthcoming Volumes of *Something about the Author*

Abels, Harriette S.
Allard, Harry
Allen, Agnes B. 1898-1959
Allen, Jeffrey 1948-
Anders, Rebecca
Anderson, Leone C. 1923-
Andrist, Ralph K. 1914-
Appleby, Ellen
Ardley, Neil (Richard) 1937-
Austin, R. G.
Axeman, Lois
Ayme, Marcel 1902-1967
Bains, Rae
Baker, Olaf
Balderson, Margaret 1935-
Barkin, Carol
Bartlett, Margaret F. 1896-
Barton, Harriett
Bassett, Jeni 1960(?)-
Bauer, Caroline Feller 1935-
Bauer, John Albert 1882-1918
Beckman, Delores
Beim, Jerrold 1910-1957
Beim, Lorraine 1909-1951
Bernheim, Evelyne 1935-
Bernheim, Marc 1924-
Betancourt, Jeanne 1941-
Birnbaum, Abe 1899-
Bloom, Lloyd
Boegehold, Betty 1913-1985
Boning, Richard A.
Bonners, Susan
Bourke, Linda
Bowen, Gary
Bracken, Carolyn
Brewton, Sara W.
Bridgman, Elizabeth P. 1921-
Bromley, Dudley 1948-
Bronin, Andrew 1947-
Bronson, Wilfrid 1894-
Brooks, Ron(ald George) 1948-
Brown, Roy Frederick 1921-
Brownmiller, Susan 1935-
Buchanan, William 1930-
Buchenholz, Bruce
Budney, Blossom 1921-
Burchard, Marshall
Burke, David 1927-
Burstein, Chaya M.
Butler, Dorothy 1925-
Butler, Hal 1913-
Calvert, Patricia
Camps, Luis 1928-
Carley, Wayne

Carlson, Nancy L.
Carrie, Christopher
Carris, Joan D. 1938-
Carroll, Ruth R. 1899-
Cauley, Lorinda B. 1951-
Chang, Florence C.
Charles, Carole
Charles, Donald 1929-
Chartier, Normand
Chase, Catherine
Chessare, Michele
Cline, Linda 1941-
Cohen, Joel H.
Cole, Brock
Cooper, Elizabeth Keyser 1910-
Cooper, Paulette 1944-
Cosgrove, Margaret 1926-
Coutant, Helen
Dabcovich, Lydia
D'Aulnoy, Marie-Catherine 1650(?)-1705
David, Jay 1929-
Davies, Peter 1937-
Davis, Maggie S. 1942-
Dawson, Diane
Dean, Leigh
Degens, T.
Deguine, Jean-Claude 1943-
Dentinger, Don
Deweese, Gene 1934-
Ditmars, Raymond 1876-1942
Drescher, Henrik
Dumas, Philippe 1940-
East, Ben
Edelson, Edward 1932-
Edens, Cooper
Edwards, Linda S.
Eisenberg, Lisa
Elder, Lauren
Elwood, Roger 1943-
Endres, Helen
Eriksson, Eva
Erwin, Betty K.
Etter, Les 1904-
Everett-Green, Evelyn 1856-1932
Falkner, John Meade 1858-1932
Fender, Kay
Filson, Brent
Fischer, Hans Erich 1909-1958
Flanagan, Geraldine Lux
Flint, Russ
Folch-Ribas, Jacques 1928-
Foley, Louise M. 1933-
Fox, Thomas C.

Freschet, Berniece 1927-
Frevert, Patricia D(endtler) 1943-
Funai, Mamoru R. 1932-
Gans, Roma 1894-
Garcia Sanchez, J(ose) L(uis)
Garrison, Christian 1942-
Gathje, Curtis
Gelman, Rita G. 1937-
Gemme, Leila Boyle 1942-
Gerber, Dan 1940-
Goldstein, Nathan 1927-
Gould, Chester 1900-1985
Graeber, Charlotte Towner
Greenberg, Polly 1932-
Gregory, Diana 1933-
Grimm, Cherry Barbara 1930-
Gross, Alan 1947-
Gutman, Bill
Haas, Dorothy F.
Harris, Marilyn 1931-
Hayman, LeRoy 1916-
Healey, Larry 1927-
Heine, Helme 1941-
Henty, George Alfred 1832-1902
Herzig, Alison Cragin
Hicks, Clifford B. 1920-
Higashi, Sandra
Hockerman, Dennis
Hollander, Zander 1923-
Hood, Thomas 1779-1845
Howell, Troy
Hull, Jessie Redding
Hunt, Clara Whitehill 1871-1958
Hunt, Robert
Inderieden, Nancy
Irvine, Georgeanne
Iwamura, Kazuo 1939-
Jackson, Anita
Jackson, Kathryn 1907-
Jackson, Robert 1941-
Jacobs, Francine 1935-
Jameson, Cynthia
Janssen, Pierre
Jaspersohn, William
Johnson, Harper
Johnson, Maud
Johnson, Sylvia A.
Jukes, Mavis
Kahn, Joan 1914-
Kalan, Robert
Kantrowitz, Mildred
Kasuya, Masahiro 1937-
Keith, Eros 1942-
Kirn, Ann (Minette) 1910-

13

Koenig, Marion
Kohl, Herbert   1937-
Kohl, Judith
Kramer, Anthony
Kredenser, Gail   1936-
Kurland, Michael   1938-
Lawson, Annetta
Leach, Christopher   1925-
Lebrun, Claude
Leckie, Robert   1920-
Leder, Dora
Le-Tan, Pierre   1950-
Lewis, Naomi
Lindgren, Barbro
Lindman, Maj (Jan)
Lines, Kathleen
Livermore, Elaine
Lye, Keith
MacKinstry, Elizabeth   (?)-1956
Mali, Jane Lawrence
Marks, Burton   1930-
Marks, Rita   1938-
Marron, Carol A.
Marryat, Frederick   1792-1848
Marsh, Carole
Martin, Dorothy   1921-
Marxhausen, Joanne G.   1935-
May, Dorothy
Mayakovsky, Vladimir   1894-1930
McKim, Audrey Margaret   1909-
McLoughlin, John C.   1949-
McReynolds, Ginny
Melcher, Frederic G.   1879-1963
Miller, J(ohn) P.   1919-
Molesworth, Mary L.   1839(?)-1921
Molly, Anne S.   1907-
Moore, Lilian
Moskowitz, Stewart
Muntean, Michaela
Murdocca, Sal
Nickl, Peter
Nicoll, Helen
Obligado, Lillian Isabel   1931-
Odor, Ruth S.   1926-
Oppenheim, Shulamith (Levey)   1930-
Orr, Frank   1936-
Orton, Helen Fuller   1872-1955
Overbeck, Cynthia

Owens, Gail   1939-
Packard, Edward   1931-
Parker, Robert Andrew   1927-
Paterson, A(ndrew) B(arton)   1864-1941
Patterson, Sarah   1959-
Pavey, Peter
Pelgrom, Els
Peretz, Isaac Loeb   1851-1915
Perkins, Lucy Fitch   1865-1937
Petersen, P(eter) J(ames)   1941-
Peterson, Jeanne Whitehouse   1939-
Phillips, Betty Lou
Plowden, David   1932-
Plume, Ilse
Poignant, Axel
Pollock, Bruce   1945-
Pollock, Penny   1935-
Polushkin, Maria
Porter, Eleanor Hodgman   1868-1920
Poulsson, Emilie   1853-1939
Powers, Richard M.   1921-
Prager, Arthur
Prather, Ray
Pursell, Margaret S.
Pursell, Thomas F.
Pyle, Katharine   1863-1938
Rabinowitz, Solomon   1859-1916
Rappoport, Ken   1935-
Reese, Bob
Reich, Hanns
Reid, Alistair   1926-
Reidel, Marlene
Reiff, Tana
Reiss, Elayne
Reynolds, Marjorie   1903-
Robert, Adrian
Rohmer, Harriet
Rosier, Lydia
Ross, Pat
Roy, Cal
Rudstrom, Lennart
Sadler, Marilyn
Satchwell, John
Schneider, Leo   1916-
Sealy, Adrienne V.
Seidler, Rosalie
Shea, George   1940-
Silbert, Linda P.

Slepian, Jan(ice B.)
Smith, Alison
Smith, Betsy Corington   1937-
Smith, Catriona (Mary)   1948-
Smith, Ray(mond Kenneth)   1949-
Smollin, Michael J.
Steiner, Charlotte
Stevens, Leonard A.   1920-
Stine, R. Conrad   1937-
Stubbs, Joanna   1940-
Sullivan, Mary Beth
Suteev, Vladimir Grigor'evich
Sutherland, Robert D.   1937-
Sutton, Jane   1950-
Sweet, Ozzie
Thaler, Mike
Thomas, Ianthe   1951-
Timmermans, Gommaar   1930-
Todd, Ruthven   1914-
Tourneur, Dina K.   1934-
Treadgold, Mary   1910-
Velthuijs, Max   1923-
Villiard, Paul   1910-1974
Vincent, Gabrielle
Wagner, Jenny
Walker, Charles W.
Walsh, Anne Batterberry
Walter, Mildred P.
Watts, Franklin   1904-1978
Wayne, Bennett
Weston, Martha
Whelen, Gloria   1923-
White, Wallace   1930-
Wild, Jocelyn
Wild, Robin
Winter, Paula   1929-
Winterfeld, Henry   1901-
Wolde, Gunilla   1939-
Wong, Herbert H.
Woolfolk, Dorothy
Wormser, Richard   1908-
Wright, Betty R.
Wright, Bob
Yagawa, Sumiko
Youldon, Gillian
Zaslow, David
Zistel, Era
Zwerger, Lisbeth

In the interest of making *Something about the Author* as responsive as possible to the needs of its readers, the editor welcomes your suggestions for additional authors and illustrators to be included in the series.

Acknowledgments

Grateful acknowledgment is made to the following publishers, authors, and artists for their kind permission to reproduce copyrighted material.

ABINGDON PRESS. Illustration by Val Biro from *100 Bible Stories,* retold by Norman J. Bull. Copyright © 1980 by The Hamlyn Publishing Group Ltd. Reprinted by permission of Abingdon Press.

HARRY N. ABRAMS, INC. Illustration by Norman Rockwell from *Norman Rockwell's Americana ABC* by George Mendoza. Copyright © 1975 by Harry N. Abrams, Inc. Illustrations copyright © by Curtis Publishing Co. Reprinted by permission of Harry N. Abrams, Inc.

ADDISON-WESLEY PUBLISHING CO., INC. Illustration by True Kelley from *Let's Give Kitty a Bath!* by Steven Lindblom. Text copyright © 1982 by Steven Lindblom. Illustrations copyright © 1982 by True Kelley. Reprinted by permission of Addison-Wesley Publishing Co., Inc.

AMERICAN LIBRARY ASSOCIATION. Sidelight excerpts from *British Children's Authors,* edited by Cornelia Jones and Olivia R. Way. Copyright © 1976 by American Library Association. Reprinted by permission of American Library Association.

AMERICAN WEST PUBLISHING CO. Sidelight excerpts from *My Dear Wister: The Frederic Remington-Owen Wister Letters.* Copyright © 1972 by American West Publishing Co. Reprinted by permission of American West Publishing Co.

ARIEL BOOKS. Illustration by Ruth Sanderson from *Heidi* by Johanna Spyri. Copyright © 1984 by The Tempest Co. Reprinted by permission of Ariel Books.

ATHENEUM PUBLISHERS. Jacket painting by Sarah E. Edgar from *Footfalls* by Elizabeth Harlan. Copyright © 1982 by Elizabeth Harlan./ Illustration by Ruth Sanderson from *The Season of Silence* by Mary Francis Shura. Copyright © 1976 by Mary Francis Shura./ Illustration by Ruth Sanderson from *Don't Hurt Laurie!* by Willo Davis Roberts. Copyright © 1977 by Willo Davis Roberts./ Jacket illustration by Neil Feigeles from *Earth Song* by Sharon Webb. Text copyright © 1983 by Sharon Webb. Illustrations copyright © 1983 by Neil Feigeles. All reprinted by permission of Atheneum Publishers.

AVON BOOKS. Illustrations by Tove Jansson from *Moominland Midwinter* by Tove Jansson. Translated by Thomas Warburton. Copyright © by Tove Jansson. English translation copyright © 1958 by Ernest Benn Ltd./ Cover illustration by Norman Walker from *The Executioner* by Jay Bennett. Copyright © 1982 by Jay Bennett. All reprinted by permission of Avon Books.

ERNEST BENN LTD. Illustration by Tove Jansson from *The Exploits of Moominpappa* by Tove Jansson. Translated by Thomas Warburton./ Illustration by Tove Jansson from *Tales from Moominvalley* by Tove Jansson. Translated by Thomas Warburton. Copyright © by Tove Jansson. English translation copyright © 1963 by Ernest Benn Ltd. All reprinted by permission of Ernest Benn Ltd.

THE BODLEY HEAD LTD. Illustration by Victor Ambrus from *The Song of Caedmon* by Arthur Scholey. Music by Donald Swann. Text copyright © 1971 by Arthur Scholey. Music copyright © 1971 by Donald Swann. Reprinted by permission of The Bodley Head Ltd.

BOUNTY BOOKS. Illustration by Frederic Remington from *The Song of Hiawatha* by Henry Wadsworth Longfellow. Copyright © 1982 by Crown Publishers, Inc. Reprinted by permission of Bounty Books.

CAMELOT PUBLISHING CO., INC. Illustration from *Some People Just Won't Believe a Computer* by Donald D. Spencer. Copyright © 1978 by Camelot Publishing Co., Inc. Reprinted by permission of Camelot Publishing Co., Inc.

JONATHAN CAPE LTD. Illustration by Wayne Anderson from "The Christmas Country," in *The Magic Inkstand, and Other Stories* by Heinrich Seidel. Translated by Elizabeth Watson Taylor. Translation copyright © 1982 by Elizabeth Watson Taylor. Illustrations copyright © 1982 by Wayne Anderson. Reprinted by permission of Jonathan Cape Ltd.

CAROLRHODA BOOKS, INC. Illustration by Nancy L. Carlson from *Halloween* by Joyce K. Kessel. Copyright © 1980 by Carolrhoda Books, Inc./ Illustration by Karen Ritz from *Valentine's Day* by Joyce K. Kessel. Copyright © 1981 by Carolrhoda Books, Inc. Both reprinted by permission of Carolrhoda Books, Inc.

CHELSEA PUBLISHING CO., INC. Editorial cartoon by Winsor McCay from *The World Encyclopedia of Cartoons,* Volume I, edited by Maurice Horn. Copyright © 1980 by Maurice Horn and Chelsea House Publishers. Reprinted by permission of Chelsea Publishing Co., Inc.

WILLIAM COLLINS PUBLISHERS, INC. Jacket illustration by Allen Davis from *First Offender* by Michael Harrah. Copyright © 1980 by Michael Harrah. Reprinted by permission of William Collins Publishers, Inc.

COWARD, McCANN & GEOGHEGAN, INC. Illustration by Jerry Pinkney from *Apples on a Stick: The Folklore of Black Children,* collected and edited by Barbara Michels and Bettye White. Text copyright © 1983 by Barbara Michels and Betteye White. Illustrations copyright © 1983 by Jerry Pinkney./ Jacket illustration by Jerry Pinkney from *Rainbow Jordan* by Alice Childress. Both reprinted by permission of Coward, McCann & Geoghegan, Inc.

CROWELL-COLLIER. Illustration by Jo Polseno from *To Catch a Bird* by Jay Williams. Copyright © 1968 by Jay Williams. Reprinted by permission of Crowell-Collier.

THOMAS Y. CROWELL, INC. Illustration by Ronald Himler from *Conquista!* by Clyde Robert Bulla and Michael Syson. Copyright © 1978 by Clyde Robert Bulla and Michael Syson./ Illustration by Leonard Weisgard from *White Bird* by Clyde Robert Bulla. Copyright © 1966 by Clyde Robert Bulla./ Illustrations by Ruth Sanderson from *The Beast of Lor* by Clyde Robert Bulla. Copyright © 1977 by Clyde Robert Bulla./ Illustration by Chris Conover from *The Wish at the Top* by Clyde Robert Bulla. Text copyright © 1974 by Clyde Robert Bulla. Illustrations copyright © 1974 by Chris Conover./ Illustration by Michele Chessare from *The Cardboard Crown* by Clyde Robert Bulla. Text copyright © 1984 by Clyde Robert Bulla. Illustrations copyright © 1984 by Michele Chessare./ Illustration by Trina Schart Hyman from *The Moon Singer* by Clyde Robert Bulla. Text copyright © 1969 by Clyde Robert Bulla. Illustrations copyright © 1969 by Trina Schart Hyman./ Illustration by Judy Glasser from *Mr. Radagast Makes an Unexpected Journey* by Sharon Nastick. Text copyright © 1981 by Sharon Nastick. Illustrations copyright © 1981 by Judy Glasser./ Illustration by Jerry Pinkney from *Mary McLeod Bethune* by Eloise Greenfield. Text copyright © 1977 by Eloise Greenfield. Illustrations copyright © 1977 by Jerry Pinkney./ Illustration by Jerry Pinkney from *Childtimes: A Three-Generation Memoir* by Eloise Greenfield and Lessie Jones Little. Copyright © 1971 by Pattie Ridley Jones./ Illustration by Reynold Ruffins from *Camels: Ships of the Desert* by John F. Waters. Text copyright © 1974 by John F. Waters. Illustrations copyright © 1974 by Reynold Ruffins./ Illustration by Satomi Ichikawa from *Keep Running, Allen!* by Clyde Robert Bulla. Text copyright © 1978 by Clyde Robert Bulla. Illustrations copyright © 1978 by Satomi Ichikawa. All reprinted by permission of Thomas Y. Crowell, Inc.

DELL PUBLISHING CO., INC. Jacket painting by Gary Watson from *Wilhemina Jones, Future Star* by Dindga McCannon. Text copyright © 1980 by Dindga McCannon. Illustrations copyright © 1980 by Gary Watson. Reprinted by permission of Dell Publishing Co., Inc.

ANDRE DEUTSCH LTD. Illustration by Doris Susan Smith from *Need a House? Call Ms. Mouse!* by George Mendoza. Copyright © 1981 by Grosset & Dunlap, Inc. and Librairie Ernest Flammarion. Reprinted by permission of Andre Deutsch Ltd.

DIAL BOOKS FOR YOUNG READERS. Illustration by Frederic Remington from *Frederic Remington's Own Outdoors* by Frederic Remington. Copyright © 1964 by Douglas Allen./ Jacket illustration by Jerry Pinkney from *Roll of Thunder, Hear My Cry* by Mildred D. Taylor. Copyright © 1976 by Mildred D. Taylor. Reprinted by permission of Dial Books For Young Readers.

DODD, MEAD & CO. Illustration by Susan Bonners from *Spring Peepers Are Calling* by Charlene W. Billings. Text copyright © 1978 by Charlene W. Billings. Illustrations copyright © 1978 by Susan Bonners./ Illustration by Gerald McCann from *Famous Negro Heroes of America* by Langston Hughes. Copyright © 1958 by Langston Hughes./ Photograph by Richard B. McPhee from *Rounds with a Country Vet* by Richard B. McPhee. Copyright © 1977 by Richard B. McPhee. All reprinted by permission of Dodd, Mead & Co.

DOUBLEDAY & CO., INC. Illustration by Victor Ambrus from *The Farthest-Away Mountain* by Lynne Reid Banks. Copyright © 1976 by Lynne Reid Banks./ Illustration by Paul Hogarth from *Majorca Observed* by Robert Graves and Paul Hogarth. Text copyright 1954, © 1955, 1956, 1957, 1965 by International Authors N. V. Illustrations copyright © 1965 by Paul Hogarth./ Illustration by Gahan Wilson from "The Milk Tooth," in *The Good Luck Spider and Other Bad Luck Stories* by George Mendoza. Copyright © 1970 by George Mendoza./ Sidelight excerpts from *Frederic Remington: A Biography* by Peggy and Harold Samuels. Copyright © 1982 by Peggy and Harold Samuels./ Illustration by Frank Frazetta from "A Fighting Man of Mars," in *Master Mind of Mars* by Edgar Rice Burroughs. All reprinted by permission of Doubleday & Co., Inc.

DOVER PUBLICATIONS, INC. Illustration by Winsor McCay from *Dreams of the Rarebit Fiend* by Winsor McCay. Copyright © 1973 by Dover Publications, Inc. Reprinted by permission of Dover Publications, Inc.

E. P. DUTTON, INC. Illustration by Ruth Sanderson from *Into the Dream* by William Sleator. Text copyright © 1979 by William Sleator. Illustrations copyright © 1979 by Ruth Sanderson./ Illustration by Mercer Mayer from "The Skunk in the Pond," in *The Crack in the Wall and Other Terribly Weird Tales* by George Mendoza. Text copyright © 1968 by George Mendoza. Illustrations copyright © 1968 by Mercer Mayer./ Illustration by Jerry Pinkney from "Wastewin and the Beaver," in *Tonweya and the Eagles, and Other Lakota Indian Tales,* retold by Rosebud Yellow Robe. Text copyright © 1979 by Rosebud Yellow Robe Frantz. Illustrations copyright © 1979 by Jerry Pinkney./ Illustration by Jerry Pinkney from *The Patchwork Quilt* by Valerie Flournoy. Text copyright © 1985 by Valerie Flournoy. Illustrations copyright © 1985 by Jerry Pinkney. All reprinted by permission of E. P. Dutton, Inc.

LES EDITIONS LA COURTE ECHELLE. Illustration by Félix Vincent from *Les Saisons* by Raoul Duguay. Text copyright by Raoul Duguay. Illustrations copyright by Félix Vincent. Reprinted by permission of Les Editions La Courte Echelle.

FABER & FABER LTD. Illustration by Jill Bennett from "The Shadow" by Walter de la Mare in *Once Upon a Rhyme: 101 Poems for Young Children,* edited by Sara and Stephen Corrin. Copyright © 1982 by Faber & Faber Ltd. Reprinted by permission of Faber & Faber Ltd.

FARRAR, STRAUS & GIROUX, INC. Illustration by Jamie Wyeth from *The Stray* by Betsy James Wyeth. Text copyright © 1979 by Betsy James Wyeth. Illustrations copyright © 1979 by Jamie Wyeth. Reprinted by permission of Farrar, Straus & Giroux, Inc.

FOUR WINDS PRESS. Illustration by Mercer Mayer from *Everyone Knows What a Dragon Looks Like* by Jay Williams. Text copyright © 1976 by Jay Williams. Illustrations copyright © 1976 by Mercer Mayer./ Illustration by Lucinda McQueen from *The Water of Life* by Jay Williams. Text copyright © 1980 by Barbara G. Williams. Illustrations copyright © 1980 by Lucinda McQueen./ Jacket illustration by Jerry Pinkney from *Ji-Nongo-Nongo Means Riddles* by Verna Aardema./ Illustration by Mercer Mayer from *The Reward Worth Having* by Jay Williams. Text copyright © 1977 by Jay Williams. Illustrations copyright © 1977 by Mercer Mayer. All reprinted by permission of Four Winds Press.

BERNARD GEIS ASSOCIATES, INC. Illustration by Paul Hogarth from *Brendan Behan's New York* by Brendan Behan. Copyright © 1964 by Beatrice Behan and Paul Hogarth. Reprinted by permission of Bernard Geis Associates, Inc.

DAVID R. GODINE, PUBLISHERS, INC. Sidelight excerpts from *A Grain of Wheat: An Autobiography* by Clyde Robert Bulla. Reprinted by permission of David R. Godine, Publishers, Inc.

VICTOR GOLLANCZ LTD. Illustration by Hans Helweg from *Oggy at Home* by Ann Lawrence. Text copyright © 1977 by Ann Lawrence. Illustrations copyright © 1977 by Hans Helweg. Reprinted by permission of Victor Gollancz Ltd.

GROSSET & DUNLAP, INC. Illustration by Norman Rockwell from *Norman Rockwell's Four Seasons* by George Mendoza. Copyright © 1982 by Ruth Diana Mendoza./ Cover illustration by N. C. Wyeth from *The Return of Tarzan* by Edgar Rice Burroughs. Both reprinted by permission of Grosset & Dunlap, Inc.

HARCOURT BRACE JOVANOVICH, INC. Illustration by Stephen Gammell from *Leo Possessed* by Dilys Owen. Text copyright © 1975 by Dilys Owen. Illustrations copyright © 1979 by Harcourt Brace Jovanovich, Inc. Reprinted by permission of Harcourt Brace Jovanovich, Inc.

HARPER & ROW, PUBLISHERS, INC. Jacket illustration by Melanie Willa Winsten from *What's the Matter Girl?* by Elizabeth Brochmann. Copyright © 1980 by Elizabeth Brochmann./ Illustration by Joan Sandin from *Daniel's Duck* by Clyde Robert Bulla. Text copyright © 1979 by Clyde Robert Bulla. Illustrations copyright © 1979 by Joan Sandin./ Illustration by Ronald Himler from *Wind Rose* by Crescent Dragonwagon. Text copyright © 1976 by Crescent Dragonwagon. Illustrations copyright © 1976 by Ronald Himler./ Illustration by Robert Andrew Parker from *When Light Turns into Night* by Crescent Dragonwagon. Text copyright © 1975 by Crescent Dragonwagon. Illustrations copyright © 1975 by Robert Andrew

Parker./ Illustration by Ben Shecter from *Will It Be Okay?* by Crescent Dragonwagon. Text copyright © 1977 by Crescent Dragonwagon. Illustrations copyright © 1977 by Ben Shecter./ Illustration by Dick Gackenbach from *I Hate My Brother Harry* by Crescent Dragonwagon. Text copyright © 1983 by Crescent Dragonwagon. Illustrations copyright © 1983 by Dick Gackenbach./ Illustration by Susan Jeschke from *A Mitzvah Is Something Special* by Phyllis Rose Eisenberg. Text copyright © 1978 by Phyllis Rose Eisenberg. Illustrations copyright © 1978 by Susan Jeschke./ Illustration by Steven Kellogg from "The Hairy Toe," in *Gwot! Horribly Funny Hairticklers* by George Mendoza. Text copyright © 1967 by George Mendoza. Illustrations copyright © 1967 by Steven Kellogg. All reprinted by permission of Harper & Row, Publishers, Inc.

HASTINGS HOUSE, PUBLISHERS, INC. Illustration by Victor Ambrus from "The Conceited Prince," in *The Book of Magical Horses* by Margaret Mayo. Copyright © 1976 by Margaret Mayo. Reprinted by permission of Hastings House, Publishers, Inc.

HEFFER & SONS LTD. Illustration from *The Taylors of Ongar* by Doris Mary Armitage./ Illustration by Ann Taylor from *The Taylors of Ongar* by Doris Mary Armitage. Both reprinted by permission of Heffer & Sons Ltd.

HILL & WANG. Illustration by Paul Hogarth from *London à la Mode* by Malcolm Muggeridge. Copyright © 1966 by Paul Hogarth and Malcolm Muggeridge. Reprinted by permission of Hill & Wang.

HOUGHTON MIFFLIN CO. Illustration by Bill Peet from *Big Bad Bruce* by Bill Peet. Copyright © 1977 by William B. Peet./ Illustration by Bill Peet from *Cyrus, the Unsinkable Sea Serpent* by Bill Peet. Copyright © 1975 by William B. Peet./ Illustration by Bill Peet from *How Droofus the Dragon Lost His Head* by Bill Peet. Copyright © 1971 by William B. Peet./ Illustration by Bill Peet from *Chester the Worldly Pig* by Bill Peet. Copyright © 1965 by William B. Peet./ Illustration by Bill Peet from *Buford, the Little Bighorn* by Bill Peet. Copyright © 1967 by William Peet. All reprinted by permission of Houghton Mifflin Co.

JUDSON PRESS. Illustration by Masahiro Kasuya from *The Shoemaker's Dream,* English text by Mildred Schell. Copyright © 1980 by Shiko-Sha Co. Ltd. Illustrations copyright © 1982 by Judson Press. Reprinted by permission of Judson Press.

ALFRED A. KNOPF, INC. Illustration by Nicola Bayley from *The Patchwork Cat* by William Mayne. Text copyright © 1981 by William Mayne. Illustrations copyright © 1981 by Nicola Bayley./ Illustration by Nicola Bayley from *Polar Bear Cat* by Nicola Bayley. Copyright © 1984 by Nicola Bayley./ Illustration by Jill Bennett from *Danny, the Champion of the World* by Roald Dahl. Text copyright © 1975 by Roald Dahl. Illustrations copyright © 1975 by Alfred A. Knopf, Inc. All reprinted by permission of Alfred A. Knopf, Inc.

LITTLE, BROWN & CO. Illustration by Susan Meddaugh from *My Friend Bear* by Carol-Lynn Rössel Waugh. Text copyright © 1982 by Carol-Lynn Rössel Waugh. Illustrations copyright © 1982 by Susan Meddaugh. Reprinted by permission of Little, Brown & Co.

LOTHROP, LEE & SHEPARD BOOKS. Illustration by Imero Gobbato from *The Practical Man* by George Mendoza. Text copyright © 1968 by George Mendoza. Illustrations copyright © 1968 by Imero Gobbato./ Illustration by True Kelley from *The Mouses' Terrible Halloween* by True Kelley and Steven Lindblom. Text copyright © 1980 by Steven Lindblom. Illustrations copyright © 1980 by True Kelley. Both reprinted by permission of Lothrop, Lee & Shepard Books.

MACMILLAN, INC. Illustration by Troy Howell from *Jemima Remembers* by Crescent Dragonwagon. Text copyright © 1984 by Crescent Dragonwagon. Illustrations copyright © 1984 by Troy Howell./ Illustration by John O'Brien from *One Big Wish* by Jay Williams. Text copyright © 1980 by Barbara G. Williams. Illustrations copyright © 1980 by John O'Brien. Both reprinted by permission of Macmillan, Inc.

JULIA MacRAE BOOKS. Illustration by Ruth Sanderson from *Samantha on Stage* by Susan Clement Farrar. Text copyright © 1979 by Susan Clement Farrar. Illustrations copyright © 1979 by Ruth Sanderson. Reprinted by permission of Julia MacRae Books.

McGRAW-HILL BOOK CO. Illustration by Frederic Remington from *The Buffalo Soldiers in the Indian Wars* by Fairfax Downey. Copyright © 1969 by Fairfax Downey. Reprinted by permission of McGraw-Hill Book Co.

MODERN CURRICULUM PRESS, INC. Illustration by Diana Magnuson from *Jeanie's Valentines* by Carrie Rarick. Text copyright © 1982 by Carrie Rarick. Illustrations copyright © 1982 by Follett Publishing Co. Reprinted by permission of Modern Curriculum Press, Inc.

WILLIAM MORROW & CO., INC. Illustration by Meg Wohlberg from *The Smallest Boy* *in the Class* by Jerrold Beim. Copyright 1949 by Jerrold Beim./ Illustration by Victor Ambrus from *Grandma, Felix, and Mustapha Biscuit* by Victor Ambrus. Copyright © 1981, 1982 by Victor Ambrus. Both reprinted by permission of William Morrow & Co., Inc.

EDITORIAL NOGUER, S.A. (Spain). Illustration by Tove Jansson from *La Familia Mumin* by Tove Jansson. Copyright © 1967 by Tove Jansson. Reprinted by permission of Editorial Noguer, S.A. (Spain).

W. W. NORTON CO., INC. Illustration by Imero Gobbato from *The Good-for-Nothing Prince* by Jay Williams. Text copyright © 1969 by Jay Williams. Illustrations copyright © 1969 by Imero Gobbato./ Illustration by Ib Ohlsson from *Philbert the Fearful* by Jay Williams. Text copyright © 1966 by Jay Williams. Illustrations copyright © 1966 by Ib Ohlsson. Both reprinted by permission of W. W. Norton Co., Inc.

OXFORD UNIVERSITY PRESS. Illustration by Victor G. Ambrus from "Flambards in Summer," in *Flambards* by K. M. Peyton. *Flambards* copyright © 1967 by K. M. Peyton. "Flambards in Summer" copyright © 1969 by K. M. Peyton./ Illustration by Victor Ambrus from the "Seascapes," in *The New Dragon Book of Verse*, edited by Michael Harrison and Christopher Stuart-Clark. Copyright © 1977 by Oxford University Press./ Illustration by Eric Fraser from "O Luck of the Ugly..." in *Egyptian and Sudanese Folk-Tales*, retold by Helen Mitchnik. Copyright © by Helen Mitchnik./ Illustration by Eric Fraser from "The Old Crone Who Was More Wily than Iblees," in *Egyptian and Sudanese Folk-Tales*, retold by Helen Mitchnik. Copyright © 1978 by Helen Mitchnik. All reprinted by permission of Oxford University Press.

PARENTS MAGAZINE PRESS. Illustration by Blake Hampton from *The Cookie Tree* by Jay Williams. Text copyright © 1967 by Jay Williams. Illustrations copyright © 1967 by Blake Hampton./ Illustration by Friso Henstra from *Petronella* by Jay Williams. Text copyright © 1973 by Jay Williams. Illustrations copyright © 1973 by Friso Henstra./ Illustration by Rick Schreiter from *The Practical Princess and Other Liberating Fairy Tales* by Jay Williams. Text copyright © 1978 by Jay Williams. Illustrations copyright © 1978 by Parents Magazine Press. All reprinted by permission of Parents Magazine Press.

PENGUIN BOOKS LTD. Illustration by Christine Roche from *How We Work* by Anita Harper. Text copyright © 1977 by Anita Harper. Illustrations copyright © 1977 by Christine Roche. Reprinted by permission of Penguin Books Ltd.

CLARKSON N. POTTER, INC. Illustration by William Pène du Bois from *The Planet of Lost Things* by Mark Strand. Text copyright © 1982 by Mark Strand. Illustrations copyright © 1982 by William Pène du Bois. Reprinted by permission of Clarkson N. Potter, Inc.

PRENTICE-HALL, INC. Photograph from *Ballet for Boys and Girls* by Kathrine Sorley Walker and Joan Butler. Text copyright © 1979 by Joan Butler and Kathrine Sorley Walker. Reprinted by permission of Prentice-Hall, Inc.

G. P. PUTNAM'S SONS. Illustration by Moneta Barnett from *Fly, Jimmy, Fly!* by Walter Dean Myers. Text copyright © 1974 by Walter Dean Myers. Illustrations copyright © 1974 by Moneta Barnett. Reprinted by permission of G. P. Putnam's Sons.

RAND McNALLY & CO. Illustration by Victor G. Ambrus from *Encyclopedia of Legendary Creatures* by Tom McGowen. Copyright © 1981 by Rand McNally & Co. Reprinted by permission of Rand McNally & Co.

RANDOM HOUSE, INC. Sidelight excerpts from *A Change of Climate* by Jay Williams. Copyright © 1956 by Random House, Inc. Reprinted by permission of Random House, Inc.

THE B & R SAMIZDAT EXPRESS. Illustration by Christin Couture from *The Lizard of Oz* by Richard Seltzer. Copyright © 1974 by Richard Seltzer. Reprinted by permission of The B & R Samizdat Express.

SAN FRANCISCO BOOK CO., INC. Photograph by René Burri from *Lost Pony* by George Mendoza. Copyright © 1976 by George Mendoza. Reprinted by permission of San Francisco Book Co., Inc.

SCHOLASTIC, INC. Sidelight excerpts from *Books Are by People* by Lee Bennett Hopkins. Copyright © 1969 by Scholastic, Inc. Reprinted by permission of Scholastic, Inc.

CHARLES SCRIBNER'S SONS. Illustration by Reynold Ruffins from *That's Not Fair* by Jane Sarnoff and Reynold Ruffins. Text copyright © 1980 by Jane Sarnoff. Illustrations copyright © 1980 by Reynold Ruffins./ Illustration by Reynold Ruffins from *The Code and Cipher Book* by Jane Sarnoff and Reynold Ruffins. Text copyright © 1975 by Jane Sarnoff. Illustrations copyright © 1975 by Reynold Ruffins./ Illustration by Reynold Ruffins from *My*

Brother Never Feeds the Cat by Reynold Ruffins. Copyright © 1979 by Reynold Ruffins./ Illustration by Reynold Ruffins from *Giants! A Riddle Book and Mr. Bigperson's Side: A Story Book* by Jane Sarnoff and Reynold Ruffins. Text copyright © 1977 by Jane Sarnoff. Illustrations copyright © 1977 by Reynold Ruffins./ Illustration by Lillian Hoban from *Strawberry Dress Escape* by Crescent Dragonwagon. Text copyright © 1975 by Crescent Dragonwagon. Illustrations copyright © 1975 by Lillian Hoban./ Illustration by Reynold Ruffins from *The Monster Riddle Book* by Jane Sarnoff and Reynold Ruffins. Text copyright © 1975, 1978 by Jane Sarnoff. Illustrations copyright © 1975 by Reynold Ruffins./ Illustration by Sheila Maguire from *The Kitchen in History* by Molly Harrison. Copyright © 1972 by Molly Harrison. All reprinted by permission of Charles Scribner's Sons.

SIMON & SCHUSTER, INC. Illustration by Fred Gwynne from *The King's Trousers* by Robert Kraus. Text copyright © 1981 by Robert Kraus. Illustrations copyright © 1981 by Fred Gwynne./ Illustration by Fred Gwynne from *The King Who Rained* by Fred Gwynne. Copyright © 1970 by Fred Gwynne. Both reprinted by permission of Simon & Schuster, Inc.

UNIVERSITY OF OKLAHOMA PRESS. Illustrations by Frederic Remington from *Pony Tracks* by Frederic Remington. Both reprinted by permission of University of Oklahoma Press.

VIKING KESTREL. Illustration by Joelle Boucher from *Henri Mouse* by George Mendoza. Text copyright © 1985 by George Mendoza. Illustrations copyright © 1985 by Joelle Boucher. Reprinted by permission of Viking Kestrel.

THE VIKING PRESS. Illustration by Robert Quackenbush from "The Ghost of Bleek Manor," in *The Black Pearl and the Ghost; or, One Mystery after Another* by Walter Dean Myers. Text copyright © 1980 by Walter Dean Myers. Illustrations copyright © 1980 by Robert Quackenbush./ Jacket illustration by Diane de Groat from *The Young Landlords* by Walter Dean Myers. Copyright © 1979 by Walter Dean Myers. Both reprinted by permission of The Viking Press.

HENRY Z. WALCK, INC. Illustration by Tove Jansson from *Tales from Moominvalley* by Tove Jansson. Translated by Thomas Warburton. Copyright © by Tove Jansson. English translation copyright © 1963 by Ernest Benn Ltd./ Illustrations by Tove Jansson from *Moominsummer Madness* by Tove Jansson. Translated by Thomas Warburton. All reprinted by permission of Henry Z. Walck, Inc.

WALKER BOOKS LTD. Illustration by Will Giles from *The Prickly Plant Book* by Sue Tarsky. Copyright © 1980 by Sebastian Walker Association Ltd. Reprinted by permission of Walker Books Ltd.

FREDERICK WARNE AND CO., INC. (New York). Jacket illustration by Bob Karalus from *Johnny Stands* by Harry W. Paige. Copyright © 1982 by Harry W. Paige./ Illustration by Kate Greenaway from "Negligent Mary," in *Little Ann, and Other Poems* by Jane and Ann Taylor./ Illustration by Kate Greenaway from "The Orphan," in *Little Ann, and Other Poems* by Jane and Ann Taylor. All reprinted by permission of Frederick Warne and Co., Inc. (New York).

FREDERICK WARNE LTD. (London). Illustration by Kate Greenaway from "Negligent Mary," in *Little Ann, and Other Poems* by Jane and Ann Taylor./ Illustration by Kate Greenaway from "The Orphan," in *Little Ann, and Other Poems* by Jane and Ann Taylor. Both reprinted by permission of Frederick Warne Ltd. (London).

WATSON-GUPTILL PUBLICATIONS. Illustration by Burne Hogarth from "The God of Tarzan," in *Jungle Tales of Tarzan* by Edgar Rice Burroughs. Adapted by Burne Hogarth and Robert M. Hodes. Copyright © 1976 by Edgar Rice Burroughs, Inc. Reprinted by permission of Watson-Guptill Publications.

FRANKLIN WATTS, INC. Illustration by Victoria Chess from *Cat and Dog and the ABC's* by Elizabeth Miller and Jane Cohen. Text copyright © 1981 by Elizabeth Miller and Jane Cohen. Illustrations copyright © 1981 by Victoria Chess. Reprinted by permission of Franklin Watts, Inc.

ALBERT WHITMAN & CO. Illustration by Christa Kieffer from *You Were Born on Your Very First Birthday* by Linda Walvoord Girard. Text copyright © 1983 by Linda Walvoord Girard. Illustrations copyright © 1983 by Christa Kieffer. Reprinted by permission of Albert Whitman & Co.

WINSTON PRESS, INC. Illustration by Troy Howell from "Siegfried, Child of the Forest," in *The Immortal Dragon of Sylene, and Other Faith Tales* by Rafael Tilton. Copyright © 1982 by Rafael Tilton. Reprinted by permission of Winston Press, Inc.

Sidelight excerpts from an article "The Strength of Weakness: A Profile of Illustrator Jerry

Pinkney" by Nick Meglin, January, 1982 in *American Artist*. Reprinted by permission of *American Artist*./ Jacket illustration by Blanche Sims from *Blue Denim Blues* by Anne Warren Smith. Copyright © 1982 by Anne Warren Smith. Jacket illustration copyright © 1982 by Blanche Sims. Reprinted by permission of Carol Bancroft & Friends./ Jacket illustration by Frank Schoonover from *A Princess of Mars* by Edgar Rice Burroughs. Copyright 1917 by A. C. McClurg & Co. Reprinted by permission of Edgar Rice Burroughs, Inc./ Cover illustration by Studley O. Burroughs from *Tarzan Triumphant* by Edgar Rice Burroughs. Reprinted by permission of Edgar Rice Burroughs, Inc./ Cover illustration by Jeff Jones from *I Am a Barbarian* by Edgar Rice Burroughs. Reprinted by permission of Edgar Rice Burroughs, Inc./ Cover illustration by John Coleman Burroughs from *Synthetic Men of Mars* by Edgar Rice Burroughs. Reprinted by permission of Edgar Rice Burroughs, Inc./ Sidelight excerpts from an article "Letter from England: The Magic of the Mask," February, 1977 in *Horn Book*. Copyright © 1977 by Aidan Chambers. Reprinted by permission of Aidan Chambers./ Cover illustration by J. Allen St. John, January 15, 1984 in *The Courier-Journal* (Louisville, Kentucky). Reprinted by permission of *The Courier-Journal*./ Sidelight excerpts from an article "Meet Your Author, Clyde Robert Bulla," by Clyde Robert Bulla in *Cricket* magazine. Reprinted by permission of *Cricket* magazine.

Sidelight excerpts from an article "Jay Williams," December, 1975 in *Cricket* magazine. Reprinted by permission of *Cricket* magazine./ Sidelight excerpts from an article "Fred Gwynne, Where Are You?" by Bettelou Peterson, February 8, 1982 in *Detroit Free Press*. Reprinted by permission of *Detroit Free Press*./ Illustration by Hans Helweg from *Oggy at Home* by Ann Lawrence. Text copyright © 1977 by Ann Lawrence. Illustrations copyright © 1977 by Hans Helweg. Reprinted by permission of Hans Helweg./ Four panels from the comic strip "Little Nemo in Slumberland," 1905-11, in *The New York Herald*. Reprinted by permission of *The New York Herald*./ Illustration by Winsor McCay from *Little Nemo in Slumberland* by Winsor McCay. Copyright 1945 by McCay Features Syndicate. Reprinted by permission of McCay Features Syndicate./ Sidelight excerpts from an article "Fred Gwynne— King of Curmudgeons?" by Robert Berkvist, May, 1976 in *The New York Times Biographical Service*. Copyright © 1976 by The New York Times Co. Reprinted by permission of The New York Times Co./ Photographs from *Frederic Remington: Artist of the Western Frontier* by John Stewart. Copyright © 1971 by John Stewart. Reprinted by permission of the Remington Art Museum./ Sidelight excerpts from an article "Before You Write," by Clyde Robert Bulla, December, 1954 in *The Writer*. Copyright 1954 by The Writer, Inc. Reprinted by permission of *The Writer*.

PHOTOGRAPH CREDITS

Norman John Bull: Ron Magowan, Chandler Photography; Earl Joseph Dias: Ann Margaret Studio; Crescent Dragonwagon (at the Half Moon): Ann Wakefield; Harvey Frommer: Paul S. Weiss; Elizabeth Harlan: Ed Stoecklin; Paul Hogarth: Toby Hogarth; Tove Jansson: Hans Paul, (with Moomin home) Vesa Klemettl; Mark Strand: Lilo Raymond; Jane and Ann Taylor: National Portrait Gallery (London); Jay Williams: T. Savage; Betsy James Wyeth: Susan Gray.

SOMETHING ABOUT THE AUTHOR

AMBRUS, Gyozo (Laszlo) 1935-
(Victor G. Ambrus)

PERSONAL: Born August 19, 1935, in Budapest, Hungary; emigrated to England in 1956; son of Gyozo (a chemical engineer) and Iren (Toth) Ambrus; married Glenys R. Chapman (an illustrator), 1958; children: Mark, Sándor John. *Education:* Attended Hungarian Academy of Fine Art for three years; Royal College of Art, London, England, Diploma A.R.C.A., 1960; diplomas from Royal Engravers and from Royal Society of Arts. *Politics:* Democrat. *Religion:* Roman Catholic. *Home:* 52 Crooksbury Rd., Farnham, Surrey, England.

CAREER: Artist, designer, author and illustrator of books for children. Lecturer on illustration, West Surrey College of Art, Surrey, England, 1964-80, and other colleges; member, Council for National Academic Awards of Great Britain. Has exhibited work at the Royal Academy, Biennale of Bratislava, in Bologna, Italy, and in Belgium. Works included in permanent collections at University of Southern Mississippi, Library of Congress, and Oxford University Press, London, England. *Member:* Royal College of Art (associate member), Royal Society of Arts (fellow), Royal Society of Painters, Etchers, and Engravers (fellow). *Awards, honors:* Spind Book Festival award, 1963, for *The Cossacks,* 1964, for *Time of Trial,* 1965, for *The Maplin Bird,* 1968, for *Young Mark: The Story of a Venture;* Kate Greenaway Medal commendation from Library Association of Great Britain, 1964, for *The Royal Navy* and *Time of Trial,* and 1972, for *The Sultan's Bath;* Kate Greenaway Medal for distinguished work in illustration for children's books, 1965, for *Three Poor Tailors,* and 1975, for *Mishka* and *Horses in Battle;* Woodward Park School Book Award, 1967, for *The Bushbabies;* Australian Book of the Year Award, 1969, for *When Jays Fly to Barbmo.*

WRITINGS—Under name Victor G. Ambrus; self-illustrated; published by Oxford University Press, except as indicated: *The Three Poor Tailors* (*Horn Book* honor list), 1965, Harcourt, 1966; *Brave Soldier Janosh,* Harcourt, 1967; *The Little Cockerel,* Harcourt, 1968; *The Seven Skinny Goats,* 1969, Harcourt, 1970; (reteller) *The Sultan's Bath,* 1971, Harcourt, 1972; *Hot Water for Boris,* 1972; *A Country Wedding,* 1973, Addison-Wesley, 1975; *Horses in Battle,* 1975; *Mishka,* 1975, Warne, 1978; (adapter) Brothers Grimm, *The Valiant Little Tailor,* 1980; (adapter) *Dracula: Everything You Always Wanted to Know But Were Too Afraid to Ask,* 1981, Merrimack, 1983; *Blackbeard the Pirate,* 1981, Merrimack, 1983; (with D. Lindsay) *Under the Double Eagle: Three Centuries of History in Austria and Hungary,* 1981, Merrimack, 1982; *Dracula's Bedtime Storybook: Tales to Keep You Awake at Night,* Merrimack, 1982; *Grandma, Felix, and Mustapha Biscuit,* Morrow, 1982.

Illustrator: Joan Aiken, *The Kingdom and the Cave,* Abelard, 1959, Doubleday, 1975; Alan C. Jenkins, *White Horses and Black Bulls,* Blackie & Sons, 1960, Norton, 1963; René Guillot, *The Master of the Elephants,* Oxford University Press, 1961; William Mayne, *The Changeling,* Oxford University Press, 1961, Dutton, 1963; R. Guillot, *Fofana,* Criterion, 1962; Hester Burton, *Castors Away* (*Horn Book* honor list), Oxford University Press, 1962, World Publishing, 1963; Barbara Bartos-Hoeppner, *The Cossacks,* Oxford University Press, 1962, Walck, 1963; Frances W. Browin, *Looking for Orlando,* Oxford University Press, 1962; Shenna Porter, *Hills and Hollows,* Oxford University Press, 1962; F. Braumann, *Malik and Amina,* Oxford University Press, 1962; Mary Treadgold, *The Heron Ride,* J. Cape, 1962; Griselda Gifford, *The Youngest Taylor,* Bodley Head, 1963; Rosemary Manning, *Arripay,* Constable, 1963, Farrar, Straus, 1964; S. Porter, *Jacob's Lad-*

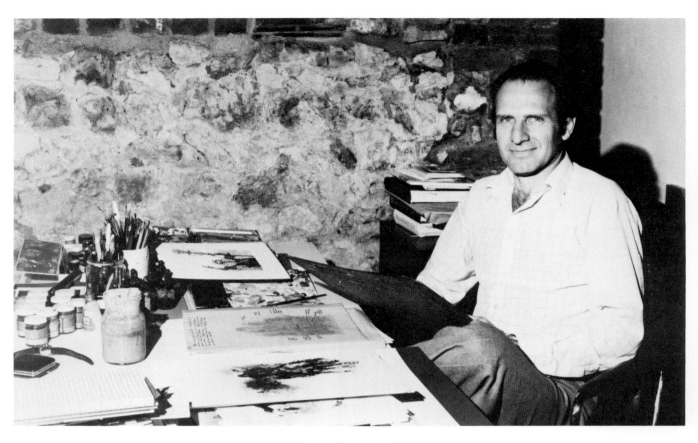

GYOZO AMBRUS

der, Oxford University Press, 1963; Elspeth Boog-Watson and Janet I. Carruthers, *Elizabethan Sailor,* Oxford University Press, 1963; H. Burton, *Seaman at the Time of Trafalgar,* Oxford University Press, 1963; K. M. Peyton, *Sea Feuer* (ALA Notable Book), World Publishing, 1963 (published in England as *Windfall,* Oxford University Press, 1963); Nicholas Kalashnikoff, *Jumper,* Oxford University Press, 1963; Peter Dawlish, *The Royal Navy,* Oxford University Press, 1963; H. Burton, *Time of Trial* (*Horn Book* honor list), Oxford University Press, 1963, World Publishing, 1964; Jane Duncan (pseudonym of Elizabeth Jane Cameron), *Camerons on the Hills,* St. Martin's Press, 1963; Rosemary Sutcliff, *The Hound of Ulster* (ALA Notable Book; *Horn Book* honor list), Bodley Head, 1963, Dutton, 1964; J. Duncan, *Camerons on the Train,* St. Martin's Press, 1963; Ruth Manning-Sanders, *The Red King and the Witch: Gypsy Folk and Fairy Tales,* Oxford University Press, 1964, Roy, 1965; Helen Griffiths, *The Greyhound,* Hutchinson, 1964, Doubleday, 1966; Eleanor Farjeon and W. Mayne, editors, *The Hamish Hamilton Book of Kings,* Hamish Hamilton, 1964, published in America as *A Cavalcade of Kings,* Walck, 1965; Richard Parker, *Private Beach* (Junior Literary Guild selection), Harrap, 1964, Duell, Sloan & Pearce, 1965; B. Bartos-Hoeppner, *Save the Khan,* translated by S. Humphries, Walck, 1964; Jenny Grace Fyson, *The Three Brothers of Ur,* Oxford University Press, 1964, Coward, 1966; H. Griffiths, *The Wild Heart,* Hutchinson, 1963, Doubleday, 1964; Jane Oliver, *Watch for the Morning,* St. Martin's Press, 1964; Barbara Sleigh, compiler, *North of Nowhere: Stories and Legends from Many Lands,* Collins, 1964, Coward, 1966; Cordelia Jones, *Nobody's Garden* (*Horn Book* honor list), Deutsch, 1964, Scribner, 1965; Edward Fitzgerald, *The British Army,* Oxford University Press, 1964; K. M. Peyton, *The*

Maplin Bird (*Horn Book* honor list), Oxford University Press, 1964, World Publishing, 1965.

John W. R. Taylor, *The Royal Air Force,* Oxford University Press, 1965; Jennifer Grace Fyson, *The Journey of the Eldest Son,* Oxford University Press, 1965, Coward, 1967; K. M. Peyton, *The Plan for Birdsmarsh* (*Horn Book* honor list), Oxford University Press, 1965, World Publishing, 1966; J. Duncan, *Camerons at the Castle,* St. Martin's Press, 1965; Veronica Robinson, *David in Silence,* Lippincott, 1965; Barbara L. Picard, *One Is One,* Oxford University Press, 1965; Francis M. Pilkington, *The Three Sorrowful Tales of Erin* (ALA Notable Book), Bodley Head, 1965, Walck, 1966; Helen Kay (pseudonym of Helen Colodny Goldfrank) *Henri's Hands for Pablo Picasso,* Abelard, 1965; Kelman Frost, *Son of the Sahara,* Roy, 1965; William Stevenson, *The Bushbabies* (ALA Notable Book; *Horn Book* honor list), Houghton, 1965; E. Farjeon and W. Mayne, editors, *A Cavalcade of Queens,* Walck, 1965 (published in England as *The Hamish Hamilton Book of Queens,* Hamish Hamilton, 1965); Robert M. Ballantyne, *The Dog Crusoe,* edited by Roger L. Green, Dutton, 1966; Barbara L. Picard, *The Young Pretenders,* Criterion, 1966; Ian Serraillier, *The Challenge of the Green Knight* (*Horn Book* honor list), 1966, Walck, 1967; J. Duncan, *Camerons Calling,* St. Martin's Press, 1966; H. Griffiths, *The Wild Horse of Santander,* Hutchinson, 1966, Doubleday, 1967; K. M. Peyton, *Thunder in the Sky,* Oxford University Press, 1966, World Publishing, 1967; S. Porter, *Deerfold,* Oxford University Press, 1966; P. Dawlish, *The Merchant Navy,* Oxford University Press, 1966; H. Burton, *No Beat of Drum,* Oxford University Press, 1966, World Publishing, 1967; Irene Byers, *Mystery at Map-*

pins, Scribner, 1966; E. M. Almedingen, *Young Mark: The Story of a Venture* (ALA Notable Book; *Horn Book* honor list), Oxford University Press, 1966, Farrar, Straus, 1968; A. C. Jenkins, *Kingdom of the Elephants*, Follett, 1966; Evelyn Ames, *A Glimpse of Eden*, Houghton, 1967; E. M. Almedingen, *Katia* (*Horn Book* honor list), Farrar, Straus, 1967; Arthur Catherall, *Prisoners in the Snow*, Lothrop, 1967; Margaret Storey, *Pauline*, Doubleday, 1967; K. M. Peyton,

Flambards (trilogy; ALA Notable Book), Oxford University Press, 1967, World Publishing, 1968; Miska Miles (pseudonym of Patricia Miles Martin) *The Pieces of Home* (Junior Literary Guild selection), Atlantic-Little, Brown, 1967; Reginald Maddock, *The Great Bow,* Rand McNally, 1968; I. Serraillier, *Robin the Greenwood: Ballads of Robin Hood,* Walck, 1968; Barbara J. Berry, *Shannon,* Follett, 1968; H. Griffiths, *Léon,* Doubleday, 1968; J. Duncan, *Camerons, Ahoy!,*

(From *The Song of Caedmon* by Arthur Scholey. Music by Donald Swann. Illustrated by Victor Ambrus.)

"I'm glad to meet you, too. Sit down, sit down. Have a fly." ■ (From *The Farthest-Away Mountain* by Lynne Reid Banks. Illustrated by Victor Ambrus.)

St. Martin's Press, 1968; R. Manning-Sanders, *The Glass Man and the Golden Bird: Hungarian Folk and Fairy Tales,* Roy, 1968; Margaret Balderson, *When Jays Fly to Barbmo* (ALA Notable Book), Oxford University Press, 1968, World Publishing, 1969; H. Burton, *In Spite of All Terror* (ALA Notable Book), Oxford University Press, 1968, World Publishing, 1969; Madeleine Polland, *Stranger in the Hills,* Doubleday, 1968; A. Catherall, *Kidnapped by Accident,* Lothrop, 1969; K. M. Peyton, *Flambards in Summer* (ALA Notable Book; *Horn Book* honor list), Oxford University Press, 1969, World Publishing, 1970; David Walker, *Big Ben,* Houghton, 1969; Winifred Fin-

lay, *Folk Tales from the North,* F. Watts, 1969; Patricia Lynch, *Knights of the God: Tales and Legends of the Irish Saints,* Holt, 1969; Lavinia Russ, editor, *Forever England: Poetry and Prose about England and the English,* Harcourt, 1969; Geza Gardonyi, *Slave of the Huns,* Bobbs, 1969; William Cowper, *The Diverting History of John Gilpin,* Abelard-Schuman, 1969; R. Manning-Sanders, *Jonniken and the Flying Basket: French Folk and Fairy Tales,* Dutton, 1969; K. M. Peyton, *The Edge of the Cloud,* World Publishing, 1969; Franklyn M. Branley, *The Mystery of Stonehenge* (*Horn Book* honor list), Crowell, 1969.

LeRoy Allen, *Shawnee Lance,* Delacorte, 1970; Kathleen Fidler, *Haki, the Shetland Pony,* Rand McNally, 1970; A. Catherall, *Red Sea Rescue,* Lothrop, 1970; Ladislav Grosman, *Shop on Main Street,* translated by Iris Urwin, Lothrop, 1970; I. Serraillier, *Robin and His Merry Men: Ballads of Robin Hood,* Walck, 1970; E. M. Almedingen, *Fanny,* Farrar, Straus, 1970; R. J. Unstead, *The Story of Britain,* T. Nelson, 1970; H. Burton, *The Henchmans at Home,* Oxford University Press, 1970, Crowell, 1972; H. Burton, *Beyond the Weir Bridge* (ALA Notable Book), Crowell, 1970; W. Finlay, *Folk Tales from Moor and Mountain,* Roy, 1970; Arthur Scholey, *The Song of Caedmon* (music by Donald Swann), Bodley Head, 1971; Joseph Jacobs, editor, *Celtic Fairy Tales,* World Publishing,

1971; Robert J. Unstead, *Living in a Crusader Land,* Addison-Wesley, 1971; R. Sutcliff, *Tristan and Iseult* (ALA Notable Book), Dutton, 1971; H. Burton, *The Rebel* (ALA Notable Book), Oxford University Press, 1971, Crowell, 1972; Joan Aiken, *The Kingdom and the Cave,* Doubleday, 1972; Ronald Welch, *Tank Commander,* Oxford University Press, 1972; Bernard Miles, editor, *Favorite Tales from Shakespeare,* Hamlyn, 1972, Rand McNally, 1977; (with wife, Glenys Ambrus) Carolyn Haywood, *A Christmas Fantasy,* Morrow, 1972; B. Picard, *Tales of Ancient Persia,* Oxford University Press, 1972, Walck, 1973; Bonnie Highsmith, *Kodi's Mare,* Criterion, 1972; R. Sutcliff, *Heather, Oak, and Olive: Three Stories,* Dutton, 1972; H. Burton, *Riders of the Storm,* Oxford

(From "The Conceited Prince," in *The Book of Magical Horses* by Margaret Mayo. Illustrated by Victor Ambrus.)

University Press, 1972, Crowell, 1973; Roger L. Green, compiler, *A Cavalcade of Magicians*, Walck, 1973; Alexander Cordell, *The Traitor Within*, T. Nelson, 1973, Globe Books, 1975; Charles P. May, *Left by Themselves*, Scholastic Book Service, 1973; Nan Chauncy, *Hunted in Their Own Land*, Seabury, 1973; W. Finlay, *Cap O'Rushes and Other Folk Tales*, Kaye & Ward, 1973, Harvey House, 1974; John Tully, *The Glass Knife*, Methuen, 1974; Barbara Sleigh, *Spin Straw to Gold: Book of Fairy Tales and Legends*, Lions, 1974; R. J. Unstead, *Living in a Castle*, Addison-Wesley, 1974; H. Burton, *Kate Rider*, Oxford University Press, 1974, Crowell, 1975; R. J. Unstead, *Living in the Time of the Pilgrim Fathers*, Addison-Wesley, 1974.

H. Griffiths, *Just a Dog*, Holiday House, 1975; H. Griffiths, *The Mysterious Appearance of Agnes*, Holiday House, 1975; (with David Smee) Peter Dickinson, *Chance, Luck, and Destiny*, Gollancz, 1975, Atlantic-Little, Brown, 1976; (with G. Ambrus) C. Haywood, *A Valentine Fantasy*, Morrow, 1976; Sara Corrin and others, *Stories for Tens and Over*, edited by Stephen Corrin, Faber, 1976; Robert Swindells, *Voyage to Valhalla*, Hodder & Stoughton, 1976; Roger L. Green, editor, *The Hamish Hamilton Book of Other Worlds*, Hamish Hamilton, 1976; M. A. Wood, *The Year the Raiders Came*, Anderson Press, 1977; R. Swindells, *The Very Special Baby*, Hodder & Stoughton, 1977, Prentice-Hall, 1978; Margaret Mayo, *The Book of Magical Horses*, Hastings House, 1977;

H. Griffiths, *Running Wild*, Holiday House, 1977; Richard Moody, *The World of Dinosaurs*, Grosset, 1977; Robert Selbie, *The Anatomy of Costume*, Mills & Boon, 1977; H. Griffiths, *Pablo*, Hutchinson, 1977; K. M. Peyton, *The Right-Hand Man*, Oxford University Press, 1977; Antonia Fraser, *Robin Hood*, Sidgwick & Jackson, 1977; Lynne R. Banks, *The Farthest-Away Mountain*, Doubleday, 1977; Tobi Tobias, *Chasing the Goblins Away*, Warne, 1977; Joseph E. Chipperfield, *Hunter of Harter Fell*, Hutchinson, 1977; Michael Harrison and Christopher Stuart-Clark, editors, *The New Dragon Book of Verse*, Oxford University Press, 1977; Pamela Oldfield, *The Terrible Plain Princess*, Hodder & Stoughton, 1977; H. Burton, *Tim at the Fur Fort*, Hamish Hamilton, 1978; Nora Rock, *Monkey's Perfect*, Anderson-Hutchinson, 1978, State Mutual Bank, 1981; B. Miles, adapter, *Robin Hood: Prince of the Outlaws*, Rand McNally, 1978; M. Mayo, *The Book of Magical Cats*, Kaye & Ward, 1978; B. Sleigh, *Grimblegraw and the Wuthering Witch*, Hodder & Stoughton, 1978; Peter Carter, *Madatan*, Oxford University Press, 1979; H. Griffiths, *The Last Summer* (Junior Literary Guild selection), Holiday House, 1979; W. Finlay, *Tales from the Borders*, Kaye & Ward, 1979; M. A. Wood, *Master Deor's Apprentice*, Anderson, 1979.

Geoffrey Hindley, *Under Siege*, Angus & Robertson, 1980; H. Griffiths, *Blackface Stallion*, Holiday House, 1980; C. Haywood, *The King's Monster*, Morrow, 1980; N. Rock, *Rope*

(From "Seascapes," in *The New Dragon Book of Verse*, edited by Michael Harrison and Christopher Stuart-Clark. Illustrated by Victor Ambrus.)

If someone could manage to sneak up on a Leprechaun and grab hold of him, that person's fortune might be made. ■ (From *Encyclopedia of Legendary Creatures* by Tom McGowen. Illustrated by Victor G. Ambrus.)

around the Wind, Anderson-Hutchinson, 1980, State Mutual Bank, 1981; R. J. Unstead, *The Life of Jesus*, Hamlyn, 1981; Tom McGowen, *Encyclopedia of Legendary Creatures*, Rand McNally, 1981; Norman Bull, *My Little Book of Jesus*, Hamlyn, 1981; R. Sutcliff, *Eagle's Egg*, Hamish Hamilton, 1981; Elyne Mitchell, *Snowy River Brumby*, Hutchinson, 1981; W. Finlay, *Tales of Fantasy and Fear*, Kaye & Ward, 1982; Rudyard Kipling, *Just So Stories*, Rand McNally, 1982; James Riordan, *Tales of King Arthur*, Rand McNally, 1982; (with Glenys Ambrus) C. Haywood, *Santa Claus Forever!*, Morrow, 1983; J. Riordan, *Tales from the Arabian Nights*, Rand McNally, 1983; Michael De Larrabeiti, *Jeeno, Heloise and Igamor, the Long, Long Horse*, Merrimack, 1984; J. Riordan, *Stories from the Ballet*, Rand McNally, 1984; *Canterbury Tales*, Rand McNally, 1985.

Also illustrator of *The Stories of Exploration*, Benn; *The Hamish Hamilton Book of Magicians*, Hamish Hamilton; and Charles P. May's *Stranger in the Storm*, Abelard.

ADAPTATIONS: "The Three Poor Tailors" (filmstrip with cassette), Weston Woods, 1972; "The Sultan's Bath" (filmstrip with cassette or phonodisc), Weston Woods, 1974.

WORK IN PROGRESS: Illustrating *Peter and the Wolf* for Oxford University Press, and *More Tales from Shakespeare* for Hamlyn.

SIDELIGHTS: "I know that when I was a young boy, I always used to be very influenced by the illustrations in a book. In

fact, I remember picking up books in the library and looking at the illustrations, deciding whether to read a book or not on the basis of the drawings." [Cornelia Jones and Olivia R. Way, editors, *British Children's Authors*, American Library Association, 1976.¹]

"I came from a family of three brothers and two sisters. We lived in Budapest with summer visits into the countryside, which was a magical place to me and influences my artwork even today, particularly my colors. My father was a research chemist and my two brothers followed similar careers in chemical engineering and architecture. I, on the other hand, began drawing as a small child and maintained that interest through grammar school and eventually into the Hungarian Academy of Fine Art.

"During World War II as a child of eight, I experienced war at close range, as the fighting went on all around us like a recurring nightmare. The same thing happened again in 1956, when I left Hungary at the age of twenty and was accepted into the Royal College of Art in London from which I graduated in 1960. The combination of the Hungarian Academy, an excellent school with classical traditions in teaching, and that of the more or less easy-going Royal College of Art gave me a unique training for which I am very grateful.

"I illustrated my first book, which was reviewed in the *London Times Literary Supplement*, during the last year of my college training. The article published one of my drawings and stimulated interest in my work among publishers. I am presently

He had a half-filled glass of bitter in his hand which he set down on the table. Christina had her port. . . . ▪
(From "Flambards in Summer," in *Flambards* by K. M. Peyton. Illustrated by Victor G. Ambrus.)

in the happy position of proposing ideas to my English publisher Oxford University Press, for whom I have worked for about twenty-five years, and for whom I do most of my work, particularly color work."

Ambrus's interest in book illustration started "right at the beginning, when I started reading books. As soon as I read a story, I was immediately inspired to do a drawing. I was also very interested in the books I saw that were illustrated by other artists, and I tried to imitate their drawings.

"I think I work in the colors that I use because they appeal to me more than anything else. I hope they also appeal to children, but I enjoy using brilliant colors enormously because I find them exciting to use. I like to use clear colors, anyway, because I think if you mix colors—with big blacks and whites, for instance—you get a lot of gray. I don't particularly like to use color the way painters would use it, mixing it up too much. I like to put the colors straight down, whether it's ink or poster paint. Also, I feel that folktales are a form of folk art, like embroidery or painting on wooden furniture, and they are always done with brilliant colors. It's only natural that books should also be illustrated in bright colors.

"I suppose other artists must have influenced my work. I am very interested in Victorian illustrators' work, particularly Arthur Rackham's books. I have enormous admiration for them. So probably the way they work appeals to me, and I like to be influenced by them."[1]

"I am also very lucky to be married to Glenys, whom I met at the Royal College of Art. She was trained as a painter, so she has wonderful color-sense. We have lively exchanges of opinions about our work. Our youngest son, Sándor, also joins in, giving an expert child's-eye point of view."

"It is always a difficult problem to illustrate books by other authors, because you've got to try and work out what is in the mind of an author, what type of character he has in mind. But generally speaking, the better the book, the easier to illustrate. If I read a very good description of a character, then I immediately get an idea of the character without any difficulty. Often I get books where the characters are vaguely described and the reader does not get an immediate and definite idea of what they would look like and how they would behave. Then I am in great trouble illustrating the different characters. I firmly believe if you get a good story you get good illustrations, and if you get a mediocre story or a bad story you can end up with bad drawings. The artist doesn't have much of an idea of what the character is really like. Therefore, the artist is guessing, and he will probably draw very average characters rather than a real believable person. I have talked to authors about the illustrations I have done for their books. At the same time I had an author who said my illustrations influenced her writing. It was Mrs. Peyton. She said that she was surprised to see some of the drawings I did of characters, and then later on she thought perhaps that's the way they should be, and she molded that character in the next book to match the drawings in a way. I always feel very pleased if I hear that I managed to portray a character as the author pictured him.

"Quite often I have to go to the location of the setting of a book before I do the illustrations. If I have the time, I try to. But, of course, when you get books on Africa it's a bit difficult. I have gone to the location of several of the books, which is very exciting. In fact, I've done some of the drawings on the spot, and they always seem to have much more of a feeling of reality about them. I remember once drawing in a town in the bitter cold when my hands were absolutely numb—I could just about hold a pen—but those drawings have a feeling of reality about them which is lacking in the drawings I did in the comfort of my house. So it's always a good thing to go to the location of a place and get the feeling of that place.

"Generally speaking, I choose which events I illustrate in a story. Very occasionally, when there is a small amount of space available in the book, you get restricted by the publisher. The editor determines exactly the places where drawings are needed, and you have to illustrate the text exactly, on the opposite side. I learned the hard way that the illustrator should always choose his subject. I remember that the second or third book I illustrated was a folktale which had a character in it, a girl with a spotted dress. There were twelve illustrations in the book—twelve full-page illustrations—and on every single page there was this girl in the spotted dress. Of course, the whole book became rather boring because every time you turned a page and you saw a drawing, there was this poor thing sitting in a spotted dress. The other thing was that out of the dozen drawings, she was sitting down in probably half of them. She was either sitting down in the kitchen or sitting down outside. Certainly the drawings became rather boring. I certainly was very bored with them. So if I can, I always ask the publishers to let me choose the incidents to illustrate.

"There are two ways of deciding how many illustrations might be in a book. First, it depends on the amount of space available in the book after the type is placed. You're always given a

Nearly every kind of sport is available on board: walking the plank, keel-hauling, shark-baiting, and deep sea-fishing. ■ (From *Blackbeard the Pirate* by Victor G. Ambrus. Illustrated by the author.)

Into the cage went the plumpest, tastiest-looking little thing that Felix had ever seen. ■ (From *Grandma, Felix, and Mustapha Biscuit* by Victor Ambrus. Illustrated by the author.)

guideline by the publisher of roughly how many pages can be spared for illustration. Other than that, the number of illustrations is the artist's own decision and depends upon the individual book. Some books dealing with sea stories or large-scale battles need double-spread illustrations that run across two pages. Obviously when you are doing an illustration that runs across two pages, there's not going to be very much space left for other illustrations, so the illustrations tend to be rather large-scale and few in number. But when you have a book with several small chapters, then you really need to do roughly a drawing each. So you are going to end up with a lot of small illustrations, probably chapter-head size or even smaller. I think the important thing is that the illustrations should be spaced out evenly through the book, so you don't have dull passages where there isn't any drawing at all.

"I think that probably the most important thing to me in il-

lustrating a book is to liven up the story and help it along. I think the illustration shouldn't just be a support of the text, but should take it a stage further. The illustration of a story should be very much a part of the book itself. It should also tell its own story. For instance, I once illustrated a book set in the period of the Battle of Trafalgar. I included in my illustrations some drawings of an incident on board Lord Nelson's battleship the *Victory,* which the author didn't deal with specifically, just mentioned on the side. When I had done the illustrations, she questioned my right to include drawings which didn't exactly tally with the text that she wrote. I explained to her I felt that at that particular part, the drawing was essential to bring out the atmosphere of the battle and the tragedy of what was happening, and in some way I felt I was obliged to contribute to her story and take it along a stage further.''[1]

"My favorite books range from picture books, particularly the folk tales, and more recently I've taken interest in 'Dracula,' to realistic historical illustrations as found in *Under the Double Eagle, The Legends of King Arthur,* and *Shakespeare Tales.*

"My wife and I both work in the studio of our home, but visit London and publishers frequently. I enjoy taking lovely country walks. Living near the old 'Pilgrims Way' route to Canterbury, was a constant inspiration while working on *Canterbury Tales.* I also enjoy traveling through 'old' Europe—France, Austria, Spain, Germany—viewing the old cities and buildings, museums of fine art, examining history and military history. Along with these influences stands music—Mozart and Vivaldi. I play records constantly and am also prone to some good old fashioned Viennese light music, but when I draw folk tales I play Gipsy music from Hungary—full blast!

"For relaxation I paint in oil and also draw from life in art classes. I frequently exhibit etchings and prints in London."

Ambrus's works are included in the Kerlan Collection at the University of Minnesota and in the de Grummond Collection at the University of Southern Mississippi.

HOBBIES AND OTHER INTERESTS: Military history (especially the Napoleonic wars), collecting arms, armor, and antique weapons, travel, old architecture, paintings.

FOR MORE INFORMATION SEE: Junior Bookshelf, June, 1966; Lee Kingman and others, compilers, *Illustrators of Children's Books: 1957-1966,* Horn Book, 1968; Brian Doyle, *The Who's Who of Children's Literature,* Schocken, 1968; Bettina Hurlimann, *Picture-Book World,* translated and edited by Brian W. Alderson, World Publishing, 1969; Diana Klemin, *The Illustrated Book,* Clarkson Potter, 1970; Doris de Montreville and Donna Hill, editors, *Third Book of Junior Authors,* H. W. Wilson, 1972; Martha E. Ward and Dorothy A. Marquardt, *Illustrators of Books for Young People,* 2nd edition, Scarecrow, 1975; Cornelia Jones and Olivia R. Way, *British Children's Authors: Interviews at Home,* American Library Association, 1976; Lee Kingman and others, editors, *Illustrators of Children's Books: 1967-1976,* Horn Book, 1978; *Who's Who in Art,* Art Trade Press, 1982.

APFEL, Necia H(alpern)   1930-

BRIEF ENTRY: Born July 31, 1930, in Mount Vernon, N.Y. Author and lecturer in astronomy. Apfel graduated from Tufts University in 1952 and continued graduate study at Harvard University until 1954. The following year she became a research analyst for Standard Oil Co. in Chicago. In the early 1960s she began further graduate study at Northwestern University as a student of astronomy. "This was a field I had always been interested in since childhood," Apfel revealed, "but was discouraged from pursuing." In 1973 she became associate director of the Astro/Science Workshop at Adler Planetarium, remaining there until 1979 when she became a full-time writer.

Among Apfel's works are five juvenile books on astronomy, including *It's All Relative: Einstein's Theory of Relativity* (Lothrop, 1981). *School Library Journal* commended her use of "lots of down-to-earth examples with familiar objects to help elucidate difficult concepts," while *Booklist* found her explanation of the theory to be "bolstered with concrete anal-

ogies." Although Apfel found this book "especially difficult" to write, she believes that "it is important for young people to be exposed to these concepts as early as possible so that they will be more comfortable with them later on." Her other juvenile books are *Stars and Galaxies* (F. Watts, 1982), *The Moon and Its Exploration* (F. Watts, 1982), *Astronomy and Planetology* (F. Watts, 1983), and *It's All Elementary: From Atoms to the Quantum World of Quarks, Leptons, and Gluons* (Lothrop, 1985). Apfel is also the author of "Ask Ulysses," a monthly question-and-answer column for children featured in *Odyssey.* In addition to writing, she has taught courses in astronomy to children at Adler Planetarium and has lectured at elementary and junior high schools. *Home and office:* 3461 University Dr., Highland Park, Ill. 60035.

FOR MORE INFORMATION SEE: Contemporary Authors, Volume 107, Gale, 1983.

BARNES, Malcolm   1909(?)-1984

OBITUARY NOTICE: Born about 1909; died following a sudden illness, September 12, 1984. Publisher, editor, translator, and author. Barnes embarked on a publishing career with the firm of Chapman & Hall and in 1936 joined Allen & Unwin publishers, from which he retired in 1974 as editorial director. He worked for the Ministry of Information on Press Censorship during World War II. His best known translation was the children's classic *Le Ballon rouge* by Albert Lamorisse published in English as *The Red Balloon* in 1957. A skier and mountaineer in his free time, Barnes edited and translated a portion of the Swiss Mountaineering Federation book, *The Mountain World,* worked on Thor Heyerdahl's *Tigris Expedition,* and produced a translation of *Alpine Tragedy* by Charles Gos. His abridgement of author Augustus Hare's autobiography, *The Story of My Life,* appeared in two volumes titled *The Years with Mother* and *My Solitary Life.* Just prior to his death, Barnes completed a biography of Hare.

FOR MORE INFORMATION SEE— Obituaries: *Times* (London), September 18, 1984.

BATEY, Tom   1946-
(Jasper Tomkins)

BRIEF ENTRY: Born December 19, 1946, in Des Moines, Iowa. Batey received his B.F.A. from the University of Washington in 1971 and has worked as a staff artist for Bantam Books and as art director for Great Northwest Publications. Since 1978 he has been employed as a free-lance writer and artist. Under the pseudonym Jasper Tomkins, Batey is both author and illustrator of three picture books published by Green Tiger. His first, *The Catalog* (1981), is the whimsical story of three mountains in a remote desert area who order an assortment of giraffes, turtles, and bears from a catalog. *Publishers Weekly* called it an "exhilarating flight of fancy, a love of a book . . . so cleverly drawn that the author makes one eager to believe his tale." *The Catalog* was listed among the five best children's books in the world at the 1981 International

Children's Book Fair in Bologna, Italy. When Batey traveled to Italy to receive his award, he found the trip "overwhelming," an experience that led him to realize "the incredible responsibility held in the hands of children's writers for the well-being of young people everywhere. . . ." Batey continued to share that responsibility with *Nimby: A Remarkable Cloud* (1983) and *The Hole in the Ocean: A Daring Journey* (1984). He is currently anticipating the publication of two additional picture books, *The Catalog: Part Two* and *The Tiger and the Whale. Home:* 25516 Southeast 27th, Issaquah, Wash. 98027.

FOR MORE INFORMATION SEE: Contemporary Authors, Volume 107, Gale, 1983.

BAYLEY, Nicola   1949-

PERSONAL: Born August 18, 1949, in Singapore, China; part of childhood spent in Hampshire, England; daughter of Percy Howard (a company director) and Ann Barbara (Crowder) Bayley; married John Hilton (a barrister), December 21, 1979; children: Felix Percy Howard. *Education:* Attended St. Martin's School of Art; Royal College of Art, diploma, 1974. *Residence:* London, England.

CAREER: Illustrator of books for children. *Exhibitions:* St. Martin's School of Art, 1967-71; Royal College of Art Graduate Exhibition, 1971-74. *Awards, honors: The Patchwork Cat* received a Kate Greenaway Medal commendation and was selected one of International Reading Association's "Children's Choices," both 1982, and received the Bologna Fair Prize, 1983.

WRITINGS—Compiler; all for children: *Nicola Bayley's Book of Nursery Rhymes,* J. Cape, 1975, Knopf, 1977; *One Old*

NICOLA BAYLEY

I would slide on my tummy down hills of snow, I would be colored snow-white. . . . ■ (From *Polar Bear Cat* by Nicola Bayley. Illustrated by the author.)

Oxford Ox (counting book), Atheneum, 1977; *Copycats* (includes *Parrot Cat, Polar Bear Cat, Elephant Cat, Spider Cat,* and *Crab Cat*), Knopf, 1984.

Illustrator; all for children: Richard Adams, *The Tyger Voyage,* Knopf, 1976; Christopher Logue, adapter, *Puss in Boots* (pop-up book), J. Cape, 1976, Greenwillow, 1977; Russell Hoban, *La Corona and the Tin Frog, and Other Tales,* J. Cape, 1978, Merrimack, 1981; William Mayne, *The Patchwork Cat,* Knopf, 1981; W. Mayne, *The Mouldy,* Knopf, 1983.

WORK IN PROGRESS: A book of nonsense rhymes and a book of lullabies, to be published by Walker Books.

SIDELIGHTS: Bayley was born in Singapore on August 18, 1949. Her childhood was spent in both China and Hampshire, England. As a student at an English boarding school, she was excused from games in favor of art. "I had growing pains so wasn't allowed to do hockey and lacrosse. I spent all my afternoons in the art room." [Lee Kingman and others, compilers, *Illustrators of Children's Books: 1967-1976,* Horn Book, 1978.[1]]

Encouraged by an art teacher, Bayley applied to various art schools with a portfolio of fashion and textile designs. Her original ambition was to be a fashion designer, not an illustrator. At St. Martin's School of Art in London, she took graphic design courses and concentrated in her final years on illustration with John Farman and Fritz Wegner. After St. Martin's, Bayley continued her education at the Royal College of Art in London where her style of illustration was encouraged by Quentin Blake. Following graduation she worked for Jon-

Rats wake up and gnash their teeth at her and flash their eyes. ▪ (From *The Patchwork Cat* by William Mayne. Illustrated by Nicola Bayley.)

athan Cape, the publisher of her first book of nursery rhymes. Her second book for Jonathan Cape was Richard Adams's *The Tyger Voyage* for which she provided the illustrations. The book was written as the result of Bayley's illustration for the old rhyme "Three Thick Thumping Tigers Taking Toast for Tea." When Adams saw that illustration, he was so inspired that he composed his narrative poem around it.

Bayley lives and works in London. She prefers to work in water color on cartridge paper. The most difficult part of her work is at the rough draft stage. "I use my brain for them. After that it's mindless though absorbing. It's almost painting by numbers. I just fill in what I've drawn."[1]

The stippled look of her pictures is produced by dotting on paint with a brush in thousands of tiny dabs. Her drawings of animals are quite popular. Of these, her favorite subject is the cat; she enjoys keeping them as pets. "We used to have three but now there's only Desdemona left. I don't think it's fair to keep them, myself, in London till I'm really settled. Then I shall gather them round me like anything."[1]

FOR MORE INFORMATION SEE: Lee Kingman and others, compilers, *Illustrators of Children's Books: 1967-1976,* Horn Book, 1978.

BENNETT, Jay   1912-

PERSONAL: Born December 24, 1912, in New York, N. Y.; son of Pincus Shapiro (a businessman) and Estelle Bennett; married Sally Stern, February 2, 1937; children: Steven Cul-

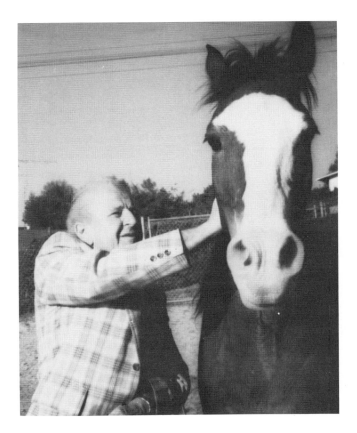

JAY BENNETT

len, Randy Elliott. *Education:* Attended New York University. *Home:* 402 Ocean Parkway, Brooklyn, N. Y. 11218.

CAREER: Writer and lecturer. Has worked as a farmhand, factory worker, lifeguard, mailman, salesman, and senior editor of an encyclopedia. *Wartime service:* English features writer and editor, Office of War Information, 1942-45. *Member:* Mystery Writers of America, Dramatists Guild, Writers Guild of America, Authors League of America. *Awards, honors:* Edgar Allan Poe Award from Mystery Writers of America for best juvenile mystery novel, 1974, for *The Long Black Coat,* and 1975, for *The Dangling Witness.*

WRITINGS: Catacombs, Abelard-Schuman, 1959; *Death Is a Silent Room,* Abelard-Schuman, 1965; *Murder Money,* Fawcett, 1963; *Deathman, Do Not Follow Me* (juvenile mystery), Meredith Press, 1968; *The Deadly Gift* (juvenile mystery; Junior Literary Guild selection), Meredith Press, 1969; *The Killing Tree* (juvenile mystery), F. Watts, 1972; *Masks: A Love Story,* F. Watts, 1972; *The Long Black Coat* (juvenile mystery), Delacorte, 1973; *Shadows Offstage,* Nelson, 1974; *The Dangling Witness* (juvenile mystery), Delacorte, 1974; *Say Hello to the Hit Man,* Delacorte, 1976; *The Birthday Murderer,* Delacorte, 1977; *The Pigeon,* Methuen, 1980; *The Executioner,* Avon, 1982; *Slowly, Slowly, I Raise the Gun,* Avon, 1983; *I Never Said I Loved You,* Avon, 1984.

Plays: "No Hiding Place" (three-act), first produced in New York at President Theatre, November 10, 1949; "Lions after Slumber" (three-act), first produced in London at Unity Theatre, June 2, 1951.

Also author of radio scripts, including "Miracle before Christmas" and "The Wind and Stars Are Witness," broadcast on major networks; author of television scripts for "Alfred Hitchcock Presents," "Crime Syndicated," "Wide, Wide World," "Cameo Theater," and "Monodrama Theatre."

SIDELIGHTS: "I am a New Yorker, born and bred; attended New York University, but never got any degree. I consider myself a well-educated man, but it would all have been much easier had I stayed on and finished at New York University.

"I have been married a long time to a girl I fell in love with the instant I saw her. We have two sons, Steve, an architect, and Randy, a doctor of education. I have an abiding love of literature, music (all kinds of phases), art, and ballet. I am also a fan of basketball, football, and baseball. I played some football at one time in my youth. My wife and I love to travel and to see and talk with other people. We also love to lie on beaches in the sun and get into the warm waters and swim.

"I wanted to be a writer from an early age, but had a very, very hard time breaking in—some fourteen years of writing and writing and not getting a single word of encouragement. Then I sold a suspense drama to NBC-TV and that launched me. I wrote for all the networks and one of my dramas was sent as representative of American radio writing to some forty countries by diplomatic pouch. I wrote over a million words for television. I left a lucrative career to devote my full time to writing for the young adult because I believed then and still believe that this readership is the most vital and alive of all readerships in American literature. I feel very strongly that the best writing done today is in that genre.

"I'm often asked how I get my ideas for my books. Well, let me cite one example. I wrote a book, *The Deadly Gift,* which has as its central character a young Mohawk Indian, the son

(Cover illustration by Norman Walker from *The Executioner* by Jay Bennett.)

of steelworkers who have a community in Brooklyn. I should say had a community, because I understand that most of the Indian community has been thinned out.

"I always thought the idea and central character of the book came to me intuitively one morning as I sat at the typewriter. I distinctly remember the character and central situation just kind of bursting into life. It was almost like automatic writing. And I thought it all must have come from my walking around the neighborhood and talking to some of the Mohawk steelworkers.

"But now I know that it was not that at all. I know the very experience from which the book emerged.

"I know because one night for no reason at all, sitting alone, it came back to me, vivid and very forceful.

"I remember it all.

"Many years ago I was riding a freight train from Kansas to Colorado. Sitting with me in the empty boxcar was a young Navaho. He had hopped on just as the train was clearing Junction City and starting its slow climb to Denver. We sat and talked a good way through the night. And then the train stopped dead and a big guy with a club and a gun came along and threw us out into the rain.

"There was a look on the Navaho's face. A hard, hopeless look. He never said another word to me as we walked along the tracks. I saw his eyes, the hat, the dungarees tight and wet on his legs.

"I never saw him again.

"But I know now that I never forgot him and all he said to me in the boxcar, and all he said when we walked to the dawn, and he didn't speak a word. I know now how I came to write *The Deadly Gift,* and why I feel the way I do about Indians. You see, I went back to New York and became a writer. And he went on to nowhere.

"The young adult reader should be encouraged and guided to the best of standards. If he picks up a suspense book, he should first demand that it be an entertaining one, a sight more thrilling and engrossing than most suspense television shows . . . and, above all, the book should have a strong and sustaining theme. I firmly believe this. Whenever I go out to meet my readers or when I read the letters they send me, I find that the themes I choose make my books extremely popular with them. For example, I deal with the loner in our society and show that it is impossible to survive alone. One must come to a decision, the decision to relate to the rest of humanity. The reader identifies with my 'loner' character and enjoys the crisis of decision and at the same time finds his sensibilities opened up. The reader thinks and feels as he enjoys, and whether or not he knows it consciously, he has learned something about the world he is living in."

FOR MORE INFORMATION SEE: Contemporary Authors, New Revision Series, Volume II, Gale, 1984.

BENNETT, Jill (Crawford) 1934-

PERSONAL: Born August 3, 1934, in Johannesburg, South Africa; part of childhood spent in Jamaica; married; children: Adam, Catherine. *Education:* Attended Wimbledon School of Art, London, England, and Slade School of Art, London; received National Diploma of Theatre Design, 1958. *Residence:* Putney, London, England.

CAREER: Illustrator of books for children, designer for the theater, and dollmaker.

ILLUSTRATOR: Roald Dahl, *Fantastic Mr. Fox,* Puffin, 1974 (Bennett was not associated with earlier edition); R. Dahl, *Danny, the Champion of the World,* Knopf, 1975; Dorothy Edwards, *The Magician Who Kept a Pub, and Other Stories,* Kestrel Books, 1975; Rosemary Harris, *I Want to Be a Fish,* Kestrel Books, 1977; Joan Aiken and others, *The Cat-Flap and the Apple Pie, and Other Funny Stories,* compiled by Lance Salway, W. H. Allen, 1979; Charles Causley, *Figgie Hobbin,* Puffin, 1979 (Bennett was not associated with earlier edition); Frances Gapper, *Jane and the Kenilwood Occurrences,* Faber, 1979; Helen Cresswell, *Bagthorpes v. the World,* Faber, 1979; Catherine Sefton (pseudonym of Martin Waddell), *The Ghost and Bertie Boggin,* Faber, 1980; Griselda Gifford, *Earwig and Beetle,* Gollancz, 1981; Sara Corrin and Stephen Corrin, editors, *Once Upon a Rhyme: 101 Poems for Young Children,* Faber, 1982; D. Edwards, *Misk and Magic,* Lutterworth, 1982; Carolyn Sloan, *Shakespeare, Theatre Cat,*

I twist and turn,
I creep, I prowl,
Likewise does he,
The crafty soul. . . .

■ (From "The Shadow" by Walter de la Mare in *Once Upon a Rhyme: 101 Poems for Young Children*, edited by Sara and Stephen Corrin. Illustrated by Jill Bennett.)

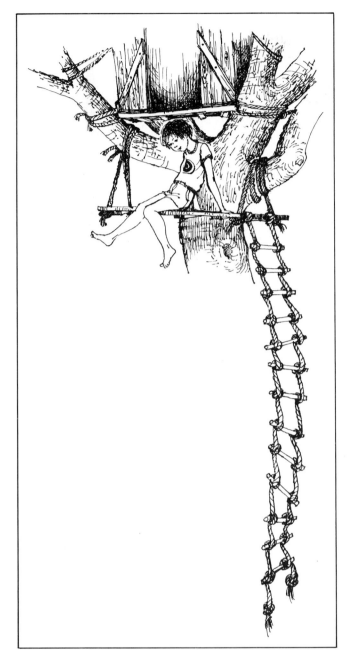

Then there was the treehouse which we built high up in the top of the big oak at the bottom of our meadow. ■ (From *Danny, the Champion of the World* by Roald Dahl. Illustrated by Jill Bennett.)

Macmillan, 1982; Storr, *Tales of Polly and the Hungry Wolf*, Faber, 1982; C. Sefton, *The Emma Dilemma*, Faber, 1982; Dick King-Smith, *The Queen's Nose*, Gollancz, 1983; S. Corrin and S. Corrin, editors, *Round the Christmas Tree*, Faber, 1983; Angela Bull, *The Accidental Twins*, Faber, 1983; June Counsel, *A Dragon in Class Four*, Faber, 1984; D. King-Smith, *Harry's Mad*, Gollancz, 1984; S. Corrin and S. Corrin, *The Faber Book of Christmas Stories*, Faber, 1984.

WORK IN PROGRESS: Illustrating Sara and Stephen Corrin's *The Faber Book of Stories for Pets;* illustrating Fay Samson's *Chris and the Dragon,* for Gollancz.

SIDELIGHTS: "Ever since I learned to read I have wanted to draw. My rather solitary childhood in Jamaica was 'peopled' with books. Later, in South Africa, I fell in love with the theatre. I realised with delight that in designing for the stage I could combine my two obsessions. I passed my National Diploma for Theatre Design and in 1958 got married. Now both my children are grown and I can concentrate on my doll-making along with illustration. I am lucky to have drawn for wonderful writers who make it exciting to draw the pictures they create with their words. It is also stimulating to see the excellent illustrative work of all kinds that is being done today."

BILLINGS, Charlene W(interer)   1941-

PERSONAL: Born January 11, 1941, in Manchester, N.H.; daughter of George E. (a power company employee) and Alice (a nurse; maiden name, Labbee) Winterer; married Barry A. Billings (an electrical engineer), December 16, 1961; children: Cheryl, Sharon. *Education:* University of New Hampshire, B.A. (cum laude), 1962; Rivier College, M.S., 1973. *Agent:* Janet D. Chenery, Chenery Associates Literary Agency, 440 E. 23rd St., New York, N.Y. *Residence:* Nashua, N.H.

CAREER: Hopkinton High School, Hopkinton, N.H., science teacher, 1962-63; University of New Hampshire, Durham, research assistant in biochemistry, 1963-64; writer. *Member:* Society of Children's Book Writers, American Society of Journalists and Authors, Sigma Xi Scientific Research Society (honorary associate member), Phi Beta Kappa, Phi Kappa Phi, Phi Sigma. *Awards, honors: Microchip: Small Wonder* was chosen an outstanding children's science trade book by the National Association of Science Teachers, 1984.

*WRITINGS—*Nonfiction for children: *Spring Peepers Are Calling* (illustrated by Susan Bonners), Dodd, 1978; *Salamanders,* Dodd, 1981; *Scorpions,* Dodd, 1983; *Microchip: Small Wonder,* Dodd, 1984.

WORK IN PROGRESS: Books about marine worms, the common loon, fiber optics, and the space station NASA expects to launch in the 1990s.

SIDELIGHTS: "Writing about science and writing for children bring together my love for both. The boundless enthusiasm and curiosity of young people continues to motivate me. Well-written science books for children are of the utmost importance. They must be accurate and should convey the excitement of science. They provide the opportunity to discover, understand, and appreciate the natural and technical world we all share. Besides writing, I enjoy cooking, photography, camping, swimming, and walks in the country. Many of these activities include my family."

FOR MORE INFORMATION SEE: Kirkus Reviews, February 1, 1979; *School Library Journal,* April, 1979, August, 1983; *Nashua Telegraph,* May 12, 1979; *Instructor,* May, 1979; *Science and Children,* January, 1980; *Appraisal: Children's Science Books,* spring, 1980, fall, 1981, winter, 1984; *Booklist,* April, 1981, August, 1983, January 1, 1985; *Bulletin of the Center for Children's Books,* June, 1981.

(From *Spring Peepers Are Calling* by Charlene W. Billings. Illustrated by Susan Bonners.)

Our days, our deeds, all we achieve or are,
Lay folded in our infancy; the things
Of good or ill we choose while yet unborn.
—John Townsend Trowbridge

Some of my best friends are children. In fact, all of my best friends are children.
—J.D. Salinger

BLASSINGAME, Wyatt Rainey   1909-1985 (W. B. Rainey)

OBITUARY NOTICE—See sketch in *SATA* Volume 34: Born February 6, 1909, in Demopolis, Ala.; died January 8, 1985, in Bradenton, Fla. Author. A free-lance writer since 1933, Blassingame produced sixty books throughout his lifetime, both fiction and nonfiction for children and adults. Nearly fifty of those books are juvenile nonfiction works covering a variety of topics, including histories (*The U.S. Frogmen of World War II, Men Who Opened the West, The Incas and the Spanish*

Conquest), biographies (*Stephen Decatur, Eleanor Roosevelt, Joseph Stalin and Communist Russia*), animal lore (*Wonders of Alligators and Crocodiles, Wonders of Raccoons, Wonders of the Turtle*), and books of general interest (*Great Trains of the World, Look It Up Book of Presidents, Story of the United States Flag*). Blassingame also wrote several stories for children based on American folklore heroes like *John Henry and Paul Bunyan Play Baseball, How Davy Crockett Got a Bearskin Coat,* and *Pecos Bill Rides a Tornado.* In addition to adult novels like *For Better, for Worse* and *Halo of Spears,* Blassingame contributed over six hundred stories and articles to national magazines, anthologies, and textbooks. His first short stories, mainly mystery and detective tales, appeared during the 1930s under the name W. B. Rainey.

FOR MORE INFORMATION SEE: Contemporary Authors, New Revision Series, Volume 3, Gale, 1981; *The Writers Directory: 1984-1986,* St. James Press, 1983. Obituaries: *Sarasota Herald-Tribune,* January 10, 1985.

BROCHMANN, Elizabeth (Anne) 1938-

PERSONAL: "Ch" in surname is pronounced "k"; born August 30, 1938, in Alberni, Vancouver Island, British Columbia, Canada; daughter of Edward John (a logger, mill owner, and landlord) and Alice (a landlady; maiden name, Schwarz) Luckhurst; married Harold Brochmann (a mathematics teacher and computer consultant), September 3, 1961; children: John Craig, Alice Kari. *Education:* Received teaching certificate from Victoria College, 1968. *Home:* 3264 St. George's Ave., North Vancouver, British Columbia, Canada V7N 1V3.

CAREER: Teacher at Old Fort Nelson in British Columbia, in Nova Scotia, in Ghana, West Africa, and in North Vancouver;

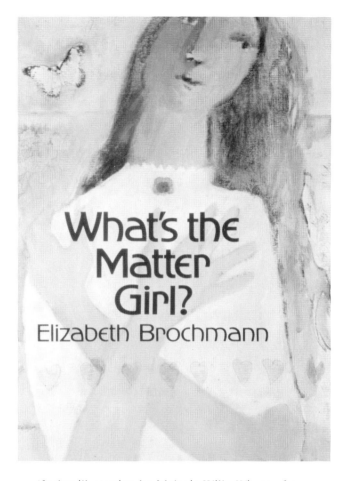

(Jacket illustration by Melanie Willa Winsten from *What's the Matter Girl?* by Elizabeth Brochmann.)

ELIZABETH BROCHMANN

teacher of writing in continuing education division at University of British Columbia, Vancouver, and at Langava College; writer. Volunteer worker with the mentally ill in St. Vincent, West Indies. *Member:* Writers Union, Ontario Arts Council. *Awards, honors:* Canada Council Grant, 1979.

WRITINGS: What's the Matter Girl? (juvenile novel), Harper, 1980; *Nobody Asked Me* (juvenile novel), James Lorimer, 1984.

Also author of six radio pieces for the "Peter Gzowski Show," Canadian Broadcasting Company (CBC), 1976, and of short stories "The Camping Trip," 1978, and "The Candy Man," 1979, for the "Hornby Collection," CBC.

WORK IN PROGRESS—Three novels: *Me and My Brother, My Brother and Me, Summer Job at the Greasy Spoon;* two adult novellas: *Also Man* and *Ga;* and *Turn Left for Utopia.*

SIDELIGHTS: "It takes me a very long time to finish a book. At first it comes quickly, often the whole book in a rush—but as if hidden in a cloud or a lot of wrapping paper, I have to wait and to dig for it.

"Writing is an act of discovery, so I write for self-illumination, that moment when the cloud disperses or the last sheet of wrapping paper is torn off to reveal the truth. If I am lucky it is a recognized truth for others. Often these are the old truths, small and ordinary, haltingly felt but clearly observed—at least that is what I try for.

"For me, remembering how as a child I entered the world of a book, writing for children has a special appeal. Anna appears in my first book at maybe five. I plan on writing seven or eight others, for I am following her life from the age of five to eighty-five or so. All books will be adult books, but also books for readers the age of Anna in the story. So when Anna is five, the reader (or listener) is five. She is only somewhat like myself, born in a town very much like my hometown. All the characters are composites of people, especially any that might resemble my relatives.

"I owe a great deal to my family. They put up with my writing, at times joining in, and then generously let me borrow bits of them to help make my characters. I also owe a great deal to my first editor, Elaine Edelman, and my Canadian editor, Shelly Tanaka—both consistently work for excellence in children's literature."

BULL, Norman John   1916-

PERSONAL: Born October 19, 1916, in Portsmouth, Hampshire, England; son of Edward George and Alice Henrietta Bull; married Margaret Ellen Humm, May, 1942; children: Margaret Jennifer, Peter Edward. *Education:* Trinity College, Oxford, B.A., 1938, M.A., 1949; University of Reading, D. Phil., 1967. *Home:* 21 Wonford Rd., Exeter, Devon, EX2 4LH, England.

CAREER: Teacher and involved in parish and youth work, 1938-48; St. Luke's College of Education, Exeter, England,

lecturer, 1948-58, senior lecturer, 1958-62, principal lecturer in education, 1962-75, head of religious education department, 1948-75; writer, 1952—. Member of Canterbury City Council, 1947-48. Honorary editor of *Devon Oakleaves* (a quarterly magazine of the National Trust). *Member:* Society of Authors, Rotary International.

WRITINGS: Book of Bible Activities, Hulton Educational Publications, 1955; *First Bible Dictionary,* Hulton Educational Publications, 1955; (with V. D. Whitburn) *God Speaks to Man,* Hulton Educational Publications, Book 1: *Call of the Hebrews,* 1957, Book 2: *Life of Jesus,* 1957, Book 3: *Heroes of Faith,* 1957, Book 4: *Prophets of God,* 1958, Book 5: *Teaching of Jesus,* 1958, Book 6: *The Church Marches On,* 1958; *From Prophecy to Law* (teachers guide), Religious Education Publications, 1958; *Religious Education in the Primary School,* Macmillan, 1958; *People of God* (dramatic Bible reader), Heinemann Educational, 1959; *Life of Christ* (dramatic Bible reader), Heinemann Educational, 1959.

Great Christians, Hulton Educational Publications, 1960, Book 1: *The Early Saints,* Book 2: *New Life in the Church,* Book 3: *Workers for God,* Book 4: *The Church in All the World; Kingdom of God* (dramatic Bible reader), Heinemann Educational, 1961; *Prophets* (dramatic Bible reader), Heinemann Educational, 1961; *Rise of the Prophets* (teachers guide), Religious Educational Publications, 1961; *Children of the Bible,* Evans, 1961; *Old Testament Church* (dramatic Bible reader), Heinemann Educational, 1963; *My Catechism Book,* National Society/Society for Promoting Christian Knowledge, 1963; *Church of Christ* (dramatic Bible reader), Heinemann Educational, 1964; *The Bible Story and Its Background* (juvenile), Hulton Educational Publications, Book 1: *Founders of the Jews,* 1965, Book 2: *Kings of the Jews,* 1966, Book 3: *Prophets of the Jews,* 1966, Book 4: *The Church of the Jews,* 1967, Book 5: *Jesus the Nazarene,* 1968, Book 6: *The Parables of Jesus,* 1969, Book 7: *The Church of Jesus Begins,* 1970, Book 8:

David's sling was a fine weapon, too. Sometimes a wild beast came after his sheep. ■ (From *100 Bible Stories,* retold by Norman J. Bull. Illustrated by Val Biro.)

NORMAN JOHN BULL

The Church of Jesus Grows, 1970; *The Rise of the Church,* Heinemann Educational, 1967; *Symbols* (juvenile), edited by Ronald J. Goldman, four volumes, Hart-Davis Educational, 1967, Morehouse, 1970; *Stories Jesus Told* (juvenile; illustrated by Graham Byfield), Augsburg, 1969; *Moral Education,* Routledge, 1969, Sage Publications, 1970; *Moral Judgment from Childhood to Adolescence,* Routledge, 1969, Sage Publications, 1970.

The Way of Wisdom (juvenile), Longman, Book 1: *Living with Others,* 1970, Book 2: *Myself and Others,* 1970, Book 3: *Rulers,* 1971, Book 4: *Drivers,* 1973, Book 5: *Persons,* 1976; *One Hundred Great Lives* (juvenile), Hulton Educational Publications, 1972, Dufour, 1975; *Colours* (juvenile), Burke Books, 1973; *The Bible Data Book,* Evans Brothers, 1975; *Food and Drink,* Wheaton, 1979; *You and Me,* Wheaton, 1979; *Light and Darkness* (juvenile), Wheaton, 1979; *Festivals and Customs* (juvenile), Wheaton, 1979.

The Story of Jesus (juvenile), Hamlyn, 1980, Abingdon, 1983; *100 Bible Stories* (juvenile), Hamlyn, 1980, Abingdon, 1983; *My Little Book of Prayers* (juvenile), Hamlyn, 1980; *100 New Testament Stories,* Hamlyn, 1981, Abingdon, 1984; *My Little Book of Jesus* (illustrated by Victor Ambrus), Hamlyn, 1981; (with R. J. Ferris) *Stories from World Religions,* Oliver & Boyd, 4 books, 1982-83; *A Modern Saint Francis: The Story of Brother Douglas* (juvenile), Arnold-Wheaton, 1983; *How Things Began* (juvenile; series of six books), Basil Blackwell, in press.

WORK IN PROGRESS: Research on mythology.

SIDELIGHTS: "I took up writing as an integral part of my professional work in education. I have published books for children of all ages, for students and teachers, and, in the publication of my research, for educational psychologists. All my writing has been educational, in the widest sense."

HOBBIES AND OTHER INTERESTS: Music, gardening.

BULLA, Clyde Robert   1914-

PERSONAL: Born January 9, 1914, in King City, Mo.; son of Julian and Sarah (Henson) Bulla. *Education:* "Largely self-educated." *Home:* Los Angeles, Calif. *Agent:* Bill Berger Associates, 444 E. 58th St., New York, N.Y. 10022.

CAREER: Professional writer of children's books. Composer of music for children. *Tri-County News,* King City, Mo., linotype operator and columnist, 1943-49. *Member:* Authors Guild, Society of Children's Book Writers. *Awards, honors:* Boys' Club of America Gold Medal, 1955, for *Squanto, Friend of the White Men;* Authors Club of Los Angeles award for outstanding juvenile book by Southern California author, 1961, for *Benito;* Southern California Council on Children's Liter-

CLYDE ROBERT BULLA

He looked up. The animal stood nearby, watching him. . . . ▪ (From *Conquista!* by Clyde Robert Bulla and Michael Syson. Illustrated by Ronald Himler.)

(From the movie "Shoeshine Girl," based on the book by Clyde Robert Bulla. Released by Learning Corporation of America, 1980.)

ature award, 1962, for distinguished contribution to field of children's literature, and 1976, for *Shoeshine Girl;* George F. Stone Center for Children's Books award, 1968, for *White Bird;* Commonwealth Club of California Silver medal, 1970, for *Jonah and the Great Fish;* Christopher Award, 1971, for *Pocahontas and the Strangers; Noah and the Rainbow: An Ancient Story* was selected as a Children's Book Showcase title, 1973; Charlie May Simon Award, 1978, Sequoyah Children's Book Award, 1978, and South Carolina Children's Book Award, 1980, all for *Shoeshine Girl; A Lion to Guard Us* was selected as a Notable Children's Trade Book in Social Studies, 1982.

WRITINGS—Juvenile, except as indicated; published by Crowell, except as indicated: *These Bright Young Dreams* (adult novel), Penn, 1941; *The Donkey Cart* (illustrated by Lois Lenski), 1946; *Riding the Pony Express* (illustrated by Grace Paull), 1948; *The Secret Valley* (illustrated by G. Paull), 1949.

Surprise for a Cowboy (illustrated by G. Paull), 1950; *A Ranch for Danny* (illustrated by G. Paull), 1951; *Song of St. Francis* (illustrated by Valenti Angelo), 1952; *Johnny Hong of Chinatown* (illustrated by Dong Kingman), 1952; *Eagle Feather* (illustrated by Tom Two Arrows), 1953; *Star of Wild Horse Canyon* (illustrated by G. Paull), 1953; *Down the Mississippi* (illustrated by Peter Burchard), 1954; *Squanto, Friend of the White Men* (illustrated by P. Burchard), 1954, published as *Squanto, Friend of the Pilgrims,* 1969; *White Sails to China* (illustrated by Robert Henneberger), 1955; *The Poppy Seeds* (illustrated by Jean Charlot), 1955; *A Dog Named Penny* (illustrated by Kate Seredy), Ginn, 1955; *John Billington: Friend of Squanto* (illustrated by P. Burchard), 1956; *The Sword in the Tree* (illustrated by Paul Galdone), 1956; *Old Charlie* (illustrated by P. Galdone), 1957; *Ghost Town Treasure* (illustrated by Don Freeman), 1957; *Pirate's Promise* (illustrated by P. Burchard), 1958; *The Valentine Cat* (illustrated by Leonard Weisgard), 1959; *Stories of Favorite Operas* (illustrated by Robert Galster), 1959.

Three-Dollar Mule (illustrated by Paul Lantz), 1960; *A Tree Is a Plant* (illustrated by Lois Lignell), 1960; *The Sugar Pear Tree* (illustrated by Taro Yashima), 1960; *Benito* (illustrated by V. Angelo), 1961; *The Ring and the Fire: Stories from Wagner's Nibelung Operas* (illustrated by Clare Ross and John Ross), 1962; *What Makes a Shadow?* (illustrated by Adrienne Adams), 1962; *Viking Adventure* (illustrated by Douglas Gors-

His mother and father were proud. ∎ (From *Daniel's Duck* by Clyde Robert Bulla. Illustrated by Joan Sandin.)

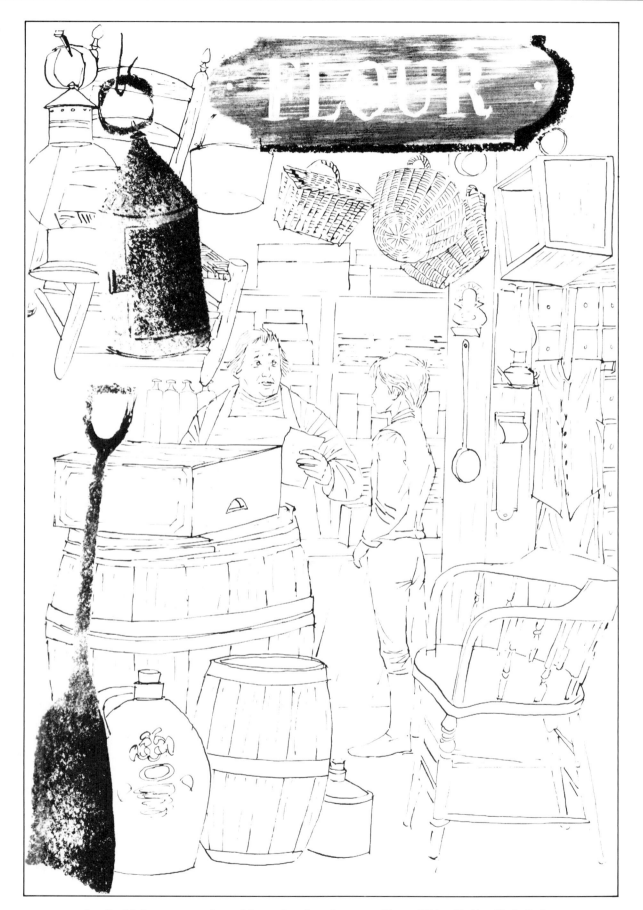

Joe Roddy's store was a log cabin on the edge of town. ■ (From *White Bird* by Clyde Robert Bulla. Illustrated by Leonard Weisgard.)

line), 1963; *Indian Hill* (illustrated by James J. Spanfeller), 1963; *St. Valentine's Day* (illustrated by V. Angelo), 1965; *More Stories of Favorite Operas* (illustrated by Joseph Low), 1965; *Lincoln's Birthday* (illustrated by Ernest Crichlow), 1966; *White Bird* (illustrated by L. Weisgard), 1966; *Washington's Birthday* (illustrated by Don Bolognese), 1967; *Flowerpot Gardens* (illustrated by Henry Evans), 1967; *The Ghost of Windy Hill* (illustrated by D. Bolognese), 1968; *Mika's Apple Tree: A Story of Finland* (illustrated by Des Asmussen), 1986; *Stories of Gilbert and Sullivan Operas* (illustrated by James McCrea and Ruth McCrea), 1968; *New Boy in Dublin: A Story of Ireland* (illustrated by Jo Polseno), 1969; *The Moon Singer* (illustrated by Trina Schart Hyman), 1969.

Jonah and the Great Fish (illustrated by Helga Aichinger), 1970; *Pocahontas and the Strangers* (illustrated by P. Burchard), 1971; *Joseph the Dreamer* (illustrated by Gordon Laite), 1971; *Open the Door and See All the People* (illustrated by Wendy Watson), 1972; (translator) Max Bolliger, *Noah and the Rainbow: An Ancient Story* (illustrated by H. Aichinger), 1972; *Dexter* (illustrated by Glo Coalson), 1973; *The Wish at the Top* (illustrated by Chris Conover), 1974; *Shoeshine Girl* (illustrated by Leigh Grant), 1975; *Marco Moonlight* (illustrated by Julia Noonan), 1976; *The Beast of Lor* (illustrated by Ruth Sanderson), 1977; (with Michael Syson) *Conquista!* (illustrated by Ronald Himler), 1978; *Keep Running, Allen!* (illustrated by Satomi Ichikawa), 1978; *Last Look* (illustrated by Emily A. McCully), 1979; *Daniel's Duck* (illustrated by Joan Sandin), Harper, 1979.

The Stubborn Old Woman (illustrated by Anne Rockwell), 1980; *My Friend, the Monster* (illustrated by Michele Chessare), 1980; *Lion to Guard Us* (illustrated by M. Chessare), 1981; *Almost a Hero* (illustrated by Ben Stahl), Dutton, 1981; *Dandelion Hill* (illustrated by Bruce Degen), Dutton, 1982; *Poor Boy, Rich Boy* (illustrated by Marcia Sewall), Harper, 1982; *Charlie's House* (illustrated by Arthur Dorros), 1983; *The Cardboard Crown* (illustrated by M. Chessare), 1984; *A Grain of Wheat: A Writer Begins* (autobiography), Godine, 1985. Contributor of stories and articles to periodicals, including *Women's Day, American, The Writer*.

Composer of music for song books, with lyrics by Lois Lenski: *Cotton in My Sack*, Lippincott, 1949; *I Like Winter*, Walck, 1950; *Prairie School*, Lippincott, 1951; *We Are Thy Children*, Crowell, 1952; *Mamma Hattie's Girl*, Lippincott, 1953; *On a Summer Day*, Walck, 1953; *Corn-Farm Boy*, Lippincott, 1954; *Songs of Mr. Small*, Oxford University Press, 1954; *A Dog Came to School*, Oxford University Press, 1955; *Songs of the City*, Edward B. Marks Music Corp., 1956; *Up to Six: Book I*, Hansen Music, 1956; *Flood Friday*, Lippincott, 1956; *Davy and Dog*, Walck, 1957; *I Went for a Walk*, Walck, 1958; *At Our House*, Walck, 1959; *When I Grow Up*, Walck, 1960.

Composer of incidental music for plays; all written by Lois Lenski; all published by the National Council of Churches, 1952; *The Bean-Pickers; A Change of Heart; Strangers in a Strange Land*. Composer of librettos for two unproduced operas.

ADAPTATIONS: "The Moon Singer" (orchestration), music by William Winstead, first performed at The Academy of Music, Philadelphia, Pa. by the Philadelphia Orchestra, November 11, 1972; "Shoeshine Girl" (movie), Learning Corporation of America, 1980.

WORK IN PROGRESS: The Redbud Tree, a novel for young adults.

At night he slept in the forks of trees, where he was safe from wild beasts. ■ (From *The Beast of Lor* by Clyde Robert Bulla. Illustrated by Ruth Sanderson.)

SIDELIGHTS: "I was born on a farm near King City, Missouri, on **January 9, 1914.** Besides my mother and father, I had two sisters and a brother.

"I didn't know until later that King City was a town. I thought it was a great city. On Saturday night the main street was crowded with people. I had my first nickel bag of candy there, and my first ice cream cone. (I bit off the end of the cone, and the ice cream ran down my shirt.) I saw my first movie there, but I can't remember what it was. It was probably a cowboy picture.

"There were interesting things to see and do in town, but I was soon ready to go home. It seemed to me that was where I belonged. I liked our house with its little rooms—two upstairs and three down. My father told me it was almost a hundred years old.

"In the back yard were trees—peach, cherry, pear, and black walnut. The vegetable garden was there, too. And there were hollyhocks. Hundreds of them came up and bloomed every spring, with bees buzzing among them.

"In the front yard were four mulberry trees, an evergreen, and a big box-elder. I used to climb the mulberry trees, and I had a swing in the box-elder.

"Our front porch faced west. I could sit there and see the barnlot with the big barn and small sheds. I could see the

"They sent me away," said Torr. ■ (From *The Moon Singer* by Clyde Robert Bulla. Illustrated by Trina Schart Hyman.)

pasture and the woods. Beyond the woods I could see Will Sutton's little brown house half a mile away.

"My dog Carlo would be with me on the porch. He was a collie. He was the family dog before I was born, but as soon as I was old enough to play outside, he became my dog.

"Most of our storms came out of the west. I liked to sit on the porch and watch them. The sky would turn dark, almost black. Lightning would split the clouds and thunder would crash. Wind would blow and bend the trees, and I would see

the rain like a gray curtain falling over the woods. It would sweep across the barnlot and onto the porch, onto my dog and me.

"Carlo was afraid of storms. He would shiver and push against me. I remember the smell of his wet fur. I would put by arms around him and he would sit there until my mother opened the door and found us.

"My mother didn't worry about me as long as Carlo and I were together. She didn't know about the dangerous game we played. We chased the horses in the pasture. I waved a stick, and Carlo barked at their heels.

"One day I ran too close behind them. One of them kicked me. Corrine [my sister] found me in the pasture. I was covered with blood, and the mark of a horse's hoof was on my forehead. For weeks I lay in bed. When I began to get well, my mother cut out maps and made me a geography book. I kept it for a long time." [Clyde Robert Bulla, *A Grain of Wheat: A Writer Begins,* Godine, 1985.[1]]

1920-1926. Educated at Bray School. "Those were the days of country schools. Ours was the Bray School. My sister Louise had taught there before she was married. My sister Corrine had just finished high school and was ready to take her place.

"Corrine was teaching for the first time. I was going to school for the first time. It was a two-mile walk to school. We started off together. Almost always it rained on the first day of school, but this was a sunny September day. I had my new dinner

He and Olivia waited on the platform. She looked different this morning. ■ (From *The Cardboard Crown* by Clyde Robert Bulla. Illustrated by Michele Chessare.)

bucket. There was a beef sandwich in it, and a boiled egg and a banana and a piece of cake. But this gave me no joy.

"I said, 'I know I'll get a whipping.'

"'I'll be the teacher,' Corrine said. '*I'm* not going to whip you.'

"Later we learned to cut across pastures and through woods to make the way shorter. On this day we took the road. Past Otis King's, past John King's and Mag Elliott's, over the iron bridge and up the clay hill, past George Haynes's, and there was the school lane.

"At the end of the lane was the schoolyard, with the schoolhouse in the middle. The schoolhouse was white with a red brick chimney. It had only one room. The blackboard was up front, along with the teacher's desk and the library. The library was a tall, green cupboard with a door. There were rows of seats and desks for the boys and girls. In the back of the room was a big, iron stove.

"Corrine and I were the first ones there. She wrote 'Welcome' on the blackboard. Boys and girls began to come from the farms in the neighborhood. There were nine boys and nine girls. Two or three rode horses to school, but most of them walked.

"I was in the first grade with three other boys—Leonard, Lawrence, and Harold. Later Lawrence and Harold moved away, but Leonard and I were in school together for years.

"... I liked school. I was surprised at how much I liked it, although I was sometimes sorry my dog couldn't be there. Every day he started off with me. Every day I had to send him back.

"It took our whole school to make two baseball teams. Besides baseball, we played ante-over, kick-the-can, dare-base, and Indian. In winter we played fox-and-geese in the snow.

"In first grade we had spelling, numbers, reading, and writing. I was slow at numbers, better at spelling. What I really liked were reading and writing. I wanted to learn new words. I wanted to write them and put them together to see what I could make them say.

"Words were wonderful. By writing them and putting them together, I could make them say whatever I wanted them to say. It was a kind of magic.

"Reading was a kind of magic, too. In a book I would meet other people and know what they were doing and feeling and thinking. From a book I could learn about life in other places. Or I could learn everyday things like tying a knot or building a birdhouse.

"By the time I was ready for the third grade, I had read most of the books in our school library. There weren't many. I wanted more. I began reading whatever I could find at home.

"There was always work to be done on a farm. Boys and girls had their special chores. My first ones were filling the woodbox and feeding the animals.

"The woodpile was in the barnlot. There were big pieces of wood to be burned in the heating stove. Smaller pieces were for the cook stove. Sometimes I carried the wood in my arms.

Sometimes I hauled it in a little wagon or the two-wheeled cart. I brought it to the back door and piled it in the woodbox in the kitchen.

"I took corn to the pigs and chickens. I fed skim milk to the calves. In summer I hoed weeds out of the vegetable garden and sometimes out of the cornfield.

"But there was time to play, time for long walks in the woods. I looked for rocks along the creek. I knew where to find May apples. They grew on plants that looked like little green umbrellas. The apples were yellow and squashy. They smelled better than they tasted. Ripe gooseberries were good. (Not green ones; they were so sour I could never eat one without making a face.) Wild blackberries were even better. Wild raspberries were best of all."[1]

1924. "I wanted to be a writer. I was sure of that. . . . I went from the second grade to the third to the fourth, and I hadn't changed. I still knew what I wanted to be. . . .

"In the paper I read about a contest for boys and girls—'Write the Story of a Grain of Wheat in five hundred words or less.' First prize was $100. There were five second prizes of $20 each. After that there were one hundred prizes of $1 each.

"I began to write my story. It went something like this: 'I am a grain of wheat. I grew in a field where the sun shone and the rain fell.'

"I didn't tell anyone what I was doing. When my story was finished, I made a neat copy. I mailed it in our mailbox down the road.

"Time went by. I began to look for the paper that would tell who had won the contest. At last it came.

"There was a whole page about the contest. I saw I hadn't won the first prize. I hadn't won a second prize either. That was a disappointment. I had thought I might win one of the second prizes.

"I read down the long list at the bottom of the page—the names and addresses of the boys and girls who had won the $1 prizes. Surely my name would be there. It *had* to be!

"I read more and more slowly. Only a few names were left. And one of them was mine! 'Clyde Bulla, King City, Missouri.'

"I had written a story that was all mine. No one had helped me. I had sent it off. How many other boys and girls had sent their stories? Maybe a thousand or more. But my story had won a prize, and my name was here in the paper. I was a writer. No matter what anyone else might say, I was a writer."[1]

Besides books and writing, Bulla was interested in opera, history, and in traveling to other parts of the world. "We didn't have many books in our school library, and there were no swings or slides on the playground. But we had something wonderful in our schoolroom—a world globe.

"To some of the boys and girls it was a toy, and they spun it like a top. It was never a toy to me. It was a marvelous picture of the world. I turned it slowly, reading the names on it and learning the shapes of the countries and continents. All those places were out there, waiting for me. I said to myself, 'I'm

going to travel. I'm going everywhere!'" [Clyde Robert Bulla, "Meet Your Author, Clyde Robert Bulla," *Cricket*, November, 1980.[2]]

After finishing one year at King City High School in 1927, Bulla left school and worked as a farmer until 1943.

1946. Published first story for children, *The Donkey Cart.* Bulla had no formal training as a writer. "I began very young and proceeded by trial and error. At first I wrote magazine stories, articles, and a novel for adults. I also worked on a hometown newspaper and wrote a weekly column. A friend, who was an elementary teacher and a writer, saw the column and told me the style of it suggested children's stories. So I wrote my first story for children, *The Donkey Cart.*" [Lee Bennett Hopkins, *Books Are By People,* Citation Press, 1969.[3]]

Several of Bulla's subsequent books grew out of his travels. "Until I was grown, I lived in the Middle West. Then I moved to the West, first to Arizona and then to California, where I met Indians for the first time and became interested in them

He came upon his mother with her head bowed over the kitchen table. ■ (From *The Wish at the Top* by Clyde Robert Bulla. Illustrated by Chris Conover.)

and in their history. One of my most memorable vacations was spent at an isolated trading post on an Indian reservation. I have Indian friends here in Los Angeles.''[3]

"There have been more trips—by land, sea, and air—within my own country as well as to foreign ones. A story has come out of almost every one. Sometimes it is waiting to be written as soon as I am home again. Sometimes it comes to me long afterward.

"So I travel and write, write and travel. It is a good life.''[2]

Bulla's numerous books for young people combine his vivid imagination with his interests in travel, opera and music, and history. ". . . I retold the stories of twenty-three operas, and the collection was published under the title *Stories of Favorite Operas*. It was hard to limit the number to twenty-three. It

was especially hard to omit the four operas in Wagner's 'Ring' cycle, and three years later I told the stories of these music dramas in a separate book, *The Ring and the Fire*.

"Even before the second book was finished, I was planning a third. . . . The retelling of the stories is meant to help listeners follow the operas with greater understanding and enjoyment." [Clyde Robert Bulla, "Introduction," *More Stories of Favorite Operas*, Crowell, 1965.[4]]

Regarding his work habits, Bulla remarked: "I like to carry an idea in the back of my mind for awhile, allowing it to develop in its own way and in its own time. One day, when the story seems complete, I begin writing; I write first in longhand, slowly and painfully. The opening paragraph is the hardest; sometimes I write as many as 50 or 60 before turning out one I can use. Every manuscript goes through several complete

Jenny lay down. She leaned back. "Maybe it is a little like grapes. A little like watermelons, too," she said. "Oh, look up there! Look at that cloud. It's a frog."

(From *Keep Running, Allen!* by Clyde Robert Bulla. Illustrated by Satomi Ichikawa.)

drafts. Sometimes I try out ideas on children. I hope the boys and girls know from my books that I have sympathy for them and that I remember what it is like to be a child."[3]

"I ask myself questions. What kind of person is the hero? What is his environment and how does he react to it? How do he and the heroine feel toward each other? Is she giddy or serious? What is her background?

"When I've lived with my characters long enough to know them and their relationship to each other and have my story line well in mind, I'm ready to begin writing. Certainly this approach doesn't eliminate all the work, but it does eliminate a lot of the uncertainty. If you know how your characters talk, you are not going to have so much trouble with dialogue. If you know what their reactions will be to a situation, you can be pretty sure your motivation will be sound. [Clyde Robert Bulla, "Before You Write," *The Writer*, December 1954.[5]]

Bulla has lived in California for over thirty years in a big, old house in Los Angeles. "Sometimes I complain about Los Angeles' smog, traffic, and high taxes, but all in all I'm happy and contented here. The mountains, the ocean, and the desert are all nearby. There are theatres, museums, libraries, and concert halls. Many writers and illustrators of children's books live in the area, and some of them are among my best friends. I love the theatre—plays, operas, concerts—and I love to travel too. My idea of a good vacation is a long voyage on a freighter. I play the piano and write music. I paint in oils and water-colors, not very well but with enthusiasm! The longer I live, the more I value peace and quiet. I am not a person who is easily bored."[3]

Bulla's works are included in the Kerlan Collection at the University of Minnesota and in the de Grummond Collection at the University of Southern Mississippi.

HOBBIES AND OTHER INTERESTS: Music, painting in oils and water colors, travel.

FOR MORE INFORMATION SEE: The Writer, December, 1948, December, 1954; Huck and Young, *Children's Literature in the Elementary School,* Holt, 1961; Muriel Fuller, editor, *More Junior Authors,* H. W. Wilson, 1963; May Hill Arbuthnot, *Children and Books,* 3rd edition, Scott, Foresman, 1964; *The Children's Bookshelf,* Child Study Association of America, 1965; *Books for Children, 1960-1965,* American Library Association, 1966; Nancy Larrick, *A Teacher's Guide to Children's Books,* Merrill, 1966; Lee Bennett Hopkins, *Books Are by People,* Citation Press, 1969; *Elementary English,* November, 1971; Miriam Hoffman and Eva Samuels, *Authors and Illustrators of Children's Books,* Bowker, 1972; *American Bi-Centennial Reading,* Children's Book Council, 1975; D. L. Kirkpatrick, *Twentieth-Century Children's Writers,* St. Martin's Press, 1978; *Cricket,* November, 1980; Clyde Robert Bulla, *A Grain of Wheat: A Writer Begins,* Godine, 1985.

BURROUGHS, Edgar Rice 1875-1950

PERSONAL: Born September 1, 1875, in Chicago, Ill.; died March 19, 1950, in Encino, Calif.; son of George Tyler and Mary Evaline (Zieger) Burroughs; married Emma Centennia Hulbert, January 31, 1900; married second wife, Florence Gilbert, 1935 (divorced, 1942); children: (first marriage) Joan,

Hulbert, John Coleman. *Education:* Attended several private schools, including Phillips Academy, Andover, Mass., and Michigan Military Academy, Orchard Lake. *Home:* Encino, Calif.

CAREER: Author. Michigan Military Academy, Orchard Lake, assistant commandant, 1895-96; American Battery Co., Chicago, Ill., treasurer, 1899-1903; Sears, Roebuck & Co., department manager, 1906-08; A. W. Shaw Co. (publishers of *System*), department manager, 1912-13; writer, since 1911. War correspondent for United Press International and Los Angeles *Times* in the Pacific Islands, 1942-46. Also worked at various times as a gold miner, storekeeper, cowboy, and railroad policeman. *Military service:* U.S. Army, 7th U.S. Cavalry, Fort Grant, Ariz.; discharged as under age. Later served in the Illinois Reserve Militia; became major. *Member:* Loyal Legion Club.

WRITINGS—Science fiction and adventure: *The Mucker* (illustrated by J. Allen St. John), Grosset, 1921, reissued, Ace Books, 1974; *The Girl from Hollywood*, Macaulay, 1923, reissued, Ace Books, 1977; *The Land That Time Forgot* (illustrated by J. A. St. John), A. C. McClurg, 1924, reissued, Ace Books, 1975; *The Bandit of Hell's Bend*, A. C. McClurg, 1925, reissued, Ace Books, 1977; *The Cave Girl*, A. C. McClurg, 1925, reissued, Ace Books, 1975; *The Eternal Lover*, A. C. McClurg, 1925, reissued as *The Eternal Savage*, Ace Books, 1977; *The Mad King*, A. C. McClurg, 1926, reissued, Ace Books, 1976; *The Moon Maid*, Grosset, 1926, reissued, Ace Books, 1977; *The Outlaw of Torn*, A. C. McClurg, 1927, reprinted, Buccaneer Books, 1976.

The Monster Men, A. C. McClurg, 1929, reissued, Ace Books, 1977; *Jungle Girl* (illustrated by Studley Burroughs), E. R. Burroughs, 1932, reissued as *The Land of Hidden Men*, Ace Books, 1977; *Apache Devil* (illustrated by S. Burroughs), E. R. Burroughs, 1933, reprinted, Buccaneer Books, 1976; *Back to the Stone Age* (illustrated by his son, John Coleman Burroughs; originally published as "Seven Worlds to Conquer" in *Argosy* magazine, January-February, 1937), E. R. Burroughs, 1937, reissued, Ace Books, 1975; *The Oakdale Affair* [*and*] *The Rider* (illustrated by J. C. Burroughs), E. R. Burroughs, 1937, reprinted separately, Buccaneer Books, 1976; *The Lad and the Lion* (illustrated by J. C. Burroughs), E. R. Burroughs, 1938, reissued, Ace Books, 1974.

The Deputy Sheriff of Comanche County (illustrated by J. C. Burroughs), E. R. Burroughs, 1940, reissued, Ace Books, 1975; *Land of Terror*, E. R. Burroughs, 1944, new edition illustrated by Roy G. Krenkel, Canaveral, 1963; *Beyond Thirty* [*and*] *The Man-Eater*, Science-Fiction & Fantasy Publications, 1957 [*Beyond Thirty* was reissued as *The Lost Continent*, Ace Books, circa 1964]; *Beyond the Farthest Star*, Ace Books, 1964, reissued, 1973; *Tales of Three Planets* (illustrated by R. G. Krenkel), Canaveral, 1964, reissued, 1975; *Out of Time's Abyss* (first published in *Blue Book Magazine*, 1918), Ace Books, circa 1964, reissued, 1973; *The People That Time Forgot* (first published in *Blue Book Magazine*, 1918), Ace Books, circa 1964, reissued, 1977; *The Girl from Farris's* (first published in *All-Story Weekly*, September-October, 1916), House of Greystoke, 1965; *The Efficiency Expert* (first published in *Argosy All-Story Weekly*, October, 1921), House of Greystoke, 1966; *I Am a Barbarian*, E. R. Burroughs, 1967, reissued, Ace Books, 1975.

"Tarzan" series: *Tarzan of the Apes*, A. L. Burt, 1914, reissued (illustrated by Burne Hogarth), Watson-Guptill, 1972; *The Return of Tarzan*, Grosset, 1915, reissued, Ballantine, 1975; *The Beasts of Tarzan* (illustrated by J. A. St. John), A.

EDGAR RICE BURROUGHS

C. McClurg, 1916, reissued, Ballantine, 1975; *The Son of Tarzan* (illustrated by J. A. St. John), A. C. McClurg, 1917, reissued, Ballantine, 1975; *Tarzan and the Jewels of Opar* (illustrated by J. A. St. John), Grosset, 1918, reissued, Ballantine, 1975; *Jungle Tales of Tarzan* (illustrated by J. A. St. John), Grosset, 1919, reissued (illustrated by Burne Hogarth), Watson-Guptill, 1976; *Tarzan the Untamed* (illustrated by J. A. St. John), A. C. McClurg, 1920, reissued, Ballantine, 1976; *Tarzan the Terrible* (illustrated by J. A. St. John), A. C. McClurg, 1921, reissued, Ballantine, 1976; *Tarzan and the Golden Lion* (illustrated by J. A. St. John), A. C. McClurg, 1923, reissued, Ballantine, 1976; *Tarzan and the Ant Men,* Grosset, 1924, reissued, Ballantine, 1976; *The Tarzan Twins* (illustrated by Douglas Grant), P. F. Volland, 1927, reissued as *Tarzan and the Tarzan Twins,* Canaveral, 1963; *Tarzan, Lord of the Jungle* (illustrated by J. A. St. John), A. C. McClurg, 1928, reissued, Ballantine, 1976; *Tarzan and the Lost Empire,* Metropolitan Books, 1929, reissued, Ballantine, 1976.

Tarzan at the Earth's Core, Metropolitan Books, 1930, reissued, Ballantine, 1975; *Tarzan the Invincible* (illustrated by S. Burroughs), E. R. Burroughs, 1931, reissued, Ballantine, 1964; *Tarzan Triumphant* (illustrated by S. Burroughs), E. R. Burroughs, 1932, reissued, Ballantine, 1975; *Tarzan and the City of Gold* (illustrated by J. A. St. John), E. R. Burroughs, 1933, reissued, Ballantine, 1975; *Tarzan and the Lion Man* (illustrated by J. A. St. John), E. R. Burroughs, 1934, reissued, Ballantine, 1975; *Tarzan and the Leopard Men* (illustrated by J. A. St. John), E. R. Burroughs, 1935, reissued, Ballantine, 1975; *Tarzan's Quest* (illustrated by J. A. St. John), E. R. Burroughs, 1936, reissued, Ballantine, 1975; *Tarzan and the Forbidden City* (illustrated by J. C. Burroughs), E. R. Burroughs, 1938, reissued, Ballantine, 1975; *Tarzan the Magnificent* (illustrated by J. C. Burroughs), E. R. Burroughs, 1939, reissued, Ballantine, 1976; *Tarzan and the "Foreign Legion"* (illustrated by J. C. Burroughs), E. R. Burroughs, 1947, reissued, Ballantine, 1975; *Tarzan and the Castaways* (illustrated by Frank Frazetta), Canaveral, 1965, reprinted, 1975; *Tarzan and the Madman* (illustrated by Reed Crandall), Canaveral, 1964, reprinted, 1975.

"Mars" series: *A Princess of Mars* (illustrated by Frank E. Schoonover), A. C. McClurg, 1917, new edition illustrated by F. Frazetta, Doubleday, 1970; *The Gods of Mars,* A. C. McClurg, 1918, reprinted, Canaveral, 1975; *The Warlord of Mars,* A. C. McClurg, 1919, reprinted, Buccaneer Books, 1976; *Thuvia, Maid of Mars* (illustrated by J. A. St. John), A. C. McClurg, 1920, reissued, Ballantine, 1973; *The Chessmen of Mars* (illustrated by J. A. St. John), A. C. McClurg, 1922, reissued, Ballantine, 1973; *The Master Mind of Mars* (illustrated by J. A. St. John), A. C. McClurg, 1928, reissued (illustrated by Frank Fravetta), Doubleday, 1973; *A Fighting Man of Mars,* Metropolitan Books, 1931, reissued, Ballantine, 1976; *Swords of Mars* (illustrated by J. A. St. John), E. R. Burroughs, 1936, reissued, Ballantine, 1973; *Synthetic Men of Mars* (illustrated by J. C. Burroughs), E. R. Burroughs, 1940, reissued, Ballantine, 1973; *Llana of Gathol* (illustrated by J. C. Burroughs), E. R. Burroughs, 1948, reissued, Ballantine, 1973; *John Carter of Mars* (illustrated by R. Crandall), Canaveral, 1964, reissued, Ballantine, 1973.

"Pellucidar" series: *At the Earth's Core* (illustrated by J. A. St. John), A. C. McClurg, 1922, reissued, Manor Books, 1976; *Pellucidar* (illustrated by J. A. St. John), A. C. McClurg, 1923, reissued, Ace Books, 1975; *Tanar of Pellucidar,* Metropolitan Books, 1930, reissued, Ace Books, 1973; *Savage Pellucidar* (illustrated by J. A. St. John), Canaveral, 1963, reissued, Ace Books, 1975.

"Venus" series: *Pirates of Venus* (illustrated by J. A. St. John), E. R. Burroughs, 1934, reprinted, Canaveral, 1975; *Lost on Venus* (illustrated by J. A. St. John), E. R. Burroughs, 1935, reissued, Ace Books, 1973; *Carson of Venus* (illustrated by J. C. Burroughs), E. R. Burroughs, 1939, reissued, Ace Books, 1975; *Escape on Venus* (illustrated by J. C. Burroughs), E. R. Burroughs, 1946, reissued, Ace Books, 1977; *The Wizard of Venus,* Ace Publishing, 1970.

ADAPTATIONS—Movies: "The Lad and the Lion," Selig Polyscope Co., 1917; "Tarzan of the Apes," starring Elmo Lincoln, First National, 1918; "The Romance of Tarzan," star-

Ron Ely, star of the 1966-68 NBC-TV series "Tarzan," insisted on doing his own stunts. Here he displays combat badges from the first season.

(From the movie "Tarzan of the Apes," starring Elmo Lincoln, the first Tarzan. Produced by First National, 1918.)

ring E. Lincoln, First National, 1918; "The Oakdale Affair," World Film Corp., 1919; "The Return of Tarzan," Numa Pictures Corp., 1920; "Tarzan and the Golden Lion," R-C Pictures Corp., 1927; "Tarzan, the Ape Man," starring Johnny Weissmuller and Maureen O'Sullivan, Metro-Goldwyn-Mayer, 1932, starring Denny Miller, Metro-Goldwyn-Mayer, 1959; "Tarzan, the Fearless," starring Buster Crabbe, PRI, 1933; "The New Adventures of Tarzan," starring Herman Brix, 1935, re-edited as "Tarzan and the Green Goddess," PRI, 1938; "Tarzan and His Mate," starring J. Weissmuller and M. O'Sullivan, Metro-Goldwyn-Mayer, 1934; "Tarzan Escapes," starring J. Weissmuller and M. O'Sullivan, Metro-Goldwyn-Mayer, 1936; "Tarzan's Revenge," starring Glenn Morris, Twentieth Century-Fox, 1938; "Tarzan Finds a Son," starring J. Weissmuller, M. O'Sullivan, Johnny Sheffield, and Cheetah (the chimp), Metro-Goldwyn-Mayer, 1939; "Tarzan In Exile," starring J. Weissmuller, M. O'Sullivan, and J. Sheffield, Metro-Goldwyn-Mayer, 1939; "Tarzan's Secret Treasure," starring J. Weissmuller and M. O'Sullivan, Metro-Goldwyn-Mayer, 1941; "Tarzan's New York Adventure," starring J. Weissmuller and M. O'Sullivan, Metro-Goldwyn-Mayer, 1942; "Tarzan's Desert Mystery," starring J. Weissmuller and J. Sheffield, RKO Radio Pictures, 1943; "Tarzan Triumphs," starring J. Weissmuller, RKO Radio Pictures, 1943;

"Tarzan and the Amazons," starring J. Weissmuller, J. Sheffield and Brenda Joyce, RKO Radio Pictures, 1945; "Tarzan and the Leopard Woman," starring J. Weissmuller, J. Sheffield and B. Joyce, RKO Radio Pictures, 1945; "Tarzan and the Huntress," starring J. Weissmuller and B. Joyce, RKO Radio Pictures, 1947; "Tarzan and the Mermaids," starring J. Weissmuller and B. Joyce, RKO Radio Pictures, 1948; "Tarzan's Magic Fountain," starring Lex Barker and B. Joyce, RKO Radio Pictures, 1949.

"Tarzan and the Slave Girl," starring L. Barker, RKO Radio Pictures, 1950; "Tarzan's Peril," starring L. Barker, RKO Radio Pictures, 1951; "Tarzan's Savage Fury," starring L. Barker, RKO Radio Pictures, 1952; "Tarzan and the She-Devil," starring L. Barker and Raymond Burr, RKO Radio Pictures, 1953; "Tarzan's Hidden Jungle," starring Gordon Scott, Vera Miles and Jack Elam, RKO Radio Pictures, 1955; "Tarzan and the Lost Safari," starring G. Scott, Metro-Goldwyn-Mayer, 1957; "Tarzan's Fight for Life," starring G. Scott, Metro-Goldwyn-Mayer, 1958; "Tarzan and the Trappers," starring G. Scott and Cheetah (the chimp), RKO Radio Pictures, 1958; "Tarzan's Greatest Adventure, starring G. Scott, Metro-Goldwyn-Mayer, 1959; "Tarzan the Magnificent," starring G. Scott, Paramount Pictures, 1960; "Tarzan Goes to

(From the movie "The New Adventures of Tarzan," starring Herman Brix, 1935. Re-edited as "Tarzan and the Green Goddess." Released by PRI, 1938.)

India," starring Jock Mahoney, Metro-Goldwyn-Mayer, 1962; "Tarzan's Three Challenges," starring J. Mahoney, Metro-Goldwyn-Mayer, 1963; "Tarzan and the Valley of Gold," starring Mike Henry, American International Pictures, 1965; "Tarzan and the Great River," starring M. Henry, Paramount Pictures, 1967; "Tarzan and the Jungle Boy," starring M. Henry, Paramount Pictures, 1968; "The Land That Time Forgot," starring Douglas McClure and John McEnery, American International Pictures, 1975; "Tarzan, the Ape Man," starring Miles O'Keefe and Bo Derek, Metro-Goldwyn-Mayer/United Artists, 1981; "Greystoke: The Legend of Tarzan, Lord of the Apes," starring Christopher Lambert, Warner Bros., 1984.

Serials: "The Son of Tarzan" (series of fifteen motion pictures), National Film Corp., 1920-21; "The Adventures of Tarzan" (series of fifteen motion pictures), Great Western Producing Co., 1921; "Tarzan, the Mighty" (series of fifteen motion pictures), Universal Pictures, 1928; "Tarzan, the Tiger" (series of fifteen motion pictures), Universal Pictures, 1929-30; "Jungle Girl" (series of fifteen motion pictures), Republic Pictures, 1941; "Tarzan" (television series), starring Ron Ely, NBC-TV, Banner Productions, 1966-68.

SIDELIGHTS: **September 1, 1875.** Born in Chicago, Ill., the son of a successful businessman and former Civil War major. Young Burroughs received his education from various schools. He attended Brown School until an outbreak of diphtheria forced his removal to Miss Coolie's Maplehurst School for Girls, followed by Harvard School and Phillips Andover. Finally, in 1895, he graduated from Michigan Military academy, an institution he described as "a polite reform school." Academically, Burroughs's standing was unremarkable. He took little interest in his studies and allowed many interruptions for the quest of adventure. At one time, while attending Harvard School, he left in mid-semester to follow his brothers to their newly acquired ranch in Idaho. "Somewhere along the line I went to Idaho and punched cows. I greatly enjoyed that experience, as there were no bathtubs in Idaho at that time. I recall having gone as long as three weeks when on a round-up without taking off my boots and Stetson. I wore Mexican spurs inlaid with silver: they had enormous rowels and were equipped with dumbbells. When I walked across a floor, rowels dragged behind and the dumbbells clattered: you could have heard me coming for a city block. Boy! was I proud!

"After leaving Orchard Lake (Michigan Military Academy), I enlisted in the 7th U.S. Cavalry and was sent to Fort Grant,

WHY WERE ALL THE PEOPLES OF THE JUNGLE NOT TREES? WHY WERE THE TREES NOT SOMETHING ELSE? WHY WAS TARZAN DIFFERENT FROM TAUG, AND TAUG DIFFERENT FROM BARA, THE DEER, AND BARA DIFFERENT FROM SHEETA, THE PANTHER, AND WHY WAS NOT SHEETA LIKE BUTO, THE RHINOCEROS?

WHERE AND HOW, ANYWAY, DID THEY ALL COME FROM -- THE TREES, THE FLOWERS, THE INSECTS, THE COUNTLESS CREATURES OF THE JUNGLE?

QUITE UNEXPECTEDLY, AN IDEA POPPED INTO TARZAN'S HEAD. IN FOLLOWING OUT THE MANY RAMIFICATIONS OF THE DICTIONARY DEFINITION OF GOD HE HAD COME UPON THE WORD CREATE -- "TO CAUSE TO COME INTO EXISTENCE; TO FORM OUT OF NOTHING."

(From "The God of Tarzan," in *Jungle Tales of Tarzan* by Edgar Rice Burroughs. Adapted by Burne Hogarth and Robert M. Hodes. Illustrated by Burne Hogarth.)

Edgar Rice Burroughs with his highly prized Cord automobile, 1933.

Arizona, where I chased Apaches, but never caught up with them. After that, some more cow punching, a storekeeper in Pocatello, Idaho; a policeman in Salt Lake City; gold mining in Idaho and Oregon; various clerical jobs in Chicago; department manager for Sears, Roebuck & Co.; and, finally, *Tarzan of the Apes.''* [Richard A. Lupoff, *Edgar Rice Burrougs: Master of Adventure,* Canaveral Press, 1965.[1]]

Burroughs's preliterary life was punctuated with adventurous trips to the West where he joined his brothers in a variety of business ventures.

January 31, 1900. Married Emma Centennia Hulbert in Chicago. Began writing the first of his science fiction stories, *Under the Moons of Mars,* in 1911 after the birth of two children. ''I had no idea how to submit a story or what I could expect in payment. Had I known anything about it at all, I would never have thought of submitting half of a novel, but that is what I did. Thomas Newell Metcalf, then editor of *All-Story Magazine,* published by The Frank A. Munsey Co., wrote me that he liked the first half of the story and, if the second was as good, he thought he might use it. Had he not given me this encouragement, I would never have finished the story and my writing career would have been at an end, since I was not writing because of any urge to write nor for any particular love of writing. I was writing because I had a wife and two babies, a combination which does not work well without money.'' [Thomas E. Hudgeons III, *The Official Price Guide to Comic and Science Fiction Books,* The House of Collectibles, n.d.[2]]

Submitted *Under the Moons of Mars* to *All-Story Magazine* in two installments under the pen name Normal Bean. The printer, thinking the name was misspelled, changed it to Norman Bean.

1912. Wrote *Tarzan of the Apes* which became an astonishing success when it appeared in *All-Story Magazine.* After being rejected by every major book publisher, it was finally accepted by A. C. McClurg & Co. and became a 1914 best-seller. Years later Burroughs reflected on his creation. ''. . . It was my third novel and the first to appear under my own name, which was unknown outside of a radius of six feet from my back porch.

''Bob Davis of the Munsey Company liked the story and it appeared in the October, 1912 issue of *All-Story Weekly,* whereupon I commenced to have visions of earning three thousand dollars a year and affluence in the writing game.

''Sharing a common weakness with one hundred and twenty million other Americans, I got a great kick out of seeing my name in print, and as an all-fiction magazine is anything but an enduring monument I commenced to look up the addresses of book publishers.

''During the next couple of years, every reputable publisher in the United States had an opportunity to turn down *Tarzan of the Apes,* and did.

''I was not surprised; in fact, the only thing about the marketing of my stories that ever surprises me is when they sell.

(From the movie "Tarzan and the Jungle Boy." starring Mike Henry. Produced by Paramount Pictures, 1968.)

(From the movie "Tarzan and the Lost Safari," starring Gordon Scott. Produced by Metro-Goldwyn-Mayer, 1957.)

(From the movie "Tarzan Goes to India," starring Jock Mahoney. Produced by Metro-Goldwyn-Mayer, 1962.)

(From the movie "Tarzan and the Slave Girl," starring Lex Barker. Produced by RKO Radio Pictures, 1950.)

A vintage Tarzan by illustrator J. Allen St. John. ■ (From the cover of *Courier Journal* [Louisville, Kentucky], January 15, 1984.)

I have never written a story yet but that deep down in my heart I was positive that it would be refused.

"It was the newspaper that created the demand for Tarzan. Unless I am mistaken, the *New York Evening World* started it; and then it was syndicated in cities of all sizes all over the United States and finally in boiler plate form in several thousand small town newspapers.

"The result was that A. C. McClurg & Company had so many inquiries from their retail customers for *Tarzan of the Apes* that, after having refused the story a year before, they now wrote me asking for the book rights.

"The book had about the same experience in England, some thirteen publishers turning it down before Sir Arthur Methuen undertook its publication there; but it achieved possibly a greater success in England than in the United States until the death of Sir Arthur.

"Contracts have been entered . . . for the translation of *Tarzan of the Apes* into Arabic, Czecho-Slovakian [*sic*], Danish, Dutch (Holland), Finnish, French, German, Hungarian, Icelandic, Italian, Norwegian, Polish, Roumanian, Russian, Spanish, Swedish, Portuguese and Urdu; and it has been printed in Braille for the blind.

"*Tarzan of the Apes* has had many adventures that are between the covers of no book. Having been pirated in Soviet Russia, he gained such popularity among the proletariat that the Soviet government was forced to take official cognizance of him. Whether they murdered him in a cellar or knouted him to Siberia, I do not know; but they got all het up because groups of illiterate peasants gathered in the street while a more educated fellow, oftentimes a soldier, read Tarzan out loud to them instead of Soviet propaganda or the intriguing dream books of Mr. Marx.

"In Germany he aroused the jealousy of a publisher because of his popularity, and this good sportsman dug up a story that I had written during the heat of anti-German propaganda in this country following the sinking of the Lusitania. He had a book written and published, telling all about the two horrible creatures, *Tarzan of the Apes* and Edgar Rice Burroughs; and

he distributed it so effectively that the German press made Tarzan an issue, lambasting him editorially and advising all good Germans to throw their Tarzan books into the garbage cans . . . which they did.

"Little boys have broken into the newspapers all over the world by falling out of trees and breaking something while emulating Tarzan, and one little boy, Jackie Strong of Gresham, Oregon, who was lost three days and nights on the wooded slopes of Mount Hood, attributed his ability to take care of himself and come through alive and well to the fact that he had been a student of *Tarzan of the Apes*.

"*Tarzan of the Apes* was not written primarily for children and my files contain letters of appreciation from men and women of all ages and from all walks of life . . . school teachers, librarians, college professors, priests, doctors, lawyers, soldiers, sailors, and business men, among which are names internationally famous; but possibly the greatest pleasure that I have derived from the publication of my stories has come through the knowledge that they have appealed also to children and that I have given them a character, however improbable he may seem, that will set for them a higher standard of manliness, integrity and sportsmanship.

"In addition to the Tarzan stories, I have written forty-eight other stories, thirty-one of which are in book form, and for

(Cover illustration by Fred J. Arting from *Tarzan of the Apes* by Edgar Rice Burroughs.)

(Cover illustration by John Coleman Burroughs from *Synthetic Men of Mars* by Edgar Rice Burroughs.)

some years it has been my policy to write one Tarzan and one other type of story, which I call a non-Tarzan.

"What seems to me one of the remarkable things about the Tarzan books, and for that matter of all my other novels is that they have never been out of print and that there is a constant demand for them, requiring reprinting every year since the first one was published. . . .

"All in all, Tarzan has done far better than I possibly could have dreamed at the time that I created him." [Edgar Rice Burroughs, "The Story of Tarzan," Department of Rare Books and Special Collections, University of Louisville, Louisville, Kentucky.[3]]

On several occasions Burroughs was asked what had inspired him to write the story of Tarzan. "As a child I was always fascinated by the legend of Romulus and Remus, who were supposed to have been suckled and raised by a she-wolf. This interest, I presume, led to conjecture as to just what sort of an individual would develop if the child of a highly civilized, intelligent and cultured couple were to be raised by a wild beast without any intercourse whatsoever with members of the human race. It was because I had played with this idea on my mind at various times, I presume, that I naturally embodied it in the story after I started writing." [Irwin Porges, *Edgar Rice Burroughs: The Man Who Created Tarzan*, Ballantine Books, 1975.[4]]

February 28, 1913. A third child, John, was born. With the birth of his son, Burroughs made the decision to quit his job and devote himself to writing full time.

January 27, 1918. *Tarzan of the Apes* came to the screen, starring Elmo Lincoln. It was the first film in history to gross over one million dollars.

"I did not like the picture, but there is little or nothing that an author can do unless he wishes to be constantly involved in expensive litigation, and as I am not much interested in anything but the royalties accruing from motion pictures and as I think they have little or no effect upon the sales of my books it is more or less a matter of indifference to me whether the picture is good or bad inasmuch as I have found that I cannot get good pictures made.

"The Universal Pictures Corporation has made a serial to be called 'Tarzan the Mighty,' supposed to be based upon *Jungle Tales of Tarzan*. Insofar as I have been able to discover it is just another serial and I am quite sure it bears little resemblance to the series of short stories from which it is supposed to be taken." [Letter to Frank Paul Schonfeld, B.E.M. (with whom Burroughs corresponded for thirty years), Croydon, Surrey, England, August 1, 1928. Taken from the Department of Rare Books and Special Collections, University of Louisville, Louisville, Kentucky.[5]]

Burroughs's attention turned to the imminent involvement of the United States in World War I. Moved by intense patriot-

(Cover illustration by Jeff Jones from *I Am a Barbarian* by Edgar Rice Burroughs.)

ism, and expecting a military appointment, he enrolled in the Los Angeles Riding Academy for a brush-up course in horsemanship. His appointment was that of captain in the reserves, but he never saw any action, nor did he get the opportunity to serve as a war correspondent.

February, 1919. Purchased a 550-acre estate in the San Fernando Valley, and christened his new home "Tarzana Ranch."

1931. In a letter to the editor of *The Bristol Times,* Burroughs addressed a charge of plagiarism which was rumored against him. "Never, with one exception, since I commenced writing have I replied to a critic, and the good Lord knows that I have had plenty of opportunities. That exception was the result of a charge of plagiarism made by some continental newspaper (I have forgotten its name) which stated that I had stolen the novel, *Tarzan of the Apes,* bodily from the French of an obscure Parisian writer, who was starving to death in an attic because of my perfidy.

"Now plagiarism is a nasty thing, which all decent men abhor, and writers, above all other men, should be most positive of their evidence before insinuating a charge of plagiarism against a fellow writer.

(Cover illustration by N. C. Wyeth from *The Return of Tarzan* by Edgar Rice Burroughs.)

"Upon many occasions I have had called to my attention what appeared to be obvious thefts of my own works, but I have never felt that the offender was guilty of plagiarism 'beyond a reasonable doubt,' since I fully realize, what every experienced waiter [*sic*] must realize, that there is nothing new under the sun and that the best we may hope to do is to garb the same old themes in new and attractive clothing.

"For some reason English reviewers have always been particularly unkind to me. I appear to be the proverbial red rag to their bullishness . . . at sight of my name they paw dirt and bellow.

"I do not know why this should be since I have never sought to make any pretensions to literary eminence. I have written many stories that have entertained millions of readers, (nor injured the morals of any) nor have I ever attempted to do more than entertain. I pose as neither prophet nor teacher.

"And now comes a writer in *The Bristol Times* of January 27th, 1931, under the caption *Life on Mars,* who accuses me, 'unintentionally perhaps,' of stealing my themes from Mr. Kipling and Mr. Wells.

"To Mr. Kipling as to Mr. Haggard I owe a debt of gratitude for having stimulated my youthful imagination and this I gladly acknowledge, but Mr. Wells I have never read and consequently his stories of Mars could not have influenced me in any way.

(Cover illustration by Studley O. Burroughs from *Tarzan Triumphant* by Edgar Rice Burroughs.)

(From the movie "Greystoke: The Legend of Tarzan, Lord of the Apes," starring Christopher Lambert. Copyright © 1984 by Warner Bros., Inc.)

(From the movie "Tarzan and the Amazons," starring Johnny Weissmuller, Johnny Sheffield, and Brenda Joyce. Copyright 1945 by Champion Productions.)

A young Tarzan with his ape mother. ■ (Photograph from the movie "Greystoke: The Legend of Tarzan, Lord of the Apes." Copyright © 1984 by Warner Bros., Inc.)

(From the movie "Tarzan, the Ape Man," starring Bo Derek and Miles O'Keefe. Released by Metro-Goldwyn-Mayer/United Artists, 1981.)

Burroughs and son John Coleman, who illustrated many of his father's books.

"And as for the originality of the Tarzan idea, one might as well accuse of pirating the idea of a book from 'Cadmus, the Phoenecian,' or whosoever it was who invented them, as to assume that I took an original idea from Mr. Kipling and exploited it to my own profit.

"The Mowgli theme is several years older than Mr. Kipling. It is older than books. Doubtless it is older than the first attempts of man to evolve a written language. It is found in the myths and legends of many peoples, the most notable, possibly, being the legend of Romulus and Remus, which stimulated my imagination long before Mowgli's creation.

"That Mr. Kipling selected a she-wolf to mother a man-child might more reasonably subject him to charges of plagiarism than the fact that I chose a she-ape should condemn me on a similar count.

"It is all very silly, and perhaps noticing such charges is sillier yet, but no man enjoys being branded a thief.

"I am glad to acknowledge any influence that my youthful reading of Mr. Kipling may have had upon my imagination, but I am also indebted to many other masters as, doubtless, Mr. Kipling would acknowledge his debt to the vast literature that preceded him, but to Mr. Wells, whom I have never read, I owe nothing.

"To the writer of the article in *The Bristol Times* I owe something. He has reawakened my interest in my set of Kipling, which I have not opened for many years, and which I may still enjoy above the works of later writers, despite the disparaging remarks that I understand Mr. Kipling has made relative to my deathless contributions to the classics." [Letter to the Editor of *The Bristol Times*, Bristol, England, February 13, 1931. Taken from the Department of Rare Books and Special Collections, University of Louisville, Louisville, Kentucky.[6]]

1932. The first successful radio adaptation of the Tarzan stories was a daily, fifteen-minute broadcast featuring his daughter,

(Jacket illustration by Frank Schoonover from *A Princess of Mars* by Edgar Rice Burroughs. Copyright 1917 by A. C. McClurg & Co.)

The most famous Tarzan family: Johnny Weissmuller, Maureen O'Sullivan, and Johnny Sheffield, first seen as Boy in "Tarzan Finds a Son." Copyright 1939 by Loews, Inc.

War correspondent Burroughs in 1945, with grandchildren John Ralston Burroughs, James Michael Pierce, and Danton Burroughs.

Joan Burroughs, and her husband, Jim Pierce, in the leading roles. Burroughs kept close watch over scripts and director.

1934. Divorced Emma.

1935. Unhappy with Hollywood's portrayals of Tarzan, Burroughs formed his own production company and released "The Adventures of Tarzan." It remains the most faithful to the original concept of the character.

April 4, 1935. Married Florence Gilbert, a divorced mother of two children, and nearly half his age.

April 18, 1940. Moved with his wife and stepchildren to the Hawaiian Islands.

1940. Financial pressures, concerns about the age difference between his wife and himself as well as other factors led to a drinking problem and ultimately to the end of his second marriage in 1942.

By the end of the year, however, his personal problems were shelved when Pearl Harbor was attacked by the Japanese. Burroughs was asked by General Army Headquarters to write a daily column for distribution to local newspapers and press services as a civilian morale booster.

Throughout the duration of the war in the South Pacific, he concerned himself with what he termed "the Japanese problem," and at one point even advocated the elimination of all Japanese from the Hawaiian Islands. But by the end of the war, his views became more liberal.

1949. Suffered a serious heart attack, but with determination recovered physically and emotionally.

March 19, 1950. Burroughs died at home at the age of seventy-four. "... My stories are written for entertainment and not to compete with the Old Masters as literary achievements." [Letter to book reviewer H. E. Jacobs, *Brooklyn Daily Eagle*, Brooklyn, New York, June 9, 1919. Taken from the Department of Rare Books and Special Collections, University of Louisville, Louisville, Kentucky.[7]

"Reviewing books, such as I write, on the basis of literary merit is absurd as no such claim is made for them either by the publisher or the author. It is merely a question as to whether or not they are clean, decent entertainment and they should be reviewed from this standpoint only as there is unquestionably a place in literature for light fiction, written purely for pur-

poses of entertainment." [Letter to Frank Paul Shonfeld, B.E.M., Croydon, Surrey, England, October 20, 1926. Taken from the Department of Rare Books and Special Collections, University of Louisvile, Louisville, Kentucky.[8]

FOR MORE INFORMATION SEE: Bradford M. Day, *Edgar Rice Burroughs: A Bibliography,* Science-Fiction, 1962; Henry Hardy Heins, *Golden Anniversary Bibliography of Edgar Rice Burroughs,* The Author, 1962; Richard A. Lupoff, *Edgar Rice*

(From "A Fighting Man of Mars," in *Master Mind of Mars* by Edgar Rice Burroughs. Illustrated by Frank Frazetta.)

Burroughs: Master of Adventure, Canaveral, 1965, reissued, Ace Books, 1975; Gabe Essoe, *Tarzan of the Movies: A Pictorial History of More Than Fifty Years of Edgar Rice Burroughs' Legendary Hero,* Citadel, 1968; Irwin Porges, *Edgar Rice Burroughs: The Man Who Created Tarzan,* Brigham Young University Press, 1975; J. Seeyle, "Edgar Rice Burroughs," *New York Times Book Review,* October 26, 1975; R. A. Lupoff, *Barsoom: Edgar Rice Burroughs and the Martian Vision,* Mirage Press, 1976; *Library Review 30,* University of Louisville, May, 1980; F. W. Woolsey, "Tarzan Swings Back," *The Courier-Journal Magazine,* January 15, 1984.

Obituaries: *New York Times,* March 20, 1950; *Illustrated London News,* March 25, 1950; *Newsweek,* March 27, 1950; *Time,* March 27, 1950; *Publishers Weekly,* April 1, 1950; *Wilson Library Bulletin,* May, 1950.

CAZET, Denys 1938-

BRIEF ENTRY: Born March 22, 1938, in Oakland, Calif. Director of media center, author, and illustrator. Cazet has held numerous positions during his career, including those as elementary school teacher, elementary librarian and media specialist, and high school teacher. He is currently director of St. Helena Elementary Media Center in St. Helena, Calif. In addition to his educational career, Cazet has written and illustrated several children's books. Among them is *The Duck with Squeaky Feet* (Bradbury, 1980) which *Booklist* called "a hearty chuckle from start to finish." *School Library Journal* noted the book's "humorously detailed pen-and-ink cartoons [which] invite . . . more than one-time scrutiny. . . ." In a similar manner *Booklist* described *Mud Baths for Everyone* (Bradbury, 1981) as a "jolly tale" with illustrations that "are brimming with fun."

Among Cazet's other works are three books, all featuring rabbits, which focus on relationships between family members. *Big Shoe, Little Shoe* (Bradbury, 1984) shows what happens when Louie switches shoes with his grandfather. *School Library Journal* found it a "warm story" with "rabbit characters [that are] beguiling and lovable." In *You Make the Angels Cry* (Bradbury, 1983), Albert's mother blames him for knocking over the cookie jar, when the culprit is actually a gust of wind. Exasperated, she screams, ". . . You make the angels cry!" It soon begins to rain and Albert is convinced that he really did make the angels cry. *Booklist* found the story "sweetly and simply told" and commented on its "expressive watercolors." *Christmas Moon* (Bradbury, 1984) tells the story of Patrick, a bunny who is sad because his recently-deceased grandfather will not be with the family for Christmas. Other books by Cazet are: *Requiem for a Frog* (Sonoma State College, 1971), *The Non-Coloring Book: A Drawing Book for Mind Stretching and Fantasy Building* (Chandler & Sharp, 1973), *Lucky Me* (Bradbury, 1983). and *Saturday* (Bradbury, 1985). *Home:* 1666 Whitehall La., St. Helena, Calif. 94574.

FOR MORE INFORMATION SEE: Contemporary Authors, Volume 108, Gale, 1983.

Of all people children are the most imaginative.
—Thomas Babington Macaulay

COONEY, Caroline B. 1947-

BRIEF ENTRY: Born May 10, 1947. Cooney began her writing career with the publication of *Safe as the Grave* (Coward, 1979), a mystery for children which received the 1980 North Carolina American Association of University Women's Award for juvenile literature. It was followed by *Rear-View Mirror* (Random House, 1980), the first of many novels Cooney has since written for young adults. Set in the back roads of North Carolina, *Rear-View Mirror* relates the ordeal of young Susan Seton who becomes the hostage of two brutal men after happening upon a murder in progress. "The suspense is all but unbearable," noted *Publishers Weekly.* "A taut, icy, tough performance." *Library Journal* agreed, calling the book "a highly emotive tale of terror . . . without a single lapse." Following another children's mystery entitled *The Paper Caper* (Coward, 1981), a sequel to *Safe as the Grave,* Cooney began writing a number of young adult romance novels. She now has twelve to her credit, including *April Love Story* (Scholastic Inc., 1981), *A Stage Set for Love* (Archway, 1983), *I'm Not Your Other Half* (Putnam, 1984), and *Sun, Sea, and Boys* (Archway, 1984). In addition to her writing career, Cooney is a musician who plays the organ and piano and serves as a vocalist and choir director. *Home address:* P.O. Box 1312, High Point, N.C. 27261.

FOR MORE INFORMATION SEE: Contemporary Authors, Volumes 97-100, Gale, 1981.

DAVIS, Gibbs 1953-

BRIEF ENTRY: Born November 16, 1953, in Milwaukee, Wis. Davis received a B.A. from the University of California at Berkeley in 1976. During her career she has worked as a member of an editorial staff, a coordinator of public relations, a copywriter, a professional model, and as a free-lance writer. The author of four juvenile books, Davis has been praised by critics for her fine characterizations. *Booklist* said of *Fishman and Charly* (Houghton, 1983): "Davis's characters are distinctive in a [Betsy] Byars-like fashion. . . ." In the book young Tyler Hawkins seeks to gain a sense of self-worth, among other things, by swimming the mile across Echo Bay to Macaroon Island. Although he fails to accomplish the swim on his own, he does help to capture some poachers who have been slaughtering the area's sea cows. *Booklist* observed, "Tyler's slow discovery of his worth is credibly accomplished. . . ." In *Maud Flies Solo* (Bradbury, 1981), eleven-year-old Maud faces the changing relationship between herself and her older sister who has just entered adolescence. *School Library Journal* found that "*Maud* abounds with lively characters . . . [including] Maud herself, feisty, clever and in love with flying."

Critics have also been favorable toward Davis's use of humor in her stories. *Booklist* observed that in *Maud Flies Solo* "amusing incidents are naturally woven into an inventive story of a young girl's coming into her own." Similarly, her young adult novel *Swann Song* (Bradbury, 1982) was described by *Booklist* as "a bittersweet story laced with enough leavening humor to ward off sentimentality." Davis also wrote a children's picturebook, *The Other Emily* (Houghton, 1984), in which a little girl is shocked when she discovers that she is not "the one and only Emily." She is currently working on a young adult novel, tentatively titled *Play It Again, Samantha.* *Agent:* Curtis Brown Ltd., 575 Madison Ave., New York, N.Y. 10022.

FOR MORE INFORMATION SEE: Contemporary Authors, Volume 111, Gale, 1984.

DEARY, Terry 1946-

BRIEF ENTRY: Born January 3, 1946, in Sunderland, England. Educator and novelist. Now a drama teacher and department head at Hetton School in Hetton, England, Deary previously worked in the theater as both an actor and a director. He also has been employed as a high school teacher and a theater education officer. The author of over ten novels for children and young adults, Deary began writing when he discovered a lack of suitable material for his needs as a teacher. "I wanted a story with pace and humor written in accessible language," he explains. "But I also wanted sufficient depth of characterization for readers to *care* about . . . the protagonist." He has used this approach to fiction in children's novels like *The Custard Kid, The Lambton Worm,* and *The Windmills of Nowhere,* as well as novels for young adults, including *Hope Street* and *I Met Her on a Rainy Day.* Among Deary's current projects are a textbook on teaching drama and an adult thriller entitled *Play Dead. Home:* Board Inn, Burnhope, Durham DH7 0DP, England.

FOR MORE INFORMATION SEE: Contemporary Authors, Volume 110, Gale, 1984.

EARL JOSEPH DIAS

DIAS, Earl Joseph 1916-

PERSONAL: Born March 23, 1916, in New Bedford, Mass.; son of John Felisberto (an insurance agent) and Virginia (Alexander) Dias; married Edith G. Kenny (a teacher), August 18, 1951. *Education:* Bates College, A.B. (magna cum laude), 1937; Boston University, M.A., 1938; Southeastern Massachusetts University, L.H.D., 1983; also studied summers at Shakespeare Institute, Stratford-on-Avon, England, 1957, 1960, and University of London, 1960. *Home:* 52 Walnut St., Fairhaven, Mass. 02719. *Office:* Southeastern Massachusetts University, North Dartmouth, Mass. 02747.

CAREER: High school teacher of English, Fairhaven, Mass., 1939-57; New Bedford Institute of Technology, New Bedford, Mass., associate professor of English, 1958-63; Southeastern Massachusetts University, North Dartmouth, professor of English, 1963—, chairman of department, 1971-81, professor emeritus, 1981. *New Bedford Standard-Times,* drama and music critic, 1947—, regular Sunday columnist, "A Look at the Arts," 1948—. Reader in English composition, College Entrance Examination Board. Corporator, Fairhaven Institution for Savings; member, Fairhaven Town Meeting; chairman of board of trustees, Millicent Library, Fairhaven; member of board of directors, New Bedford Symphony Orchestra and New Bedford Concert Series. *Member:* College English Association, Shakespeare Association of America, American Association of University Professors, Thoreau Society, Phi Beta Kappa.

WRITINGS: Melodramas and Farces for Young Actors, Plays, 1956; *One-Act Plays for Teen-Agers: A Collection of Royalty-Free Comedies,* Plays, 1961, revised edition, 1971; *New Comedies for Teen-Agers: A Collection of One-Act, Royalty-Free Comedies, Farces, and Melodramas,* Plays, 1967, 2nd edition, 1970; *Henry Huttleson Rogers: Portrait of a 'Capitalist,'* Millicent Library, 1974. Also author of *Mark Twain's Letters to the Rogers Family,* 1970. Plays anthologized in *A Treasury of Christmas Plays,* Plays, 1956; *A Treasury of Holiday Plays,* Plays, 1963; *Basic Reading,* Book 7, Lippincott, 1965; *Favorite Plays for Classroom Reading,* Plays, 1965; *Fifty Plays for Holidays,* Plays, 1968; *Patriotic and Historical Plays for Young People,* Plays, 1975; *On Stage for Christmas,* Plays, 1978; *Space and Science Fiction Plays for Young People,* Plays, 1981; *Mark Twain and H. H. Rogers: An Odd Couple,* Millicent Library, 1984. Contributor to *Coronet, Drama Critique, New England Quarterly,* and other journals.

WORK IN PROGRESS: Brains to Brawn: A History of Detective Fiction; How to Use Shakespeare in Daily Life, or Banking on the Bard.

SIDELIGHTS: "I grew up surrounded by books. My father was an avid reader and encouraged me to browse through a wide variety of literature. In my high school days I worked as a page in the local library, putting away books on their shelves, and reading those that caught my fancy. It seemed to me then that a writer's life must be the ideal existence; that was before I learned what hard and demanding work writing really is.

"In college, I became singularly interested in drama; in graduate school I specialized in Shakespeare. Full of enthusiasm about the Bard, I began my teaching career on a high school faculty, came to know teenagers well, and utilized this knowledge in the more than 100 plays I have written for young actors.

"As chairman of the department of English now at a large university, and as a teacher of courses in Shakespeare, modern drama, American drama, and comparative drama, I have to turn my writing occasionally to scholarly articles and books. But always I come back to my first love—plays for young people. I listen carefully to my students and their interests and often derive an idea for a play from conversations with them. Through extensive travel throughout the world, I have also gained many ideas for my writing. Best of all, of course, the constant teaching of drama helps one to learn exactly how to put a play together, how to mount to a climax, how to prepare an occasional surprise.

"Fortunately, I have in my household an experienced and helpful listener. My wife is not only an astute critic but also a source of continuous encouragement."

DICKINSON, Mary 1949-

BRIEF ENTRY: Born January 12, 1949, in Brighton, England. Since 1975 Dickinson has been a part-time storyteller at Lambeth Library in London, England. Discovering what she called a "lack of good 'everyday' stories" for children, she decided to write some of her own. *Alex's Bed* (1980) is the first of five picture books that focus on the relationship between a small boy and his mother. All published by Deutsch, the titles are: *Alex and Roy* (1981), *Alex and the Baby* (1982), *Alex's Outing* (1983), and *New Clothes for Alex* (1984). Accompanied with illustrations by Charlotte Firmin, the simple texts realistically explore the ups and downs of childhood. Dickinson's goal as a writer is two-fold, namely, "to show [children] incidents that they will recognize" and "to show [adults] what a difficult job being a parent is." *Address:* c/o Andre Deutsch, 105 Great Russell St., London WC1, England.

FOR MORE INFORMATION SEE: Contemporary Authors, Volume 110, Gale, 1984.

DIETZ, David H(enry) 1897-1984

OBITUARY NOTICE—See sketch in *SATA* Volume 10: Born October 6, 1897, in Cleveland, Ohio; died of Parkinson's disease, December 9, 1984, in Cleveland Heights, Ohio. Educator, journalist, and author best known for his numerous science writings. Dietz taught general science at Western Reserve University (now Case Western Reserve University) from 1927 to 1950 and retired from the Scripps-Howard newspaper chain in 1977 after fifty-six years as science writer. Among his works are four books for children: *All about Satellites and Space Ships, All about Great Medical Discoveries, All about the Universe,* and *Stars and the Universe*. His adult writings include *The Story of Science, Medical Magic, Atomic Energy in the Coming Era,* and *The New Outline of Science*. He also wrote articles on the atomic bomb for *Encyclopaedia Britannica*.

FOR MORE INFORMATION SEE: Contemporary Authors, New Revision Series, Volume 2, Gale, 1981; *International Authors and Writers Who's Who [and] International Who's Who in Poetry,* 9th edition, Melrose, 1982; *American Men and Women of Science: The Physical and Biological Sciences,* 15th edition, Bowker, 1982. Obituaries: *New York Times,* December 11, 1984; *Chicago Tribune,* December 12, 1984; *Washington Post,* December 13, 1984.

DRAGONWAGON, Crescent 1952-

PERSONAL: Born November 25, 1952, in New York, N.Y.; daughter of Maurice (a biographer) and Charlotte (a children's book writer; maiden name, Shapiro) Zolotow; married Crispin Dragonwagon (an archaeologist), March 20, 1970 (divorced August 10, 1975); married Ned Shank (an architectural marketing consultant), October 20, 1979. *Education:* Educated in Hastings-on-Hudson, N.Y., and Stockbridge, Mass. *Home address:* c/o Dairy Hollow House, Rte. 2, Box 1, Eureka Springs, Ark. 72632.

CAREER: Writer. *Member:* Authors Guild of Authors League of America, Poets and Writers, American Society of Journalists and Authors, Women in Film.

CRESCENT DRAGONWAGON

WRITINGS: Rainy Day Together, Harper, 1970; *The Commune Cookbook,* Simon & Schuster, 1971; *The Bean Book,* Workman Publishing, 1973; *Putting Up Stuff for the Cold Time,* Workman Publishing, 1973; *Strawberry Dress Escape,* Scribner, 1975; *When Light Turns into Night* (illustrated by Robert A. Parker), Harper, 1975; *Wind Rose* (illustrated by Ronald Himler), Harper, 1976; *Will It Be Okay?* (illustrated by Ben Schecter), Harper, 1977; *Your Owl Friend* (illustrated by Ruth Bornstein), Harper, 1977; *If You Call My Name* (illustrated by David Palladini), Harper, 1981; *Message from the Avocadoes* (poetry), August House, 1981; (with Paul Zindel) *To Take a Dare* (novel; ALA Notable Book), Harper, 1982; *I Hate My Brother Harry* (illustrated by Dick Gackenbach), Harper, 1983; *Katie in the Morning* (illustrated by Betsy Day), Harper, 1983; *Coconut* (illustrated by Nancy Tafuri), Harper, 1984; *Jemima Remembers* (illustrated by Troy Howell), Macmillan, 1984; *Always, Always* (illustrated by Arieh Zeldich), Macmillan, 1984; *Alligator Arrived with Apples: A Thanksgiving Potluck Alphabet,* Macmillan, 1985; *The Year It Rained* (novel), Macmillan, 1985; *Just Like in the Movies* (novel), Macmillan, 1986; *Half a Moon and One Whole Star,* Macmillan, 1986. Contributor to popular magazines, including *Cosmopolitan, Seventeen, Organic Gardening, McCall's, Ladies' Home Journal,* and *New Age.*

ADAPTATIONS—Movies: "Wind Rose," Phoenix Films, 1983.

WORK IN PROGRESS: I Hate My Sister Maggie; Dairy Hollow House Cookbook, coauthored with Jan Brown and illustrated by Jacqui Froelick; and magazine articles.

SIDELIGHTS: Dragonwagon was born in New York City. Her father, Maurice Zolotow, worked as a Broadway theater critic when she was young and often brought Dragonwagon along on opening nights. ''I remember 'Carousel' and 'West Side Story,' 'Oklahoma,' and 'One Hundred Ten in the Shade.' I used to wear a black velvet party dress with a little white, lace placket in the front.

''I have one brother, Stephen, nine years older than me. We fought all the time. It's all told in *I Hate my Brother Harry.* It was a relief to see him grow up and move out.

''Growing up in New York didn't affect my development as a writer. If someone has the writer's bent, he is going to write wherever he lives. Of course, geographical roots, original and transplanted, do show up in one's work as background.

''If writing is a gift, it is not one you possess as such. It is loaned to you. The desire to write is more important than actual talent. From the time I learned the alphabet I wrote stories, beginning with drawing accompanied by a few words.

Everything says *leaving, going away.* . . . ■ (From *Jemima Remembers* by Crescent Dragonwagon. Illustrated by Troy Howell.)

When we come out again,
there is a tiny row of cabbage seedlings."

(From *Will It Be Okay?* by Crescent Dragonwagon. Illustrated by Ben Shecter.)

Most of life since has been focused in my writing: strong feelings and experiences, interesting people, overheard bits of conversation, almost everything that strikes me has a way of turning up in my work, sometimes surprising me greatly. Actually, my best work is that which does surprise me. At such times I don't feel like I'm writing; the writing is just happening on its own. The deep impulse to put occurrences into words, the discipline to back up this impulse, and the sense of surprise are what combine to make a writer.

"Both my parents are vivid, creative and supportive people. I grew up with lots of freedom, was allowed to define the perimeters, and was able to discover what was true for myself. Since my parents are both writers, I can't say they would have been as supportive had I decided to pursue mathematics instead of writing, but they did leave me room to explore my own bent.

"I attended public school until seventh grade, went to Stockbridge School for a year, followed by an experimental school in Manhattan for six months. Then, at age sixteen, I quit altogether. I did not do well with authority. Once, in seventh grade, we read Ernest Hemingway and were assigned to write our own short story. The teacher scolded me for not using complete sentences. 'But it was dialogue!' I said. 'People don't talk in complete sentences and anyway, Hemingway didn't use complete sentences.' My teacher, condescension oozing from his voice, said, 'Publish some books of your own, then we'll talk about Hemingway.' Why do people talk to kids that way? Still, I'm sure such incidents were factors which led me to

submit my writing at such an early age, a kind of 'Well, I'll show them' thing. In fact, *Rainy Day Together,* was accepted for publication in 1969, the year I quit school. I attended an alternative university for a while but am largely self-educated. I read all the time, and always have. My parents were tolerant of my decision to leave school.

"After I quit school, I lived in a collective in Brooklyn—eight of us altogether, everyone else much older than me. We'd stay up late, talking heatedly over cups of hot herb tea, arguing and learning, reading books and discussing ideas. In those years, I thought about, felt, lived, and breathed the imperative of changing society, achieving justice for everyone, and putting an end to war. My social beliefs were strong, as they were for many people at the time. It has since become fashionable to deny what our generation felt and fought for. But it was important to society, and to the individuals who participated. It was a very exciting time to be a teenager, and certain values—the value of individual vision, yet the knowledge that no individual is separate from his or her world—stay with me.

"Because my parents are writers, it seemed evident to me that when things happen to you in life, you write about them, and eventually they become books. Writing seemed natural, not esoteric or difficult. My parents were influential but not in the sense of role models. In some ways they were both role models of how *not* to be writers. My father worked at home in his office upstairs. We weren't allowed to disturb him and if we did, we were in trouble. My mother's desk was in a corner of the bedroom. We could run up and bother her any time we

Right now this is all there is. . . . ■ (From *When Light Turns into Night* by Crescent Dragonwagon. Illustrated by Robert Andrew Parker.)

wanted. The truth is the writer needs self-protection as well as openness and human compassion. My father cut himself off from us too much and my mother didn't do it enough.

"When I was little I loved *Kenny's Window,* the Laura Ingalls Wilder books, and, of course, *The Secret Garden.* As a young adult, I felt a void settle in the library. I remember browsing restlessly, never finding anything that seemed right for me. Then came my revolutionary years, and the influences of the writings of Wilhelm Reich, Carl Jung and such feminist writers as Robin Morgan. During the last ten years Eastern philosophy has dominated my nonfiction reading, while good contemporary fiction has been the mainstay of my fun reading: Gail Godwin, Nancy Thayer, Judith Rossner, Anne Rice, John Yount and many others. My life has thus lead me from the artistic to the political and finally to the spiritual: a spirituality that is down to earth and includes all aspects of daily life— art, work, social concerns."

In 1982 Dragonwagon collaborated on *To Take a Dare* with author Paul Zindel. "I had started a number of novels but never finished them. I knew that Paul worked with other writers. One day, I bit the bullet and wrote him a letter asking if he would work with me. He agreed. I wanted his assurance

to finish my novel if I reached the point that I couldn't, and he gave it to me. As it turned out ninety-eight percent of *To Take a Dare* is my writing, but I feel I couldn't have written it without his encouragement. He was willing to talk to me, to help me over every fearful little hump. In that sense, it is truly his book as well. He responded to me and would cheer me on."

Dragonwagon's first novel is not especially autobiographical. "At sixteen, I was much more sophisticated than Christa in *To Take a Dare.* I came out of a more educated, liberal background than she did. Where some of the events in our lives are similar, our responses to them are quite different. Still, many kids are living through that story. When I last drove from Arkansas to Georgia, for instance, I picked up a girl hitchhiker much like Christa. Unfortunately, the kids who are living with such struggles are not necessarily reading these books. But as the novel points out, you never know when or how you are going to touch someone's life.

"I don't consciously try to touch people through my writing. I write for myself—it is a need, a compulsion. The writer becomes the instrument through which words flow, and sometimes the words themselves become the instrument which touches someone else's life. I'm hesitant to say this because it sounds self-serving, but it is true that at times the writing I've done for my own satisfaction has an effect on the reader. When it does, it's something extra; the writer can be glad it happened, but cannot really claim to have had anything to do with it.

"My primary satisfaction comes from the writing itself. The secondary satisfaction is being able to support myself with my writing. It's great to be paid for something I feel I have to do anyway. There have been times when I've had to support myself in other ways: waitressing, delivering flowers, even proofreading telephone books. Through it all I continued to write. I know how special it is to be able to make a living, and to be published. When I'm told by someone 'I've always wanted to be a writer,' I cringe a little. But when I hear 'I've always written,' my ears perk up. There's a big difference. 'Being a writer' is about wanting other people to see you a certain way; it's about image. 'Writing' is about a private, deep self-satisfying labor, about reality.''

When Dragonwagon's life is fairly organized, she gets up every morning and "makes a nice hot cup of tea. I need the caffeine to get started. Then I disappear into the office with my cat and work all day. This routine is often broken up by

teaching, lecturing, visiting schools, and working with both children and teachers. I'm also connected with the Artists in Education program both in Georgia and Arkansas.

"We just bought a wonderful house with much potential, but it needs a lot of work which was disruptive. I'm happy my office is almost finished now, even though I've always managed to write in spite of upheavals. I wrote *Half a Moon and One Whole Star* when I was in India last fall living in a grass hut and I've written on the road in motel rooms, wherever I happened to be.

"Inspiration is only a small percentage of all the writing I do, although it is probably most of the writing that sells. It seems you still have to do all the uninspired writing that doesn't pan out and that doesn't sell. It's the pick and shovel work that softens the grounds for the inspirational seed. The ground must be ready for the seed to take root. For every piece of work I've had published, I've written at least ten others which have been turned down. This irrational urge keeps me writing and sending things out. One also needs discipline, because writers do not write only when inspired.

"In the past I kept journals, and had daily exercises I'd do at the typewriter for an hour to warm up. My work habits are better now. There were long periods between projects when I

Your papa and I birthed you then, in this very bed, right here. ■ (From *Wind Rose* by Crescent Dragonwagon. Illustrated by Ronald Himler.)

would beat myself over the head. 'Why aren't you working harder?' I'd ask myself. This was intensified by my involvement in children's literature, because when I do get an idea, I write very quickly. Writing for children differs from writing for adults because it is briefer in duration. Psychologically, I'm still in touch with my childhood. Stillness, oversensitivity, and poetry come easily to me, all of which are essential to children's books.''

Dragonwagon has recently written some adult novels. ''Most of the novels I have written are borderline adult/young adult fiction. I like writing about adolescence, an interesting time of life to explore. You have to be beyond the age that you're writing about, done with digesting that period in your own life, to write an interesting and mature piece of work.

''When the idea for a book comes to me, my mind returns to it again and again. There is an attraction to the idea, an incident, or, in the case of an adult book, attraction to a character. I never begin with an issue. I'm not interested in proselytizing in my work. There are issues that are of concern to me, but I wouldn't deal with them in a book as such. My concerns surface unconsciously, through my obsessional interest in a character, or an event. The amount of research I do varies with each book. I've also written nonfiction for adults and magazine articles so I'm not afraid of research. I like it.''

Dragonwagon discussed her writing process. ''For years I wrote first drafts by hand. I finally bought a word processor, and I'm totally sold on it, though I'm generally pretty low tech.

''When I've completed an initial draft, I show it first to my husband, then to my mother. Sometimes my father will see an early draft, but he is diffident about reading fresh work. Reading unpublished work to him is like looking in my underwear drawer. It makes him feel a little overly fastidious. Every so often I've forced him to listen to something before it's been published, but he is almost superstitious. I'm superstitious too. While I'm developing a new work, there is a real temptation to talk about it. But if I talk too much, I run the risk of losing the desire to write it. There is a point at which I won't show my work to anybody, but I have a deep need to share it with at least one person, chapter by chapter, and that is my husband, Ned Shank.

''I would rarely submit a first draft. I usually submit a second or third, then prepare myself to do a fourth and a fifth. Sometimes I say 'no' to an editor's suggestion. My most disastrous book was *Katie in the Morning*. It was my favorite when I wrote it, but I let the editors make changes and I allowed them to use an illustrator whose pictures I didn't like. It has ruined the book for me. I still would rather read the original manuscript of *Katie in the Morning* than the published version.

''It's important for the illustrations of my books to work with the text. The illustrations for *Wind Rose* and *When Light Turns into Night* work well with the text. The pictures in *I Hate My Brother Harry* are perfect, and the illustrations for *Your Owl Friend, Jemima Remembers,* and *Always, Always* work very well. Visually, those are my favorite books.''

Dragonwagon's book *Wind Rose* was inspired by ''the actual birth of a baby named Wind Rose. *Wind Rose* is typical of my writing process, beginning with an incident which sparked the idea. Never having had a child myself, I took my own feelings

Emily stood up and slipped away. ■ (From *Strawberry Dress Escape* by Crescent Dragonwagon. Illustrated by Lillian Hoban.)

I wish a giant frog would catch him and make him into frosting. ■ (From *I Hate My Brother Harry* by Crescent Dragonwagon. Illustrated by Dick Gackenbach.)

CRESCENT DRAGONWAGON

about being in love and attached them to the actual conception and birth of this child and wrote the book.''

A movie adaptation of *Wind Rose* was released through Phoenix Films in 1983. ''The production was faithful to the text, and I feel the movie was very well done, though I was not directly involved.''

Dragonwagon includes writing as one of her hobbies and many interests. ''Though 'hobbies' doesn't quite fit, there's no real line for me between work and play. For fun I write, I garden, I cook. I watch 'Hill Street Blues' every week. I'm constantly reading. At any given time I'm in the middle of a number of books. I go to the theater whenever I'm in a metropolitan area. I listen to a wide range of music from classical to British Isles, from folk to jazz. I love National Public Radio's 'All Things Considered' and 'Prairie Home Companion.'''

With two partners, Dragonwagon owns Dairy Hollow House, a country inn in the Ozark Mountains. Although not the full-time innkeeper, she is able to indulge her interests in cooking and gardening by working out the inn's landscaping and testing recipes served for breakfasts and dinners. ''Dairy Hollow House was a little Ozark farmhouse in Eureka Springs that had been abandoned. With his background in historic preservation, Ned knew about saving old buildings. We purchased the house in 1979 with a friend, Bill Haynes, and began to restore it, deciding that it would make a fine country inn. We planned to live across the way and take care of it. That was the theory, and it was very successful. We hired some great people to work for us—we were lucky to find them. Since the inn is located in Dairy Hollow, we called the girls, who came in every morning to fix breakfast and clean the house, the 'Dairy Maids.' When we needed to move to Atlanta for Ned's work, one of the original Dairy Maids, Jan, moved up to a managerial position and became innkeeper. She and her husband live in what was formerly our house and run the business. When Jan and her husband go on vacation, I come and innsit. I live part of each year in Atlanta with Ned and part in Eureka Springs.

''The Dairy Hollow House is sweetly warm: handmade quilts on the beds, regional antiques. We completely landscaped the driveway and planted a beautiful flower garden. It is an enchanting place. People love it, and come back time and again. We also serve dinners by reservation, and while Jan is on vacation I cook. I made some wonderful dinners there last month: chocolate mousse cakes, feta cheese and fresh sage tartlets, French black raspberry shortcakes, chicken breasts stuffed with mushrooms and white wine, grilled chicken with lemon and herbs, six layer vegetable tortes and a grilled rainbow trout with sour cream and dill. . . . The list goes on and on. Dairy Hollow House is one of the favorite things in my life.''

Dragonwagon advises that young people interested in writing should ''keep writing. When I teach, I tell my students that you can't drive with the emergency break on. When you're trying to be creative and free flowing, you can't worry about how your parents or your teachers will react, or worry about grades, or winning the prize for your poem. You can't worry about whether every sentence is perfect or every word is just right. You have to jump in and write. Basically I teach the difference between writing a first draft and editing. To bring together the intellectual mind and the imaginative, intuitive mind, you must learn to separate the two. It's easier to get into the editing mode than the free form mode. It's a challenge to write without patching up as you go along. It's something I've tried to teach myself over the years. The reason I could

never finish a novel was my impulse to perfect it as I went along. On a first draft, write all the way through, then come back later and straighten it out.

''If you decide to start writing, the main thing to remember is that writing is *work*—hard work. But for those of us who feel we must write, there's nothing we'd rather be doing and nothing else we're really fit for.''

EISENBERG, Phyllis Rose   1924-

PERSONAL: Born June 26, 1924, in Chicago, Ill.; daughter of Lewis (in retail business) and Frances (in retail business; maiden name, Remer) Rose; married Emanuel M. Eisenberg, September 2, 1945; children: Bart. *Education:* Attended Los Angeles Valley College, 1965-66, and University of California, Los Angeles, 1975. *Home and office:* 5703 Ventura Canyon Ave., Van Nuys, Calif. 91401.

CAREER: East Valley Young Men's Christian Association (YMCA), Van Nuys, Calif., remedial tutor in reading and math, 1972-74; Los Angeles Valley Community College, Los Angeles, Calif., instructor in creative writing, 1973-75; Los Angeles Pierce College, Los Angeles, instructor in creative writing, 1976-79; Crossroads Hospital, Los Angeles, journal therapist, 1981. Founders Guild for San Fernando Valley Child Guidance Clinic; editor, 1965-68, executive secretary, 1966-70. *Member:* P.E.N., Authors Guild, Society of Children's Book Writers, Southern California Council of Literature for

PHYLLIS ROSE EISENBERG

Dorrie has a very long hair growing out of her chin that you can see only in bright light. ■ (From
A Mitzvah Is Something Special by Phyllis Rose Eisenberg. Illustrated by Susan Jeschke.)

Children. *Awards, honors:* "I'm I.Q." won Unitarian-Universalist National Playwriting Competition, 1975; *A Mitzvah Is Something Special* was listed as one of twelve outstanding works of fiction for children in *World Book Encyclopedia Yearbook 1979* and headed a list of one hundred books selected for free children by *Ms.*, 1979; *Don't Tell Me a Ghost Story* was named an All Choice List Book and was displayed at the International Youth Library's 34th International Children's and Youth Exhibition in Munich, West Germany, 1983.

WRITINGS: A Mitzvah Is Something Special (juvenile; illustrated by Susan Jeschke), Harper, 1978; (contributor) Tristine Rainer, *The New Diary: How to Use a Journal for Self-Guidance and Expanded Creativity*, J. P. Tarcher, 1978; *Don't Tell Me a Ghost Story* (juvenile; illustrated by Lynn Munsinger), Harcourt, 1982. Work represented in anthologies, including *Stories for Free Children*, edited by Letty Cottin Pogrebin, McGraw, 1982. Also author of "I'm I.Q.," a one-act play for adults. Contributor of fiction, nonfiction and poetry to newspapers and magazines, including *Cricket, Instructor, Progressive, Los Angeles Times, Woman's World, Ms.*, and *School Magazine* (Sydney, New South Wales).

WORK IN PROGRESS: A Mensch Is Something Special, sequel to *A Mitzvah Is Something Special; Becky Big Enough*, a picture book; *Stovie*, a short story for adults; a novel for adults.

SIDELIGHTS: "Unlike many authors, I did not always know that I would one day put most of my energy into writing. The only thing that I recall writing during my childhood was a four-line poem that was published in the school newspaper when I was in kindergarten. I was a quiet and rather shy child, who lived in Chicago with my parents, older sister, and younger brother. We moved often (oh, how I dreaded transferring schools) to whatever section of the city in which my parents could earn a living. My parents divorced when I was eleven. Although commonplace now, divorce was rather a rarity when I was growing up. I worried about being different from my friends and consequently became more withdrawn. I didn't know it then, but the seeds of a compelling need to express myself had been planted.

"During my adolescence I became an avid letter writer. My letters were usually long and quite detailed, and recipients would often tell me that they'd read and reread these letters and that often I made them laugh and cry. I was married and the mother of my own kindergartener before I took writing seriously. I noticed one of those "Tell in twenty-five words or less' sponsor-type contests in a magazine. I entered, won a vacuum cleaner, and became addicted to contests, winning thirty-five out of every hundred. Later, I wrote and sold greeting card verses and gaglines, and eventually I moved into the medium I enjoy most: writing stories for children and adults.

"How people feel and behave is important to me, and that interest, combined with personal experience, is behind most of the material I write. The idea behind *A Mitzvah Is Something Special* occurred when my son was fifteen. I had no idea that a comment of his would lead to my first children's book a dozen years later, but it did. As a teenager, he often appeared bored when visiting relatives, but one day he said, 'I have the best of two worlds in my grandmothers.' I didn't realize he was aware of their differences, and I was impressed with his accurate appraisal. Without realizing it, I kept his observation at the back of my mind until one day the book sprang to life. I consider the book to be about love and differences in people. The book has an ethnic flavor, but the theme is a universal one.

"*Don't Tell Me a Ghost Story* is for all children and adults who like to invent, tell, and listen to ghost stories. I had fun writing this story and the idea behind it is just that—pure and simple fun.

"My advice to aspiring authors is to become more aware of the details in life and to become a skilled observer and eavesdropper. How do people look when they are enthusiastic, wary, joyful, intimidated? Do they giggle nervously? Stand straighter? Stare at the floor? I love to listen to people at the marketplace and to people sitting near me in a restaurant. I sometimes create stories (that don't always find their way to paper) about what people's lives might be like based solely upon what I see and hear.

"Keeping a journal and recording in it all the things and incidents that feel especially memorable to you is a wonderful aid to writing. Whether it's how the fog looked to you at dawn, the way the freckles were 'arranged' on a child's nose, or how the shopkeeper squinted at you when you returned merchandise, you never know when those ideas will find their way into a novel, a story, or a poem. You can't forget them if you record them in a journal. The things that strike you as poignant, breathtaking, funny, or sad make you the unique person you are, and it is your unique view of the world that readers will be drawn to and value. I have kept a journal for many years and that pursuit has helped me to understand myself more and, subsequently, other people. I also find that journal keeping helps me to tap my creativity and allows me to 'get inside' of my book characters' minds and hearts. I became so intrigued with the benefits a journal provides that I began to teach the process to others.

"The practice of writing ultimately helps you find your own style and helps you to decide what is appropriate to the subject matter you've chosen. Most writers have many styles, depending on what they choose to write about. The question 'How do I find my own style?' is the one I'm most frequently asked as a teacher. My answer is always the same: 'By experimenting through writing.'

"Another trait that most successful writers share is perseverance. I once sold a story that was sent to twenty-two publishers, but I have a friend who easily topped my record: She sold a book after it had been rejected forty-one times. So 'don't give up' is an understatement in the writing field."

HOBBIES AND OTHER INTERESTS: Reading, folk dancing, textile painting, yoga, ice skating, and theatre.

FRIEDMAN, Ina R(osen) 1926-

BRIEF ENTRY: Born January 6, 1926, in Chester, Pa. In two books for young adults, Friedman explores the demoralizing effect of racial bigotry through the true life stories of those who have lived through it. *Black Cop: A Biography of Tilman O'Bryant* (Westminster Press, 1974) is an account of one man's struggle to overcome the adversities of black racial prejudice in America. Friedman describes how perseverance and determination eventually led O'Bryant from a poverty stricken childhood to the hard-earned position of Assistant Chief of Police in Washington, D.C. "As a study of prejudice and resistance," observed *Bulletin of the Center for Children's Books*, "this is provocative. . . ." On a much more chilling note is *Escape or Die: True Stories of Young People Who Survived the Holocaust* (Addison-Wesley, 1982). In preparation for the book, Friedman traveled to five continents while conducting interviews with over one hundred survivors of the Holocaust. Ultimately, twelve first-person narratives were chosen to comprise the final work. "These are tales of strength and hope," noted *Voice of Youth Advocates,* "the stuff of which legends are born."

Friedman's latest work is a book for children entitled *How My Parents Learned to Eat* (Houghton, 1984). In a much lighter vein, it also explores racial differences as an American sailor and a Japanese girl fall in love and encounter cultural difficulties, best exemplified by the problem of knife and fork versus chopsticks. A 1985 Christopher Award winner, the book was described by *New York Times Book Review* as "a quiet yarn . . . [that] offers an engaging introduction to the idea that there are many ways to do something so basic as eating." Friedman is also a translator of adult books from Hebrew to English and has contributed to several collections of poetry for Hebrew schools.

FOR MORE INFORMATION SEE: Contemporary Authors, Volumes 53-56, Gale, 1975.

HARVEY FROMMER

FROMMER, Harvey   1937-

PERSONAL: Born October 10, 1937, in Brooklyn, N.Y.; son of Max and Fannie (Wechsler) Frommer; married Myrna Katz (a writer, teacher, and free-lance editor), January 23, 1960; children: Jennifer, Freddy, Ian. *Education:* New York University, B.S., 1957, M.A., 1961, Ph.D., 1974. *Religion:* Jewish. *Residence:* North Woodmere, N.Y.

CAREER: United Press International (UPI), Chicago, Ill., sportswriter, 1957-58; New York public schools, New York City, high school English teacher, 1960-70; City University of New York, New York City, associate professor, 1970—. As a sports nostalgia and trivia expert, has appeared on television and radio talk shows. *Military service:* U.S. Army, 1958-59. *Member:* Association of American University Professors, Society of American Baseball Research. *Awards, honors:* Honored by the chancellor of the City University of New York in annual salute to scholars "who have brought distinction to themselves and to their university during the past year," 1984.

WRITINGS: A Baseball Century: The First 100 Years of the National League, Macmillan, 1976; (with Ronald Weinmann) *A Sailing Primer,* Atheneum, 1977; *The Martial Arts: Judo and Karate,* Atheneum, 1978; *Sports Lingo,* Atheneum, 1979; *Sports Roots: How Nicknames, Namesakes, Trophies, Competitions, and Expressions Came to Be in the World of Sports,* Atheneum, 1979; *The Great American Soccer Book,* Atheneum, 1980; *New York City Baseball: The Last Golden Age, 1947-1957,* Macmillan, 1980; *The Sports Date Book,* Grosset, 1981; *Rickey and Robinson: A Dual Biography,* Macmillan, 1982; *Sports Genes,* Ace, 1982; *Baseball's Greatest Rivalry,* Atheneum, 1982; *Basketball My Way—Nancy Lieberman,* Scribner, 1982; *Baseball's Greatest Records, Streaks, and Feats,* Atheneum, 1983; *Jackie Robinson,* F. Watts, 1984; (with wife, Myrna Frommer) *The Games of the Twenty-Third Olympiad: Los Angeles 1984 Commemorative Book,* International Sports, 1984; *Baseball's Greatest Managers,* F. Watts, 1985; *Na-*

tional Baseball Hall of Fame, F. Watts, 1985; *Primitive Baseball,* Atheneum, in press.

WORK IN PROGRESS: Autobiography with Red Holzman of Holzman's forty years in baseball.

SIDELIGHTS: In 1974 Frommer wrote his doctoral dissertation in English on the influence of sports on television and of television on sports. His efforts to have the work published resulted in the opportunity to write *A Baseball Century,* the official centennial history of the National League.

"Sports and work and writing fascinate me, and gardening acts as a release. I am involved all the time with one of these or another. I have written seventeen books on sports in ten years and look forward to doing many more. An auto accident—for a few frightening moments—made me wonder if I would ever do anything again. However, after a long healing process, I am starting to engage in all my projects again at full speed.

"I enjoy my dual careers—as professor of writing and speech and as sports author and lecturer. One acts as a change of pace for the other. Also, there is my wonderful family, my wife, Myrna—my editor, adviser, organizer, and inspirer—and my lovely children. My two boys are totally involved in the world of sports, and we are able to share anecdotes and happy times playing games—especially baseball. I still find myself anchored in my own childhood world of games and fanhood. Perhaps that is what inspired *New York City Baseball* and

Rickey and Robinson—both books deal with the golden heroes and my growing up years, when the world we all knew was very different.

"I am very pleased when reviewers say nice things about my writings. I try to give my work every ounce of effort and intelligence that I possess. I am especially pleased when I receive a fan letter or when I meet someone or hear of someone who has read one of my books and has expressed his or her appreciation. I look back over these things and am happy at how far a poor kid from a seedy neighborhood in Brooklyn came in the United States of America. I dream now of other journeys, other accomplishments, other big and significant books for the future."

As the result of a nationwide search, Frommer was selected to be the major author and editor of the official commemorative book of the 23rd Olympic Games.

FOR MORE INFORMATION SEE: New York Times, April 13, 1980; *New York Times Book Review*, June 15, 1980.

GATER, Dilys 1944-
(Dilys Owen; Olwen Edwards, Lys Holland, Clover Sinclair, Katrina Wright, Vivien Young, pseudonyms)

PERSONAL: Born April 17, 1944, in Wrexham, North Wales; daughter of Edward (a clerk) and Olwen (Jones) Binnion; married Dennis Owen, September 27, 1963 (divorced, 1969); married Philip Gater (a bank messenger), May 21, 1977; children:

DILYS GATER

(first marriage) Judith. *Education:* Attended Grove Park Grammar School for Girls, Wrexham, North Wales. *Home:* 31 Carlton Rd., Shelton, Stoke-on-Trent, Staffordshire, England.

CAREER: Author and free-lance journalist. Before becoming a full-time writer, worked variously as a library assistant, shop assistant, receptionist and barmaid. *Awards, honors:* Women's Institute Festival Award, 1972, for "The Day Before"; Best Original Play award from Stoke Festival, 1979, for "Mirage," and 1983, for "The Cavern."

WRITINGS—Under name Dilys Owen: *Crowen and the Vale of Edeyrnion: The Official Guide* (travel), Wynn Williams, 1970; *Caroline Comes for Tea* (one-act play), Evans Brothers, 1973; *Percival, the Performing Pig* (one-act play), Evans Brothers, 1973; *Sophy* (adult novel), Muller, 1974; *The Casebook of Inspector Samson* (juvenile; illustrated by Ivan Ripley), Muller, 1974; *Leo Possessed* (juvenile), Muller, 1975, (illustrated by Stephen Gammell), Harcourt, 1979; *Play-Games* (juvenile), Muller, 1977.

"Mr. Munch" series; all published by Muller; all for young people: *Mr. Munch: Milk* (illustrated by Claude Kailer), 1974; *. . . Cereals* (illustrated by C. Kailer), 1974; *. . . Sugar* (illustrated by C. Kailer), 1974; *. . . Fish* (illustrated by Angela Lewer), 1976; *. . . Salt and Spices* (illustrated by A. Lewer), 1976; *. . . Meat* (illustrated by A. Lewer), 1976.

Under pseudonym Olwen Edwards; adult novels: *The Devil's Own*, Hale, 1975; *The Devil's Daughter*, 1976.

Under name Dilys Gater; all for adults: *Fugitive Like the Wind* (one-act play), French, 1979; *The Witch-Girl* (novel), Hale, 1979; *Emily* (novel), Hale, 1980; *The Singing Swans* (two-act play), New Playwrights' Network, 1980; *The Dark Star* (novel), Hale, 1981; *Prophecy for a Queen* (historical novel), Hale, 1982; *Turnabout* (one-act play), New Playwrights' Network, 1982.

Under pseudonym Lys Holland: *A Man of Honour* (novel), Hale, 1983; *Sing No Sad Songs* (novel), Hale, 1983.

Under pseudonym Clover Sinclair: *Venetian Romance* (historical romance), Hale, 1982; *Lallie* (historical suspense), Hale, 1983.

Under pseudonym Vivien Young: *Jenni* (contemporary novel), Hale, 1982; *Castle of Love* (novel), Hale, 1983.

Under pseudonym Katrina Wright; all romantic suspense novels; all published by D. C. Thomson: *Susannah's Secret*, 1983; *A Dangerous Love*, 1983; *From Greece with Love*, 1984; *Shadow of Clorinda*, 1984; *The Spy in Petticoats*, 1984; *Love on the Nile*, 1984.

Unpublished plays: "Will the Real Anne Smith Stand Up Please?," first produced at Wrexham Little Theatre, Wrexham, North Wales, November 19, 1971; "The Day Before," first produced at Gresford V. A. School, North Wales, April 28, 1972; "Circle of Fear," and "Heaven Forbid!," first produced at Mitchell Memorial Theatre, Stoke-on-Trent, England, April 28, 1983.

Also contributor to over thirty newspapers and magazines, as well as to local radio stations.

WORK IN PROGRESS: More romances for D. C. Thomson; work for two local radio stations, including a script for a monthly book news program and a weekly poetry-reading broadcast; educational projects on Shakespeare's plays for schools; recording books on audio-cassette.

SIDELIGHTS: "I have written ever since I could hold a pen. I think though that the most valuable gift a writer can possess is experience. Live life to the full. I would like to contribute something really original and worthwhile to the world of young people's books. Also, I believe in making people forget their everyday problems and letting them enjoy themselves through books. I am interested in studying speech and drama, have acted widely (amateur) and done ballet. I love opera.

"I find that nearly everything I do, and many incidents, things and places I have seen come into my work—sometimes they even spark off a whole book—but only after enough time has passed for them to have spent a long time in the melting pot. I leave a lot of planning of plots, etc., to my subconscious—I believe in letting your mind work for you and I have trained myself to sort out problems while I am asleep.

"I find that I go through patches when everything seems to go right with my work, and it is as easy as falling off a log; but there are other times when I doubt whether I will ever be able to write another word, never mind anything good. For-

tunately, these bad patches do not come along too often, but I am always conscious that it does not matter how many books, articles, or stories, I have written over the years, the one that always matters most is the next one—the one I am just about to write. I try to look forward and to do the best I can even with the simplest little script or story. It does not have to be great literature for you to put your best into it, you should do it with everything, and try to write with your whole self whatever you are tackling. I can tell when my work is bad, and I throw it away. I don't believe in hoarding things and constantly revising, because if there is a basic flaw, all the revision in the world will not put it right. Better to turn to something else, and try to do better next time. I keep hoping that one day I'll write something that is really memorable—but I don't think I would believe it even if people told me that I'd achieved this ambition. I would always be thinking 'The next one must be better.'"

FOR MORE INFORMATION SEE: Liverpool Daily Post, February 18, 1974; Chester Chronicle, February 22, 1974; Cheshire Observer, February 22, 1974; Hanley Evening Sentinel (Stoke-on-Trent), July 29, 1977.

Peta lay in bed, blinking in the sudden flood of bright light and looking indignant. "What did you do that for?" she demanded. ▪ (From *Leo Possessed* by Dilys Owen. Illustrated by Stephen Gammell.)

GIRARD, Linda Walvoord 1942-

PERSONAL: Born November 16, 1942, in Amsterdam, N.Y.; daughter of Christian Herman (a minister) and Marie (a teacher; maiden name, Verduin) Walvoord; married Delmar W. Girard (a futures trader), January 4, 1969; children: Aaron. Education: Hope College, B.A., 1964; University of Chicago, M.A., 1966, graduate study, 1968, 1970-71, and 1974. Home: 24499 Kelsey Rd., Barrington, Ill. 60010.

CAREER: Millikin University, Decatur, Ill., instructor, 1966-68; North Central College, Naperville, Ill., assistant professor, 1970-71; Cook Publishing Co., Elgin, Ill., editor for teacher education publications, 1977-78. President, Barrington Writer's Workshop, 1980-81; membership chairman, Off-Campus Writer's Workshop, 1981-83. Member: Authors Guild, Society of Children's Book Writers, American Association of University Professors, Modern Language Association of America. Awards, honors: Ford Foundation fellow, University of Chicago, 1964-65; fellow, University of Chicago, 1965-66; fellow, U.S. Office of Education, 1971-74; fellow in poetry, Illinois Arts Council, 1985.

WRITINGS: You Were Born on Your Very First Birthday (illustrated by Christa Kieffer), edited by Kathy Tucker, A. Whitman, 1983; My Body Is Private, edited by K. Tucker, A. Whitman, 1984; Who Is a Stranger and What Should I Do? (illustrated by Helen Cogancherry), edited by Abbey Levine, A. Whitman, 1984; Halley's Comet, A. Whitman, 1985.

Contributor of poetry to numerous literary quarterlies, including Spoon River Quarterly, Ascent, Mississippi Valley Review, Cottonwood Review, Nimrod, and Midwest Quarterly.

WORK IN PROGRESS: A historical novel; poetry; juvenile biography of Edmond Halley.

SIDELIGHTS: Girard was born in Amsterdam, New York, and grew up as the middle child in a minister's family, living in small towns in New York, Michigan, and New Jersey. She graduated from high school in Oradell, New Jersey, and was

LINDA WALVOORD GIRARD

educated further at Hope College in Holland, Michigan and the University of Chicago.

But most of her childhood was spent in Holland, Michigan "where the tulips bloom in the boulevards and along the streets as well as on the huge acres of tulip farms. In this town, about eighty per cent of the people still have Dutch roots, and in the town of about 20,000, there are over seventy-five churches of the two Dutch Protestant denominations. So being a minister's child was nothing special in *that* place!

"At home, we had a merry household, talking all the time. There was a combination of reserve and warmth, and a corny sense of humor. We lived in three different parsonages while I was growing up, and in those days, they tended to be big, and their yards tended to have big bushes and hedges, perfect for hideaways, cops and robbers and such. I remember secret clubs with complicated rules, gangs, coded messages, and I remember having the freedom to roam at a fairly young age.

"I remember writing a lot as a child. I taught myself to type in sixth grade, on my dad's typewriter no longer good enough for sermons, and I wrote a play, which my teacher later sold to a magazine. For $10. That teacher thought you could do great things. So you did.

"There was great expressiveness in our household. I heard my parents tell each other 'I love you' or 'You're beautiful' many times. And there was a very modern lifestyle between my parents in the 1940's. Not many ministers would vacuum, do housework, or cook, but my Dad did. He also baked all our bread. My mother was active in speaking regionally and writing for publication, as a role she had aside from my Dad.

Before you were born
you had a special place
where you curled up inside your mommy.
For nine months
while the weather and the seasons changed outside
and the wind blew in the trees
it was always exactly the same every day
in your place. Safe. Floating. Warm.

(From *You Were Born on Your Very First Birthday* by Linda Walvoord Girard. Illustrated by Christa Kieffer.)

"Telling stories, as well as writing and speaking, surrounded me all the time as I grew up. I have one grandfather who stole on board a freight train at the age of eighteen, and stowed away to South Dakota to homestead, with no neighbors for miles. I have another grandfather who at eighteen was a very proper Edwardian and cared about his collars, and was studying to become a very reserved minister. But both of these grandfathers told stories well—one with a set of favorites, of danger and dark nights, decorated with the calls of wild wolves on the plains of South Dakota. The other grandfather wrote his memoirs in a graceful, easy, homey style, of growing up on a Wisconsin dairy farm in the 1890's, and his book is warm and reserved at the same time. And it tells what you want to know, instead of how Uncle Henry died or who a second cousin married.

"I'd say the best part of a writer's childhood is always with her. I hope each of my books and poems have behind them a certain warmth and a sense of a person speaking, a voice. In my books for children, I try to give the reader something to remember, like a taste or flavor—not just ideas or information. Even though two of my books are about 'educational' subjects (strangers and abuse), I try to give them rhythm and tone. A book should be an experience, not just a report or directions.

"I sit each day at our home in Barrington, Illinois, looking out a second-story window overlooking a marsh and pond and some hills and sheds, and write, at the moment, about Edmond Halley. So many books about Halley's approaching comet talk about comets. To me, the interesting story is the personal story of a discoverer.

"I write every day, and like the process of writing itself. Poems usually go through many revisions. Though I did not do any creative writing in the years between my college days and about five years ago (about a fifteen-year gap, in which I taught, and edited books, as well as raised a family), I did write a lot as a child, and also made up stories often. Today, I still like to make up stories *ad lib* for my son at bedtime. Sometimes these become kernels for new books. But whether they do or not, I try to think of the person it's for, and the fun of the story and language itself. Sometimes, that gives a writer his best ideas."

GLOBE, Leah Ain 1900-

PERSONAL: Born March 14, 1900, in Narevke, Russia (now U.S.S.R.); brought to United States in 1906; daughter of Wolf and Sarah (Cohen) Ain; married Jacob Globe, August 9, 1925; children: Rena Quint. *Education:* Jewish Theological Seminary of America Teachers Institute, teacher's certificate, 1920; attended Hunter College (now of the City University of New York), Brooklyn Museum Art School, and Columbia University. *Religion:* Jewish.

CAREER: Editor. Hebrew Institute, book editor, 1920-30. *Member:* Mizrachi Women's Organization (chairman of national cultural committee, 1946-49).

WRITINGS: (Editor with Azriel Eisenberg) *The Bas Mitzvah Treasury* (young adult), Twayne, 1965; (translator and editor with A. Eisenberg) *The Secret Weapon, and Other Stories of Faith and Valor* (illustrated by Joan Kiddell-Monroe), Son-

cino, 1966; (translator and editor with A. Eisenberg) *Sabra Children: Stories of Fun and Adventure in Israel* (juvenile; illustrated by Gabe Josephson), Jonathan David, 1970; (editor with A. Eisenberg) *Home at Last,* Bloch Publishing, 1977.

GORDON, Shirley 1921-

BRIEF ENTRY: Born December 29, 1921, in Geneva, Ill. Employed as a full-time writer since 1955, Gordon also has worked as a reporter for *TV-Radio Life* magazine and as a network publicist for Columbia Broadcasting System, Inc. Radio and Television. She has written scripts for network radio shows, including "Suspense," "The Whistler," and "Hollywood Radio Mystery Theatre," as well as for television shows like "You Are There," "Courtship of Eddie's Father," and "Bewitched." The author of seven juvenile books, she has written three about Susan and her best friend Crystal. In *Crystal Is the New Girl* (Harper, 1976), Crystal joins Susan's third-grade class. At first Susan rejects the idea of making friends with Crystal, but is soon won over by the girl's unique personality and behavior. *Booklist* described the book as "a warm story of a growing friendship," while *Publishers Weekly* commented on its "likeable . . . pair of heroines." The girls also appear in *Crystal Is My Friend* (Harper, 1978) and *Happy Birthday, Crystal* (Harper, 1981).

In *The Boy Who Wanted a Family* (Harper, 1980), Michael goes to live with Miss Graham, a single woman who would like to adopt him. He has been "almost adopted" twice before and fears that the same thing may happen again. In the end, however, he's happy to learn that he has a new mom. *School Library Journal* found the book's characters "warm and real." Gordon's other books are *The Green Hornet Lunchbox* (Houghton, 1970), *Grandma Zoo* (Harper, 1978), and *Me and the Bad Guys* (Harper, 1980). *Home:* 6122 Myosotis St., Los Angeles, Calif. 90042.

FOR MORE INFORMATION SEE: Contemporary Authors, Volumes 97-100, Gale, 1981.

GWYNNE, Fred(erick Hubbard) 1926-

PERSONAL: Born July 10, 1926, in New York, N.Y.; married Jean Reynard, 1952; children: four. *Education:* Attended Phoenix School of Design; Harvard University, B.A., 1951. *Residence:* New York, N.Y.

CAREER: Actor, illustrator and writer. Began acting career performing Shakespeare in Cambridge, Mass., 1951, and made Broadway debut as Stinker in "Mrs. McThing," 1952; has made numerous stage appearances since then, including roles in "Love's Labour's Lost," 1953, "The Frogs of Spring," 1953, "Irma la Douce," 1960, "Here's Love," 1963, "The Lincoln Mask," 1972, "The Enchanted," 1973, "More Than You Deserve," 1973, "Twelfth Night," 1974, "Cat on a Hot Tin Roof," 1974, "Our Town," 1975, "The Winter's Tale," 1975, "A Texas Trilogy," 1976, "Angel," 1978, "Grand Magic," 1979, "Salt Lake City Skyline," 1982, and "Who-

FRED GWYNNE

dunnit?,'' 1983. Played Francis Muldoon in the television series ''Car 54, Where Are You?,'' NBC-TV, 1961-63, and Herman Munster in ''The Munsters,'' CBS-TV, 1964-66; has also appeared in numerous television productions, including ''Harvey,'' 1958, ''The Hasty Heart,'' 1958, ''The Old Foolishness,'' WNTA-TV, 1961, ''The Lesson,'' WNDT-TV, 1966, ''Infancy,'' WNET-TV, 1967, ''Guess What I Did Today,'' NBC-TV, 1968, ''Arsenic and Old Lace,'' ABC-TV, 1969, ''The Littlest Angel,'' NBC-TV, 1969, ''Paradise Lost,'' WNET-TV, 1971, ''The Police,'' KCET-TV, 1971, ''Dames at Sea,'' NBC-TV, 1971, ''Harvey,'' NBC-TV, 1972, and ''Any Friend of Nicholas Nickleby's Is a Friend of Mine,'' PBS-TV, 1982; appeared in motion pictures ''On the Waterfront,'' Columbia, 1954, ''Munster, Go Home,'' Universal, 1966, ''Luna,'' Twentieth Century-Fox, 1979, ''Simon,'' Orion, 1980, ''Jack-a-Boy,'' Phoenix Films, 1980, and ''The Cotton Club,'' Paramount, 1984. Has also worked as copywriter for J. Walter Thompson (advertising agency), 1955-60. *Military service:* U.S. Navy, 1944-46. *Member:* Actor's Equity Association, American Federation of Television and Radio Artists, Screen Actor's Guild. *Awards, honors:* Obie Award for best actor, *Village Voice,* about 1980, for performance in stage play ''Grand Magic.''

WRITINGS—All self-illustrated; all for children, except as indicated: *Best in Show,* Dutton, 1958; *What's Nude?* (adult humor; introduction by Nathaniel Benchley; photographs by Peter Basch), I. Obolensky, 1960; *God's First World* (adult humor), Harper, 1970; *The King Who Rained,* Windmill Books, 1970; *Ick's ABC,* Windmill Books, 1971; *The Story of Ick,* Windmill Books, 1971; *A Chocolate Moose for Dinner,* Windmill Books, 1976; *The Sixteen-Hand Horse,* Windmill Books, 1980.

Illustrator; for children: George W. Martin, *The Battle of the Frogs and the Mice: An Homeric Fable,* Dodd, 1962; Robert Kraus, *The King's Trousers,* Windmill Books, 1981.

SIDELIGHTS: Actor and author Fred Gwynne is probably best known for his roles in the popular television series, ''The Munsters'' and ''Car 54, Where Are You?'' Neither a writing nor an acting career was his childhood ambition, however. ''The thing I always wanted to be, ever since I can remember, was a portrait painter.'' [Robert Berkvist, ''Fred Gwynne—King of Curmudgeons?,'' *New York Times Biographical Service,* May, 1976.[1]]

Gwynne, the son of a stockbroker who retired to Palm Beach, Florida for health reasons, had an ideal childhood. ''I fished for ten years and never caught a damn thing.''[1]

After his father's death, his mother moved to New York and Gwynne was sent to prep school at Groton. ''I got the highest number of black marks of any boy who'd ever been there, I think, and I was lucky I wasn't kicked out. It was a very straitlaced place in those days, but it was good for me. It took my father's place, in a way.''[1]

Besides drawing, Gwynne found an interest in the acting society at school. ''I auditioned by making up a scene that, even today, makes me cry when I think of it. It was *terribly* good, but the teacher sneered at it and I went away.''[1] By the following year, however, he had become president of the Groton dramatic society.

Following graduation from Groton, Gwynne joined the Navy. After his discharge he returned to New York and entered commercial art school, but only for a short time. Realizing that art just wasn't the perfect career choice for him, he left art school and entered Harvard University. '' . . . I took up acting again. I was in the Hasty Pudding Society and got involved with the Brattle Theater, where I worked my way up from walk-ons and one-liners to bigger roles. It was a very valuable experience.''[1]

After graduation from Harvard, Gwynne made his Broadway debut in 1952 with a small part in the Mary Chase comedy, ''Mrs. McThing,'' which starred Helen Hayes. Acting, however, was not enough to support himself. He worked as an advertising copywriter on the Ford Motor Company account at the J. Walter Thompson agency and acted when and where he could for five years.

Gwynne made his television debut in the series, ''Car 54, Where Are You?'', which ran from 1961 to 1963. In 1964 he starred in the series ''The Munsters.'' As Herman Munster, Gwynne gained fame, but also became type cast as a loveable monster. ''I didn't get very rich, but I did make money on that show, even though I was working for Universal under what they called a minimum residual deal. That means I got paid for the first years of reruns, but that's all. I didn't make money from residuals, but I did invest a lot in Xerox while I was doing the show and I got out of the market at the right time, after several stock splits. So in that way 'The Munsters' made me enough money to survive on, which made it an interesting ballgame. The money let me pursue what I wanted.

''I was having a pretty tough time in my head, figuring out what I was going to do. I was drooping pretty badly, because I didn't feel I was right for anything and I didn't think that anyone else felt I was right for anything either. Then a friend of mine suggested I go over to Stratford, Conn., and try out

(From the stage revival of "Cat on a Hot Tin Roof," starring Elizabeth Ashley and Fred Gwynne. The Off-Broadway production opened at the ANTA Theatre, September 24, 1974.)

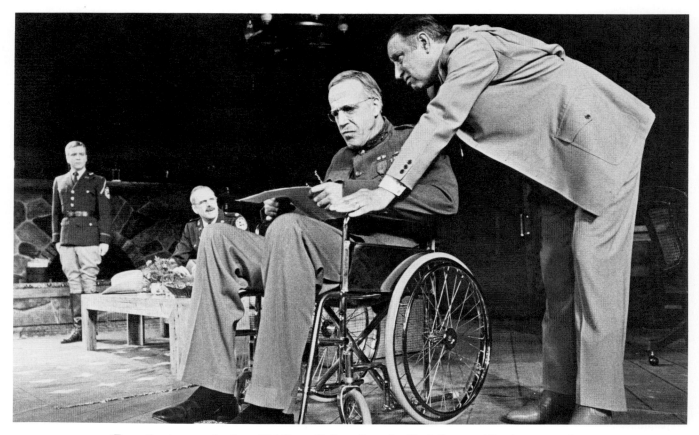

(From the stage production of "A Texas Trilogy," starring Fred Gwynne. The show opened on Broadway at the Broadhurst Theater, September 21, 1976.)

(From the television series "The Munsters," starring Fred Gwynne and Yvonne De Carlo. First broadcast on CBS-TV, September 24, 1964.)

for one of their Shakespeare productions. I did, and it was wonderful.''[1]

At the Shakespearean theater in Stratford, Connecticut, Gwynne successfully played in "Twelfth Night," "A Winter's Tale," and in Thornton Wilder's, "Our Town." He also wrote and illustrated children's books. Acting in the theater and writing for children became far more appealing to Gwynne than working in a television series. '' . . . I was at Rutgers once, for a film discussion, and wound up sitting beside Fay Wray. She was absolutely charming to me, and I decided to let it all out. I said things about alienation, and feeling like a household product, and she looked at me in a kindly way that made me go on and on. 'I mean I really like "The Munsters,'" I told her, 'but I feel I'm typed forever,' and so on.

"Fay Wray just kept smiling. Finally I was finished, and she knew I was finished. She looked at me quite casually and said, 'Honey, you've got "The Munsters" and I've got "King Kong" and we're in the same boat. We can't live with it and we can't live without it.' That kept me going.''[1]

Gwynne has continued to successfully manage two careers. He has illustrated several of his children's books, including

The King Who Rained, A Chocolate Moose for Dinner, and, most recently, *The Sixteen-Hand Horse*. He has also illustrated children's books by other writers.

Besides acting in the theater, Gwynne has worked in several television productions and has appeared in numerous movies. '' . . . I never could figure whether I went into acting in the first place to become famous or to get away from working as a bank teller. I have the feeling it was to get away from the bank.

"If I do TV now, it's PBS stuff because that's the most interesting. . . .

'' . . . Actors usually are very critical of themselves. There's been only one time I thought I did well in . . . years of acting, the Bertolucci film, 'Luna' with Jill Clayburgh. It was a small part, but I thought for those few minutes on the screen I wasn't playing any tricks.

"That probably was because of Bertolucci. Working with him is very much magic time. You feel absolutely free, so easy. Yet, if you think about it, you're probably doing exactly what he wants you to do.

Once upon a time, in the Kingdom of Ethelbert, there lived a proud and haughty king. His name was King Ivor the Third. ■ (From *The King's Trousers* by Robert Kraus. Illustrated by Fred Gwynne.)

Mommy says little children always have bear feet.

(From *The King Who Rained* by Fred Gwynne. Illustrated by the author.)

" . . . As I get older, I realize the thought of going down to a theater every night to do the same role has become slightly onerous. Only something like Big Daddy in 'Cat on a Hot Tin Roof,' which I did a few years ago, would make it seem worthwhile. That kind of role gives you back so much." [Bettelou Peterson, "Fred Gywnne, Where are You?," *Detroit Free Press*, February 8, 1982. ²]

FOR MORE INFORMATION SEE: *Variety*, November 11, 1970; Robert Berkvist, "Fred Gwynne—King of Curmudgeons?," *New York Times Biographical Service*, May, 1976; *New York Times*, May 7, 1978; Bettelou Peterson, "Fred Gwynne, Where Are You?," *Detroit Free Press*, February 8, 1982; *People*, January 25, 1985.

HAAS, Merle S.   1896(?)-1985

OBITUARY NOTICE: Born about 1896 in Portland, Ore.,; died of pneumonia, January 7, 1985, in New York, N.Y. Hospital worker and translator. The wife of Random House publishing executive Robert K. Haas, Haas was best-known for her translations of French author Laurent de Brunhoff's Babar books for children. The stories, now considered classics, detail the adventures of an elephant king named Babar. Haas, a Red Cross worker during World War I, also worked for hospitals throughout her lifetime. She spent twenty years as a nurse's aide at hospitals in White Plains, New York, and worked for several years at a children's hospital in Vahalla, New York. In addition, she was closely associated with the Howard R. Rusk Institute for Rehabilitation Medicine, where she established a library and an art department for the patients. Haas served on the Institute's placement committee for discharged patients and was the head of the hospitality committee.

FOR MORE INFORMATION SEE—Obituaries: *New York Times*, January 8, 1985.

HAMALIAN, Leo   1920-

PERSONAL: Born January 13, 1920, in New York, N.Y.; son of Thomas, (a photoengraver) and Rose (Taranto) Hamalian; married Catherine Spraker, 1943; married Linda Bearman, April 10, 1974; children: (first marriage) Jeffrey, Derek, Leslie. *Education:* Cornell University. B.S., 1942; Columbia University, M.A., 1947, Ph.D., 1954. *Home:* 530 East 90th St., New York, N.Y. 10028. *Office:* Department of English, City College of the City University of New York, New York, N.Y. 10031.

CAREER: New York University, New York City, instructor in English, 1941-53; City College of the City University of New York, New York City, assistant professor, 1954-65, associate professor, 1965-70, dean of curricular guidance, 1965-68, professor of English, 1970—, director of creative writing graduate program, 1972-74. Smith-Mundt Lecturer in Syria, 1962-64; dean, California Institute of the Arts, 1970-72; exchange professor, University of Paris VIII, 1983. *Member:* Amnesty International, Modern Language Association of America, Americans for Democratic Action, National Council of Teachers of English, Freedom to Write Committee, P.E.N. *Awards, honors:* Fulbright grants, University of Damascus, 1962-64, University of Tehran, 1974-75, and University of Hamburg, 1980.

WRITINGS: (Editor) *Reading and Rhetoric from Harper's*, Harper, 1963; (editor with Vera Von Wiren-Garczynski) *Seven Russian Short Novel Masterpieces*, Popular Library, 1967; *The Secret Careers of Samuel Roth*, Harian Press, 1969; (editor with Arthur Zeiger) *In the Modern Idiom: An Introduction to Literature*, Crowell, 1973; (editor) *D. H. Lawrence: A Collection of Criticism*, McGraw, 1973; (editor) *Franz Kafka: A Collection of Criticism*, McGraw, 1974; (editor with wife, Linda Hamalian) *Solo: Stories by Women about Women Alone*, Delacorte, 1977; *Burn after Reading*, Ararat Press, 1978; (editor with John Yohanan) *New Writing from the Middle East*,

LEO HAMALIAN

New American Library, 1978; (editor) *Rogues: Stories of Swindlers, Thieves and Confidence Men* (juvenile), Crowell, 1979; *As Others See Us: The Armenian Image in Literature,* Ararat Press, 1980; (editor) *In Search of Eden,* New American Library, 1981; (editor) *Ladies on the Loose: Women Travellers of the 18th and 19th Centuries,* Dodd, 1981; *D. H. Lawrence in Italy,* Taplinger, 1982.

Editor with Edmond L. Volpe: *Ten Modern Short Novels,* Putnam, 1958, 2nd edition, published as *Eleven Modern Short Novels,* 1970; *Great Stories by Nobel Prize Winners,* Noonday Press, 1959; *Essays of Our Time,* McGraw, 1960; *Grammar in Context,* Putnam, 1960, revised edition, with Valerie Krishna, Capricorn, 1976; *Great Essays by Nobel Prize Winners,* Noonday Press, 1960; *Pulitzer Prize Reader,* Popular Library, 1961; *Seven Short Novel Masterpieces,* Popular Library, 1961; *Noble Prize Reader,* Popular Library, 1965; *International Short Novels: A Contemporary Anthology,* Wiley, 1974.

Editor with Frederick R. Karl: *Short Fiction of the Masters,* Putnam, 1963, 2nd edition, 1973; *The Existential Imagination,* Fawcett, 1963; *The Shape of Fiction: British and American Short Stories,* McGraw, 1967; *The Radical Vision: Essays for the Seventies,* Crowell, 1970; *The Naked I: Fictions for the Seventies,* Fawcett, 1971; *The Fourth World: The Imprisoned, the Poor, the Sick, the Elderly and Underaged in America,* Dell, 1976; *Everything You Need to Know about Grammar,* Fawcett, 1979.

Contributor to numerous periodicals, including *Nation, New York Times, New York Times Book Review, Accent, Blackwood's Magazine, University Bookman, Journal of Modern Literature, American Book Review, The Literary Review, Colorado Quarterly, English Journal, Book Forum, Aramco World, D. C. Gazette, Art News,* and *Chicago Jewish Forum.* Editor of *Ararat,* 1972—.

WORK IN PROGRESS: Editor of *The View from Ararat: Another Decade of Armenian-American Writing;* a book about the influence of D. H. Lawrence on fiction and poetry.

SIDELIGHTS: "Most of my writing arises from my immediate experience and nearby needs. For instance, when I returned from a Fulbright year of teaching in Iran (1975), I embarked upon a book about contemporary writing from the Middle East, drawing as well upon information I had absorbed while living in Damascus (1962-64). Two of my books, *Burn after Reading* and *As Others See Us,* developed out of my rediscovery of ethnic identity, a process which began while I was physically close to my parents' roots and which, incidentally, led me to accept the position of editor of *Ararat,* a quarterly journal of arts and letters devoted to Armenian life and culture. The other side of the coin—what it means to be an American—stimulated me to put together *In Search of Eden.*

"My political sympathies, like those of my colleague Frederick Karl, produced my favorite two anthologies: *The Fourth World,* about America's forgotten people; and *The Radical Vision,* about the intellectual, political and cultural currents of the Sixties. After I became aware of the urgent issues underlying the women's movement, I collaborated with my wife, Linda, on a book about women who have to cope with living alone, *Solo.* This concern, combined with the inspiration provided by some extensive travel at this time, spurred me to do a book about women who travelled alone in the eighteenth and nineteenth centuries as a way of liberating themselves from the confines of conventional society.

"On occasion, I have been invited by a publisher to prepare texts suited to the college classroom—*Essays of Our Time, The Shape of Fiction,* and *Eleven Modern Short Novels* were among the results. Out of my interest in modern and *avant-guarde* literature grew *The Existential Imagination, The Naked I,* and *In the Modern Idiom.* In an age lacking heroes, I am planning a book about Sir Richard Burton, the legendary adventurer of the last century."

HARE, Norma Q(uarles) 1924-

BRIEF ENTRY: Born July 10, 1924, in Dadeville, Mo. Educator and author of books for children. Hare graduated from California State University at Fresno in 1958 and received her M.A. from the same institution in 1963. During the late 1950's and 1960's she taught at various schools in California; since 1967 she has been employed as principal at Hillside Elementary School in South San Francisco, Calif. Hare is the author of three books for children, all published by Garrard: *Who Is Root Beer?* (1977), *Wish Upon a Birthday* (1979), and *Mystery at Mouse House* (1980). As a former teacher, she realizes that "for many children, learning to read is hard work." Thus, she strives to write books that children will find "fun to spend time with, ones they can clearly understand on their own...." *Home address:* P.O. Box 161, Millbrae, Calif. 94030.

FOR MORE INFORMATION SEE: Contemporary Authors, Volume 101, Gale, 1981.

ELIZABETH HARLAN

HARLAN, Elizabeth 1945-

PERSONAL: Born November 11, 1945, in New York, N.Y.; daughter of Irving Arthur (a surgeon) and Hortense (a professor and weaver; maiden name, Schachtel) Sarot; married Robert S. Mandel, June 9, 1965 (divorced, December, 1968); married Leonard M. Harlan (a real estate developer), August 27, 1969; children: (second marriage) Joshua David, Noah Michael. *Education:* Barnard College, B.A., 1967; Yale University, M. Phil., 1971. *Home:* Windmill Farm, Cranbury, N.J. 08512. *Agent:* Rosalie Siegel, 111 Murphy Dr., Pennington, N.J. 08534.

CAREER: Full-time writer.

WRITINGS: Footfalls (young adult novel), Atheneum, 1982. Also contributor of articles to newspapers and periodicals.

WORK IN PROGRESS: Summer of the Cicada Killer, a young adult novel.

SIDELIGHTS: "I have always been interested in children in my writing. My work, like my life, is a matter of self development. I have never forgotten my childhood, and I have never turned my back on the child within me. Consequently, I rec-

Some day I intend to be a marathon racer like the Norwegian runner, Grete Waitz. ▪ (Jacket illustration by Sarah E. Edgar from *Footfalls* by Elizabeth Harlan.▪

ognize that everyone is always growing and changing, that 'growing up' means moving on, not standing still. I have tried to capture this in all my writing."

In *Footfalls,* Harlan explored the relationship of Stevie Farr with her father who is dying of cancer. Although a fictional work, the book is based on the author's own relationship with her father. "This is, after all, the story of my loving and losing my father when I was a child. All my story. All painfully true. But all enclosed within myself. How could I share this with my readers to make it happen for them as well as for me? How could I convey the tenderness of my love for my father, the stoicism with which I faced his dying, the private pain I felt when he was gone, and the deep and life-changing growth that I experienced through my loss?

"As I look outside and beyond my study window at the pin oak turning colors in the fall, I see the lesson made visible that I had to learn in order to write my novel. The colors of the leaves—bright green, almost electric green running to brown with all the middle range of autumn oranges and golds—are true and real. I see them and I know they are there—vibrant, living, almost technicolor in the cool clear sun of this late October afternoon.

"But if I were to take a picture, and if the picture were to reproduce the exact visual impression of the leaves and their real-life colors, no one would believe the photograph had not been retouched, made more glorious by artifice. Maybe it's shadow and tone we need, perhaps backdrop, or a special angle to make believable the splendor of this tree in fall.

"And so it was with my story *Footfalls,* and with all stories. We need to find a lens which enlarges what one person sees so that others can share the view.

"The seasons of our lives, like leaves that fall from trees, come and go, but faithful impressions live on. The permanence of print is, I think, my greatest joy in being published. Something which began within now lives outside of and beyond myself."

HARPER, Anita 1943-

PERSONAL: Born April 25, 1943, in Bradford-on-Avon, Wiltshire, England; daughter of Wilfred and Dorothy (Smart) Jones; married Rod Harper, March 5, 1966 (divorced, 1978); children: Joseph, Emily. *Education:* Polytechnic of North London, associate of the Library Association, 1966; Institute of Psychotherapy and Social Studies, diploma, 1982. *Home:* 48 Falkland Rd., London NW5 2XA, England.

CAREER: Librarian, writer, and psychotherapist.

WRITINGS— Juvenile: Mummy is a Health Visitor (illustrated by Gloria Timbs,) Blackie & Son, 1973; *Mummy Runs a Cafe* (illustrated by Trevor Ridley), Blackie & Son, 1973; *Daddy Drives a Bus* (illustrated by T. Ridley), Blackie & Son, 1973; *Daddy Builds Houses* (illustrated by G. Timbs), Blackie & Son, 1973; *The Robot, the Dinosaur, and the Hairy Monster* (illustrated by Sara Silcock), Blackie & Son, 1975; *Ella Climbs a Mountain* (illustrated by Michael Jackson), Kestrel Books, 1977; (with Christopher Rawson and Heather Amery) *Disguise*

ANITA HARPER

and Make-Up (illustrated by Colin King and Juliet Stanwell-Smith) Usborne Publishing, 1978; *How We Live* (illustrated by Christine Roche), Harper, 1977; *How We Work* (illustrated by C. Roche), Harper, 1977; *How We Feel* (illustrated by C. Roche), Kestrel Books, 1979; *How We Play* (illustrated by C. Roche), Kestrel Books, 1979.

WORK IN PROGRESS: "I am particularly interested now in writing books which recognise and help children deal creatively with the emotional experiences of childhood."

SIDELIGHTS: "My first books for children grew out of sharing my days with my son and later my daughter and seeing the world through their eyes. I recognised that one of the mysteries of life for very young children was the 'work' which parents and other adults disappeared to and reappeared from each day. I also saw the lack of connection in children's books at that time and in my children's minds between the tasks that they saw being performed in the world and the 'work' that so often took away the adults they knew.

"Letters from readers of those first books and my involvement in the Women's Liberation Movement raised my awareness of the sexist assumptions in so many books for children, and made me want to write books which showed adults and children in less stereotyped ways and, in particular, which gave girl readers more positive and varied models to identify with.

"I was part of the Kids Book Group—a collective of women writers and illustrators whose concern was also with this. The 'How We' books grew out of a concern that children be presented on the page with the variety of ways in which we live and that a variety of responses to situations we encounter be validated.

"In retrospect I can see that I was creating the books I would have welcomed as a child.

"I grew up an only child in the country and books were important companions and windows on the world, but I sensed even then that there was so much they left out. *Alice in Wonderland* and *Alice through the Looking Glass,* with their recognition of the bizarre and irrational that is all around us, were particular favourites.

"The bulk of my time and energy over the last three years has been taken up with training to become a feminist psychotherapist. I hope to actively return to the field of children's books in the near future."

Some people like their work.
Some people find it boring.

■ (From *How We Work* by Anita Harper. Illustrated by Christine Roche.)

HARRAH, Michael 1940-

PERSONAL: Born February 19, 1940, in Marion, Ind.; son of Walter S. (a carpenter) and Mary (Bailey) Harrah; married Wendy Watson (a book illustrator and author), December 19, 1970 (divorced, 1981); children: Mary Cameron, James. *Education:* University of Toledo, B.A., 1962, M.A., 1979. *Home:* 3157 Glanzman, Toledo, Ohio 43614. *Agent:* Curtis Brown Ltd., 575 Madison Ave., New York, N.Y. 10022. *Office:* 136 Huron St., Toledo, Ohio 43692.

CAREER: Actor and singer with various companies, including ensemble work with the New York City Opera and principal roles in regional companies with performers such as Bert Lahr, Judith Anderson, Robert Merrill, and Roberta Peters, 1965—; Lucas County Juvenile Court, Toledo, Ohio, Summerfield Schools, Petersburg, Mich. and Toledo Public Schools, Toledo, Ohio, counselor, 1977-83; University of Toledo, Toledo, Ohio, writing instructor, 1981—; WGTE-FM Radio Station, Toledo, Ohio, and WGLE Radio Station, Lima, Ohio, producer-host, 1984—. High school teacher of writing, 1962-64.

WRITINGS: First Offender (young adult), Philomel Books, 1980.

WORK IN PROGRESS—Two novels: A story about a "nineteenth-century rogue," and a novel in a contemporary setting.

SIDELIGHTS: "I am the youngest of two brothers. Motivation for writing *First Offender* came from the experience of work-

MICHAEL HARRAH

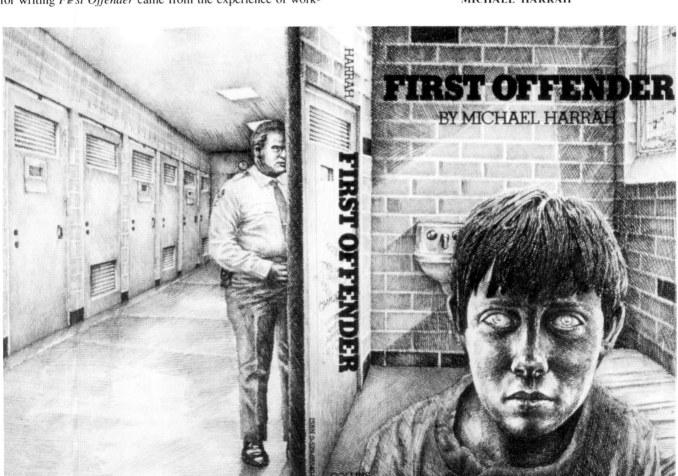

Freddy sat on his bed waiting to be locked in. ■ (Jacket illustration by Allen Davis from *First Offender* by Michael Harrah.)

ing in juvenile court and also the desire to tell a story that would appeal to the sense of isolation that many adolescents experience. I have traveled mostly in the southwest United States, where my parents lived before their deaths, and lived for several years in New York City. I see a unity in writing, acting, and singing, in that all share the purpose of telling a story.''

HOBBIES AND OTHER INTERESTS: Acting and singing.

HARRISON, Molly   1909-

PERSONAL: Born in 1909, in Stevenage, Hertfordshire, England; daughter of Ernest Charles and Ethel Hodgett; married Gordon Frederick Harrison, 1940; children: three daughters. *Education:* Attended the Sorbonne, Paris, France. *Home:* The Coach House, Horse Leas, Bradfield, Berkshire, England.

CAREER: Early in career, taught at various schools; Geffrye Museum, London, England, assistant to curator, 1939-41, cu-

rator, 1941-69; Routledge & Kegan Paul, London, editor of ''Routledge Local Search'' series, 1969-77. Member of Council Museums Association, 1953-56, and Council of Industrial Design, 1958-61. Lecturer on educational topics. *Member:* Museum Association (fellow), Royal Society of the Arts (fellow), Society of Authors (member of management committee, 1969-70; chairman of educational writers group, 1970-71). *Awards, honors:* Order of the British Empire, 1967.

WRITINGS—All nonfiction: *Museum Adventures: The Story of the Geffrye Museum,* University of London Press, 1950; *Furniture* (juvenile), Educational Supply Association, 1953, 4th edition, 1961; *Learning Out of School: A Brief Guide to the Educational Uses of Museums,* Educational Supply Association, 1954, revised edition, Ward Lock, 1970; *Food* (juvenile), Educational Supply Association, 1955, 2nd edition, 1961; *Children in History* (juvenile; illustrated by Sheila Maguire), Hulton, Volume I: *The Middle Ages,* 1958, Volume II: *Sixteenth and Seventeenth Centuries,* 1959, Volume III: *The Eighteenth Century,* 1960, Volume IV: *The Nineteenth Century,* 1961, revised editions, 1976-78.

Homes (juvenile), Educational Supply Association, 1960; *Your Book of Furniture* (illustrated by S. Maguire), Faber, 1960;

Anglo-Saxon cooking. ■ (From *The Kitchen in History* by Molly Harrison. Illustrated by Sheila Maguire.)

MOLLY HARRISON

(compiler with O. M. Royston) _How They Lived,_ Volume II (Harrison was not associated with Volume I, Barnes & Noble, 1962; _Shops and Shopping_ (illustrated by S. Maguire and others), Ward Lock, 1965; _Changing Museums: Their Use and Misuse,_ Longmans, 1967; _Hairstyles and Hairdressing_ (juvenile; illustrated by Elizabeth Clarke), Ward Lock, 1968, Dufour, 1969. _The English Home_ (juvenile; illustrated by S. Maguire), Routledge & Kegan Paul, 1969.

People and Furniture: A Social Background to the English Home, Rowman & Littlefield, 1971; _The Kitchen in History_ (illustrated by S. Maguire), Osprey, 1972; _Homes_ (juvenile; "Now and Then" book; illustrated by Kenneth Day), Benn, 1973; _Museums_ (juvenile; illustrated by Christine Robins), Mills & Boon, 1973; _Museums and Galleries,_ Routledge & Kegan Paul, 1973; _Home Inventions_ (juvenile), Usborne Publishing, 1975; _Homes in Britain,_ Allen & Unwin, 1975; _People and Shopping: A Social Background,_ Benn, 1975; _Markets and Shops,_ Macdonald Educational, 1978; _Growing Up in Victorian Days_ (juvenile), Wayland, 1980.

"Picture Source Book for Social History" series; juvenile; all published by Allen & Unwin: (With Anne A. M. Wells) _Picture Source Book for Social History: The Seventeenth Century,_ 1953; (with A.A.M. Wells) ... _The Eighteenth Century,_ 1955; (with A.A.M Wells) ... _Early Nineteenth Century,_ 1957; (with A.A.M. Wells) ... _From the Conquest to the Wars of the Roses,_ 1958; (with O. M. Royston) ... _Late Nineteenth Century,_ 1961; (with Margaret E. Bryant) ... _Sixteenth Century,_ 1962; (with O. M. Royston) ... _The Twentieth Century,_ 1967.

HOBBIES AND OTHER INTERESTS: Writing and gardening.

FOR MORE INFORMATION SEE: Times Literary Supplement, February 20, 1964; _Christian Science Monitor,_ April 28, 1964.

HARTLEY, Fred Allan III 1953-

PERSONAL: Born March 22, 1953, in Morristown, N.J.; son of H. Allan (an artist and writer) and Hermine (Peppinger) Hartley; married Sherry Dykstra, June 14, 1974; children: Fred Allan IV, Andrea Joy. _Education:_ Wheaton College, Wheaton, Ill., B.A., 1975; Gordon-Conwell Theological Seminary, M.Div., 1979. _Home:_ 1736 Northwest Eighth Terr., Homestead, Fla. 33030. _Office:_ South Dade Alliance Church, 29501 Kingman Rd., Leisure City, Fla. 33033.

CAREER: Ordained Christian & Missionary Alliance minister, 1980; associate pastor of village church in Fort Myers, Fla., 1976-78; South Dade Alliance Church, Leisure City, Fla., senior pastor, 1979—. Lecturer and conference speaker.

WRITINGS: Update: A New Perspective on Christian Dating (young adult), Revell, 1977; _Dare to Be Different,_ Revell, 1979; _Growing Pains: First-Aid for Teenagers,_ Revell, 1981; _One Hundred Per Cent Discipleship_ (young adult), Revell, 1983.

SIDELIGHTS: "When I was nineteen years of age, I accompanied my father to an editorial conference at the Fleming H.

FRED ALLAN HARTLEY III

Revell Co. (publishers). There, conversation obviously centered on books—particularly my father's work. Over dessert they turned to me and asked, 'What have you ever published?' I chuckled and replied, 'A term paper for college.' They responded that they were always looking for new authors and would be glad to have me submit some material. I had just finished writing a short story on a dating relationship I had had, so I sent it to them.

"Soon after, they sent me a contract for a book that was to become my first publication, *Update: A New Perspective on Christian Dating.* I have since been impressed with the powerful medium of printed copy. As a Christian writer, I work from the philosophical base of absolute truth and the conviction that God has spoken in history through his son, Jesus Christ . . . the Incarnate Word. In my publications I have sought to transcribe eternal truths into concrete realities that are livable for today's adolescents. I trust I have been at least partially successful.''

HOGARTH, Paul   1917-

PERSONAL: Born October 4, 1917, in Kendal, Westmorland, England; son of Arthur and Janet (Bownass) Hogarth; married Phyllis Daphne Pamplin (marriage ended); married Patricia Douthwaite, February 14, 1959; children: (second marriage) Toby. *Education:* Attended Manchester College of Art, 1936-38, St. Martin's School of Art, 1938-40. *Home and office:* The Studio, 61 Auden Place, Manley St., London NW1 8ND,

The Baroness has been a char, busker, cook and night nurse. ■ (From *London à la Mode* by Malcolm Muggeridge. Illustrated by Paul Hogarth.)

England. *Literary agent:* Georges Borchardt, Inc., 145 East 52nd St., New York, N.Y. 10022. *Art agent:* Edward T. Riley, 215 East 31st St., New York, N.Y. 10016.

CAREER: Free-lance artist and illustrator. London County Council Central School of Arts and Crafts, London, England, visiting lecturer, 1951-54; Royal College of Art, London, tutor, 1964-70, visiting lecturer in Department of Illustration, Faculty of Graphic Design, 1971—. Visiting associate professor, Philadelphia College of Art, 1968-69. *Exhibitions:* Francis Kyle Gallery, London, 1980 and 1983. *Military service:* Royal Engineers, 1940-42. *Member:* Association of Illustrators (honorary president), Royal Designers for Industry, Royal Academy of Fine Arts (academician), Society of Industrial Artists and Designers (fellow), Chelsea Arts Club (London), Reform Club (London). *Awards, honors:* Francis Williams Illustration Award, 1982, for *Poems.*

WRITINGS: Defiant People: Drawings of Greece Today, Lawrence & Wishart, 1953; *Drawings of Poland*, Wydawnictwo Artystczno-Graficzne (Warsaw), 1953; *Looking at China*, Lawrence & Wishart, 1956; *People Like Us: Drawings of South Africa and Rhodesia*, Dobson, 1958, published as *The Sons of Adam*, T. Nelson, 1960; *Irish Sketchbook*, Verlagder Kunst,

PAUL HOGARTH

(From *Majorca Observed* by Robert Graves and Paul Hogarth. Illustrated by Paul Hogarth.)

1962; _Creative Pencil Drawing_, Watson, 1964; _Creative Ink Drawing_, Watson, 1968; _The Artist as Reporter_, Reinhold, 1967, revised enlarged edition, Gordon Fraser, 1985; _Drawing People_, Watson, 1971; _Artists on Horseback: The Old West in Illustrated Journalism, 1857-1900_, Watson, 1972; _Drawing Architecture_, Watson, 1973; _Paul Hogarth's American Album_, Lion and Unicorn Press, 1974; _Paul Hogarth's Walking Tours of Old Philadelphia_, Barre Publishing, 1976; _Paul Hogarth's Walking Tours of Old Boston_, Dutton, 1978; (with Stephen Spender) _America Observed_, Clarkson N. Potter, 1979; _Arthur Boyd Houghton_, Gordon Fraser, 1982.

Illustrator: Charlotte Brontë, _Jana Eyrova_ (title means "Jane Eyre"), Mlada Fronta (Prague), 1953; Charles Dickens, _Pan

(From _Brendan Behan's New York_ by Brendan Behan. Illustrated by Paul Hogarth.)

Pickwick, Statni Nakladatelstvi Detske Knihy (Prague), 1956; Doris Lessing, _Going Home_, M. Joseph, 1957; Arthur Conan Doyle, _The Adventures of Sherlock Holmes_, Folio Society, 1958; R. Haggard, _King Solomon's Mines_, Penguin, 1958; P. Knight, _The Gold of the Snow Geese_, T. Nelson, 1958; O. Henry, _Selected Short Stories_, Folio Society, 1960; Elizabeth Gaskell, _Marie Bartonová_ (title means "Mary Barton"), Mlada Fronta, 1960; Olive Schreiner, _The Story of an African Farm_, Limited Editions, 1961; Jean Jacques Salomon, _Prehistory: Civilization Before Writing_, Dell, 1962; Brendan Behan, _Brendan Behan's Island_, Geis, 1962; B. Behan, _Brendan Behan's New York_, Geis, 1964; Robert Graves, _Majorca Observed_, Doubleday, 1965; (and author of captions) Malcom Muggeridge, _London a la Mode_, Hill & Wang, 1967; Alaric Jacob, _A Russian Journey_, Hill & Wang, 1969; James D. Atwater and R. E. Ruiz, _Out from Under_, Doubleday, 1969; Doris Whitman, _The Hand of Apollo_, Follett, 1969; Elizabeth Sheppard-Jones, _Stories of Wales: Told for Children_, Academy Chicago, 1978; Siegfried Sassoon, _Memoirs of a Fox-Hunting Man_, Limited Editions, 1978; James Joyce, _Ulysses_, Franklin Library, 1978; Nigel Buxton, _America_, Cassell, 1979; R. Graves, _Poems_, Limited Editions, 1980; S. Sassoon, _Memoirs of an Infantry Officer_, Limited Editions, 1981; Hugh Johnson, _Hugh Johnson's Wine Companion_, Simon & Schuster, 1984; Joseph Conrad, _Nostromo_, Folio Society, 1984.

Contributor to _Penrose Annual_ of Hastings House, and to _Fortune_, _Daily Telegraph Magazine_, _Sports Illustrated_, _Illustrated London News_, and other periodicals. Art editor, _Contact_, 1950-51.

WORK IN PROGRESS: Illustrations for a book about the city of London by Sir David Piper, to be published by Faber & Faber.

SIDELIGHTS: "Many of my books—especially, _Creative Pencil Drawing_, _Creative Ink Drawing_, _Drawing People_, _Drawing Architecture_— are 'how to' books which attempt to explain the function of technique in relation to the art of drawing.

"My other books, which I have also written and illustrated, cover aspects of the role of a thinking artist-observer. These include _The Artist as Reporter_ which attempts to make editors, art directors, and artists more aware of the superior, imaginative potential of the artist as illustrator, _Artists on Horseback_, a survey of Victorian artists reporting the Old West for the British picture press and two walking tour books of Boston and Philadelphia, which were aimed at making Americans more aware of their historic past.

"As an illustrator, I have decorated the pages of many books published in both the United States and Europe. These range from nineteenth-century classics like _Jane Eyre_, _Pickwick Papers_ and Mrs. Gaskell's _Mary Barton_.

"I particularly enjoy bringing the past to life and have continued to do this in books such as _Out from Under_, _Memoirs of a Fox-Hunting Man_, _Memoirs of an Infantry Officer_ and _Ulysses_. Much of the background material for the illustrations in these books derive from actual observation. For example, the Dublin in _Ulysses_ I got to know intimately from my explorations with Brendan Behan when we worked together on _Brendan Behan's Island_. Essentially, my illustrative work with authors falls into two graphic idioms each of which fertilizes the other."

FOR MORE INFORMATION SEE: Architectural Review, August, 1955; _Graphis_, September/October, 1962; Robin Jacques, _Illustrators at Work_, Studio Books, 1963; Diana Klemin, _The

Illustrated Book, Clarkson N. Potter, 1970; *Designer* (London), November, 1979; *Financial Times* (London), March 31, 1980.

HOLT, Rochelle Lynn   1946-
(Rochelle Holt DuBois)

PERSONAL. Born March 17, 1946, in Chicago, Ill.; daughter of Russell Thomas and Olga (Kochick) Holt. *Education:* University of Illinois at Chicago Circle, B.A., 1967; University of Iowa, M.F.A., 1970; Columbia Pacific University, Ph.D., 1980. *Residence:* Westfield, N.J. and Phoenix, Ariz. *Agent:* Jim Haughey, Eastview Editions, 1185 Morris Ave., Union, N.J.

CAREER: Morningside College, Sioux City, Iowa, instructor of English, 1973; Rust College, Holly Springs, Miss., instructor of Spanish, 1973-74; Mississippi Industrial College, Holly Springs, assistant professor of English, 1974-75; Daniel Payne College, Birmingham, Ala., assistant professor of English, 1975-76; Union College, Cranford, N.J., adjunct English teacher, 1984-85. Co-owner of Ragnarok Press, 1970-78, and coordinating editor, Merging Media, 1978—. Has also been a professional book reviewer for over twenty years for *Small Press Review, Telewoman, Women Sense, New Jersey TV Weekly,* and other periodicals. *Member:* National Association for Poetry Therapists, Associated Writers Program, New Jersey Society of Poets, Feminist Writers Guild (national steering committee, 1981-83), International Women Writers Guild, Poetry Society of America, Academy of American Poets. *Awards, honors:* National Endowment for the Arts writer in residence grant, 1976-77; play production grant, Office of Advanced Drama of University of Minnesota, fall, 1975, for production, "Walking into the Dawn: A Celebration"; recipient of three grants from the Coordinating Council of Literary Magazines, 1976, 1978, 1979, for literary magazine, *Valhalla.*

WRITINGS: All poetry, except as indicated; published by Ragnarok, except as indicated: *To Make a Bear Dance,* 1970; *The Human Omelette,* 1971; *A Seismograph of Feeling,* 1972; *The Bare Tissue of Her Soul,* 1972; *Wing Span of an Albatross,* 1972; *A Ballet of Oscillations,* 1973; *A Peaceful Intent,* 1973; *Holly Springs: A Letter,* 1974; (with Margaret Taylor) *Landscapes,* 1974 *Poems for Amaefula,* 1974; *The Sun and the Moon,* 1974; *Yellow Pears: Smooth as Silk,* 1975; *Love in Spring,* 1975 (with D. H. Stefanson) *Gold Fantasy,* 1975; *The Song of the Robin* (juvenile), 1975; (contributor) Bill Henderson, editor, *The Publish-It-Yourself Handbook,* Pushcart, 1975; *Love in the Year of the Dragon,* Northwoods Press, 1976; *The Tender Touch of a Leaf,* 1976; *With Veils of Rain,* 1977; *Plum Blossoms in the Mist,* 1977; *Eulogy for Anahita,* C. P. Graham Press, 1977; *From One Bird,* 1978; *With Flowers and Kiss,* 1978; (under name Rochelle Holt DuBois) *Second Skin,* Merging Media, 1978; *Ecstasy,* Merging Media, 1979; *Living Memories,* Merging Media, 1979; *Boxing with River and Wind: Pen and Ink Poems,* Merging Media, 1979.

A Legend in His Time (juvenile novella), Merging Media, 1980; *Pangs* (novella), Lawton Press, 1981; *The Invisible Dog* (miniature book), Mosaic Press, 1981; *Timesharing: A Consumer's Guide to a New Vacation Concept* (nonfiction), Somrie Press, 1981; *The Train in the Rain,* Timberline Books, 1982; (with Diane Stein) *The Unicorn Moon,* Merging Media, 1982; (with

ROCHELLE LYNN HOLT

Virginia Love Long-Glasscock) *Moon Log-Ocean Waves,* Merging Media, 1982; *The Woman in the Moon* (short story), Geryon Press, 1983; *Timelapse,* Lunchroom Press, 1983; (with Adele Kenny) *Dialogue of Days,* Merging Media, 1983; (with Megan Terry) *Two by Terry Plus One* (plays; contains "Walking Into Dawn: A Celebration"), I. E. Clark, 1984; *The Blue Guitar,* Northwoods Press, 1984; (with V. Love Long-Glasscock) *Letters of Human Nature* (illustrated by Julie Ball), Merging Media, 1985; *Prescriptions for Psyche,* Timberline Press, 1985; *Extended Family* (illustrated by Carol del Guidice), American Studies Press, 1985; *The Elusive Rose* (chapbook), Aquila Press (Scotland), 1985; (with Linda Zeiser) *Mendsongs and Soulspace* (illustrated by J. Ball), Merging Media, 1985; *A Little of the Sea* (Caribbean stories), Bahamas International Publishers, 1986; (with Linda Ball) *Haiku of Desire* (illustrated by J. Ball), Merging Media, 1986; (with V. Love Long-Glasscock) *Shared Safari* (illustrated by Sudie Rakusin), Merging Media, 1986; *How to Cope with Depression Psychically* (nonfiction chapbook; illustrated by J. Ball), Merging Media, 1986.

Plays: "Walking Into Dawn: A Celebration" (multi-media play; see above), first produced in Omaha, Neb., at the Magic Theatre, November 7, 1975; "Golden Pyramids at Ohama: Egyptian Comedy" (multi-media play), produced in Towson, Md., at Goucher College, 1977; "Sharper than a Serpent's Tooth" (multi-media play), produced in Tarpon Springs, Fla., at the Florida Recreation Center Theater, 1978; (author of libretto) Jean Toomer, "Cane," produced in Philadelphia, Pa., at the Oracles Theatre, 1983.

Editor; all published by Ragnarok, except as indicated: *Eidolons,* 1972; *Children of the Moon,* 1973; *Sprays of Rubies,* 1975; (and translator) Leonora Carrington, *The Oval Lady* (short story translations from the Spanish), Capra Press, 1975. Also editor of *Valhalla 7 Networks,* a special Anais Nin tribute issue, 1978. Editor of *Valhalla* magazine, 1970-78, and *Search,* 1978—.

Contributor to anthologies: *Convocation: Women in Writing,* United Sisters, 1975; *Love in New York,* Alternative Press, 1976; *First Person Intense,* Mudborn Press, 1978; *Gargoyle 12 and 13,* Paycock Press, 1979; *Obsidian: Black Lit in Review,* Wayne State, 1980; *Critical Studies of Short Fiction,* Salem Press, 1981.

ADAPTATIONS: "Yellow Pears, Smooth as Silk" (recording), Ragnarok, 1977.

WORK IN PROGRESS: Novels: *My House,* a family saga written with Olga G. Holt; *Halcyon; The Suitcase Gypsy: An Intimate Portrait of America; Scars; Eye of the Mash;* (with Susan Sheppard) *Invocation of Hands.* Poetry: *Stream of Consciousness* (a scrambled alphabet of poems and stories; calligraphy by Joanne Preston; illustrated by Conchita), *Web of Breath* and *Stalking the Gaps.*

SIDELIGHTS: "I have been encouraged and inspired by my friends, Anais Nin, Virginia Love Long-Glasscock, Susan Sheppard, Linda Zeiser, Julie Ball, and Lili Bita, to continue my interest in a multi-media type of writing (poetry, plays, stories, novellas) and to explain my sense of poetic reality in a changing world of innovative arts. I have been a painter for over a decade, a dancer for thirty years and recently (1982) began sculpting under the influence of Esi Wortzel, a sculptor and formerly known opera singer."

Holt has given over 250 poetry readings in twenty-two states in nineteen years with at least five a year since 1967. Her juvenile chapbooks, *A Legend in His Time* and *Song of Robin,* have been translated into Spanish. She has been a teacher of English and writer for over a decade, and is a registered poetry therapist. She is also a monthly columnist for *Feminine Connections.* Since 1983 Holt has been judge of West Virginia Writer's Society in the children's literary category.

JANSSON, Tove (Marika) 1914-

PERSONAL: Born August 9, 1914, in Helsinki, Finland; daughter of Viktor (a sculptor) and Signe (an artist; maiden name, Hammarsten) Jansson. *Education:* Studied book design in Stockholm, 1930-33; painting in Helsinki, 1933-36, and at Atelier Adrien Holy, Paris, France, 1938, and in Florence, Italy. *Home:* Helsinki, Finland.

CAREER: Finnish artist, author and illustrator, whose oil paintings have been shown at seven exhibitions in Helsinki; creator of the "Moomins," appearing in her books for children and, earlier, in cartoon strips. Works at her studio in Helsinki in the winter, and at a cabin-retreat on a small island off the Finnish coast about five months a year; writes in Swedish (member of the Swedish-speaking minority in Finland), but all of her books for children have also been published in English. *Member:* Painter's Society (Helsinki), Author's Club (Helsinki), Pen Club. *Awards, honors:* Stockholm Award for

best childrens' book, 1952, Nils Holgersson Plaque, 1953, and Selma Lagerlöf Medal, 1953, all for *Hur gick det sen? (The Book about Moomin, Mymble and Little My);* *Moominsummer Madness* was nominated by the Swedish section of the International Board on Books for Young People for the International Hans Christian Andersen Award, 1956; an award from the Academy (Finland), Hans Christian Andersen Diploma of the International Council of Youth (Florence), Rudolf Koivu plaquette (Finland), and the Elsa Beskow Award (Malmö), all 1958, all for *Trollvinter (Moominland Midwinter);* Swedish Culture Prize (Helsinki) for body of work, 1958, 1963, and 1970; Hans Christian Andersen Diploma of the International Council of Youth, 1962, for *Who Will Comfort Toffle?,* and 1964, for *Tales from Moominvalley;* Langman's Prize, 1965; Hans Christian Andersen Medal, Author Award, 1966; *Expressen* [Stockholm's daily paper] Winnie-the-Pooh Prize for *Moominvalley in November,* 1970; Prize of the Finnish State for *Moominvalley in November,* 1971; Selma Lagerlöf Prize for *Sculptor's Daughter,* 1972; Bonniers Publishing House, Sweden, scholarship award, 1972; Prize of Swedish Academy, 1972; Werner Söderström Publishing House and Grafia Society (Finland) scholarship and medal for illustration, 1973; given the "Order of Smile" medal by the Polish children, 1976; Austrian State Prize for Children's and Juvenile Literature, 1978, for *Wer soll den Lillan trösten?* (Austrian edition of *Vem ska trösta Knyttet? ("Who Will Comfort Toffle?")*]; honorary doctorate from Abo Academy, 1978; Le Grand Prix des

(From *Moominland Midwinter* by Tove Jansson. Illustrated by the author.)

TOVE JANSSON

Treize, for *Sommarboken* (*The Summer Book*), 1979; awarded the "Prize of Dunce's Hat," by the Finnish Comic Strip Society, 1980.

WRITINGS—All self-illustrated; juvenile, except as noted: *Smaatrollen och den stora översvämningen* (title means "The Small Trolls and the Large Flood"), Söderström, 1945; *Kometjakten*, Söderström, 1945, published in Sweden as *Mumintrollet på Kometjakt*, Sorlins, 1946, translated by Elizabeth Portch, and published in England, 1951, revised edition published as *Kometen Kommer*, Schildt, 1968, published in America as *Comet in Moominland*, Walck, 1968; *Trollkarlens hatt*, Schildt, 1949, published in England as *The Finn Family Moomintroll*, Benn, 1950, published in America as *The Happy Moomins*, Bobbs Merrill, 1952, and as *The Finn Family Moomintroll*, Walck, 1965; *Moominpappans bravader*, Schildt, 1950, published in America as *The Exploits of Moominpappa*, Walck, 1966, revised edition, published as *Muminpappans*

memoarer, Schildt, 1968; *Hur gick det sen?*, Schildt, 1952, published in England as *The Book about Moomin, Mymble and Little My*, Benn, 1953; *Farlig midsommar*, Schildt, 1954, published in America as *Moominsummer Madness*, Walck, 1961; *Trollvinter*, Schildt, 1957, translated by T. Warburton, published in England as *Moominland Midwinter*, Benn, 1958, published in America, Walck, 1962; *Vem ska trösta Knyttet?*, Schildt, 1960, translated by Kingsley Hart, published in England as *Who Will Comfort Toffle?*, Benn, 1961, published in America, Walck, 1969; *Det osynliga barnet och andra berättelser*, Schildt, 1962, translated by Thomas Warburton, published in America as *Tales from Moominvalley*, Walck, 1964; *Pappan och Havet*, Schildt, 1965, translated by K. Hart, published in America as *Moominpappa at Sea*, Walck, 1967; *Bildhuggarens Dotter* (autobiographical), Schildt, 1968, published in England as *Sculptor's Daughter*, Benn, 1969, translated by K. Hart, published in America, Avon/Flare, 1976; *Sent i November*, Schildt, 1970, translated by K. Hart, published in America as *Moominvalley in November*, Walck, 1971; *Lys-*

The houseboat was quite red when he had finished, and so was the ground, and most of the shipyard, too. . . . ■ (From *The Exploits of Moominpappa* by Tove Jansson. Illustrated by the author.)

snerskan (adult short stories; title means ''The Listener''), Schildt, 1971; *Sommarboken* (adult fiction), Schildt, 1972, translated by Thomas Teal, published in America as *The Summer Book*, Pantheon, 1975; *Solstaden* (adult fiction), Schildt, 1974, translated by T. Teal, published in America as *Sun City*, Pantheon, 1976; *Den Farliga Resan*, Schildt, 1977, translated by K. Hart, published in England as *The Dangerous Journey*, Benn, 1978; *Dockskapet* (adult short stories), Schildt, 1978; *Moominstroll* (contains Volume 1, *Comet in Moominland*, Volume 2, *Finn Family Moomintroll*, Volume 3, *Moominland Midwinter*, Volume 4, *Moominpappa at Sea*, Volume 5, *Moominsummer Madness*, Volume 6, *Moominvalley in No-*

vember, Volume 7, *Tales from Moominvalley)*, Avon, 1978; *Skurken i Muminhuset*, Schildt, 1980; *Den A´rliga Bedragaren* (adult novel), Schildt, 1982; *Stenakern* (adult novel), Schildt, 1984. Writer of two plays for children; writer and designer of strip-cartoon, ''Moomin, '' *The Evening News,* London, 1953-60.

Illustrator: Lewis Carroll (pseudonym of Charles Lutwidge Dodgson), *Alice's Adventures in Wonderland,* Delacorte, 1977. Also illustrator of Swedish editions of *Alice in Wonderland, The Hobbit,* and *The Hunting of the Snark.*

SIDELIGHTS: **August 9, 1914.** Born in Helsinki, Finland. "We lived in a large, dilapidated studio in Helsinki and I pitied other children who had to live in ordinary flats, nothing like the mysterious jumble of turn-tables, sacks with plaster and cases with clay, pieces of wood and iron constructions where one could hide and build in peace. A home without sculptures seemed as naked to me as one without books."

"How remarkably complex my upbringing was,—although I never noticed it—my parents gave their children the impression of growing up in a wealthy, generous, problem-free home, although one comes to understand in later years how 'troublesome' it really was, both financially and in other ways. At that time, one only had hopes of possibilities, excitement and great variety; everything was important, but nothing was necessary; everything could be treated as play, but never, ever meaningless. My mother, especially, had an unusual quality; a mixture of strict morals and almost endless unparralled tolerance." [Eva von Zweigbergk, *Barnboken i Sverige 1750-1950,* Rabén & Sjögren, 1965.[1]]

Jansson's parents were both artists: her mother, a designer; her father, a sculptor. "To get peace for their work they gave me a pencil to handle as soon as I was old enough to hold it. We lived in Finland, Helsingfors, during the summer in the archipelago farthest out into the sea—as we do now. When I was small we went for summer journeys to Sweden and also to the islands. If something has influenced my books it may be these summer islands and, of course, the sea." [Lee Kingman and others, compilers, *Illustrators of Children's Books: 1957-1966,* Horn Book, 1968.[2]]

"My mother made illustrations and dustcovers for books all day long and well into the night. Sometimes she told me stories in front of the fire in the Dutch-Tile stove. The studio was in darkness, there was only the fire and we and our unreal, completely safe world. But it was my father who gave the necessary background of excitement. When there was a fire in town he would wake us up in the middle of the night and hurry us along dark streets to look. He played the balalaika at his parties which lasted for several days. Summers he brought us along to a desolate island where he rented a fisherman's cabin, he took us out sailing whenever the weather was bad enough, he salvaged smuggled canisters of liquor and driftwood from the bays, and loved thunderstorms above anything else. Without a happy childhood I would never have started writing."

The Snork Maiden had come across the first brave nose-tip of a crocus. ■ (From *Moominland Midwinter* by Tove Jansson. Illustrated by the author.)

Papá Mumin examinó el sombrero pensativamente. ■ (From *La Familia Mumin,* a Spanish translation of *Trollkarlens hatt* by Tove Jansson. Illustrated by the author.)

Reading was an early and favorite activity. Since Jansson's mother designed numerous Swedish books, her daughter had easy access to many books. "One of the books I read the most when I was approximately nine years old was *Poes sällsamma berättelser* ('Poe's Strange Stories'). [Another book was] *Arosenius kattresa* ('Arosenius Cat Trip') by Elsa Beskow. I didn't like the characters Pelle Snusk, Max and Moritz, and the Grimm brothers. I did, however, like Bauer's *Bland tomtar och troll* ('Among Elfs and Trolls'), because of the pictures. And [Zachrias] Topelius too, of course. When all else failed, I could always pick up one of the romantic and naive Topelius story books, unless I chose science fiction or horror stories. They calmed me down.

". . . I did not have much spare time to read girl's books. I read Kipling, Stevenson, Conrad, Lagerlöf, London and, as I said, Poe.

"After I was thirteen, I became a bookworm. I read everything I could get my hands on. My mother 'Ham,' in her work, made book covers. She obtained free samples of many to bring home and I read them all from cover to cover. If there was a book she thought unsuitable for me, and she seldom did, she would simply say: 'This is a very fruitful, historical novel, you must read it,' and I never read that book. When I was forced to go outside for fresh air, I would continue reading behind a trash container in the yard. At night I would read by flashlight under the covers. I read a lot of Victor Hugo and Thomas Hardy to understand . . . [his] 'landscapes.'" [Bo Carpelin, translation of "Tove Jansson," *Min väg till barnboken,* edited by B. Strömstedt, Bonniers, 1964.[3]]

1930-1936. Studied book design and then painting in Stockholm, Helsinki, Paris, and Florence. "In 1939, I wrote (in Swedish) my first children's book. When I illustrate my stories

I never get this feeling I have when I write, of walking in a strange world that was my own long ago. I don't draw for myself, but for those who shall read the stories, and I draw to clarify, to emphasize or to alleviate.''

1945. First of many ''Moomin'' books was published. The troll book, which introduced the bizarre ''Moominworld,'' was first written in Swedish and then translated into Finnish, English, German, Hebrew, Japanese and Polish. The books were inspired by visits to an island off the coast of Finland, where young Jansson and her family used to go. ''Far out from the coast there's an uninhabited island which I used to think was more dangerous than the other islands. Every time my father took us out to sea, I hoped he would sail there. And every

time we got there, the wind increased or there was a thunder-storm, and Father said, looking very pleased, 'Now we must stay the night.' He never went out sailing if the weather was too fine.

''The forest on that island was an impenetrable tangle of trees, many of which had fallen during the winter gales. We pulled up the boat and, when it got dark, crept under the sail and tried to sleep. The gale was full of strange noises, shouts, whispers, and something scurrying over the sailcloth, and I was certain the island was full of trolls. So I asked how big and angry trolls were. 'They're small,' my mother said, 'small and nice. They like gales, just as we do.'

Moomintroll was lying in his customary place (or one of his places) curled up on the green-and-yellow moss with his tail carefully tucked in under him. ■ (From *Moominsummer Madness* by Tove Jansson. Illustrated by the author.)

"Much later, I moved out to that same island and sat listening to the gales in my cabin, and one day I felt the urge to write about trolls. I called them Moomintrolls. Perhaps I wrote mostly for myself, as a sort of secret game and a way to return to my adventurous summers of long ago. At the time I wasn't a writer at all—I was a painter and designer. But through writing about my summers it was as if I could build my first raft again, find the fantastic cave yet again, pry very small rubies out of the rock, hunt for a hidden treasure (which actually existed although I never found it), dive in night-dark waters, climb, forever climb in trees and hills, and find hidden places where nobody had ever been before.

"I let the trolls experience my own happy summers, or maybe I experienced theirs, take it how you will. Anyway the location was always the islands in the Gulf of Finland, the best landscape I know.... Those places are where one can feel secure and alone in the right way, and that is where one can have ideas that lead to just about anything." ["Meet Your Author: Tove Jansson," *Cricket,* volume 8, number 4, December, 1980.[4]]

"Before I started writing—I didn't know much about children; it was the Moomintroll who introduced them to me. The children who you meet in radio interviews etc. are, as a rule, polite and well groomed. I have become acquainted with some of them and I talk to them as I do with my friends. They sometimes come to the studio and, among other things read...." [3]

1952-1953. Won the Stockholm Award, the Nils Holgersson Plaque, and the Selma Lagerlöf Medal, all for her book *The Book about Moomin, Mymble and Little My.* When asked for whom she writes, Jansson responded: "I write for myself first, not children. But *if* my stories are directed toward a certain type of reader, then it has to be to a 'skrutt.' By that, I mean those who have a hard time fitting in somewhere; those on the fringe, the lost ones. We all try to avoid being viewed as a 'skrutt.'

"If I don't write to entertain . . . little children, then, I guess, I must write for my own childishness. Either I have lost only half of my childhood or I can't fit in with a grown society; a rather unnoticed form of escapism. I also definitely see the Moomin Valley as a part of a northern, Finnish landscape. In the beginning, my writing included too many exotic palm trees, but now they have disappeared. I now try to follow a specific course of events, for example the seasons. Children are very particular about that. The moon must rise in the right place—but it can, naturally, be as large as you want. It's not out of the question that I see my Moominworld very realistically, yes, naturalistically, in regard to the environment and the scenery.

"I don't consciously try to educate. I have no general 'philosophy.' I try to describe what fascinates me, what I see and remember, and to let everything happen around a family setting, in which the family members get along, unusually well."[3]

Only the snout bore some resemblance to the troll's. But possibly, a thousand years ago. . .? ■
(From *Moominland Midwinter* by Tove Jansson. Illustrated by the author.)

Tove Jansson with Moomin home. The house, constructed of wood, has glass windows and electricity. The Moomin home kitchen is a replica of Jansson's island cottage kitchen.

I built it by the brook, where the grass was green and soft and exactly suitable for a Moomingarden. ■ (From *The Exploits of Moominpappa* by Tove Jansson. Illustrated by the author.)

1966. Won the Hans Christian Andersen Medal for writing her "Moomintroll" books. "Being awarded the medal bearing Hans Christian Andersen's name is a great responsibility. But, rather amazingly, I don't feel the usual burden that follows responsibility. I just feel very happy.

"Sometimes I wonder why people who have left their childhood quite far behind should suddenly start writing stories for children. And do we actually write for children at all? Don't we rather write for our own pleasure—or vexation—whether we write tragedies or nursery rhymes?

"... Pleasure needn't always be the impetus for a nursery rhyme. Perhaps one tries to rid oneself of nonessential ballast, that childishness that can find no room in a grown-up community. Or perhaps one tries to portray something that is fading away. One may write to save oneself, as an attempt to return to that taken-for-granted world where there is no responsibility, no rigidity.

"The world of children is a landscape in strong colors where safety and catastrophe run on paralled courses, nourishing each other. In that world there is room for everything, all is possible.... The illustrations are simply an attempt at explaining what I have perhaps failed to express in words, a kind of footnote. Also they are there out of consideration. What is too frightening can be intensified, a happy moment can be lengthened. What the self-absorbed writer has skipped because it jarred his style, the illustrator can portray in minute detail to amuse the reading child. And the illustrator can simply omit those pictures that would only impede the child's own fantasies. How could anybody portray the unmentionable face of the Snark? How could anybody draw transcendental beauty?

"Now and then the writer has botched the job and then the illustrator gently comes forward and tries to set things right. Sometimes lines and planes can say more than words. And in the blessed blacks of China ink the child can see its own enchanted danger, tempered to the desired degree of terror. The writer generally introduces his own fear into the story. No child can, of course, be fascinated by a story that doesn't frighten him occasionally. But even so I think a writer must be very careful when he re-shapes his dreads into fairy tales. It may be that he writes for himself. It may be that the book becomes better, more real that way.

"There is a plethora of very fine children's books that mainly portray the writer's disappointments, phobias, and depressions, tales of punishment, injustice, and loneliness. But *one* thing he anyway owes his readers, a happy ending, some kind of happy ending. Or a way left open for the child to spin the tale further." [Tove Jansson, "On Winning the Andersen Award," *Top of the News,* April, 1967.⁵]

Besides winning the medal itself, Jansson's books have been on the honor list of the Hans Christian Andersen Medal Books numerous times. She has won many awards for both her illustrations and her writings. Jansson's books have been translated into twenty-eight languages including German, Italian, Norwegian, Danish, Polish, Hebrew, Japanese, Spanish, Finnish, Icelandic, Dutch, French, Russian, Ukranian, and Yugoslavian.

FOR MORE INFORMATION SEE: B. Strömstedt, editor, *Min väg till barnboken* (title means "My Way to the Children's Book"), Bonniers, 1964; Eva von Zweigbergk, *Barnboken i Sverige, 1750-1950* (title means "The Children's Book in Sweden, 1750-1950"), Rabén & Sjögren, 1965; Tove Jansson, "Winners of the Hans Christian Andersen Award 1966," *Bookbird,* number 4, 1966; T. Jansson, "On Winning the Andersen Award," *Top of the News,* April, 1967; Lee Kingman

She took a scrap of paper, and then with a trembling paw drew a picture of a theatre for Moominmamma. ■ (From *Moominsummer Madness* by Tove Jansson. Illustrated by the author.)

An overpowering longing and melancholy had gripped Moominpappa, and the only thing he knew for certain was that he didn't want any tea on the verandah. ■ (From *Tales from Moominvalley* by Tove Jansson. Illustrated by the author.)

and others, compilers, *Illustrators of Children's Books: 1957-1966*, Horn Book, 1968; Brian Doyle, *The Who's Who of Children's Literature*, Schocken Books, 1968; Eleanor Cameron, *The Green and Burning Tree*, Atlantic-Little, Brown, 1969; Doris de Montreville and Donna Hill, editors, *Third Book of Junior Authors*, H. W. Wilson, 1972; Mary Orvig, "A Collage: Eight Women Who Write Books in Swedish for Children," *Horn Book*, February, 1973; Mary Orvig, *Children's Books in Sweden 1945-1970*, Austrian Children's Book Club (Vienna), 1973; *Children's Literature Review*, Volume 2, Gale, 1976; L. Kingman and others, compilers, *Illustrators of Children's Books: 1967-1976*, Horn Book, 1978; T. Jansson, "Meet Your Author," *Cricket*, December, 1980.

JEWELL, Nancy 1940-

BRIEF ENTRY: Born August 12, 1940, in Washington, D.C. Author of picture books for children. A 1962 graduate of Goucher College, Jewell has been employed as a reader for Harper & Row Publishers in New York City since 1966. Reviewers have praised her simple yet effective texts in eight books, all published by Harper. *Publishers Weekly* described her first book, *The Snuggle Bunny* (1972), as "an endearing story of a wandering snuggle bunny. . . . perfectly suited for sharing with your favorite small child." It was followed by *Try and Catch Me* (1972), *Calf, Goodnight* (1973), and *Cheer Up, Pig* (1975). In *The Family under the Moon* (1976), Jewell focuses on one family during a spring night, creating what *New York Times Book Review* called "a lovely little cameo. . . . a simple, pleasant, euphoric mood. . . . [in] recognition of small, uneventful, but luminous moments." *Bus Ride* (1978) is the equally simple story of a young girl traveling alone at night to visit her grandfather. The author again creates a special mood, as *School Library Journal* observed: "Descriptions of scenes at night and the cave-like darkness of the big bus itself are sensitively matched in the realistic illustrations [by Ronald Himler]. . . ." Jewell's latest works are *Time for Uncle Joe* (1981) and *ABC Cat* (1983). *Office:* Harper & Row Publishers, Inc., 10 East 53rd St., New York, N.Y. 10022.

KELLEY, True Adelaide 1946-

PERSONAL: Born February 25, 1946, in Cambridge, Mass.; daughter of Mark E. (an illustrator) and Adelaide (an artist; maiden name, True) Kelley; married Steven Lindblom (a writer and illustrator of children's books); children: Jada Winter. *Education:* University of New Hampshire, B.A., 1968; attended Rhode Island School of Design, 1968-70. *Home:* Old Denny Hill, Warner, N.H. 03278.

CAREER: Free-lance illustrator, 1971—; writer, 1978—. *Member:* Audubon Society, Warner Raconteur's Association. *Awards, honors: A Valentine for Fuzzboom* was chosen as a "Children's Choice" by the International Reading Association, 1982.

WRITINGS—For children; self-illustrated: (With husband, Steven Lindblom) *The Mouses' Terrible Christmas*, Lothrop, 1978; (with S. Lindblom) *The Mouses' Terrible Halloween*, Lothrop, 1980; *A Valentine for Fuzzboom*, Houghton, 1981; *Buggly Bear's Hiccup Cure*, Parents Magazine Press, 1982; (picture book; with S. Lindblom) *Let's Give Kitty a Bath*, Addison-Wesley, 1982.

Illustrator: Ann Cole, Carolyn Haas, Faith Bushnell, and Betty Weinberger, *I Saw a Purple Cow*, Little, Brown, 1972; Franklyn Branley, *Sun Dogs and Shooting Stars: A Skywatcher's Calendar*, Houghton, 1980; Michael Pellowski, *Clara Joins the Circus*, Parents Magazine Press, 1981; A. Cole, C. Haas, and B. Weinberger, *Purple Cow to the Rescue*, Little, Brown, 1982; F. Branley, *Water for the World*, Crowell, 1982; Gilda Berger and Melvin Berger, *The Whole World of Hands*, Houghton, 1982; Joanne Oppenheim, *James Will Never Die* (Junior Literary Guild selection), Dodd, 1982; *Sunshine and Snowflake*, Western, 1983; F. Branley, *Shivers and Goose Bumps: How We Keep Warm*, Crowell, 1984; Joyce S. Mitchell, *My Mommy Makes Money*, Little, Brown, 1984; Joanna Cole, *Cuts, Breaks, Bruises, and Burns: How Your Body Heals*, Harper, 1985. Also illustrator of numerous textbooks.

WORK IN PROGRESS: "I'm working on books for babies inspired by my daughter."

SIDELIGHTS: "I have illustrated children's books since 1971, but my interest in illustrating began as a child. My mother illustrated children's books and my father was art director for *Child Life* magazine. My first published self-illustrated story appeared there when I was four years old. After graduating from college with a degree in elementary education, I attended

(From *Let's Give Kitty a Bath!* by Steven Lindblom. Illustrated by True Kelley.)

Soon Dad was standing before the mirror in his costume, trying to look mean. ■ (From *The Mouses' Terrible Halloween* by True Kelley and Steven Lindblom. Illustrated by True Kelley.)

Rhode Island School of Design. I began working as an advertising illustrator and was greatly influenced by my father who is still an illustrator. My interest in children led me to doing textbook illustrations, and now I write and illustrate my own books as well.''

HOBBIES AND OTHER INTERESTS: Skiing, birdwatching, bicycling and travel.

KENT, Deborah Ann 1948-

BRIEF ENTRY: Born October 11, 1948, in Little Falls, N.J. Kent graduated from Oberlin College in 1969 and received a M.S.W. from Smith College and a M.F.A. from the Instituto Allende. Now a writer, she was formerly associated with the University Settlement in New York City and the Centro de Crecimiento in San Miguel de Allende, Mexico. Among her seven books for young people is *Belonging* (Dial, 1978), a novel about a blind teenager who decides to attend a regular high school instead of a special school for the blind. Based on the author's own life, the book details the experience and emphasizes the emotional struggle of a blind person trying to enter into the mainstream of society. *Horn Book* called it ''a provocative first novel . . . charged with an intense yet controlled emotion . . . ,'' while *Kliatt* commented that ''the authenticity of the experience described is evident.''

Among Kent's other books is the romance *Te Amo Means I Love You* (Bantam, 1983). In the book Lena moves with her family from Chicago's El Barrio to the wealthy suburb of Wyndham Glen. There she meets and becomes attracted to Eric. A romance develops between them, but eventually ends when Eric's parents put a stop to it. ''The ending is realistic . . . ,'' said *Kliatt*. ''Both El Barrio and Wyndham Glen are well realized and the characters are believable.'' Other books by Kent are: *Cindy* (Scholastic, Inc., 1982), *That Special Summer* (Silhouette Books, 1982), *Jody* (Wishing Star Books, 1983), *Heartwaves* (Ace Books, 1984), and *Honey and Spice* (New American Library, 1985). Kent is also a contributor to *Disabled U.S.A.* and *Journal of Visual Impairment and Blindness*. *Home:* 1 Morningside Circle, Little Falls, N.J. 07424.

FOR MORE INFORMATION: Contemporary Authors, Volume 103, Gale, 1982.

KESSEL, Joyce Karen 1937-

PERSONAL: Born January 27, 1937, in Kulm, N.D.; daughter of Theodore F. (a lawyer) and Esther (Stephens) Kessel. *Education:* University of Minnesota, B.S., 1960, M.A., 1966. *Politics:* Democrat. *Home:* 6405 Colony Way, Unit C, Edina, Minn. 55435. *Office:* Lerner Publications Co., 241 First Ave. N., Minneapolis, Minn. 55401.

CAREER: Ramey Air Force Base, Aguadilla, P.R., civilian speech therapist and special reading teacher, 1966-68; Caribbean Consolidated Schools, San Juan, P.R., special reading teacher, 1968-70, director of admissions and assistant to superintendent, 1971-78; Lerner Publications Co., Minneapolis,

(From *Halloween* by Joyce K. Kessel. Illustrated by Nancy L. Carlson.)

Minn., writer and sales representative, 1978—. *Awards, honors:* Children's Choice Award from Children's Book Council and International Reading Association, 1981, for *Halloween*.

WRITINGS—For children; all published by Carolrhoda: *Halloween* (illustrated by Nancy L. Carlson), 1980; *Valentine's Day* (illustrated by Karen Ritz), 1981; *St. Patrick's Day* (illustrated by Cathy Gilchrist), 1981; *Squanto and the First Thanksgiving* (illustrated by Lisa Donze), 1981; *Careers in Dental Care* (photographs by Milton J. Blumenfeld), Lerner, 1984.

Adult: (With Tom Hamilton) ''Archy and Mehitabel'' (two-act play; adaptation), first produced in Minneapolis, Minn., at Hennepin Performing Arts Center, June 20, 1981.

WORK IN PROGRESS: Two more holiday books; *Mardi Gras: History of Carnival in Louisiana*.

SIDELIGHTS: ''I began selling books for Lerner Publications after having written two books for them. These books were purchased but never published. As I had the opportunity to speak with many librarians and school personnel, I began to recognize areas that were requested with great frequency. One of these was factual information concerning popular holidays. This suggestion was taken by the editor of Carolrhoda Books,

He could pick violets through his jail window. He wrote messages on the leaves. The birds delivered the messages. ■ (From *Valentine's Day* by Joyce K. Kessel. Illustrated by Karen Ritz.)

JOYCE KAREN KESSEL

a subsidiary of Lerner Publications, and thus began the research and writing of this series of books.

"I am also interested in writing adult material, and have written many short stories, plays, and poems, none of which have been published, with the exception of 'Archy and Mehitabel.' I would also like to write a novel of the Caribbean and the people, if time ever permits."

HOBBIES AND OTHER INTERESTS: Classical music, painting, theatre, reading, biking, travel, judo, writing poetry, short stories, and plays.

KORMAN, Gordon　1963-

BRIEF ENTRY: Born October 23, 1963, in Montreal, Quebec, Canada. Korman is the author of nine books for junior high school readers, all published by Scholastic Book Services. *This Can't Be Happening at Macdonald Hall* (1978), the result of a seventh-grade writing assignment, is the first in a series featuring the antics of two young boys at boarding school. Bruno and Boots cavort their way through three additional adventures—*Go Jump in the Pool!* (1979), *Beware the Fish!* (1980), and *The War with Mr. Wizzle* (1982)—all written by Korman before he finished high school. As a reviewer for *Maclean's* observed: "He is undoubtedly successful, because . . . [he] writes not as a grown-up to a child, but as one young adult to another." In addition to the Bruno and Boots series, Korman created a rock-music-crazed adolescent in *Who Is Bugs Potter?* (1980) and *Bugs Potter: Live at Nickaninny* (1983). His other books are *I Want to Go Home* (1981), *Our Man Weston* (1982), and *No Coins Please* (1984).

Korman believes that "kids' concerns are important, and being a kid isn't just waiting out the time between birth and the age of majority," a feeling he strives to inject into all his works. In 1981 he received the Air Canada Award from the Canadian Authors Association for his first five books. While still in high school, Korman served as writer-in-residence in Edmonton and participated in the Children's Book Festival in British Columbia. Currently, he is a student at New York University where he is studying film and television. *Home and office:* 20 Dersingham Cres., Thornhill, Ontario, Canada L3T 4E7.

FOR MORE INFORMATION SEE: Profiles 2, Canadian Library Association, 1982; *Contemporary Authors,* Volume 112, Gale, 1985.

KRENSKY, Stephen (Alan) 1953-

BRIEF ENTRY: Born November 25, 1953, in Boston, Mass. A free-lance writer and critic, Krensky graduated from Hamilton College in 1975. He credits his abilities as a writer to "the part of me that was once twelve and nine and six . . . [and] not neatly boxed and tucked away in some dusty corner of my mind." The essence of his own childhood is kept alive in fifteen books for young readers, many of them centering on the fantasy world of trolls, witches, and dragons. Using familiar folkloric themes, Krensky injects his own brand of humor into books like *A Big Day for Scepters, The Perils of Putney, Castles in the Air and Other Tales,* and *A Troll in Passing.* In *The Dragon Circle, The Witching Hour,* and *A Ghostly Business,* he combines a contemporary setting with fantastical elements as the five modern-day Wynd children employ their inherited powers of witchcraft against evil dragons, scheming witches, and wraithlike spirits. Fantasy, but not humor, is abandoned in *The Wilder Plot* and *The Wilder Summer.* Both feature the antics of young Charlie Wilder who finds himself embroiled in a series of troublesome adventures at school and summer camp. Krensky has also written a biography of Alexander the Great entitled *Conqueror and Hero: The Search for Alexander* as well as several books for younger children, including *My First Dictionary* and *Perfect Pigs: An Introduction to Manners,* written with Marc Brown. *Home and office:* 12 Eaton Rd., Lexington, Mass. 02173.

FOR MORE INFORMATION SEE: Contemporary Authors, New Revision Series, Volume 13, Gale, 1984.

Youth is confident, manhood wary, and old age confident again.

—Martin Farquhar Tupper

LAWRENCE, Ann (Margaret) 1942-

PERSONAL: Born December 18, 1942, in Tring, Hertfordshire, England; married Alan Smith, 1971. *Education:* University of Southampton, B.A. (with honors), 1964. *Agent:* Laura Cecil, 10 Exeter Mansions, 106 Shaftesbury Ave., London W1V 7DH, England.

CAREER: Writer of children's fiction. Worked at British Trust for Ornithology, Tring, Hertfordshire, England, 1964-66; teacher at schools in Aylesbury, Buckinghamshire, England, 1966-71, and Tring, Hertfordshire, England, 1969-71. *Awards, honors:* Guardian Award runner-up, 1981, for *The Hawk of May.*

WRITINGS—All for children: *Tom Ass; or, The Second Gift* (illustrated by Ionicus), Macmillan (London), 1972, (American edition illustrated by Mila Lazarevich), Walck, 1973; *The Half-Brothers* (illustrated by Ionicus), Walck, 1973; *The Travels of Oggy* (illustrated by Hans Helweg), David & Charles, 1973; *The Conjuror's Box* (illustrated by Brian Alldridge), Kestrel Books, 1974; *Mr. Robertson's Hundred Pounds* (illustrated by Elizabeth Trimby), Kestrel Books, 1976; *Between the Forest and the Hills* (illustrated by Chris Molan), Kestrel Books, 1977; *Oggy at Home* (illustrated by H. Helweg), Gollancz, 1977; *The Good Little Devil* (illustrated by Ionicus), Macmillan, 1978; *Mr. Fox* (illustrated by A. Maitland), Macmillan, 1979; *Oggy and the Holiday* (illustrated by H. Helweg), David & Charles, 1979; *The Hawk of May* (illustrated

Oggy grunted indistinct replies over his shoulder now and then. ■ (From *Oggy at Home* by Ann Lawrence. Illustrated by Hans Helweg.)

ANN LAWRENCE

by S. Felts, Macmillan, 1980; *Beyond the Firelight* (illustrated by G. Lewton), Macmillan, 1984.

SIDELIGHTS: Lawrence's "Oggy" books are tales of the life of a hedgehog. Gentle creatures abound in these children's stories and include such characters as a staid toad, a pretentious fox, and Tiggy the kitty. Humans play a small part in the background of these tales. Young readers are able to learn much about country animals through the reading of these stories.

Some of Lawrence's other publications have a historical background. *Mr. Robertson's Hundred Pounds* relates the adventures of a sixteenth-century Gloucester merchant who follows a robber all the way to Spain. A Roman town from the Dark Ages is the setting of *Between the Forest and the Hills. The Half-Brothers* is set in the imaginary sixteenth-century kingdom of Evernia. This tale concerns the development of self-awareness and self-identity of a young duchess courted by four half-brothers. In *The Conjuror's Box,* young readers are carried across worlds and centuries.

MARKLE, Sandra L(ee)   1946-

BRIEF ENTRY: Born November, 10, 1946, in Fostoria, Ohio. Author of books for young readers. Markle graduated magna cum laude from Bowling Green University in 1968 and taught elementary schools in Ohio, North Carolina, and Georgia during the late 1960s and 1970s. A full-time writer since 1980, she is the author of *Kids' Computer Capers* (Lothrop, 1983) and *The Programmer's Guide to the Galaxy* (Lothrop, 1984). Both books are designed to introduce young readers to the history of the computer and BASIC programming through the use of games, jokes, trivia, and puzzles. Markle's other works include *Exploring Winter* (Atheneum, 1984), a self-illustrated activities book, and a series of science and computer-related books published by Learning Works. She also writes the monthly columns "Natural Wonder Notebook" in *Instructor* and "The Learning Center" in *Teaching and Computers.* In addition to her writing, Markle presents teacher workshops and science programs for children, acts as science consultant to *Instructor* and Corporation for Public Broadcasting, and is a contributing editor of *Teaching and Computers. Home and office:* 535 Spindlewick Dr., Dunwoody, Ga. 30338.

FOR MORE INFORMATION SEE: Contemporary Authors, Volume 111, Gale, 1984

MARTIN, Ann M(atthews)   1955-

BRIEF ENTRY: Born August 12, 1955, in Princeton, N.J. Editor and author. Since 1983 Martin has been senior editor in Books for Young Readers at Bantam Books in New York City. Prior to that time, she held various editorial positions with both Scholastic Book Services and Pocket Books. Her first book, *Bummer Summer* (Holiday House, 1983), was a young adult romance novel that received the New Jersey Institute of Technology Authors Award in 1983. It was followed by another romance for young adults entitled *Just You and Me* (Scholastic Book Services, 1983). In her third young adult novel, *Inside Out* (Holiday House, 1984), Martin explores the relationship between eleven-year-old Jonno and his four-year-old autistic brother. "The subject of a child's reaction to his autistic sibling is a new one," observed *School Library Journal,* "and Martin handles it well." *Booklist* agreed, noting her "lively humor, expertly developed dialogue, and apt characterizations." She is also the author of *My Puppy Scrapbook: Featuring Fenwick* (Scholastic Book Services, 1983), a children's book written with Betsy Ryan. Currently, Martin is working on both nonfiction and a novel. Her latest published work is *Stagefright* (Holiday House, 1984). *Office:* Bantam Books, Inc., 666 Fifth Ave., New York, N.Y. 10103.

FOR MORE INFORMATION SEE: Contemporary Authors, Volume 111, Gale, 1984.

MATHEWS, Janet   1914-

PERSONAL: Born January 18, 1914, in Wollongong, New South Wales, Australia; daughter of James Wilson (a solicitor) and Mary Irene (a pianist; maiden name, McLelland) Russell; married Frank Mathews (an engineer), December 3, 1936 (died, 1982); children: Susan (Mrs. Angus Kennedy), Jane (Mrs. J. H. Wotten), Robert. *Education:* Attended Sydney Conservatorium of Music, Australia, 1930-1934. *Religion:* Presbyterian. *Home:* Unit 29, Kentwood, 37 Barry St., Neutral Bay, New South Wales, Australia 2089. *Agent:* Curtis Brown Party Ltd., P.O. Box 19, Paddington, New South Wales, Australia 2021.

CAREER: Concert pianist, Paris, France, 1935, and New South Wales, 1942-53; teacher of piano, 1953-66, retired, 1967; Australian Institute of Aboriginal Studies, Canberra, field researcher, 1963-77; author, 1972—. Occasional speaker on Aboriginal studies. *Member:* Australian Society of Authors, National Book Council of Australia, Children's Book Council of Australia.

WRITINGS: The Two Worlds of Jimmie Barker: The Life of an Australian Aboriginal 1900-1972, Humanities, 1977; *Wurley and Wommera: Aboriginal Life and Craft* (juvenile; illus-

JANET MATHEWS

trated by Walter Stackpool), Collins (Sydney), 1977, (New York), 1979; *Totem and Taboo: Aboriginal Life and Craft* (juvenile; illustrated by W. Stackpool), Collins (Sydney), 1979; *Fossils and Families: Aboriginal Life and Craft* (juvenile; illustrated by W. Stackpool), Collins (Sydney), 1981.

Contributor of "Lorna Dixon: Biography," in *Fighters and Singers,* edited by Isobel White, Diane Barwick, and Betty Meehan, Allen & Unwin (Sydney), 1985. Contributor of articles to *Australian Institute of Aboriginal Studies Newsletter.*

WORK IN PROGRESS: The Aboriginal Spirit of Life: This Does Not Die, about rare Aboriginal mythical beliefs and the relevant factual explanations of tribal life that are related to the dreamtime.

SIDELIGHTS: "I was about to do my Diploma of Music in 1935 when I was offered piano work in Paris, France, where I lived with a French family for one year. I decided exams could wait until my return, although I had passed all but the final one. I married soon after coming back to Australia and decided there was not much point in doing that exam as I had rather progressed past it.

"In about 1960, I received my Braille Writers Certificate as I had always had some sympathy for the blind and felt that I might become involved in the new system of writing music in Braille. However, as I was so busy teaching music, I decided there was almost too much music in my life so confined myself to putting numerous books into Braille. When I started work as an author, there was no time for Braille and I reluctantly retired.

"In 1963, due to my musical training, I was asked to do research in the field with Aborigines. New South Wales was my area, but the music was almost too easy and I became intensely interested in the many languages and customs. I was asked to clarify tribal boundaries and many other aspects of tribal life.

"This field research involved moving through very remote areas with tape recorders, finding Aborigines who still had linguistic or other important knowledge. Within about three months in the field, I was classified as a linguist and, as time progressed, as fairly knowledgeable in most aspects of their past. When asked to 'tidy up' a tremendous number of tapes recorded with one Aborigine in 1972, I did so. This request came from the Australian Institute of Aboriginal Studies in Canberra, for whom I had been doing the research. The 'tidying up' took two years and was then sent to the Institute who, to my surprise, said: 'This is a book—we are going to publish it.' That was the beginning of my career as an author. Field research with the Aborigines continued until 1977, and I still become involved in rather unexpected ways.

"Added to my own Aboriginal research for the myths included in my current book, *The Aboriginal Spirit of Life: This Does Not Die,* are extracts from publications written by my late husband's grandfather and an abbreviated biography of his life. Robert Hamilton Mathews did early and major research when a surveyor about one hundred years ago. His information has possibly been one of the main foundations of Aboriginal knowledge in Australia. Masses of his studies have been published in the form of monographs and are in my possession, as the only interested member of the family. This book of myths contains many noted by him that I had rewritten as his style was somewhat Victorian. When I was in the field, I kept trying to add to his research on the many aspects. When writing, I delve into his material frequently as this collection is very valuable. Eventually, it will go to the National Library in Canberra."

MATTHIAS, Catherine   1945-

BRIEF ENTRY: Born February 2, 1945, in Philadelphia, Pa. Matthias attended Temple University in the early 1960s before becoming a nursery school teacher in 1968. She has also worked as a contract supervisor and waitress and is currently employed in advertising sales. The author of five children's books published by Childrens Press, Matthias has concentrated her writing efforts on controlled vocabulary books for beginning readers. "I like to make these books fun to read," she remarked, "to hold the child's attention and help the learning process flow." *I Love Cats* (1983) is a picture book described by *Booklist* as a "bantering romp" with a red-headed boy in "rhyme [that] runs jovially along till the final spread...." In *Too Many Balloons* (1982) a small girl goes about the zoo buying balloons until she has one too many and begins to float away. *School Library Journal* observed: "The repetitive text ... becomes a game, wonderfully aided and abetted by the cheerfully colored animal cast." Matthias emphasizes the meanings of various prepositions in both *Out the Door* (1982) and *Over Under* (1984). She is also the author of *I Can Be a Police Officer* (1984). Her anticipated works include more easy-reading books and short novels for children. *Home:* 8811 18th Ave., S.W., Seattle, Wash. 98106.

FOR MORE INFORMATION SEE: Contemporary Authors, Volume 110, Gale, 1984.

McCANN, Gerald 1916-

PERSONAL: Born in 1916, in Brooklyn, N.Y.; married; children: five. *Education:* Attended Pratt Institute.

CAREER: Illustrator of books for children. Began his career as an illustrator of book covers and as a magazine illustrator. *Military service:* Served in North Africa during World War II.

ILLUSTRATOR—All for children: Sterner St. Paul Meek, *Bellfarm Star: The Story of a Pacer,* Dodd, 1955; Mary Patchett, *Tam the Untamed,* Bobbs-Merrill, 1955; Eleanor Reindollar Wilcox, *The Cornhusk Doll,* Dodd, 1956; Kitty Barne, *Rosina Copper: The Mystery Mare,* Dutton, 1956; Elizabeth Montgomery, *Half-Pint Fisherman,* Dodd, 1956; Enid L. Meadowcroft, *We Were There at the Opening of the Erie Canal,* Grosset, 1958; Charles Spain Verral, *Play Ball!,* Simon & Schuster, 1958; Iris Vinton, *The Story of Edith Cavell,* Grosset, 1959; Charles P. Graves, *Benjamin Franklin: Man of Ideas,* Garrard, 1960; Polly Anne Colver Graff, *Florence Nightingale: War Nurse,* Garrard, 1961; David R. Burleigh, *Arrow-Messenger,* Follett, 1962; Edward W. Dolch and Marguerite P. Dolch, *Once There Was a Bear,* Garrard, 1962; Mary Jo Borreson, *Let's Go to Plymouth with the Pilgrims,* Putnam, 1963; Nicholas Georgiady and Louis Romano, *Our National Anthem,* Follett, 1963; Betty Antoncich, *The Cilff House Mystery,*

Paul Cuffe spent all of his life on or near the sea. ■
(From *Famous Negro Heroes of America* by Langston Hughes. Illustrated by Gerald McCann.)

McKay, 1964; Samuel Langhorne Clemens, *Tom Sawyer Abroad,* Grosset, 1965; S. L. Clemens, *Tom Sawyer, Detective,* Grosset, 1965; Marian T. Place, *Marcus and Narcissa Whitman: Oregon Pioneers,* Garrard, 1967; Neil Grant, *English Explorers of North America,* Messner, 1970.

SIDELIGHTS: After high school McCann attended Pratt Engineering School at night. "... After a year I discovered myself drawing more than working on drafting—so I went across the street to Pratt Art School. I was very fortunate to have as an instructor a Mr. Baker. Some of the illustrators we had whom I particularly remember were Nick Riley, Irving Nurick and Harold Scott." [Bertha M. Miller and others, compilers, *Illustrators of Children's Books: 1946-1956,* Horn Book, 1958.]

McCann began his career in illustration working for magazines including *Outdoor Life* and doing covers for Bantam Books. This eventually led to his illustrating both adult and children's books for various publishers.

McCANNON, Dindga Fatima 1947-

PERSONAL: Born in 1947, in Harlem, N.Y.; daughter of Ralph and Lottie (Porter) Miller; married Percival E. McCannon in 1967; children: Afrodesia, Harmarkhis. *Education:* Studied at the Bob Blackburn Workshop, the Nyumba Ya Sanaa Galleries, and under artists Charles Alston, Richard Mayhew, Al Hollingsworth and Abdullah Aziz. *Home and office:* 800 Riverside Dr., New York, N.Y. 10032.

CAREER: Painter, printmaker, author, illustrator, fashion designer, quiltmaker, teacher, and muralist. Work has been shown in many exhibitions, including group shows: Harlem Outdoor Art Show, 1964-71; Greenwich Village Outdoor Art Show, 1965-68; Nyumba Ya Sanaa Galleries, New York City, 1969-72; Bedford-Stuyvesant Restorations Gallery, Brooklyn, New York, 1970-79: Mount Morris Park; Countee Cullen Library; Acts of Art Gallery, New York City, 1971-72; Johnson Publishing Co., Chicago, Ill., 1972; Galeria Mehu, Port-au-Prince, Haiti, 1972-75, 1979; Henry Street Settlement Gallery, 1975; Black Enterprise Gallery, 1975; First National African American Crafts Jubilee, Memphis, Tenn., 1979; The Gallery, New York City, 1979; Downtown Gallery, Mt. Vernon, N.Y., 1980; Grinnell Gallery, N.Y., 1980; Salmagundi Club Gallery, N.Y., 1980; Baruch College Gallery, N.Y., 1981; Bishop College Gallery, Dallas, Tex., 1981; Benin Gallery, N.Y., 1981; New Muse Gallery, N.Y., 1982, 1983, 1984; Bergen Community Museum, N.J., 1983; Cork Gallery, Lincoln Center, New York City, 1983-84; Jamaica Arts Center, N.Y., 1984; Local 1199 Gallery, N.Y., 1984; AC-BAW Gallery, N.Y., 1984.

One-woman shows: Truth Coffee Shop, N.Y., 1965; Acts of Art Gallery, N.Y., 1972; Melca Gallery, Brooklyn, N.Y., 1974; Gallery One, New York City, 1975; Irene Gandy Gallery, N.Y., 1976; Studio Gallery, N.Y., 1978, 1979; Benin Gallery, N.Y., 1978; Pyramid Gallery, N.Y., 1979, 1981; Djuna Bookstore Gallery, 1980; Harlem State Office Building, N.Y., 1982; Black Renaissance Gallery, Washington, D.C., 1982; Mehu Gallery, 1983.

Commissions include: a poster, "Dilemma of a Ghost," Harlem School of the Arts Community Theatre, N.Y., 1972; Murial environment, "Spirits Come Arising," Haitien Memoirs, Center for Multihandicapped Children, New York City, 1972;

(Jacket painting by Gary Watson from *Wilhemina Jones, Future Star* by Dindga McCannon.)

posters for New York Shakespeare Festivals, "Les Femmes Noires," 1974, and "La Gente," 1975; designed and executed mural with others, Houston St. and 2nd Ave., New York City, 1976; designed mural at 24 Furman Ave., Brooklyn, N.Y., 1982; designed and printed poster for Kings Court Block Association, N.Y., 1983.

Work is represented in permanent collections, including: Johnson Publishing Co. (Chicago, Ill.), August Heckler Collection, Leroy Anderson Collection, Studio Museum in Harlem Permanent Collection, Acts of Art Gallery Collection, Herve Mehu Gallery Collection, Cinque Gallery Collection. *Member:* Black Women Artists (co-founder and board member). *Awards, honors:* Westchester Outdoor Art Show, Green Gallery, second prize for graphics, 1966; Harambee Arts and Cultural Heritage Festival, Tallahasee, Fla., second prize for quilts, 1982.

WRITINGS: Peaches (young adult; self-illustrated), Lothrop, 1974; *Wilhemina Jones, Future Star: A Novel* (young adult; self-illustrated), Delacorte, 1980.

Illustrator; all fiction for children, except as indicated; all published by Lothrop: Edgar White, *Sati, the Rastifarian,* 1973; E. White, *Omar at Christmas,* 1973; E. White, *Children of Night,* 1974; Kofi Asare Opoku, compiler, *Speak to the Winds: Proverbs from Africa,* 1975.

WORK IN PROGRESS: Two young adult novels; wall quilts.

SIDELIGHTS: "I have been an active artist since age seventeen. The only degree I have is the degree of hard work, long hours and faith to continue. I have learned everything I know from doing, experimenting, messing up over and over until I achieve success, and by working with other artists.

"I enjoy a variety of things and in order to function solely as an artist it is necessary to be able to work in many different media. I love my work and the idea of working a nine to five routine would ruin me.

"I've traveled to Bermuda, Trinidad, Guyana, South Africa, Haiti, Senegal and Gambia in addition to many of the fifty states. I am also a co-founder and board member of Where We At, Black Women Artists, a group of thirty-two artists committed to helping women artists exhibit and find work, and to bringing art and art workshops to the entire community. I've taught children of all ages, the elderly, the mentally/physically handicapped and people incarcerated in New York prisons."

FOR MORE INFORMATION SEE: Chelsea Clinton News, April 15, 1971; *New York Post,* August 25, 1971; *Feminist Art Journal,* April, 1972; *Sunday Daily News,* June 18, 1972; *Ms. Magazine,* July, 1973; *School Library Journal,* October, 1973, November, 1973, April, 1974; *Black Creation: A Quarterly Review of Black Arts and Letters,* fall, 1973; *New York Times Book Review,* September 7, 1974; *New York Age,* September 14, 1974; *New York Times,* July 17, 1975; *New York Daily News,* October 11, 1975; *Players Magazine,* September, 1976; *The Black American,* January, 1977; *Westchester County Press,* November 22, 1979; *Garnett Weekend Magazine,* April 11, 1980; *News World,* July 28, 1980; *Art News,* October, 1980; *Tallahassee Democrat,* February, 1983.

McCAY, Winsor   1869-1934 (Silas)

PERSONAL: Born September 26, 1869, in Spring Lake, Mich.; died July 26, 1934 of a cerebral hemorrhage; son of a lumberjack; married Maude Dufour, 1891; children: Marian, Robert Winsor. *Education:* Studied art in Ypsilanti, Mich., and Chicago, Ill.

CAREER: Cartoonist and animator. At seventeen, began career by making woodcuts for traveling vaudeville shows, painting street signs, and designing posters and murals; in 1897, started newspaper career with *Cincinnati-Times Star;* in 1903, produced first comic strip "Tales of the Jungle Imps" for *Cincinnati Enquirer;* that same year, created comic strips for *Evening Telegram* under pseudonym "Silas," including "Dreams of a Rarebit Fiend" (later titled "Twas Only a Dream"); in 1904, under own name, created comic strips for *New York Herald,* including "Little Sammy Sneeze" and, in 1905, his most noted comic strip "Little Nemo in Slumberland"; in 1909, began producing animated cartoons, including "Gertie, the Dinosaur"; in 1911, worked for Hearst's *Evening Journal* producing "Little Nemo" under the new title "In the Land of Wonderful Dreams"; in 1917, produced the first feature-length cartoon "The Sinking of the Lusitania."

WRITINGS—Comic strip collections; all self-illustrated: Dreams of the Rarebit Fiend, F. A. Stokes, 1905, reprinted, Dover, 1973; *Little Sammy Sneeze,* F. A. Stokes, 1905; *Little Nemo*

Autographed photo of Winsor McCay.

(From "Gertie the Dinosaur," one of the first animated cartoons, by Winsor McCay.)

in Slumberland, McCay Features Syndicate, 1945; *Little Nemo* (originally published in Italy), Nostalgia Press, 1972, second edition, 1974, new edition, with review by Maurice Sendak, 1976; *Little Nemo in the Palace of Ice, and Further Adventures,* Dover, 1976; *Winsor McCay's Dream Days: An Original Compilation, 1904-1914,* Hyperion Press, 1977.

Films; animated cartoons; selected works: "Little Nemo" (based on the comic strip "Little Nemo in Slumberland"), first released in 1909, released as "Winsor McCay" (with filmed prologue of artist explaining production), Vitagraph, 1911; "How a Mosquito Operates" (also known as "The Story of a Mosquito"), Vitagraph, 1912, released as "Winsor McCay and His Jersey Skeeters" (with filmed prologue of artist and daughter), Universal, 1916; "Gertie, the Dinosaur," Vitagraph, 1914; "The Sinking of the Lusitania" (feature-length historical cartoon), Jewel Productions, 1918; "The Adventures of a Rarebit Eater" (series; based on the comic strip "Dreams of a Rarebit Fiend"), released in 1912 (contains "The Pet," "Bug Vaudeville," and "The Flying House").

ADAPTATIONS—Plays: "Little Nemo" (musical), opened in New York at the New Amsterdam Theatre, October 20, 1908.

Storybooks: Edna Sara Levine, *Little Nemo in Slumberland* (adapted from original "Little Nemo" cartoons), Rand McNally, 1941.

SIDELIGHTS: Born **September 26, 1869** in Spring Lake, Michigan, McCay received his only instruction in art as a student at Ypsilanti Normal School. He studied perspective under Professor John Goodison, a teacher of solid geometry. With the conclusion of his formal training, he took to the open road, landing in Chicago where he worked for a poster company. He may have worked as a sign painter with a traveling carnival which brought him to Cincinnati around 1889 and settled in as a poster and scenic artist for a resident freak show. This contact provided McCay with a taste for the fantastic, the exotic, clowns, distorted mirrors, and carnival and circus motifs. During his fifteen-year stay in Cincinnati, McCay contributed illustration to the *Cincinnati Commercial Tribune* and the *Cincinnati Enquirer.*

"... I never decided to be an artist. Simply, I couldn't stop myself from drawing. I drew for my own pleasure. I never wanted to know whether or not someone liked my drawings. I have never kept one of my drawings. I drew on walls, the

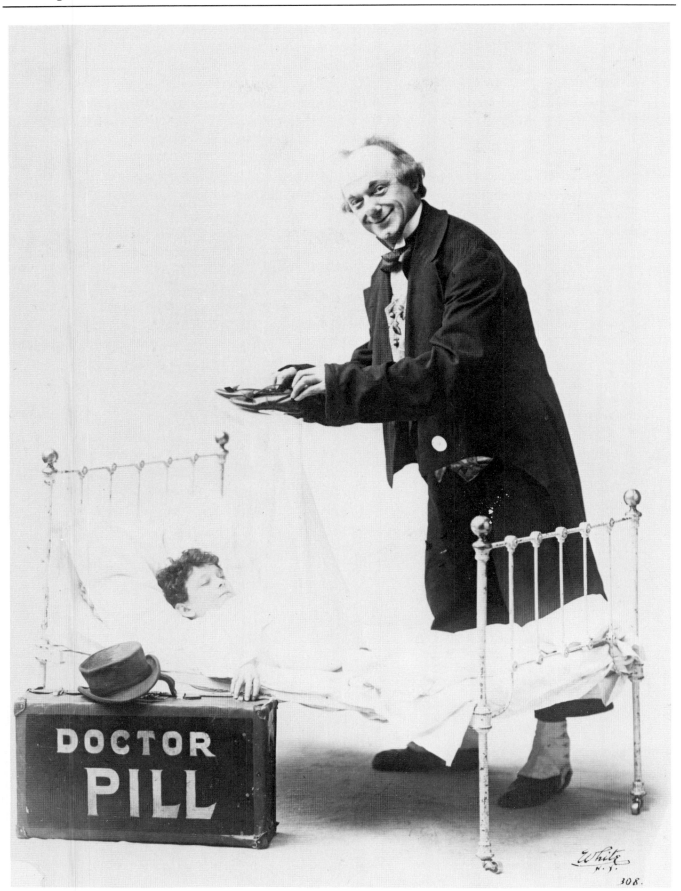

(From the Broadway musical "Little Nemo," starring Joseph Cawthorn and Master Gabriel. Based on the comic strip by Winsor McCay. The show opened at the New Amsterdam Theatre, October 20, 1908.)

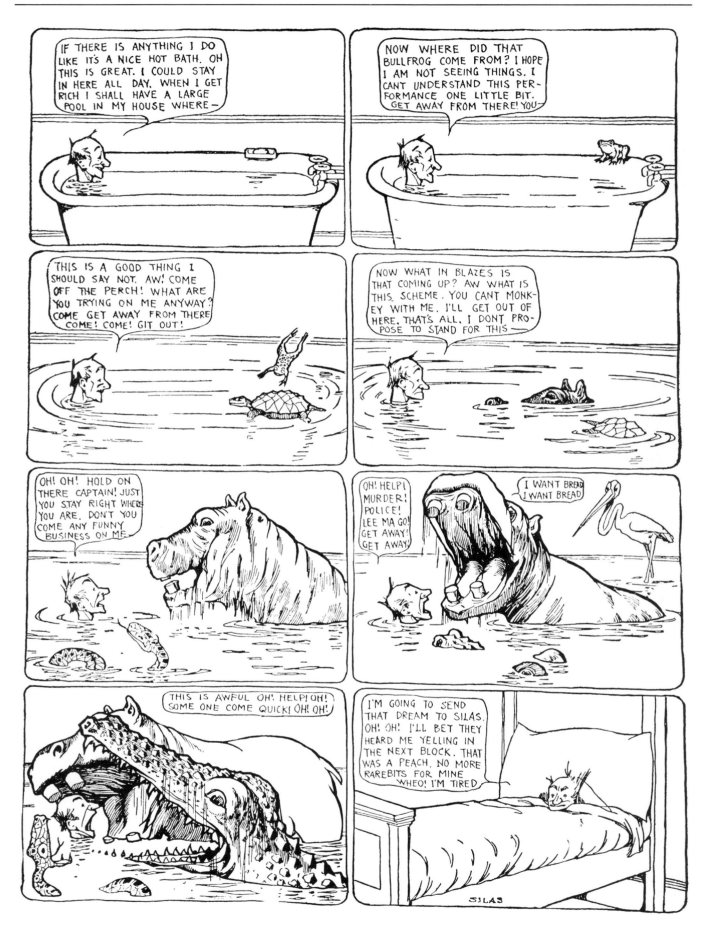

(From *Dreams of The Rarebit Fiend* by Winsor McCay. Illustrated by the author.)

Winsor McCay draws "Gertie" for his cartoonist friends including George McManus, at left.

school blackboard, odd bits of paper, the walls of barns . . . but, surprisingly as it may seem, I never thought about the money I would receive for my drawings. I simply drew them.'' [Maurice Sendak, ''Little Nemo,'' *New York Times Book Review,* November 25, 1973.[1]]

1891. Married debutante, Maude Dufour. Both his son and daughter were his models for ''Little Nemo'' and the ''Princess of Slumberland,'' respectively.

McCay's contributions to the Cincinnati papers attracted the attention of James Gordon Bennett, publisher of the *New York Herald* and the *New York Evening Telegram.* McCay traveled to New York in 1903 to work for Bennett's papers, covering crimes, trials, social events, and creating his early comic strips, ''Tales of the Jungle Imps,'' ''Hungry Henrietta,'' ''Little Sammy Sneeze,'' ''Pilgrim's Progress,'' ''Dream of the Rarebit Fiend,'' as well as the strip which established his work ''Little Nemo in Slumberland'' (*New York Herald,* October 15, 1905).

August 31, 1906. The *New York Telegraph* outlined McCay's professional schedule. ''In addition to playing twice a day at Hammerstein's for the past four weeks, Mr. McCay in that period drew four full-pages of *Little Nemo,* four one-half pages of *Rarebit Dreams,* four three column *Rarebit Dreams,* four three column *Dull Cares,* drew a twenty four sheet design, an eight sheet design, and a three sheet design for the Klaw and Erlanger production of *Little Nemo;* also designed a scene for that big spectacle, and in his odd moments while going to and

from meals dashed off a souvenir cover and a programme cover for a theatre.'' [John Canemaker, ''Winsor McCay'' in *The American Animated Cartoon,* edited by Gerald Peary and Danny Peary, Dutton, 1980.[2]]

John A. Fitzsimmons, a teenaged neighbor of the McCay family recalled how McCay made his first film as the result of a friendly bet with cartoonist-cronies George McManus, Thomas Dorgan and Tom Powers: ''. . . [T]he three or four of them were down in a saloon near the old *American* building at William and Duane Streets right under the Brooklyn Bridge. . . . I think McManus kidded McCay because he was such a fast worker. . . . Jokingly, McManus suggested that McCay make several thousand drawings, photograph them onto film and show the result in theatres. . . . McCay claimed he would produce enough line drawings to sustain a four or five minute animated cartoon showing the *Little Nemo* characters and would use the film as a special feature of his already popular vaudeville act.''[2]

As a pioneer in the field, McCay had no precedent to follow. Silent films flashed sixteen frames per second onto the screen. According to Fitzsimmons, McCay ''timed everything with split-second watches. That's how he got nice smooth action. For every second that was on the screen McCay would draw sixteen pictures. . . . He had nothing to follow, he had to work out everything for himself.

''After each drawing was completed, and a serial number assigned to it, marks [crosses] for keeping it in register with the

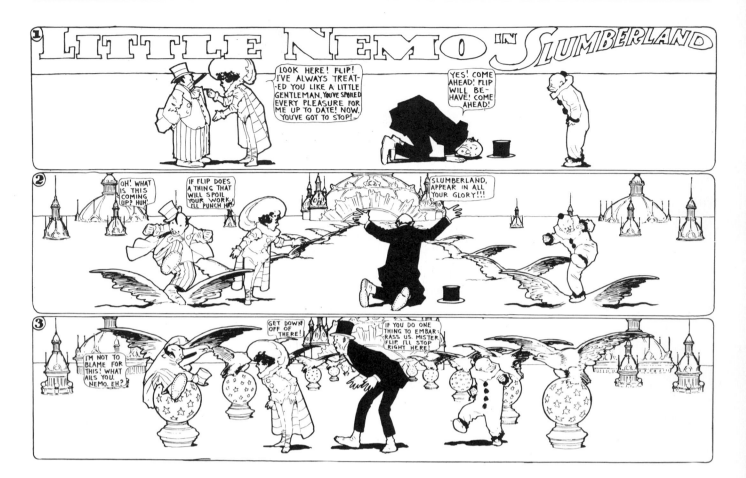

other drawings were placed on the upper right and left corners."[2]

1911. "Little Nemo", released as "Winsor McCay," appeared on the screen as an animated cartoon. In a letter to the cartoonist, Clare Briggs, McCay wrote: "I have never been as happy as when I was drawing 'Little Nemo.'" [Claude Moliterni, "Little Nemo," *Graphis*, 1972/73.[3]]

The *New York Telegraph* in its review described a live prologue but not the animation itself. "Something new in the line of novelty entertainment was provided by the sketch artist, Winsor McCay. 'Moving pictures that move' is the way the offering is described on the programme and the idea is being presented for the first time on any stage. On a screen the Vitagraph shows pictures of Mr. McCay in company with several friends at a club. He is telling them of his new idea. The idea is made a subject of ridicule. They consider such an invention impossible. The artist, undismayed by this discouragement, signs a contract, agreeing to turn out 4,000 pictures in one month's time for a moving picture concern.

"A slide is then thrown on the screen showing the artist at work in his studio. He makes good his threat and at the end of the month has fulfilled his contract. Congratulations from his friends now pour in on him and he produces his new discovery at the club, where the friends had scoffed at the idea. The fun derived from this invention in the moving picture field was thoroughly enjoyed."[2] McCay was widely regarded as the father of the animated cartoon.

McCay's audiences did not believe that the film was a series of drawings, but rather photographs of real children. Of his second film "The Story of a Mosquito," McCay wrote: "I drew a great ridiculous mosquito, pursuing a sleeping man, peeking through a key hole and pouncing on him over the transom. My audiences were pleased, but declared the mosquito was operated by wires to get the effect before the cameras."[2]

March, 1914. The first performance of "Gertie the Dinosaur" at the Palace Theatre in Chicago. "When the great Dinosaur first came into the picture the audience said it was a papier-mache animal with men inside of it and with a scenic background. As the production progressed they noticed that the leaves on the trees were blowing in the breeze, and that there were rippling waves on the surface of the water, and when the elephant was thrown into the lake the water was seen to splash. . . . I made her eat boulders and pull up trees by the roots and throw an elephant into the sea. Gertie was made to lie down and roll over and obey commands which I emphasized by a cracking whip. . . . This convinced them that they were seeing something new—that the presentation was actually from a set of drawings."[2]

McCay presented "Gertie" as a vaudeville act, in which he would appear on-stage to deliver a lecture and introduce his trained dinosaur, which would suddenly appear on-screen and respond to his commands and questions.

McCay continued to improve his animation techniques with "Gertie." "When she was lying on her side I wanted her to

(From *Little Nemo in Slumberland* by Winsor McCay. Illustrated by the author.)

breathe and I tried my watch, and also stop watch, to judge how long it took her to exhale. I could come to no exact time until one day I happened to be working where a large clock with a big second dial accurately marked the intervals of time. I stood in front of this clock and inhaled and exhaled and found that, imitating the great Dinosaur, I inhaled in four seconds and exhaled in two. The result was that when the picture was run, instead of the Dinosaur panting as you would expect, she was breathing very easily. The breathing was shown by the sides of the monster expanding and contracting like a bellows."[2]

1918. McCay's most ambitious effort, "The Sinking of the Lusitania," released by Universal-Jewel Productions. The film took twenty-two months to complete and contained approximately 25,000 drawings. According to Fitzsimmons, "McCay was especially incensed at such wanton brutality [of the sinking of the Lusitania that] he proposed to make an animated cartoon graphically depicting the horrible tragedy."[2]

McCay stopped animating films around 1921 or 1922. It was his hope to elevate animation into an art form and he was deeply disappointed when he did not see this happening. At a gathering of animators McCay exclaimed: "Animation should be an art, that is how I had conceived it . . . but as I see what you fellows have done with it is making it into a trade . . . not art, but a trade . . . *bad luck*."[2]

He advised young aspiring artists that, "It would be wise to set up a certain popular artist whom [you like] best and adopt

his 'handling' or style. You don't have to copy his drawings, but when you are puzzled with any part of your work, see how it was handled by your favorite and fix it up in a similar manner." [Michael Patrick Hearn, "The Animated Art of Winsor McCay," *American Artist,* May, 1975.[4]] He warned the young artist, however, to "never appraise your work too highly. . . . You may live to be 100 years of age, study art every day during that hundred, but you will always be a student. There is never a true artist who is not willing to learn something new."[4]

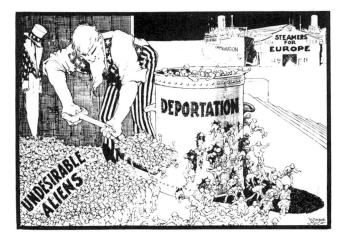

Editorial cartoon by Winsor McCay. ■ (From *The World Encyclopedia of Cartoons,* Volume I, edited by Maurice Horn.)

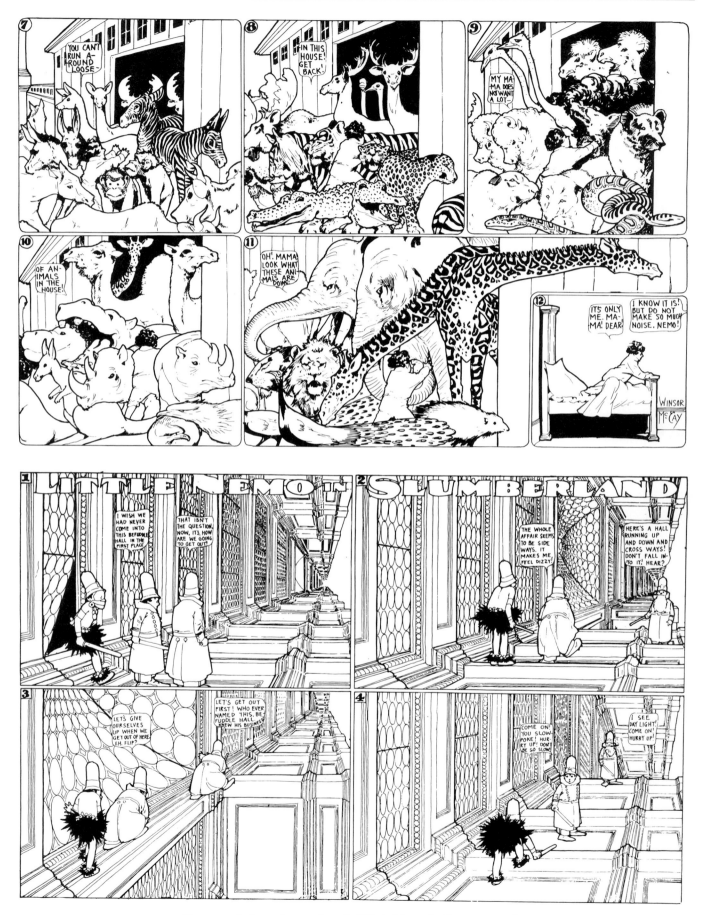

Four panels from the comic strip "Little Nemo in Slumberland."

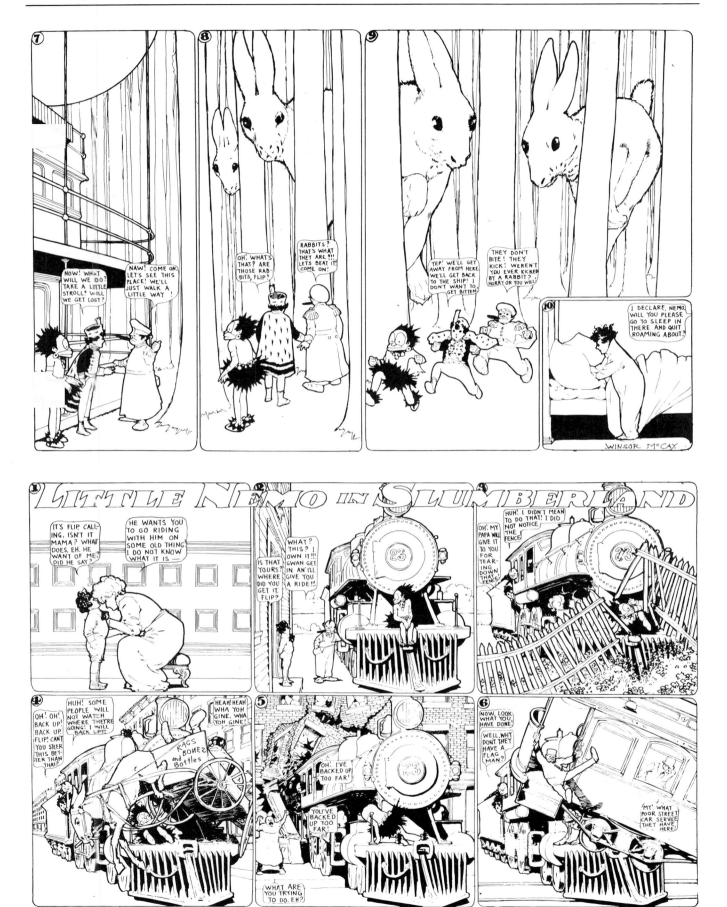

The strip first appeared in the *New York Herald*, 1905 to 1911.

July 26, 1934. Died of a massive cerebral hemorrhage at his home in Sheepshead Bay.

FOR MORE INFORMATION SEE: New York Herald, October 15, 1905; Judith O'Sullivan, editor, *The Art of the Comic Strip,* University of Maryland, Department of Art, 1971; Claude Moliterni, "Little Nemo," *Graphis,* 1972/73; *New York Times Book Review,* November 25, 1973; *Film Comment,* January, 1975; Michael Patrick Hearn, "The Animated Art of Winsor McCay," *American Artist,* May, 1975; Maurice Horn, editor, *The World Encyclopedia of Comics,* Chelsea House, 1976; Horn, editor, *The World Encyclopedia of Cartoons,* Gale, 1980; John Canemaker, *The American Animated Cartoon,* edited by Gerald Peary and Danny Peary, Dutton, 1980.

McCORD, Anne 1942-

PERSONAL—Office: University of Reading, School of Education, London Rd., Reading RG1 5AQ, England.

CAREER: Teacher, 1964-71; British Museum of Natural History, London, England, higher scientific officer, 1971-78; University of Reading, Reading, England, assistant registrar, 1978—; writer of children's nonfiction.

WRITINGS—All for children: All about Early Man, W. H. Allen, 1974; *Early Man,* EDC Publishing, 1977 (published in England as *The Children's Picture Prehistory of Early Man* [illustrated by Bob Hersey], Usborne, 1977); *Prehistoric Mammals,* EDC Publishing, 1977 (published in England as *The Children's Picture Prehistory of Prehistoric Mammals* [illustrated by B. Hersey], Usborne, 1977); *Dinosaurs,* EDC Publishing, 1977; *Children's Encyclopedia of Prehistoric Life* (illustrated by B. Hersey), Usborne, 1977.

McGRATH, Thomas 1916-

PERSONAL: Born November 20, 1916, near Sheldon, N.D.; son of James Lang and Catherine (Shea) McGrath; married Eugenia Johnson, February 13, 1960; children: Thomas Samuel Koan. *Education:* University of North Dakota, B.A., 1939; Louisiana State University, M.A., 1940; New College, Oxford, additional study, 1947-48. *Politics:* "Unaffiliated far left." *Residence:* Moorhead, Minn.

CAREER: Poet. Colby College, Waterville, Me., instructor in English, 1940-41; Los Angeles State College of Applied Arts and Sciences (now California State University, Los Angeles), assistant professor of English, 1950-54; C. W. Post College, Long Island, N.Y., assistant professor of English, 1960-61; North Dakota State University, Fargo, N.D., associate professor of English, 1962-67; Moorhead State University, Moorhead, Minn., associate professor of English, 1969—. *Military service:* U.S. Army Air Forces, 1942-45. *Member:* Phi Beta Kappa. *Awards, honors:* Rhodes Scholar, Oxford University, 1947-48; Alan Swallow Poetry Book Award, 1954, for *Figures from a Double World;* Amy Lowell travelling poetry scholarship, 1966-67; Guggenheim fellowship, 1967-68; Minnesota State Arts Council grant, 1973; National Foundation for the Arts grant, 1974; Bush Foundation fellowship, 1976-

THOMAS McGRATH

77, 1982; Minnesota Arts Board grant, 1979; National Endowment for the Arts grant, 1974, 1980.

WRITINGS—Poetry, except as indicated: First Manifesto, Swallow & Critchlow, 1940; (contributor) *The Dialectics of Love in Three Young Poets: Thomas McGrath, William Peterson, James Franklin Lewis,* edited by Alan Swallow, Press of James A. Decker, 1942; *To Walk a Crooked Mile,* Alan Swallow, 1947; *Longshot O'Leary's Garland of Practical Poesie,* International Publishers, 1949; *Witness to the Times,* privately printed, 1954; *Figures from a Double World,* Alan Swallow, 1955; *The Gates of Ivory, The Gates of Horn* (novel), Mainstream Publishers, 1957; *About Clouds* (juvenile; illustrated by Chris Jenkyns), Melmont, 1959; *The Beautiful Things* (juvenile; illustrated by C. Jenkyns), Vanguard, 1960; *Letter to an Imaginary Friend,* Volume I, Alan Swallow, 1962, Volume II, Swallow Press, 1970, Volumes III and IV, Copper Canyon Press, 1985; *New and Selected Poems,* Alan Swallow, 1962; *The Movie at the End of the World: Collected Poems,* Swallow Press, 1973; *Voyages to the Inland Sea #3,* Center for Contemporary Poetry, 1973; *Voices from beyond the Wall,* Territorial Press, 1974; *A Sound of One Hand,* Minnesota Writers Publishing House, 1975; *Open Songs,* Uzzano, 1977; *Letter to Tomasito* (juvenile), Holy Cow! Press, 1977; *Trinc: Praises II,* Copper Canyon Press, 1979; *Waiting for the Angel,* Uzzano, 1979; *Passages toward the Dark,* Copper Canyon Press, 1982; *Echoes Inside the Labyrinth,* Thunder's Mouth Press, 1983.

Also author of about twenty film scripts. Poetry included in numerous anthologies, including *Poetry for Pleasure,* edited by Ian M. Parsons, Doubleday, 1960; *Poets of Today: A New*

American Anthology, edited by Walter Lowenfels, International Publishers, 1964; *Heartland, Poets of the Midwest,* edited by Lucire Stryk, Northern Illinois University Press, 1967; *Where Is Vietnam?,* edited by W. Lowenfels, Doubleday, 1967; *Getting into Poetry,* edited by Morris Sweetkind, Rostan Holbrook Press, 1972; *Traveling America,* Macmillan, 1977; *The Norton Introduction to Literature,* second edition, Norton, 1977; *News of the Universe,* edited by Robert Bly, Sierra Club, 1980; *From A to Z: 200 Contemporary Poets,* Swallow Press, 1981. Contributor of poetry, criticism, and short stories to magazines, including *Kayak, Sixties,* and *Poetry.* Founder and editor, with wife, Eugenia McGrath, *Crazy Horse;* former assistant editor of *California Quarterly* and other literary magazines.

ADAPTATIONS—Tape recordings: Poetry readings for KUSC-radio (Los Angeles), 1958-59, and KPFK-radio (Los Angeles), February 18, 1960. Tape recordings of poetry readings also at radio station WBAI (New York) and in English departments at North Dakota State University and Moorhead State College, University of New Mexico, University of California at Berkeley, and others. Video tape of reading at St. Cloud State College, St. Cloud, Minn.

WORK IN PROGRESS: New book of poems; revisions on a novel, *All but the Last.*

SIDELIGHTS: "I've gone on with teaching—with years off when I had money to pay for writing time—and writing films. I expect to continue to give readings of my poems—which I do more and more these years—and summer workshops.

"I wrote the children's books for *particular* children I have known (including the poems of *Letter to Tomasito* who is my son) and beyond them to anyone willing to give some time for the reading. The poems and the novel are for the 'common reader' whoever that may be."

McGrath has wandered around Europe and Mexico, covered America by car, freight car, and hitchhiking, worked at odd ("some very odd") jobs to finance an interlude of writing poetry, fiction, and films, mostly documentary.

FOR MORE INFORMATION SEE: New York Times, March 7, 1948; *Saturday Review,* April 17, 1948; *New York Times Book Review,* February 21, 1965; *Antioch Review,* fall-winter, 1970-71; *New Republic,* April 21, 1973; *North Dakota Quarterly,* fall, 1982.

McPHEE, Richard B(yron)   1934-

PERSONAL: Born November 29, 1934, in New Rochelle, N.Y.; son of Harold B. (a physical education teacher) and Laura H. (a teacher; maiden name, McMillen) McPhee. *Education:* Oberlin College, B.A., 1956. *Address:* R.D. #1, P.O. Box 280, Stockton, N.J. 08559. *Agent:* Peter Miller Agency, 1021 Sixth Ave., Suite 402/403, New York, N.Y. 10018. *Office:* Technigraphic, Inc., 674 Highway 202-206 North, Bridgewater, N.J. 08807.

CAREER: Creative director for Technigraphic, Inc., Bridgewater, N.J.; author of books for children. *Member:* Author's Guild.

WRITINGS—Nonfiction; for young adults; illustrated with own

I call this picture of George's daughter *A Cow Lick for Amy.* ■ (From *Rounds with a Country Vet* by Richard B. McPhee. Photograph by the author.)

photographs: *Rounds with a Country Vet,* edited by Jennifer Anderson, Dodd, 1977; *Tom and Bear: The Training of a Guide Dog Team,* edited by J. Anderson, Crowell, 1981.

SIDELIGHTS: "I am particularly interested in how men and animals work together."

McSHEAN, Gordon   1936-

PERSONAL: Born October 7, 1936, in Glasgow, Scotland; came to the United States in 1958; son of Robert (a printer) and Margaret (Oliver) McShean; married Rae Noeline Charles, November, 1983; children: Craig Leslie. *Education:* El Camino College, A.A., 1962; University of Southern California, A.B., 1963, M.L.S., 1964, graduate study, 1969; additional graduate study at State University of New York at Albany, 1968; University of San Francisco, M.A., 1978. *Office:* Multinational Ventures, 2218 Derby Ave., Capitola, Calif. 95010; and 30 Homelands Ave., Feilding, New Zealand.

CAREER: Clydesdale Supply Co., Glasgow, Scotland, display manager, 1952-56; U.S. Army, Mannheim-Sandhofen, West Germany, civilian office administrator, 1956-57; J. J. Newberry Department Stores, Los Angeles, Calif., display manager, 1958-64; Stanford University, Stanford, Calif., documents librarian, 1964-66; Clinton Job Corps Resource Center, Clinton, Iowa, head administrator, 1967-68; Dundee Township Library, Dundee, Ill., head librarian, 1969-71; Stanislaus County Free Library, Modesto, Calif., head of programs development, 1972-76; Multinational Ventures, Capitola, Calif., owner, 1976—; Massey University, Palmerston North, New Zealand, agricultural extension officer and journalist, 1980-83; free-lance journalist, 1980—. Special coordinator of Santa Cruz Community Switchboard, 1972. *Member:* American Civil Liberties Union (member of New Mexico state board of directors, 1967), National Freedom Fund for Librarians (member of board of directors, 1969-70), New Zealand Guild of Agricultural Journalists, Organizing Committee for a National Writers Union.

WRITINGS: Operation New Zealand: My Search for a New

GORDON McSHEAN

Heart, W. H. Allen, 1970, also published as *Bum Ticker: A Hearty Traveler's Tale,* Multinational Media, 1976; *Mr. Chillhead* (juvenile; self-illustrated), Multinational Media, 1976; *Running a Message Parlor: A Librarian's Medium-Rare Memoir about Censorship* (illustrated by Terry Down), Ramparts Press, 1977. Contributor of articles to journals in the fields of library science, agriculture, and horticulture.

WORK IN PROGRESS: The Royal New Zealander, "an after-the-nuclear-holocaust novel about the struggle of Australasia to survive the 'benevolence' of a devastated and desperate America"; *Conan Doyle's Nymphs,* "a children's comedy about English brownies (girl-scout type) who photograph fairies and become involved with the famous author (based on fact)"; *Enchantment Books,* a series of booklets in photo album format; *Owner Manual,* a baby book written in the style of a new car owner manual; *Rainbowland Gets Verse,* poems about New Zealand; *A Rainbowland Christmas,* a retelling of Maori traditions.

SIDELIGHTS: "I became interested in writing very early in life, being encouraged by teachers in primary school, printing my very own broadsides on my own miniature press at eleven years old, and obtaining an antique 'Yost' typewriter—which used an ink pad instead of ribbon—at fifteen (I still hunt-and-peck!). Now I'm trying to catch up with today's technologically-advanced child writers, having bought my first word processor.

"I'm finding that New Zealand provides me with opportunities to produce smaller, creative efforts for sale to limited markets as well as the 'commercial' books to pay the bills. The 'home-grown' press is alive and well and quite respectable 'down under,' since the commercial distributors don't monopolize the booksellers' shelf space as they do in the United States. New Zealanders are great readers and are interested in the works of their neighbors and friends; booksellers carry large stocks of local authors' works regardless of imprint.

"Every now and then some New Zealand writer's less-than-commercial efforts becomes tremendously successful at which point a United States edition is produced. I like to think the American publishing scene is enriched thereby. My first commercial book reached America by that route even though I was an American writer at the time. Although I still make commercial submissions to United States publishers directly, I would be extremely pleased if one or two of my 'art-for-art's sake' New Zealand creations were to reach America through that kind of recognition.

"I always hope to make my words depict my own subjective view of life, whether I'm writing fiction, describing my own heart surgery, or writing about farm programs for newspapers. But I've learned that my 'view' must not incorporate an overt message (however well intentioned).

"Messages should be integrated into a work (as I incorporated my views on censorship in *Running a Message Parlor*) if they are to be acceptable to a reader (I still regret being a little heavy-handed with my prosocialized medicine stance in my first book, *Operation New Zealand*)."But at the same time I think that everyone should have the right to express what moves them. I'm an idealist about honesty and feel strongly that where there is censorship there is no truth. I gave up librarianship when I realized many of my colleagues mouthed intellectual freedom while secretly reserving the censors' power to themselves (it was like a religious novice discovering the clergy were really devil worshippers).

"Before our writings get to censorious librarians, however, there are editors and reviewers to wield the axe. I'm hopeful they'll enjoin the 'message' writers. Then, perhaps, librarians and the public will appreciate literary works as 'art,' not provocation, and give up their perennial witchhunts against writers."

MENDOZA, George   1934-

PERSONAL: Born June 2, 1934, in New York, N.Y.; son of George and Elizabeth Mendoza; married Nicole Sekora, 1967; children: Ashley, Ryan. *Education:* State Maritime College, B.A., 1953; graduate study at Columbia University, 1954-56. *Home:* 22 Compo Parkway, Westport, Conn. 06880.

CAREER: Poet and author, 1959—. *Awards, honors:* Lewis G. Carroll Shelf Award, 1968, for *The Hunter I Might Have Been; Need a House? Call Ms. Mouse!* was selected as a "Children's Choice" by the International Reading Association, 1982.

*WRITINGS—*All for children: *And Amedeo Asked, How Does One Become a Man?* Braziller, 1959; (with Wendy Sanford) *The Puma and the Pearl,* Walker & Co., 1962; *The Hawk Is Humming: A Novel,* Bobbs-Merrill, 1964; *A Piece of String,* Astor-Honor, 1965; *Gwot! Horribly Funny Hairticklers* (illustrated by Steven Kellogg), Harper, 1967; *The Crack in the*

GEORGE MENDOZA

Wall and Other Terribly Weird Tales (illustrated by Mercer Mayer), Dial, 1968; *A Wart Snake in a Fig Tree* (illustrated by Etienne Delessert), Dial, 1968; *The Gillygoofang* (illustrated by M. Mayer), Dial, 1968; *Flowers and Grasses and Weeds* (illustrated by Joseph Low), Funk, 1968; *The Hunter I Might Have Been: A Tale of Anguish and Love* (poem; illustrated with photographs by DeWayne Dalrymple), Astor-Honor, 1968; *The Practical Man* (illustrated by Imero Gobbato), Lothrop, 1968; *Hunting Sketches* (illustrated by Ronald Stein), Astor-Honor, 1968; *And I Must Hurry for the Sea Is Coming In . . .* (poem; illustrated with photographs by D. Dalrymple), Prentice-Hall, 1969; *A Beastly Alphabet* (illustrated by J. Low), Grosset, 1969; *The Digger Wasp* (illustrated by Jean Zallinger), Dial, 1969; *Herman's Hat* (illustrated by Frank Bozzo), Doubleday, 1969; *The Starfish Trilogy* (illustrated by Ati Forberg), Funk, 1969; (compiler) *The World from My Window: Poems and Drawings* (children's writings), Hawthorn, 1969.

Are You My Friend? (illustrated by F. Bozzo), Prentice-Hall, 1970; *The Good Luck Spider and Other Bad Luck Stories* (illustrated by Gahan Wilson), Doubleday, 1970; *The Inspector* (illustrated by Peter Parnall), Doubleday, 1970; *The Marceau Alphabet Book* (illustrated with photographs by Milton H. Green), Doubleday, 1970; *The Mist Men and Other Poems: Little Frog, Big Pond* (illustrated by P. Parnall), Doubleday, 1970; *The Thumbtown Toad* (illustrated by Monika Beisner), Prentice-Hall, 1970; *The Christmas Tree Alphabet Book* (illustrated by Bernadette Watts), World Publishing, 1971; *Big Frog, Little Pond* (illustrated by P. Parnall), McCall Pub-

lishing, 1971; *The Fearsome Brat* (illustrated by F. Bozzo), Lothrop, 1971; *Fish in the Sky*, translated by Milton Glasser, Doubleday, 1971; *Goodbye, River, Goodbye* (illustrated with photographs by George A. Tice), Doubleday, 1971; *The Hunter, The Tick, and the Gumberoo* (illustrated by Philip Wende), Cowles Book, 1971; *The Marcel Marceau Counting Book* (illustrated with photographs by M. H. Greene), Doubleday, 1971; *Moonfish and Owl Scratchings* (illustrated by P. Parnall), Grosset, 1971; *Moonstring* (illustrated by Charles Jakubowski), World Publishing, 1971; *The Scarecrow Clock* (illustrated by Eric Carle), Holt, 1971; *The Scribbler* (illustrated by Robert Quackenbush), Holt, 1971; *Poem for Putting to Sea* (illustrated by A. Forberg), Hawthorn, 1972; *The Alphabet Boat: A Seagoing Alphabet Book* (illustrated by Lawrence DiFiori), American Heritage Press, 1972; *Sesame Street Book of Opposites with Zero Mostel* (illustrated by M. Greene), Platt, 1974; (with Prasanna Rao) *Shadowplay*, Holt, 1974; *Fishing the Morning Lonely*, Freshet Press, 1974; *Lord, Suffer Me to Catch a Fish*, Quadrangle, 1974; *Norman Rockwell's Americana ABC* (illustrated with photographs by Norman Rockwell), Dell, 1975; (with Carol Burnett) *What I Want to Be When I Grow Up* (illustrated by Sheldon Secunda), Simon & Schuster, 1975; (with Howard Minsky) *Doug Henning's Magic Book*, Ballantine, 1975; *The Sesame Street Book of Jobs with Carol Burnett* (illustrated by S. Secunda), Platt, 1975; *Lost Pony* (illustrated with photographs by René Burri), San Francisco Book Co., 1976; *Norman Rockwell's Boys and Girls at Play*, Abrams, 1976; *Secret Places of Trout Fishermen*, Macmillan, 1977; *Norman Rockwell's Diary for a Young Girl* (illustrated by N. Rockwell), Abbeville Press, 1978; (with Michel Legrand) *Michel's Mixed-up Musical Bird* (illustrated by DePatie-Frelang), Bobbs-Merrill, 1978; *Norman Rockwell's Scrapbook for a Young Boy* (illustrated by N. Rockwell), Abbeville Press, 1979; *Magic Tricks* (illustrated by Colbus), Collins, 1979; (with Andrès Segovia) *Andrès Segovia, My Book of the Guitar: Guidance for the Young Beginner*, Philomel, 1979.

Need a House? Call Ms. Mouse! (illustrated by Doris Susan Smith), Grosset, 1981 (published in England as *House by Mouse*, Deutsch, 1981); *Counting Sheep* (illustrated by Kathleen Reidy), Grosset, 1982; *Alphabet Sheep* (illustrated by K. Reidy), Grosset, 1982; *Silly Sheep and Other Sheepish Rhymes* (illustrated by K. Reidy), Grosset, 1982; *The Sheepish Book of Opposites* (illustrated by K. Reidy), Grosset, 1982; *Norman Rockwell's Four Seasons*, Grosset, 1982; *Norman Rockwell's Happy Holidays*, Putnam, 1983; *Norman Rockwell's Love and Rememberance*, Dodd, 1985; *Henri Mouse*, (illustrated by Joelle Boucher), Viking, 1985; *Norman Rockwell's Patriotic Times* (introduction by President Reagan), Viking, 1985. Also author of screenplays, including "Petals from a Poem Flower," and "You Show Me Yours and I'll Show You Mine," and of scripts for "Sesame Street."

ADAPTATIONS: "Michel's Mixed-up Musical Bird," ABC-TV Afterschool Special, February, 1978.

WORK IN PROGRESS: Henri Mouse, the Juggler for Viking.

SIDELIGHTS: "In the early days I wrote many books of poetry. I don't think of myself as a poet any longer, though I do see my vision as a poetic vision and a romantic vision. I want to produce works that are meaningful, that have some beauty. I want my writing to touch people, to affect their lives. I feel that I have come closest to achieving this through my children's books. I feel highly elevated and very privileged to be working in the field. There is an innocence to children's books, and when I can no longer sit down to write with that same feeling of wonder and innocence and beauty, I'll know I'm finished.

"A children's book begins with a genuine feeling and a strong desire. I feel that I *must* write it, or else be punished. It will be more painful *not* to write than to write. It's what's called being in a double-bind. Through writing, I find the *juste milieu,* the Golden Mean."

Mendoza was raised on Long Island, New York. "I grew up on the sea. When I was twelve, I actually rebuilt an old town sloop with a couple of very knowledgeable ex-seafaring cap-

tains. She was beautiful. I often took her out on summer days and nights; I found my dreams alone in that boat.

"I did not have the strong father-son relationship that my son has with me. I had to find my own strengths. I was able to discover them through the sea, through the days of sea songs, seagulls, tides and stars. I remember more than anything the phosphorescence of the sea in the wake of my sloop as I sailed through the night. I felt I had touched the world. It was a magnificent time to grow up. I was very lucky to have created a world for myself. It was something of my own—a freedom I gave to myself. My father had forbidden me a sail boat, he

"Poor Master Simmons," was all the maidservant ever said as she patted him daily on his head while he took his meals with the grunting hogs from the sloshing trough. ■ (From "The Milk Tooth," in *The Good Luck Spider and Other Bad Luck Stories* by George Mendoza. Illustrated by Gahan Wilson.)

So he ran for his shovel and began to dig a hole to bury the trunk. ■ (From *The Practical Man* by George Mendoza. Illustrated by Imero Gobbato.)

felt that it was dangerous and that I should be thinking about other things besides sailing, but nothing could stop me. I worked to buy the boat anyway and took care of it all myself.

"There were times during late September and October when I'd take my school books along and spend a few days out on the boat, sailing through the night on the Long Island Sound. Pulling into a cove somewhere I would study my Latin, my French, or my history. When on more than one occasion, the principal of the school wanted to expel me for truancy, I'd tell him that I learned more by studying out on my sloop than in class. 'Prove it,' he'd say. And I did, by earning good grades. I've always been a loner. The sea was above all, a friend.

"At fourteen I set off for Block Island from Stony Brook. I took my sloop out too far, was lost for three weeks in the Atlantic Ocean and given up for dead. My boat was crippled with one of the sails blown out. Finally, I was picked up by the Coast Guard. I discovered a lot about myself as a young man at sea. The boat was my dream factory, enabling me to explore so many facets within myself. I found my inner

strengths, my imagination. I was young and inexperienced, but I was shaping my identity.

"At fifteen, I wanted to cross the Atlantic in the same little sloop. I didn't realize the danger—the world was my oyster. Later, in 1962 and again in 1964, I made two solo Atlantic crossings with a much larger sloop. I wrote during the voyages. It was wonderful to be alone for almost forty days.

"After reading Emlyn Williams' *Corn is Green,* I realized that I wanted to direct my life to writing. I especially remember the way the Welsh miner described the sea. Then I began to read Jack London, Dostoevsky—all the great writers I admire. I read voraciously and thought, 'That's my path.' I was young. My mother had an incredible library with all kinds of books, including Havelock Ellis. Jack London, of course, was my favorite. I worshipped him.

"The local newspaper ran my poems once a week. I felt I was no longer a transient soul. When one person has accepted you

Wherever he went he created a sensation, since he was without question the only mouse painter in Paris! ■ (From *Henri Mouse* by George Mendoza. Illustrated by Joelle Boucher.)

as a writer, it gives you faith that others will, too. Books give you a sense of permanence, of immortality.

"I studied journalism at Columbia University. I worked as a journalist writing stories for the *Herald Tribune* and later for various other magazines. I also wrote poetry and short stories which I submitted again and again to *Esquire* and *The New Yorker* without much hope. When my first book was accepted for publication by George Braziller [*And Amedeo Asked, How Does One Become a Man?*, 1956] I realized my stories were more suited to books. I was seeking a higher degree of permanency than a monthly magazine publication.

"My first opportunity with George Braziller was luck. I thought Braziller was the finest way to start, so I made an appointment

and brought him my manuscript about a boy's sea-going adventure searching for the inner seeds of manhood. George Braziller loved my allegorical fable, and so did his wife Marsha who I'm certain was instrumental in convincing him to publish the book.

"It took me several months to wrap up the deal. Braziller, a difficult man to work with, finally called me and said, 'Look, I have only a certain amount of money for your book, and since you want such a fine production, I won't have any money left to pay you. What do you want to do?' 'Publish the book, I'll wait for my money,' was my response. The finest paper was used, and Ati Forberg did the drawings. It was beautiful.

"I worked with Bobbs-Merrill on my first novel, *The Hawk*

Was Humming. After that I went to work with every publisher from A to Z.

"I'm never quite satisfied with my writing, always feeling that I haven't scratched the surface. That's frustrating. Still, there is a wonderful joy in the experience of writing.

"My style is individualistic. I see my name in anthologies, but whether I've made a contribution to children's literature is something only time will tell. When I lecture in the classroom, I make an impact. Children are very open and responsive. I talk with them about their lives, their fears, loneliness, and I read to them from my current book. I explain how a book is actually made, and I tell them that a book or a piece of writing begins with a feeling from within. A book is not something you can go out and search for. Aspiring writers must be aware of everything around them, and to become good listeners. Teachers love that! Through listening, one can grasp deeper meanings.

"My own children have influenced me tremendously. For *My Book of the Guitar: Guidance for the Young Beginner*, Andrès Segovia taught them to play the guitar. I met Segovia through a friend in Madrid. I had to court him for three years to convince him to do the book. He did not want to do a book for young people until he met my son and daughter and then agreed. He gave everything and worked harder than anyone else on the book. My wife, Nicole, who designed the book, also helped me tremendously."

"Perhaps the hardest part about being a writer is the fear that your initial vision of a book will not be realized in the final, published version. This has happened to me. A publisher did a series of mine and the finished product was awful. It happens when ideas and dreams are thought of as merchandise. I now keep control of the design of my books.

"On the other hand, I have had some great experiences with publishers. My 'Henri Mouse' series is beautiful. Children love this character who magically paints his problems away. The books were initially published in the United States and in France. French publishing companies are in tune with the finer aspects of book publishing. They take tremendous care with books."

Mendoza's *The Hunter I Might Have Been*, won the Lewis Carroll Shelf Award in 1968. *"The Hunter I Might Have Been* was a poem before it was a book. Aside from the award, the text was read into the Congressional Record by Senator Javitz as a statement against killing. Though I was drawing from something arcane, I do remember having killed a bird when I was a young boy. I always find meaning in real experience, I have to work from something pure.

"Maybe prose and poetry is one and the same. *Sailing to the Other Side* is a poem *and* a story. It began with the question, 'What would happen if suddenly, for some reason, I disappeared?' I saw my son Ryan, and I saw myself gone. I don't know if writing it was frightening as much as necessary. I felt a great need to write it." Mendoza requires absolute isolation when he works. "I don't write every day, but when I work, I work non-stop. I start with a good cup of coffee, listen to beautiful music—Bach, Vivaldi, and Pachebel—then, I create solitude. I have a place to go to where it's just me and the

Otter tells Henrietta: "Please build me a sturdy hunting and fishing lodge!"

(From *Need a House? Call Ms. Mouse!* by George Mendoza. Illustrated by Doris Susan Smith.)

Ask me what a poem is for
or what it should do
and I would tell you
go plough your hill
while I leave mine wild to grow.

■ (From *Norman Rockwell's Four Seasons* by George Mendoza. Illustrated by Norman Rockwell.)

typewriter. Many things can be going on around me—I can hear my family, the kids, the dog barking—but I still have solitude. I am able to focus. I work in a very quiet sun room near the sea, in a womb of silence. It's wonderful to know there's a gift inside you which you can give to someone else.

"I always show my first drafts to my wife who has a terrific sensibility, and knows what is going to work. I then give the manuscript to a close friend in the [publishing] business to get feedback. Ray Roberts at Little Brown is one of my closest friends. I'll always show something to Ray."

Mendoza is influenced by other art forms. "I think art has sensitized me tremendously. In my early years, I visited museums whenever I could, and studied the effects of light and shadow. I was fascinated by the contrasts—especially in the paintings by Cezanne. He reversed light and darkness, which is why his paintings are constantly surprising and fresh. Words should express contrasts with the same masterful simplicity. I often visit the Jeu de Paume museum in Paris. Inside I see a world in which I would love to live. I recently spent several days at the Gardens of Claude Monet in Giverny. He created his own paradise on earth. I came away asking, 'What is cre-

ation? What is heaven, but what we create for ourselves?' When we fall in love, we create in our own image of that which we want to love most in ourselves. Monet did that with his gardens at a great spiritual cost. The villagers in Giverny believed that their water would be polluted by the exotic plants Monet imported from China, Africa, all over the world. It took him years to fill those ponds, to convince the villagers that they would not poison the cattle, but he persisted. I was tremendously moved by his creation, and also to see his old boat, where he often painted, half submerged in the waters of those magnificent ponds.

"I used to travel a great deal. I like the feeling of being a stranger on the planet. There came a time, however, especially with children, when I felt that I needed a house. We had a house on East 64th street in New York for fifteen years, which the children knew as *their* home, but I have never owned a house. I am such a parapetetic individual, I've never really landed anywhere. I still travel but I don't like to be away from my family. I try to make the trips short, and when my kids aren't in school, they travel with me.

"When I was a boy, my father had a summer home in Ver-

There was a woman, an old gnarled stump of a woman, who went out one day to pick beans in the bean patch behind her house. . . . ■ (From "The Hairy Toe," in *Gwot! Horribly Funny Hairticklers* by George Mendoza. Illustrated by Steven Kellogg.)

George Mendoza with wife Nicole and children Ryan and Ashley.

mont. I remember the solitude I found there. I still harbor that noon-daydream of an idea, wherein I live beside Vermont ponds and streams. All my books of poetry were inspired by Vermont and the environs of streams and fields and meadows. I've dreamed about living there, but I've never been able to completely convince myself to retire from everything—to go to some Vermont farm and stay forever. I'm always moving, and so far it's worked for me. When I go to a new place, I feel that something new is going to happen. We'd only been living in Westport, Connecticut for three months when suddenly my new book, *Sailing to the Other Side,* came to me. I have a feeling of kinship with new places. Wherever I've been things happen, and I have new stories to tell. I think it's good for a

writer to have mobility—it allows him to have multiple experiences, and different outlooks.

"I don't have writers as friends. That's the last thing I want. I've known writers and I've known the professional writers who are out for the cocktail party circuit. That's just not me. I've never had intimate relationships with fellow poets either. I've gone about new projects and new ideas on my own. I am a very shy person. Actually, there are two people inside of me: the hermetic, troglodyte and the gregarious, vital, vigorous person who needs to reach out, who touches and is touched by people and life. It's tremendous to be able to touch lives and to have a good exchange with life. The best exchanges I

I am Christmas and carols that I wish would stay all year...

(From *Norman Rockwell's Americana ABC* by George Mendoza. Illustrated by Norman Rockwell.)

But he wanted to save his bread to eat in the park. . . . ■ (From *Lost Pony* by George Mendoza. Photograph by René Burri.)

know are deeply spiritual. My wife and family are my center, they keep me from getting diffused."

Of his numerous books, *Lost Pony* is Mendoza's favorite. "One Christmas, my wife bought my son a stuffed pony made in Spain. It was during the terrible recession of the 1970s. I was sent to pick up the pony and found it was very expensive, so expensive, in fact, that I called Nicole and told her that I thought it was too extravagant, especially when there were children who wouldn't find anything under their tree. My wife insisted that I bring it home. I remember cramming the beautiful hand-made pony into a taxicab. I couldn't sleep that Christmas Eve, staying up all night thinking how I wanted every child in the world to have a pony. That's where *Lost Pony* came from. I started working on it Christmas day. I saw what I wanted, I saw Paris and the Boy and knew that it had to be realized as a book.

"Why Paris? Where else? I wanted *Lost Pony* to be an iridescent story, and where else would these horses be? Not in New York City, not in Rome, not in San Francisco. Nowhere would do but Paris. The great horses are in Paris; I knew that because I had lived there. For me, the dream was for the boy I imagined, who had never had a horse, to fly out on the limbs of his dreams with the horses in Paris. I finally found the perfect character in a French orphanage. My family was very supportive. I put the whole book together myself, and when I

His nagging wife and thirteen children were all asleep in bed. ■ (From "The Skunk in the Pond," in *The Crack in the Wall and Other Terribly Weird Tales* by George Mendoza. Illustrated by Mercer Mayer.)

returned to the States, I was lucky enough to sell it in a week to San Francisco Book Company. You have to trust—in the day, the moment, and in yourself. You have to have some faith."

Tennis and work are Mendoza's relaxation. "I work all the time, but it's good for me. I just turned fifty, and I can't believe it. My doctor announced 'You're not going to have middle age . . . you'll just turn old one day.' I always had a very boyish quality—I still have a great need to see my three ribs in the mirror! But sometimes I look at myself and see that I'm changing.

"I know that like everyone, I am coming to some end. It's very curious, I find myself wondering lately, 'What is death?' I've never felt that in the past. Perhaps this feeling inspired *Sailing to the Other Side*. It is certainly one of the reasons I recently donated all of my documents to Boston University. I've dispatched all my life and now I'm ready to start all over again.

"I have no greater plans than what I am doing right now, today. There are times when I feel I've created so much, and I wonder just how large my island should be. But at the same time, I feel a certain rebirth is imminent, a nascent turn. I cherish life. Life and work are what exhilarate me."

Mendoza donated all of his works to Boston University's Special Collection Library. "I feel very proud that my books are with Boston University, and I hope that someday some soul passing through will touch upon the work that I've done and it might touch that person's life. That's why the books are here. It's so that what we've seen is not forgotten—it goes on into another's experience.

"I think young [writers] have to feel inspired by something. And I believe it's important to follow the truth inside oneself. That's why my books are here. [They] express what I felt strongly . . . and I hope they can help some other young person."

FOR MORE INFORMATION SEE: New York Times Book Review, September 19, 1970, May 2, 1971; Doris de Montreville and Donna Hill, *Third Book of Junior Authors*, H. W. Wilson, 1972; *San Francisco Examiner*, October 10, 1975; *Ms.*, July-August, 1982.

MILD, Warren (Paul) 1922-

PERSONAL: Born March 22, 1922, in Minneapolis, Minn.; son of Lawrence Albert (a bus driver) and Clara (Kumm) Mild; married Phyllis Jensen (an orders processor), August 21, 1943; children: David, Samuel, Joanne. *Education:* University of Minnesota, B.A., 1946, M.A., 1947, Ph.D., 1950. *Politics:* Democrat. *Religion:* American Baptist. *Home:* 1001 Wentz Rd., Blue Bell, Pa. 19422.

CAREER: Bethel College, St. Paul, Minn., instructor in English, 1948-50; University of Redlands, Redlands, Calif., instructor, 1950-51, assistant professor, 1951-55, associate professor of English, 1955-58, director of admissions, 1951-54; American Baptist Convention, Board of Education and Publications, Valley Forge, Pa., director of collegiate education, 1958-65; Ellen Cushing Junior College, Byrn Mawr, Pa., president, 1966-74; full-time writer, 1975—. Member of board of governors, Radnor Scholarship Committee, 1967-68. *Military service:* U.S. Army, 1942-46; became staff sergeant. *Member:* American Society for Eighteenth Century Studies, American Red Cross Chairman; Schuylkill Valley Branch). *Awards, honors:* Ford Foundation fellowship, 1954-55.

WRITINGS: What Do the Lions Eat When Daniel's Out to Lunch? (drama), Judson, 1964; *Fractured Questions* (juvenile), Judson, 1966; *Strangers Outside the Feast: A Choral Reading,* Friendship, 1967; *The Drop-Ins* (juvenile), Judson, 1968; *The Story of American Baptists,* Judson, 1976. Author of two series of church school curricula, 1980, 1982; also author of script for recording "Look Back and Dream," Friendship Press, 1969.

Filmstrips; all produced by American Baptist Churches: "Seeking the Chosen," 1975; "Furthering the Ministry," 1975; "People with a Mission," 1980; "Together in Name," 1982.

Contributor of articles to *Modern Language Quarterly* and *Proceedings of the American Philosophical Society,* Photography and layout editor of newsletter, *Ellen Cushing Way,* 1970-71.

WORK IN PROGRESS: A biography of Joseph Highmore of Holborn Row, oral history of Montgomery County Community College (Pa.) history of Calvary Baptist Church (Norristown, Pa.).

MILLER, Elizabeth 1933-

PERSONAL: Born May 25, 1933, in Istanbul, Turkey; daughter of Alfred R. (a professor) and Charlotte (Brinsmede) Bellinger; married Serge Lawrence Miller (a copper craftsman), June 29, 1957; children: Cyrus, Keith, Wendy, Chapin. *Education:* Vassar College, B.A., 1954; Western Connecticut State College, M.A., 1973. *Politics:* "Pacifist." *Home:* South St., Washington, Conn. 06793. *Office:* Washington Primary School, Washington Depot, Conn. 06794.

CAREER: Author of books for children and teacher, beginning in 1967—.

WRITINGS—For children; all written with Jane Cohen; all illustrated by Victoria Chess; all published by F. Watts; "Cat and Dog" series: *Cat and Dog Give a Party,* 1980; . . . *Have a Contest,* 1980; . . . *and the Mixed-Up Week,* 1980; . . . *Raise the Roof,* 1980; . . . *Take a Trip,* 1980; . . . *Have a Parade,* 1981; . . . *and the ABC's,* 1981.

SIDELIGHTS: "With Jane Cohen as coauthor, I have worked to develop an accelerated language arts series of books which has produced excellent results at all levels—slow learners, special education, and gifted children."

A Painter in Paris did a Portrait of him.

(From *Cat and Dog and the ABC's* by Elizabeth Miller and Jane Cohen. Illustrated by Victoria Chess.)

(From the movie "Between Two Loves," based on the novel *Two Loves for Jenny* by Sandy Miller. Presented as an ABC-TV "Afterschool Special," October 27, 1982.)

MILLER, Sandy (Peden) 1948-

PERSONAL: Born December 25, 1948, in Horton, Kan.; daughter of Norman Leslie (a television repairman) and Beckie (Wagoner) Peden; married Brian Miller (a writer and vice-president of a boys ranch), May 18, 1968; children: Ben, Jeff, Phil, Matt, Beth, Becca. *Education:* Attended Washburn University and Tulsa Junior College. *Religion:* Protestant. *Home and office:* Bethesda Boys Ranch, P.O. Box 311, Mounds, Okla. 74047. *Agent:* Merrilee Heifetz, Writers House, Inc., 21 West 26th St., New York, N.Y. 10010.

CAREER: Bethesda Missionary Society, Jamaica, West Indies, missionary, 1969-71; Bethesda Boys Ranch, Mounds, Okla., household coordinator, 1971—. *Member:* Oklahoma Writers Federation, Tulsa (Okla.) Tuesday Writers (vice-president, 1981; president, 1982), Tulsa Christian Writers (vice-president, 1981; membership chairman, 1982-83). *Awards, honors: Two Loves for Jenny* was chosen as a Children's Choice by the International Reading Association/Children's Book Council Joint Committee, 1983.

WRITINGS—For young adults: *Two Loves for Jenny,* New American Library, 1982; *Smart Girl,* New American Library, 1982; *Chase the Sun,* New American Library, 1983; *Lynn's Challenge,* New American Library, 1984; *Freddie the Thirteenth,* New American Library, 1985; *A Tale of Two Turkeys,* New American Library, 1985; *This Song Is for You,* Warner, 1985.

ADAPTATIONS—Television: "Between Two Loves" (adaptation of *Two Loves for Jenny*), ABC-TV, October 27, 1982.

SANDY MILLER

WORK IN PROGRESS: Dreamer's Legacy, a novel for young adults.

SIDELIGHTS: "I began writing poems at the age of seven and sold my first one when I was thirteen to *Grit.* When I was fifteen, I sold several more poems and two articles. I always loved to read and I would hide in my closet at night with the light on and a towel by the door to read. When I was twenty-seven, I took a correspondence course in writing which really got me started. I still enjoy reading children's and teenage books which may be why I also like to write them. With six young children, I had a hard time finding the time to write, so my first book was written from 4:30 to 6:30 in the morning.

"I was an only child for ten years, and then my mother had four more children. Consequently, I entertained myself. We lived in the country and there were always wonderful things to do such as climbing the windmill, silo, or apple tree.

"One of my favorite places was a ditch that curved through the length of our pasture. It became all kinds of things: a trench for soldiers, a creek for a wagon train crossing the prairie, or just a magic road. That must be where my imagination got such a productive start. I still love to daydream.

"When I was eleven, we moved into town. I missed the country, but I built a desk in a tree and spent a lot of time there dreaming and writing.

"When I write books now, I can remember exactly how I felt when I was a teenager. I like writing happy things because I believe children need to read positive, wholesome books."

MILLS, Claudia 1954-

BRIEF ENTRY: Born August 21, 1954, in New York, N.Y. Author and editor. Mills graduated from Wellesley College in 1976 and received a M.A. from Princeton University in 1979. Currently the editor of *QQ: Report from the Center for Philosophy and Public Policy* at the University of Maryland, she has worked at Four Winds Press as an editorial secretary and production assistant. Mills commented, "I have been writing books for children and teenagers since I was a child and a teenager." Her juvenile books include *The Secret Carousel* (Four Winds, 1983), the story of ten-year-old Lindy Webster who must remain in tiny Three Churches, Iowa while her older sister goes off to New York to study ballet. *School Library Journal* observed, "This charming short novel captures the regularity of life in a small midwestern town." *Publishers Weekly* found that "Mill's low-keyed, fluid story keeps the focus on the wistful heroine, her yearnings and conflicts. . . ." In *At the Back of the Woods* (Four Winds, 1982), Emily joins a group of ten-year-old girls who share a hideaway in the woods. Although Emily impresses one of the girls, Clarisse, with her fearlessness and other traits, she is overtaken with fear when she believes herself cursed by Mrs. Spinelli. *Library Journal* called it a "well-written, well-plotted book [that] provokes thought (and discussion)." According to *Booklist,* the "characterizations are well-drawn . . . and Clarisse's insights leave the reader much to think about."

All the Living (Macmillan, 1983) relates the trying summer of Karla and her brother Jamie. While Jamie tries to win his father's approval, Karla is obsessed with death. She decides to become a vegetarian rather than eat animals that have been killed. *Voice of Youth Advocates* remarked, "Karla and her nine-year-old brother, Jamie, have problems . . . which are sensitively explored in this novel." The same magazine had praise for Mill's young adult romance, *Luisa's American Dream* (Four Winds, 1981). "Humor blends with insight," observed the reviewer, "in a plot that intertwines an adolescent identity crisis with romance." Mills is also the coeditor of *Liberalism Reconsidered* (Rowan & Littlefield, 1983). Her most recent book is entitled *What about Annie* (Walker & Co., 1985). *Home:* 7009 Poplar Ave., Takoma Park, Md. 20912.

FOR MORE INFORMATION SEE: Contemporary Authors, Volume 109, Gale, 1983.

MILTON, Joyce   1946-

BRIEF ENTRY: Born January 12, 1946, in McKeesport, Pa. Author of adult and juvenile books. Prior to becoming a freelance writer in 1977, Milton was employed as a librarian and as a young adult editor for *Kirkus Reviews*. The titles of her books reveal a varied interest in the history of science and technology, Eastern Europe, and the history of politics in the United States. *Controversy: Science in Conflict* (Messner, 1980), her first book for young adults, is a study of science versus four areas of conflict, namely, history, society, morality, and the imagination. Covering topics such as Aztec cannibalism, eugenics, animal intelligence, and extraterrestrial life, the book was described by *School Library Journal* as "a fascinating examination of scientific argument." *Voice of Youth Advocates* agreed, noting that it provides a "stimulating view of the frontiers of science, as well as its lunatic fringe." *Bulletin of the Center for Children's Books* called Milton's second young adult book, *A Friend in China* (Hastings House, 1980), "a trenchant picture" of Agnes Smedley, the author and foreign correspondent who traveled with Communist China's Red Army and became one of the first outsiders to interview Mao Tsetung. *School Library Journal* added: "This well-researched, well-written book is. . . . an excellent complement to biographies of Mao Tse-Tung and general histories of 20th-Century China."

Milton's other works for young adults include *Here Come the Robots* (Hastings House, 1981), a history of robotics, and a novel entitled *Save the Loonies* (Four Winds, 1983). She also has written several books for younger readers like *Ruthie the Robot* (Scholastic Inc., 1983), *Secrets of the Mummies* (Random House, 1984), and *Dinosaur Days* (Random House, 1985). Among her adult titles are *Sunrise of Power: Ancient Egypt, Alexander and the World of Hellenism* (Harcourt, 1980), *Tradition and Revolt: Imperial China, Islands of the Rising Sun* (Harcourt, 1980), and *The Rosenberg File: A Search for the Truth* (Holt, 1983). *Home:* 60 Plaza St., Brooklyn, N.Y. 11238.

FOR MORE INFORMATION SEE: Contemporary Authors, Volume 106, Gale, 1982.

How beautiful is youth! how bright it gleams
With its illusions, aspirations, dreams!
Book of Beginnings, Story without End,
Each maid a heroine, and each man a friend!
                                          —Henry Wadsworth Longfellow

MITCHNIK, Helen   1901-

PERSONAL: Born February 28, 1901, in Omdurman, Sudan; daughter of Adolf (an engineer) and Hannah (Ibraheem) Mitchnik; *Education:* Attended private school in Khartoum, Sudan. *Residence:* London, England.

CAREER: Author. Has been employed as an industrial and commercial translator in England.

WRITINGS—Of interest to young readers: (Reteller) *Egyptian and Sudanese Folk-Tales* (illustrated by Eric Fraser), Oxford University Press, 1978.

WORK IN PROGRESS: Volume 2 of *Egyptian and Sudanese Folk-Tales;* a history of the author's maternal grandparents dealing with their involvement in the Mahdi's war in the Sudan; *Growing Up under a Sudanese Sun,* an extended autobiography of Mitchnik's childhood and early adolescence in the Sudan; short stories portraying the wit and humor of the people of Egypt and the Sudan, and their beliefs and superstitions.

SIDELIGHTS: "I was born in Omdurman—then the capital of the Anglo-Egyptian Sudan—on the 28th day of February, in the year 1901, shortly after the British had reconquered the country from the Mahdi and his dervish armies.

"My childhood was not in any way different from that of other children born to affluent parents, but it was certainly not typical in that I grew with harmony and ease under the conflicting influence of beliefs and traditions and habits and customs pertaining to two different worlds: the East and West from which my father and mother originated.

"Now, when distances have shrunk and changes take place from day to day, rather from year to year, my paradoxical childhood would have been of no particular importance. But

HELEN MITCHNIK

when I was growing up, distances kept people tied down for generations to their hometown, and change was so slow that it was almost imperceptible. Then the traditions and beliefs and habits and customs of East and West stood out in sharp contrast one to the other. That East and West did meet successfully is proof enough for me of my parents' liberal, tolerant attitude and their values and outlook on life, modified by their own experience of it and incessantly transmitted to us, their children.

"I had a happy childhood. And having been one of a large family of brothers and sisters, I never knew a moment of boredom or loneliness. Three of my brothers were born in quick succession after me, and I participated whole-heartedly in all their pranks and play; I climbed walls and shinned up trees and rode backwards on the bare back of a donkey, little mindful of the cuts and bruises which perpetually adorned my knees and elbows.

"I loved playing with my dolls too, and would spend many a delightful hour talking to them and decking them out in strings of colourful beads and bright bits of finery, all painstakingly collected for the purpose.

"We had many pets at home and they were an exotic variety, from a monkey and a mongoose to a tortoise and a multilingual parrot, and a full-grown snake that lived in the dark mysterious depths of the well in the backyard. Occasionally it would come out for an airing, and though we children feared it and never dared to approach it too closely, we jealously considered it our pet, and would sit riveted in awesome contemplation of its great bulk as it lay coiled up in its defence any time our elders hinted having it destroyed for reasons of our safety.

"Cats and dogs we had too, and with them I enjoyed many a frolicsome tumble on the lawn in our garden.

"But the main delights of my childhood lay in the stories my grandmother used to tell us children. My grandmother was a wonderful story teller, and she lived with us. And since in the world in which I was born there were no present day diversions in the way of cinemas and theatres, or recreation centres and the like, storytelling was the one popular entertainment with children and adults alike.

"So, come eventide, when the short tropical twilight merged into the still darkness of night, I would find my way across the rows of beds of my brothers and sisters to my grandmother's bed which stood at the head of the row. And there, secure in the warm embrace of her encircling arms, I would look up at the starry night sky above me, and sleepily listen to her tell us a story.

"That the story fairly bristled with exploits of jinn and ghoul and and ifreet did not in any way disturb my peaceful slumber; for jinn and ghoul and ifreet, together with their unusual, unsavory complement of evil spirits, were familiar characters in every day topics of conversation. And reference to them was made normally, openly, and without any inhibitions.

"There were, of course, other stories too: romantic stories of which my mother—who was also a prodigious storyteller—had an inexhaustible fund. They were stories of green oasis and flowing rivers, of moonlit nights and shy young maidens, and dashing young cavaliers on champing steeds ready to brave fire and flood in their eager quest for adventure. But though these stories were varied, the theme that ran through them

She was so appalled at her ugliness, that she decided then and there to do away with her life. ■ (From "O Luck of the Ugly. . . ." in *Egyptian and Sudanese Folk-Tales,* retold by Helen Mitchnik. Illustrated by Eric Fraser.)

never varied. It was primarily the triumph of good over evil, and basically a lesson in social morality.

"All of these stories left an indelible impression upon me, and throughout my schooldays I drew from them many a theme for my school compositions. As I grew older, my interest shifted from these stories of the world of fantasies to the stories of the realistic world about me. I was particularly interested in my own grandmother's life story and the difficult years she lived through during the era of the Mahdia. And as I listened to her story, I was at once fascinated and awed by her one unquestionable belief in the intervention of the invisible and the infinite, and in the mystic and the occult.

"The mystic and the occult were two subjects in which I became deeply engrossed early in my adolescence. And to hear my grandmother speak of them with such deep conviction, such firm assurance, my own newborn belief in them would be doubly consolidated, only to be perilously shaken, soon after, by my father whose clear, cold conception of life held no theories of the mystic and the occult, and no belief in the intervention of the invisible or the infinite.

"I was an avid reader ever since I could spell, and my father, who was an accomplished linguist, kept our bookshelves at home well stocked with every conceivable book a growing child could need. My most enjoyable readings were travel stories and mystery and detective stories, such as those of Sherlock Holmes and the *Scarlet Pimpernel*, and every time I read one of Edgar Allan Poe's new short stories, I would hasten to recount it, in Arabic, to my mother and grandmother.

"Arabic was my mother tongue. But the principal language I learned at school was English. Therefore, everything I read was in English; anything which did not emanate from our bookshelves at home was tacitly considered 'unauthorised' reading, and had, by some sort of gentleman's agreement, to be ok'd by my father first. But no child ever grew up without deviating at some time or other from this golden precept, and to this I, too, must plead guilty.

"Writing, like reading, was one other of my favourite diversions. And throughout my adolescent years I kept up an assiduous correspondence with dozens of pen-friends all over the world. We exchanged postage stamps and picture postcards and letters. Mine were always lengthy epistles describing my various interests and occupations, and to some of my favorite pen-friends I would often send a short story of my own invention, drawn along the lines of my grandmother's bedtime stories or those of Edgar Allan Poe. And that, I think, was when the urge to write first began to stir within me.

"I had no definite plans or ideas then of becoming a writer, or indeed of becoming any other sort of a career woman; for in the world in which I was born, and in the community in which I lived, the ultimate aim of all well-to-do parents was to arrange a good marriage for their growing daughters. Any other ideas would not only have been incomprehensible to them, but would have been looked upon with distaste and silent disapproval by the rest of the community.

"Nonetheless, I continued to write. Words were like pearls to me, and the paper I put them on was the string which held them together.

"The source of any material was generally a connection, albeit slight, with some sort of personal experience: a call on a friend, a visit to a new place, a festival, a celebration, indeed, even a scrap of conversation. I wrote a considerable amount of fiction too, and took particular delight in letting my characters wander unleashed into the most daunting situations in the territory of my imagination from which, with my inborn, undying optimism, I would then patiently and laboriously work out a plan to bring them back safe and unharmed. I hated sad, tragic endings, and would always wind up a story on a happy, triumphant note.

"Looking back upon it now, the time I gave to my work, and the pains I took over it, was a translation of the dormant ambition within me to become a writer. All I needed was a goad. And this came one year in the guise of a holiday to Cairo with my parents when I was still in my early teens.

"Cairo was my first experience of a big city—a dark, brilliant, warm city. And right from the start, I could sense its excitement and challenge. Its flamboyant street life was something quite unknown to us in the Sudan: the hawkers who peddled their wares, the clanging trams and open, horse-driven cabs,

cafes spilling with chattering crowds, cinemas, theatres. . . . All this held me breathless! And then it was, like the sudden burst of a volcano, that every dormant ambition within me was wildly clamouring for expression. All at once I wanted to be a writer, a journalist, a great woman traveller, doctor, a lawyer, . . . everything! And without knowing exactly where to begin or what I wanted to do, my one burning desire was *not* to go back to the stultifying sweetness of my secure, sheltered, well-organised life in the Sudan. *This* was the life for me! *This* was the world of the travel books I read! A hurried, pressing, garish world, true. But oh, how I longed to explore it!

"The logical end to all these childish dreams is, of course, anti-climatic. I did go back to the life I left. And I did suffer the miseries of frustrations and the awful black fear of the young, in the face of their unfulfilled ambitions, that life was well and truly over. But hope never really dies in the heart of the young. And under the warmth of my father's assurance that we would leave the Sudan as soon as the war (World War I) was over, and that I would be able to do all the things I wanted to do, my hope was reborn and once again life held forth the promise of fulfillment to each and every one of my young ambitions.

"Whether I could have realised them fully or in part, I have never ceased to wonder. Shortly after the war, my father and mother died suddenly within two months of each other, and grandmother died three months later. Everything did shift for me then, though not in the way I had wanted it to shift. The sun simply went out and the horizon disappeared, and in the tragic days that followed I had little or no chance of thinking about my own personal ambitions. The predominant theme in my life became the care and welfare of my younger brothers and sisters.

"Conversely, in the process of coping with the enormous changes which now began to shape my future, I aquired a wealth of experience which enriched my life and gave it the true values I really needed, particularly when times became not only more difficult, but harsh and tragic and disastrous.

"In the later years when my family commitments had considerably eased and continual parental care was no more so pressing, I needed no inducement to resort to pen and paper to fill in a pleasant leisurely hour.

"I wrote my first short story in 1958 when I was holidaying in Switzerland on my way to London where I was considering establishing my residence. It was a true story, a personal experience. And except for the last paragraph which I had to change for personal reasons, I added no fiction to it. It was called 'Train Encounter,' for it all happened one day during a seven-hour journey from Assuit (a province in Upper Egypt) to Cairo. And on the insistence of a friend who had read and liked the story, I sent it to a Swiss publisher. It appeared shortly after in a bimonthly Swiss magazine called *Die Frau* (No. 92, April, 1958) under the title *Erlebnis in der Eisenbahn* and translated into German.

"I was greatly encouraged by the success of this story for it was my first appearance in print, and I proceeded to London with high hopes of becoming a successful short story writer. But that, as I was soon to discover, was not as easy as I had anticipated. For not only the theme of my stories (and I wrote dozens of them) but the very background in which they unfolded was out of context with the established genre of the English short story magazines. And, as I knew very little of the English way of life in those days, I considered it unwise

Iblees, the Devil, was one morning sitting in the corner of a road, ...when an old crone came stumping by and asked him why he looked so pensive. ■ (From "The Old Crone Who Was More Wily than Iblees," in *Egyptian and Sudanese Folk-Tales,* retold by Helen Mitchnik. Illustrated by Eric Fraser.)

to persist in continuing to write short stories for the English magazines unless I became more familiar with the background in which I would recount them.

"Reluctantly, therefore, I gave up short story writing and, being a linguist and anxious to find myself a full-time occupation, I took up industrial and commercial translation and interpreting work. But the urge to write would not be quelled, and once again I reverted to writing in my leisure time, thus unwittingly compiling a history of my own childhood in the Sudan.

"Curtis Brown (the literary agency to whom I had sent the manuscript) were highly enthusiastic about the book. They, however, expressed their fear that publishers might find the book much too gentle to get enough notice (and I quote) 'in these days when it is mostly violence and horror which seems to attract the attention of the reviewers. . . .' How right they were!

"Ironically, it is precisely this insatiable quest for horror and violence which, over the years I have lived in the West, have made me turn more and more in nostalgic longing to the sweet, serene world of my childhood. Or was it perhaps the conflicting 'pull' of East and West upon me? I had never been consciously aware of it before, nor do I now, or would indeed at any other time, try to resist it or think of choosing between one and the other anymore than I would have thought of choosing between my father and mother. I still love their two worlds with the same deep, intense passion that I have loved them both.

"Admittedly, despite the initial difficulties and disheartening frustrations I had to contend with in striving to adjust myself to a new and unfamiliar ambience, my life in the West has been a full and rewarding life, enriched by the exciting challenge of every new day, and I can now look back upon it with a deep inner sense of quiet fulfillment.

"But I feel, at the same time, that I must preserve whole and intact that part of me which was born in the Sudan, and was shaped and moulded in the stream of its unhurried days.

"That was the spirit which moved me to write the *Folk-Tales*. And in so doing, I did relive every precious moment of my cherished world—the sweet, serene world of my childhood.

"I consider community life the very backbone of a society, and would very much like to see it revived in the present day way of life in the West. It would mean association with others, sharing ideas and ideals, all of which are sadly lacking in today's modern society where radio and television seem to have become the only focus of interest. I am greatly interested in people and outdoor life and, being a linguist fluent in English, French, Italian, Spanish, and a little German, I derive great joy in travelling to foreign lands and communicating with the local inhabitants."

MONTGOMERY, Elizabeth Rider   1902-1985

OBITUARY NOTICE—See sketch in *SATA* Volume 34: Born July 12, 1902, in Huaras, Peru; died February 19, 1985. Elementary school teacher and author. Montgomery's first book, the reading primer *We Look and See,* was written as a result of her dissatisfaction with the books available for her use as a teacher. She eventually left the teaching profession and worked as a staff writer for Scott, Foresman & Co. from 1938 to 1963. Among her more than seventy works are textbooks, fiction, nonfiction, and biographies, including *Bonnie's Baby Brother, The Mystery of Edison Brown, Two Kinds of Courage, Henry Ford: Automotive Pioneer,* and *Duke Ellington: King of Jazz.* She also wrote several plays like "Old Pipes and the Dryad" and "Knights of the Silver Shield." Montgomery received the National Presswomen and Penwomen awards as well as other prizes.

FOR MORE INFORMATION SEE: Authors of Books for Young People, 2nd edition, Scarecrow, 1971; *Contemporary Authors, New Revision Series,* Volume 3, Gale, 1981; *Who's Who of American Women,* 12th edition, Marquis, 1981; *International Authors and Writers Who's Who,* 9th edition, International Biographical Centre, 1982. Obituaries: *New London Day,* February 21, 1985.

MYERS, Walter Dean 1937-

PERSONAL: Born August 12, 1937, in Martinsburg, W.Va.; children: Karen, Michael, Christopher. *Education:* Attended State College of the City University of New York; Empire State College, B.A. *Home:* Jersey City, N.J.

CAREER: New York State Department of Labor, Brooklyn, employment supervisor, 1966-69; Bobbs-Merrill Co., Inc. (publisher), New York, N.Y., senior trade editor, 1970-77; full time writer, 1977—. Has also taught creative writing and Black history on a part time basis in New York City, 1974-75. *Military service:* U.S. Army, 1954-57. *Awards, honors:* Council on Interacial Books for Children Award, 1968, for the manuscript of *Where Does the Day Go?;* Woodward Park School Annual Book Award, 1976, for *Fast Sam, Cool Clyde and Stuff; The Young Landlords* was chosen one of American Library Association's "Best Books for Young Adults," 1979, and *Hoops* was chosen, 1982; Coretta Scott King Award, 1980, for *The Young Landlord*, 1985, for *Motown and Didi: A Love Story; The Legend of Tarik* was chosen as a Notable Children's Trade Book in Social Studies, 1982.

WRITINGS—Juvenile: *Where Does the Day Go?* (illustrated by Leo Carty), Parents Magazine Press, 1969; *The Dragon Takes a Wife* (illustrated by Ann Grifalconi), Bobbs-Merrill, 1972; *The Dancers* (illustrated by Anne Rockwell), Parents Magazine Press, 1972; *Fly, Jimmy, Fly!* (illustrated by Moneta Barnett), Putnam, 1974; *The World of Work: A Guide to*

WALTER DEAN MYERS

You ever have an idea that really sounds good until you do it and find out how stupid it was? ∎
(Jacket illustration by Diane de Groat from *The Young Landlords* by Walter Dean Myers.)

And at home
sitting loose-legged on the linoleum
in the sun slant
and fire escape shadow prison
and right in the middle of fatback
and collard greens smells
Jimmy imagined himself flying
flying and sailing and soaring

above the red-brick buildings
and the tingle-tangled antennas

(From *Fly, Jimmy, Fly!* by Walter Dean Myers. Illustrated by Moneta Barnett.)

Choosing a Career, Bobbs-Merrill, 1975; *Fast Sam, Cool Clyde, and Stuff* (ALA Notable Book), Viking, 1975; *Social Welfare,* F. Watts, 1976; *Brainstorm* (illustrated with photographs by Chuck Freedman), F. Watts, 1977; *Mojo and the Russians,* Viking, 1977. *It Ain't All for Nothin',* Viking, 1978; *The Young Landlords,* Viking, 1979; *The Black Pearl and the Ghost; or, One Mystery after Another* (illustrated by Robert Quackenbush), Viking, 1980; *The Golden Serpent* (illustrated by Alice Provensen and Martin Provensen), Viking, 1980; *Hoops,* Delacorte, 1981; *The Legend of Tarik* (illustrated by Troy Howell), Viking, 1981; *Won't Know Till I Get There,* Viking, 1982; *The Nicholas Factor,* Viking, 1983; *Tales of a Dead King,* Morrow, 1983; *Mr. Monkey and the Gotcha Bird* (illustrated by Leslie Morrill), Delacorte, 1984; *Motown and Didi: A Love Story,* Viking, 1984; *The Outside Shot,* Delacorte, 1984.

Short stories represented in anthologies, including *What We Must See: Young Black Storytellers,* edited by Orde Coombs, Dodd, 1971, and *We Be Word Sorcerers: 25 Stories by Black Americans,* edited by Sonia Sanchez, Bantam, 1973. Contributor of articles and fiction to periodicals, including *Black Creation* and *Black World.*

SIDELIGHTS: "Thinking back to my boyhood days, I remember the bright sun on Harlem streets, the easy rhythms of black and brown bodies moving along the tar and asphalt pavement, the sounds of hundreds of children streaming in and out of red brick tenements. I remember La Marketa, in East Harlem, where people spoke a multitude of languages and the Penn Central rumbled overhead. I remember playing basketball in Morningside Park until it was too dark to see the basket and then climbing over the fence to go home.

"Harlem was a place of affirmation. The excitement of city living exploded in the teeming streets. If there was a notion that as a Black child, I was to be denied easy access to other worlds, it mattered little to me if I could have this much life in the place I found myself.

"I learned to read early on. I don't actually recall the process of learning, but I do remember reading aloud to my mother from the daily newspaper as she did housework, when I was about five or six. I sensed a connection between myself and the worlds I read about in books, a connection that I was hesitant to share with my friends, perhaps because I wasn't really sure just why it seemed so important to me.

"My education bumped along. I spoke poorly, rushing words out in a bewildering jumble, hating the patience of my teachers as much as the ridicule of my classmates as I tried to express myself. I was frequently in trouble in school, sitting in the back of the room or in the principal's office. It was during one of these periods, in the fifth grade, that an already annoyed teacher caught me reading a comic book under the desk. Of course, she tore it up, but the next day she came in with a pile of books and announced that, if indeed I was going to spend so much time sitting in the back of the room and reading, I should at least read something good. Suddenly this teacher had given a direction to my reading. I still remember the first book she gave me, *East of the Sun, and West of the Moon.* Reading took on a new dimension for me.

"By high school I had a part-time job in the garment district and had purchased, with my father's help, my first typewriter. I wrote short stories and laboriously constructed poems. I enjoyed writing as I had enjoyed reading. Again, it seemed a connection with things and events that I was not part of in 'real' life. More an observer than a doer, I was on my way to becoming a writer. I just didn't know it yet.

We then hang the bowler from the ceiling and put a flashlight behind it. When the ghost wakes and sees the tiny spots of light, he will think that they are stars . . . . ■ (From "The Ghost of Bleek Manor," in *The Black Pearl and the Ghost; or, One Mystery after Another* by Walter Dean Myers. Illustrated by Robert Quackenbush.)

"My parents couldn't afford college for me, so after high school I went into the Army. I had six months' training in electronics, then spent the rest of my enlistment playing basketball.

"After the service I returned to New York and a series of jobs. By this time I had decided that what I wanted to do most was to write. Writing seemed, and still seems to be, my major involvement with life. I can reach people through my writing, and I can use that writing as a point of reference in my real-life encounters. The sense of isolation I felt as a young person is now relieved by the connecting links of my stories.

"I enjoy writing for young people because the forms are less constricting, more forgiving to the stretched imagination. I particularly enjoy writing about the city life I know best. Ultimately, what I want to do with my writing is make the connection—reach out and touch the lives of my characters and share them with a reader."

FOR MORE INFORMATION SEE: Theressa G. Rush and others, *Black American Writers: Past and Present,* Scarecrow Press, 1975.

NASH, Mary (Hughes)   1925-

PERSONAL: Born July 7, 1925, in Milwaukee, Wis.; daughter of James Hurd (a lawyer) and Caroline (Upham) Hughes; divorced; children: Norman, Hollister, Thomas. *Education:* Radcliffe College, B.A., 1951; University of Washington, Seattle, M.A., 1954. *Politics:* Democrat. *Religion:* Unitarian–Universalist. *Agent:* Russell & Volkening, Inc., 551 Fifth Ave., New York, N.Y. 10017.

CAREER: Writer, beginning 1958.

*WRITINGS—*All for children, except as indicated; all fiction, except as indicated: *While Mrs. Coverlet Was Away* (illustrated by Garrett Price), Little, Brown, 1958; *Mrs. Coverlet's Magicians* (illustrated by G. Price), Little, Brown, 1961; *The Even Temperature in the Cave, and Other Stories,* Little, Brown, 1963; *Mrs. Coverlet's Detectives* (illustrated by G. Price), Little, Brown, 1965; *The Provoked Wife: The Life and Times of Susannah Cibber* (adult biography), Little, Brown, 1977. Contributor of articles and stories to periodicals, including *Good Housekeeping, New Yorker, Pacific Spectator, Redbook,* and *Horn Book.*

SIDELIGHTS: "The great unfailing pleasure in my childhood was my books, and I have always felt a kind of debt to the authors who wrote them for me. It would be a fine feeling, in my turn, to pass this pleasure to other children today." [Martha E. Ward and Dorothy A. Marquardt, *Authors of Books for Young People,* 2nd edition, Scarecrow, 1971.]

HOBBIES AND OTHER INTERESTS: Skiing, gardening, reading, and music.

FOR MORE INFORMATION SEE: Horn Book, April, 1965; Martha E. Ward and Dorothy A. Marquardt, *Authors of Books for Young People,* 2nd edition, Scarecrow, 1971.

NASTICK, Sharon   1954-

PERSONAL: Born July 30, 1954, in Washington, D.C.; daughter of Michael J. (a federal employee) and Mary A. (a homemaker; maiden name, Summers) Nastick. *Education:* Metropolitan State College, B.A., 1977. *Politics:* Democrat. *Religion:* Catholic. *Residence:* Denver, Colo. *Address:* c/o Harper & Row, 10 East 53rd St., New York, N.Y. 10022.

CAREER: Walden Books, Aurora, Colo., sales clerk, 1978-80; Denver Public Library, Denver, Colo., clerk/typist in children's library, 1980—. *Member:* Colorado Author's League, St. James Choir.

*WRITINGS—*All for children: *Mr. Radagast Makes an Unexpected Journey* (illustrated by Judy Glasser), Harper, 1981; *So You Think You've Got Problems: Twelve Stubborn Saints and Their Pushy Parents* (illustrated by James E. McIlrath), Our Sunday Visitor, 1982.

WORK IN PROGRESS: "I'm currently working on two books. One is a ghost story about a little girl whose parents have recently divorced, and the other is about a girls' football team. No titles as yet."

SIDELIGHTS: "As early as I can remember, I was telling myself stories. I remember, after being put to bed, waiting until my door was closed, then looking at storybooks under the nightlight after I was supposed to be asleep, and making up stories of my own to go with the pictures.

"I taught myself to read when I was four, and I have read voraciously ever since, with a special fondness for fantasy and

SHARON NASTICK

"Who *dares*," the teacher rumbled in a voice quite unlike the one they knew, "to interrupt the Great Radagast in so rude and crude a fashion?..." ■ (From *Mr. Radagast Makes an Unexpected Journey* by Sharon Nastick. Illustrated by Judy Glasser.)

science fiction. Before I was twelve, I had read most of Jules Verne and Robert Louis Stevenson. Anything marked 'classic' drew me like a magnet; after all, if it was 'classic,' it had to be good, didn't it? I also read the five-volume collection of Ogden Nash's poetry which I found on my parents' bookshelves, large chunks of which I can still recite at the slightest provocation.

"What sets me off? Curiosity. Wondering what people think, why they do what they do, why 'things' are the way they are. And what would happen if some little thing, or everything, was changed.

"I first heard of the theory of immaterialism in a college literature class. I spent the rest of the period doodling in my notebook (just like Conrad!) and turning the idea over in my mind. If things existed only because we believed in them, what would happen if we stopped believing in them? Where would they go? Could they be brought back? By the time I left the class, I had the first chapter of *Mr. Radagast* written in my mind. He was not based on any teacher *I* ever had, I hasten to add; he is simply the most boring teacher I could ever

imagine. I hope he returned from his journey a little less boring.

"*So You Think You've Got Problems* is about Catholic saints who had trouble with their parents. In parochial school, I often heard of future saints who grieved their parents (such as St. Augustine), but rarely heard of parents who grieved their saintly children. Research turned up a number of saints who were drafted into the army, held prisoner in their own homes, married at an extremely early age, or, in the case of St. Catherine of Siena, forced into doing all the housework in order to discourage them from their original vocations. The format I used— a series of conversations between the author and her guardian angel—allowed me to interject humor into what otherwise could have been a grim group of biographies."

HOBBIES AND OTHER INTERESTS: "I've always been powerfully attracted to Britain, maybe because so much of my early reading was British: Arthurian legends, Sherlock Holmes, Dickens, Lewis, Tolkien. I made my first visit there last year and can't wait to go back! I'm also interested in music, from Vivaldi to Van Halen, broadway musicals, and film soundtracks. Long walks, especially near water, and bike rides are also special interests."

NURNBERG, Maxwell   1897-1984

OBITUARY NOTICE—See sketch in *SATA* Volume 27: Born December 11, 1897, in Poland; died December 22, 1984, in Brooklyn, N.Y. Educator, etymologist, playwright, and author. Nurnberg was a teacher of English and head of the English department at Abraham Lincoln High School in Brooklyn from 1930 until his retirement in 1966. Among his juvenile works are *Wonders in Words, All about Words, Fun with Words,* and *I Always Look Up the Word "Egregious."* Nurnberg's adult writings include *What's the Good Word?* and *How to Build a Better Vocabulary.* He was also the author of a play entitled *Chalk Dust,* written with Harold Clarke.

FOR MORE INFORMATION SEE: Contemporary Authors, New Revision Series, Volume 2, Gale, 1981. *Obituaries: New York Times,* December 24, 1984.

OSBORNE, Mary Pope   1949-

BRIEF ENTRY: Born May 20, 1949, in Fort Sill, Okla. Author of novels for young adults. Osborne cites her extensive traveling as one of the forces behind her writing. The daughter of a U.S. Army colonel, her childhood was spent on various Army posts in the southern United States and Salzburg, Austria. After graduating from the University of North Carolina at Chapel Hill in 1971, she moved to Europe and spent a year traveling overland through Asia to Nepal. It was while she was on a theater road tour with her husband, actor Will Osborne, that she began her writing career. In three novels for young adults, Osborne effectively reveals the difficult situations and conflicts faced by adolescents.

Booklist called *Run, Run as Fast as You Can* (Dial, 1982) "a grim but moving story," adding, "Osborne's first novel is distinguished by a clarity of writing and finely wrought characters.'' Those characters include eleven-year-old Hallie who realizes the triviality of normal sixth-grade concerns (like clothing, make-up, and popularity) when faced with the imminent death of her younger brother. In *Love Always, Blue* (Dial, 1984), Osborne explores the effect on adolescents when parents separate. Fifteen-year-old Blue Murray blames her mother for the family's break-up until she comes to terms with the severity of her father's own personal problems. *School Library Journal* noted, ''There are no bad guys here, just three people, each trying to work through their own part of a complex problem.'' Osborne's latest novel is *Best Wishes, Joe Brady* (Dial, 1984), the story of an eighteen-year-old North Carolina girl who falls in love with a summer stock actor. Currently, Osborne is working on a book for younger readers as well as a novel told through the letters and diary entries of a teenage boy. *Home and office:* 325 Bleecker St., New York, N.Y. 10014.

FOR MORE INFORMATION SEE: Contemporary Authors, Volume 111, Gale, 1984.

PAIGE, Harry W. 1922-

PERSONAL: Born September 25, 1922, in Syracuse, N.Y.; son of Montford S. and Ruth (Converse) Paige; married Ruth Killough (a high school teacher), March 16, 1946; children: Sandra P. Nelson, Judith Ann McKinnon. *Education:* Union College, A.B., 1946; State University of New York at Albany, M.A., 1953, Ph.D., 1967. *Politics:* Independent. *Religion:* Roman Catholic. *Home:* Meadow East, Apt. E-5, Potsdam, N.Y. 13676. *Agent:* Carol Mann, 174 Pacific St., Brooklyn, N.Y. 11201. *Office:* Department of Liberal Studies, Clarkson College, Potsdam, N.Y. 13676.

CAREER: Clarkson College, Potsdam, N.Y., assistant professor, 1953-60, professor of humanities, 1966—; Rockland Community College, Suffern, N.Y., associate professor, 1960-62. Tennis professional, summers, 1956-66; visiting professor of creative writing, New Mexico State University, 1973-74. *Military service:* U.S. Army Air Force, 1943-45.

WRITINGS: Songs of the Teton Sioux, Westernlore, 1970; *Wade's Place* (young adult), Scholastic Book Services, 1973; *Night at Red Mesa,* McCormick-Mathers, 1975; *The CB Mystery,* McCormick-Mathers, 1978; *Johnny Stands* (young adult), Warne, 1982; *The Summer War* (young adult), Warne, 1983; *Shadow on the Sun* (young adult), Warne, 1984.

WORK IN PROGRESS: Red Dragon, a young adult story of northern Ireland.

SIDELIGHTS: ''When I was in the third grade or so, I won a story writing contest (the prize was a book) and, although I didn't know it at the time, it set a pattern. Writing was something I always came back to, whether I was in the service, a tennis professional or a college professor. In fact, I think I chose college teaching because it gave me the time and the atmosphere in which to write.

(Jacket illustration by Bob Karalus from *Johnny Stands* by Harry W. Paige.)

HARRY W. PAIGE

"I started sending my work out in the early 50s. It was mostly poetry then and I published in the *New York Times, Saturday Review, Spirit,* and many others. Then, over the years, I wrote and published one-act plays, articles, and short stories.

"I didn't attempt a longer work until I was forced to in the writing of my doctoral dissertation. I wrote it on the *Songs of the Teton Sioux* (published by Westernlore) because of my long-standing interest in Native Americans and in the West and because I didn't want to go over the usual academic ground. To gather research, I went to the Rosebud and Pine Ridge Sioux Reservations in South Dakota, lived among the Sioux and learned their language, Lakota. The resulting work, the first literary study of the songs of the Plains' Indians, was well received.

"After that, I tried my first young adult novel, *Wade's Place,* and since its publication in 1973 it has sold over 200,000 copies. In later works, *Night at Red Mesa* and *Johnny Stands,* I returned to Indian themes.

"I like to write about the West and its people. The times spent on Indian Reservations and in Las Cruces, New Mexico have given me enough material to keep me going until I return. The fact that I know the West as an 'outsider' and an Easterner has, I feel, given me a valuable perspective, helping me to see objectively and avoid confusing the myths with the reality.

"I try not to write down to younger readers. And I try to deal with themes I consider important—the rites of passage, divided loyalties, self-betrayals—the same things I write about in my adult fiction.

"In recent years I have discovered that my paternal grandfather and some other relatives had written stories, poems, and books, and so, in the absence of more logical explanations for my own writing, I can always credit it to heredity. I feel that

writing and the other arts contain a good deal of mystery and I become inarticulate when I try to explain too much."

Paige's works are included in the deGrummond Collection at the University of Southern Mississippi.

PEET, William Bartlett   1915-
   (Bill Peet)

PERSONAL: Born January 29, 1915, in Grandview, Ind.; son of Orion Hopkins (a salesman) and Emma (a teacher; maiden name, Thorpe) Peed; married Margaret Brunst, November 30, 1937; children: Bill, Jr., Stephen. *Education:* John Herron Art Institute, 1933-36. *Home:* Studio City, Calif.

CAREER: Worked briefly as an artist for greeting card company in the Middle West, 1936-37; Walt Disney Studios, Hollywood, Calif., sketch artist and continuity illustrator for motion picture industry, then screenwriter, 1937-64; author and illustrator of children's books. *Awards, honors:* Prizes for paintings at exhibits in Indianapolis and Chicago, 1934-37; John Herron Art Institute citation, 1958, as one of the outstanding students in the history of the school; *Box Office* (magazine) Blue Ribbon award, 1961, 1964, for the best screenplay; Indiana Author's Day Award for most distinguished Hoosier book of the year for children, 1967, for *Capyboppy;* Southern California Council on Literature for Children and Young People Award for illustration, 1967, for *Farewell to Shady Glade;* Colorado Children's Book Award, 1976, for

WILLIAM BARTLETT PEET

Then, keeping an eye out for the bear, she crept along through the shadows as slinky as a fox. ∎
(From *Big Bad Bruce* by Bill Peet. Illustrated by the author.)

How Droofus the Dragon Lost His Head; California Reading Association Young Reader Medal, 1976, for *How Droofus the Dragon Lost His Head,* and 1980, for *Big Bad Bruce;* Little Archer Award from the University of Wisconsin-Oshkosh, 1977, for *Cyrus, the Unsinkable Sea Serpent;* Georgia Picture Book Award, 1979, for *Big Bad Bruce;* International Reading Association "Children's Choice" award, 1982, for *Encore for Eleanor;* California Reading Association's Significant Author Award, 1983; George G. Stone Center Recognition of Merit Award for his body of work, 1985.

WRITINGS—All self-illustrated; all published by Houghton, except as indicated: *Hubert's Hair-Raising Adventure,* 1959; *Huge Harold,* 1961; *Smokey,* 1962; *The Pinkish, Purplish, Bluish Egg,* 1963; *Ella,* 1964; *Randy's Dandy Lions,* 1964; *Chester the Worldly Pig,* 1965; *Kermit the Hermit,* 1965; *Farewell to Shady Glade,* 1966; *Capyboppy,* 1966; *Buford, the Little Bighorn,* 1967; *Jennifer and Josephine,* 1967; *Fly Homer Fly,* 1969; *The Whingdingdilly,* 1970; *The Wump World (and Pollutus),* 1970; *How Droofus the Dragon Lost His Head,* 1971; *The Caboose Who Got Loose,* 1971; *The Ant and the Elephant,* 1972; *Countdown to Christmas,* Golden Gate, 1972; *The Spooky Tail of Prewitt Peacock,* 1973; *Merle the High*

Flying Squirrel, 1974; *Cyrus, the Unsinkable Sea Serpent,* 1975; *The Gnats of Knotty Pine,* 1975; *Big Bad Bruce,* 1977; *Eli,* 1978; *Cowardly Clyde,* 1979; *Encore for Eleanor,* 1981; *The Luckiest One of All,* 1982; *No Such Things,* 1983; *Pamela Camel,* 1984; *The Kweeks of Kookatumdee,* 1985.

Screenplays; all written with others: *Pinnochio,* 1940; *Dumbo,* 1941; *Fantasia,* 1941; *Song of the South,* 1946; *Cinderella,* 1950; *Alice in Wonderland,* 1951; *Peter Pan,* 1953; *Sleeping Beauty,* 1959; *One Hundred and One Dalmations,* 1961; *The Sword in the Stone,* 1963. Also author of short subject screenplays.

SIDELIGHTS: "I was born on **January 29, 1915,** in Grandview, Indiana, a very small town on the bank of the Ohio River. My only vague memory of Grandview is the two pigs we raised in a pen in our back yard, one dull white, and the other rusty red. When I was three my family decided to move to the city of Indianapolis.

"This was the time of World War I, and our first home in Indianapolis was just a block from the railroad and I can remember the long lines of snow-covered army tanks rumbling by on flatcars during the first winter in the city.

"My father was in the Army but never in the war. Before his company could be shipped overseas, it was over. After the war he taught school for a number of years, then became a traveling salesman. Since he was on the road much of the time, selling everything from house paint to popcorn machines, we saw very little of him. My mother was a handwriting teacher and a supervisor of penmanship in the Indianapolis schools for over thirty-five years. During that time she produced a series of text books on handwriting. I have three brothers, but the youngest one, Jim, wasn't born until I was fifteen, so I really grew up with just two brothers, George and O. H., who much prefers the initials to his first and second names. Today George is a commercial artist in New York City, O. H. is a rocket test engineer at Cape Kennedy, and Jim is a furniture designer in Hickory, North Carolina.

"Looking back on those early days in Indianapolis I realize that it was as good a place as any for a boy to spend his childhood. Until I was twelve we lived near the edge of the city no more than a half-hour hike from the open countryside, with its small rivers and creeks that went winding through the rolling hills and wooded ravines. On Saturdays and all during the summer my two brothers and I along with the neighborhood boys would organize safaris to explore this region.

"One of the most memorable experiences of early childhood was a trip to my grandfather's farm in southern Indiana. It was the first train trip for me and my two brothers, something of a treat in itself. Not that it was at all eventful. The old two-car train clickety-clacked along through a hilly landscape of barns and haystacks dotted with horses, cows, and pigs. Past small towns, over rivers and creeks, and through forests. Since I was so very fond of the farm country, it was a great pleasure to see it all pass by in rapid review, and so very conveniently. A fine show to the very last scene, which was the railway station in the historic old town of Vincennes. There we were met by our grandfather in his dusty old touring car and we were off again, bouncing along for the last thirty-five miles on rambling dirt roads that were forever doubling back and forth all over the country.

"Grandfather's rustic old farm was far more exciting and spectacular than the countryside around Indianapolis, for the land that was not planted in corn and wheat was a thriving wilderness with steep-walled gullies of slate and limestone carved out by the twisting creeks, and the whole place was teeming with wildlife.

"Hawks and buzzards sailed above the treetops, rabbits scampered everywhere, and six-foot blacksnakes slithered through the fields. The dark woods swarmed with squirrels, chipmunks, weasels, opossums, and raccoons. There were foxes too, but I caught only a very brief glimpse of one—a flash of red streaking along a picket fence—and in seconds he disappeared into the brush.

"Animals have always been of special interest to me and I often regretted that Indianapolis had no zoo. My first visit to a zoo was on a trip to Cincinnati. I wanted to make the most of it, so I spent all the money I had saved from selling newspapers to buy film for a small box camera, hoping to get a picture of every animal there. Fortunately our day at the zoo was sunny and bright, just right for picture taking, and I went

A ship was about to set sail and Cyrus perked up. ■ (From *Cyrus, the Unsinkable Sea Serpent* by Bill Peet. Illustrated by the author.)

How could he eat someone just after saving his life? It didn't seem right. . . . ■ (From *How Droofus the Dragon Lost His Head* by Bill Peet. Illustrated by the author.)

clicking merrily away through the whole afternoon, never suspecting that the shutter wasn't working and not a single one of the pictures would turn out. But not all was lost, for I learned a bit of a lesson from that deceitful little camera which made all the proper clicking sounds without taking a picture. On future trips to the zoo I was armed with a sketch pad and pencil; then if the pictures didn't turn out I had only myself to blame.

"Drawing had been my main hobby from the time I was old enough to wield a crayon, and since my mother was a handwriting teacher there was always plenty of paper about the house. This hobby was especially handy in the wintertime after the first snows had turned to sleet and slush and the sledding and the snowball wars had become impossible. I drew just about anything that came to mind, all sorts of animals (including dragons, trains, fire engines, racing cars, airplanes, gladiators, pioneers fighting Indians, World War I battles, Revolutionary War battles, football games, prizefights, or what have you.

"There was an art class in grammar school, but that wasn't enough, and my drawing soon crept into the other classes. I always kept a small tablet in my desk and at every chance I would sneak a drawing into it. Quite often I'd be surprised by the teacher standing over me and my tablet would be confiscated. However, on one occasion it was different. This particular teacher snatched my tablet away just as the others had done and marched to the front of the room with it. Then turning to the class she said, 'I want you to see what William has been doing!' Then with an amused smile the teacher turned the pages for all to see. After returning the tablet she encouraged me with, 'I hope you will do something with your drawing someday.' I *did* have hopes of doing something with it, for in those days my secret ambition was to be an illustrator of animal stories. Yet, it was hard to believe that drawing could ever be practical as a career. It was too much fun and therefore it seemed wrong.

"Then at some point during high school it occurred to me that drawing was something I couldn't possibly give up, and somehow it must be turned into a profession. And upon graduation, to clinch matters, I was awarded a scholarship to the John Herron Art Institute there in Indianapolis where I studied drawing, painting, and design for the next three years. Outside of school in my spare time and during vacations I continued to

"Well, so far so bad," he muttered. . . . ■ (From *Chester the Worldly Pig* by Bill Peet. Illustrated by the author.)

sketch and paint. The subject matter of these pictures was usually the farm, the circus, the slums and shanty towns along the railroad, zoo animals, and a variety of quaint old characters.

"A number of these pictures received prizes, which was greatly encouraging, but after leaving school I realized I would have to do something else. I had met Margaret [Brunst] in art school and we were planning to be married as soon as I could figure out a way to make a living. What I needed was a steady job, and I found one at a greeting card company in Ohio. But I soon discovered it was not the job for me when I was told that rendering delicate roses and tulips for sympathy cards was my assignment for the summer.

"When I learned that there were opportunities for artists in the movie industry out in California, I headed west. There I became a sketch artist, laying out screen stories with a continuity of drawings, and as soon as the job began to show promise, Margaret and I were married."

Peet was one of many artists recruited by Disney during the Depression who served as the backbone for the Disney enterprise. "Disney got 'em for a dime a dozen." [Marshall Ing-

werson, "It's Just as if I Was Still 6—Drawing Lions in Books," *Christian Science Monitor,* November 9, 1981.[1]]

"As far as I was concerned, Disney was only going to be temporary, a way out of the dead end job I had in [the] greeting card company, but I ended up staying.

"Walt had an intuitive ability to see the better side of creative work but he rarely allowed anyone to think he was doing well. He thought he could get more out of you by keeping you in doubt." [Jim Trelease, "Disney Animator to Durable Author," *New York Times Book Review,* March 11, 1984.[2]]

1954. While still working for Disney, Peet made his first attempt to break away with a picture book, *The Luckiest One of All.* It was rejected by every publisher he approached. "I was pretty discouraged at the time but I never threw the story away and eventually, in 1982, it became my 27th book."[2]

1959. Houghton Mifflin published *Hubert's Hair-Raising Adventure.* Four books and five years later, Peet left the Disney studio for a studio of his own. "We have two sons, Bill and Steve, and when they were very small I would make up a bedtime story for them almost every night. With so much storytelling practice I began to think in terms of writing and as the years passed contributed more and more ideas to the motion picture stories. Finally I became a screenwriter, still illustrating the continuity. After all, I couldn't possibly give up the drawing habit. As a hobby I began to experiment with ideas for children's books. Once the first one was published it became more than a hobby, it grew into a second career. And just in time too. By then my bedtime story audience had grown up, Bill was in college, and Steve was in art school. Now my wife is my best audience and her interest and encouragement have been most important to the books.

"So my early ambition to illustrate animal stories was finally realized, and a little bit more, since I had never considered writing one. This way I can write about things I like to draw, which makes it more fun than work. And I still carry a tablet around with me and sneak a drawing into it now and then."

"Sometimes I feel like I'm basically doing the same thing as when I was six years old: drawing lions and tigers in books."[1]

Peet has found many fans in his large readership. "A lot of

As suddenly as that Buford became the star attraction at the Little Big Pine winter resort. ■
(From *Buford, the Little Bighorn* by Bill Peet. Illustrated by the author.)

times they think I'm about their age. They ask me what grade I'm in. They ask me which school I go to, what sports I play. . . . They say, 'If you're ever in Philadelphia please come and stay.' One wrote, 'I have read some of your funny books. They are very good. Please call me and we can talk. My dad will pay for the call.'''

Peet's titles have been published in many languages, including Swedish, German, Dutch, Japanese, French, Danish, Afrikaans, and many have been transcribed into Braille.

FOR MORE INFORMATION SEE: Books for Children, 1960-1965, American Library Association, 1966; Lee Kingman and others, compilers, *Illustrators of Children's Books: 1957-1966,* Horn Book, 1968: Nancy Larrick, *A Parent's Guide to Children's Reading,* 3rd edition, Doubleday, 1969; *Library Journal,* September, 1970; *Horn Book,* June, 1971; Doris de Montreville and Donna Hill, editors, *Third Book of Junior Authors,* H. W. Wilson, 1972; L. Kingman and others, compilers, *Illustrators of Children's Books: 1967-1976,* Horn Book, 1978; D. L. Kirkpatrick, *Twentieth-Century Children's Writers,* St. Martin's Press, 1978; *Christian Science Monitor,* November 9, 1981; *New York Times Book Review,* March 11, 1984.

PETRIE, Catherine   1947-

BRIEF ENTRY: Born October 22, 1947, in Elkhorn, Wis. Business owner and author of books for children. Petrie received her B.S. from the University of Wisconsin—Whitewater in 1969 and her M.S.E. from the same institution in 1972. She is currently continuing graduate study at the University of California in Los Angeles. From 1970 to 1981 she was employed as a reading consultant at various locations in South Dakota, Colorado, California, and Wisconsin. Since 1981 she has been owner and director of Professional Tour Consultants in Lake Geneva, Wis. As an author, Petrie utilizes short sentence structures, rhythm, rhyme, and simple vocabulary in her six books designed to aid children who are in the beginning-to-read stage. All published by Childrens Press, the titles are: *Hot Rod Harry* (1982), *Sand Box Betty* (1982), *Joshua James Likes Trucks* (1982), *Seed* (1983), *Night* (1983), and *Rain* (1983). *Home address:* Route 2, Petrie Rd., Lake Geneva, Wis. 53147.

FOR MORE INFORMATION SEE: Contemporary Authors, Volume 109, Gale, 1984.

PINKNEY, Jerry   1939-

PERSONAL: Born December 22, 1939, in Philadelphia, Pa.; married wife, Gloria; children: three sons, one daughter. *Education:* Attended Philadelphia Museum College of Art, 1957-59. *Home:* 41 Furnace Rock Rd., Croton-on-Hudson, N.Y. 10520.

CAREER: Worked as a designer/illustrator for various companies before opening his own studio, Jerry Pinkney, Inc., Croton-on-Hudson, N.Y., in 1971. Rhode Island School of Design, visiting critic, 1969-70, adjunct professor, 1971. Designer of the Harriet Tubman, Martin Luther King, Jr., Ben-

JERRY PINKNEY

jamin Banneker and Whitney Moore Young, Jr. commemorative stamps for the United States Postal Service "Black Heritage" series, and also designed the Honey Bee commemorative envelope for the postal service. Work has appeared in various exhibitions including Brooklyn Museum, National Center of Afro-American Artists, and Boston Museum of Fine Arts. *Awards, honors: Song of the Trees* won the Council on Interracial Books for Children Award, 1973, and was selected for the Children's Book Showcase, 1976; *Roll of Thunder, Hear My Cry* by Mildred D. Taylor was awarded the Newbery Medal and the *Boston Globe-Horn Book* Award, 1977; *Childtimes: A Three-Generation Memoir* and *Tonweya and the Eagles, and Other Lakota Indian Tales* were both selected for the American Institute of Graphic Arts Book Show, 1980; Carter G. Woodson Award for *Childtimes: A Three-Generation Memoir* and *Count on Your Fingers African Style; Count on Your Fingers African Style* received the Outstanding Science Book Award from the National Association of Science Teachers, 1980, and was chosen runner-up for the Coretta Scott King Award.

ILLUSTRATOR—All for children: Joyce Cooper Arkhurst, reteller, *The Adventures of Spider: West African Folk Tales,* Little, Brown, 1964; Adeline McCall, *This Is Music,* Allyn & Bacon, 1965; V. Mikhailovich Garshin, *The Traveling Frog,* McGraw, 1966; Lila Green, compiler, *Folktales and Fairytales of Africa,* Silver Burdett, 1967; Ken Sobol, *The Clock Museum,* McGraw, 1967; Harold J. Saleh, *Even Tiny Ants Must Sleep,* McGraw, 1967; John W. Spellman, editor, *The Beautiful Blue Jay, and Other Tales of India (Horn Book* honor list), Little, Brown, 1967; Ralph Dale, *Shoes, Pennies, and Rockets,* L. W. Singer, 1968; Traudl (pseudonym of Traudl Flaxman), *Kostas the Rooster,* Lothrop, 1968; Cora Annett, *Homerhenry,* Addison-Wesley, 1969; Irv Phillips, *The Twin Witches of Fingle Fu,* L. W. Singer, 1969; Fern Powell, *The Porcupine and the Tiger,* Lothrop, 1969; Ann Trofimuk, *Babushka and the Pig,* Houghton, 1969; Thelma Shaw, *Juano and the Wonderful Fresh Fish,* Addison-Wesley, 1969; K. Sobol, *Sizes and Shapes,* McGraw, 1969.

Francine Jacobs, adapter, *The King's Ditch: A Hawaiian Tale,* Coward, 1971; J. C. Arkhurst, *More Adventures of Spider,*

He stretched out on the ground and placed his head on her lap. He told her he was tired and wanted to rest. ■ (From "Wastewin and the Beaver," in *Tonweya and the Eagles, and Other Lakota Indian Tales,* retold by Rosebud Yellow Robe. Illustrated by Jerry Pinkney.)

(Jacket illustration by Jerry Pinkney from *Ji-Nongo-Nongo Means Riddles* by Verna Aardema.)

Scholastic Book Services, 1972; Adjai Robinson, *Femi and Old Grandaddie*, Coward, 1972; Mari Evans, *JD*, Doubleday, 1973; A. Robinson, *Kasho and the Twin Flutes*, Coward, 1973; Berniece Freschet, *Prince Littlefoot*, Cheshire, 1974; Beth P. Wilson, *The Great Minu*, Follett, 1974; Mildred D. Taylor, *Song of the Trees*, Dial, 1975; Cruz Martel, *Yagua Days*, Dial, 1976; M. D. Taylor, *Roll of Thunder, Hear My Cry*, Dial, 1976; Phyllis Green, *Mildred Murphy, How Does Your Garden Grow?*, Addison-Wesley, 1977; Eloise Greenfield, *Mary McLeod Bethune* (biography), Crowell, 1977; Verna Aardema, *Ji-Nongo-Nongo Means Riddles*, Four Winds Press, 1978; L. Green, reteller, *Tales from Africa*, Silver Burdett, 1979; Rosebud Yellow Robe, reteller, *Tonweya and the Eagles, and Other Lakota Indian Tales*, Dial, 1979; E. Greenfield and Lessie Jones Little, *Childtimes: A Three-Generation Memoir*, Crowell, 1979.

Virginia Hamilton, *Jahdu*, Greenwillow, 1980; Claudia Zaslavsky, *Count on Your Fingers African Style*, Crowell, 1980; Alice Childress, *Rainbow Jordan*, Coward, 1981; William Wise, *Monster Myths of Ancient Greece*, Putnam, 1981; Barbara Michels and Bettye White, editors, *Apples on a Stick: The Folklore of Black Children*, Coward, 1983; Valerie Flournoy, *The Patchwork Quilt*, Dial, 1985. Also illustrator of Helen Fletcher's *The Year Around Book*, McGraw. Contributor of illustrations to *Seventeen*, *Post*, *Boys' Life*, and *Essence*.

ADAPTATIONS: "The Patchwork Quilt" was presented on "Reading Rainbow," PBS-TV, June 25, 1985.

WORK IN PROGRESS: Illustrating Crescent Dragonwagon's *Half a Moon and One Whole Star*, for Macmillan.

SIDELIGHTS: **December 22, 1939.** Born in Philadelphia, Pennsylvania. "I was never a terrific reader and don't remember the books of my childhood. I remember comic books but never associated drawing with books and never thought of myself as an artist. I just drew anything. When I was eleven years old, I had a newspaper stand. When papers weren't selling well I'd draw what I saw around me, like the mannequins in the department store window across the street.

"Sketching and painting were new activities in our house— no one in the family had ever pursued fine art. I could draw as early as elementary school and often handled different projects through drawing. I was assigned every project that had to do with drawing, which made me feel special.

"My father was a very entertaining man with a wonderful personality, a jack-of-all trades. When my name came up in conversation, he would mention that I was an artist. People liked my father, and were willing to help me with scholarships for painting and drawing classes. I took advantage of that opportunity. During junior high and high school, I attended

Dobbins Vocational School for commercial art. As much as I enjoyed the challenge of commercial art, I never considered it a way of earning a living.

"Cartoonist, John Liney saw my work one day and invited me up to his studio, a block or two away from my newspaper stand. At that time I was using a simple sketch pad and a number two pencil and he gave me pencils, paper, and erasers. He introduced me to the possibility of making a living from art and inspired me as a young artist. I had to travel outside of my own neighborhood for art classes, and because I was often the only black kid in the class, I felt removed from the other students and the whole environment. I put up a barrier as a defense. John provided a good balance. We were able to communicate and our friendship was my first real exchange with another artist.

"My mother was also very encouraging. She was in many ways the catalyst who was always saying, 'You can do whatever you want to do.' My father, on the other hand, was a bit skeptical about the idea that his son might make a career of art. He liked the *idea* of my being an artist, and helped me at every opportunity, but when the time came for me to go off to college to study art formally, my mother had to convince him."

Attended Philadelphia Museum College of Art. "I earned a scholarship for two and one half years as a design student. It wasn't until the end of my first year of study that the Philadelphia School of Art became a college. After the switch-over, I was given the opportunity to take printmaking, painting, and drawing, even though I was an advertising design major. Had it not been for those three courses, I might have gone in another, more commercial direction.

"Art school introduced me to art on a level I had never experienced—an awareness of what my particular talents were. I was never a terrific reader or an adept speller, but when I sat down to draw, if something didn't work, I *made* it work. I loved the challenge. When I first came out of school, I freelanced in typography and worked in a flower shop in Philadelphia."

1960. "I had the opportunity to go to Boston and work for Rustcraft Greeting Card Company of Dedham, Massachusetts, in the studio card department. The type of drawing that was involved in studio cards was quite different from the kind of drawing I do now. It was more connected to design, to patterns, to textures and to lettering. I took an interest in other departments as well, and, on occasion, was asked to do more realistic drawing. I always had one foot in design and one in illustration. Though I hadn't much formal training in illustration, I had the desire to illustrate."

Began illustrating textbooks and children's books. "Boston was a good opportunity for me because it was a publishing

(Jacket illustration by Jerry Pinkney from *Rainbow Jordan* by Alice Childress.)

Jim was miserable. His favorite blue corduroy pants had been held together with patches; now they were beyond repair. ■ (From *The Patchwork Quilt* by Valerie Flournoy. Illustrated by Jerry Pinkney.)

town and I was there at a great time, a time during which publishers were reconstructing their ideas about textbooks. When I started illustrating, textbooks were illustrated in a realistic way, but suddenly, reading books and spellers became much more decorative and less realistic.

"The late part of the sixties and early seventies brought an awareness of black writers. Publishers sought out black artists to illustrate black subject matter and the work of black writers. And there I was. It was exciting, and gave me an opportunity which might have taken much longer had it not been for that movement.

"My first concern, however, was whether I was being considered for as assignment because of the merit of my work or because I was a black artist. Eventually, however, I under-

stood what the experience of being black could bring to my books."

From the very beginning of his career in illustration, Pinkney researched his material extensively and used both photographs and live models in developing his subjects. "I love detail and research everything. I enjoy research now, but in the beginning, I was very frustrated when I couldn't find the material I needed. I used to mix and match according to what I could find on a subject. The more I learned about research, the more excited I became about the possibilities. Now I do a tremendous amount of research.

"I use both photographs and models as references for my illustrations. For some of the early books, I shot Polaroids of myself, my wife Gloria, and my children. One of my skills is to be able to look at many different reference sources from which I then develop a character. Now I use models who resemble, as closely as possible, the characters I am going to portray, but I still take Polaroids. I don't work from life. I use models to explore body language rather than facial expression. Movement is very important in my work in developing a stronger relationship between the text and the illustration. As a result, my books have become more active and less designed. I have my models read the story, then I try to bring them right into it by asking them to act it out. My work with children has been a special experience. It's difficult to put kids in front of a camera, but if you can make them feel a connection between the act of modeling and the fact that they are working on a book in which they represent a specific character, they work harder.

"My drawings often give the illusion that I am approaching a subject for the first time; that is because I don't always recall how I solve problems—so each drawing has a freshness to it. I'm able to suggest mood or envision the characters for a book quickly. After reading a manuscript, I know what a character should look like. I'm terrible at perspective, however. As a result, I distort, but in a way that makes the illustrations work. I don't see things until I draw them. When I put a line down, the only thing I know is how it should feel and I know when it doesn't feel right.

"I work with a pencil in one hand and eraser in the other, not really knowing what I have until I put it down. I make very rough sketches. Finished drawings are done by putting the sketches on a light box. I draw, and when I put down a line that I don't like, I erase it, though I rarely erase it completely. You can see the process in the drawings themselves, especially those which deal with movement, such as the snake's head moving back and forth in *Kasho and the Twin Flutes*."

1969-1971. Served as a visiting critic and later as an adjunct professor at the Rhode Island School of Design. "When I was a visiting critic, I would go to the Rhode Island School of Design four times a semester to look at the work of students and talk about whatever problems they were having with it. I was not a professor or a teacher, so the input had to come from the students. It was a very informal but workable situation. I would also share my work with the students. We would sit on the floor with a pot of coffee and discuss our work. Later, I became an adjunct professor and things changed a bit because I had become part of the faculty. It wasn't as free. I enjoyed my three years there because it moved me out of the isolation of my studio and into talking and dealing with students. Bringing the students in contact with a working professional was a good policy. We shared similar problems—meeting deadlines, dealing with feelings when something was not working, and losing objectivity. I filled the gap between instructors and students. There was a communication."

1971. Moved to Croton-on-Hudson in New York, where Pinkney opened his own studio. As a freelancer, he has illustrated numerous children's books, magazine articles, record album covers, book jackets, and advertising assignments. "My studio is my home. I go to the studio in the early morning and usually work until 8:30 in the evening, five days a week, depending on how busy I am and how demanding my current project is.

"The creative process is similar for me no matter what kind of project I am working on because I always see my work as

(From *Childtimes* by Eloise Greenfield and Lessie Jones Little. Illustrated by Jerry Pinkney.)

attempting to solve a particular problem. The way I solve the problem changes, but not the fact that there are always problems to be solved. I see my work as an extension of myself; a way of getting in touch.

"The commercial projects I work on vary. I just finished a cover for *National Geographic,* four commercials for Kool Aid, and I'm working on decorating dinner plates and place settings for Dansk. Dansk chose twelve illustrators outside the area of china design in an attempt to bring a new look to their line. I designed a place setting, thirteen different individual pieces and a floral. They liked the idea of my line and my loose watercolor, but it couldn't be reproduced. We're now doing something they can produce very well. It's close to what Dansk has always been doing, but at the same time, there's me in it.

"Books give me a great feeling of personal and artistic satisfaction. *National Geographic* covers, or commemorative stamps have more to do with prestige. When I'm working on a book, I wish the phone would never ring. I love doing it. My satisfaction comes from the actual marks on the paper, and when it sings, it's magic. *National Geographic* covers mean dealing with people who want the work to meet a certain problem. Sometimes it robs you. It's hard to get a final product which is really satisfying that you love and they love.

"My wife has been a tremendous help to me. Stylistically, her influence grows out of her participation in my work process. She reads all the manuscripts I illustrate, has worked as my agent, and helped me find models. I often work from my first idea. She brings a fresh point of view or suggests new directions. The models respond to her when I'm not getting what I want. She takes the edge off and calms my craziness. Gloria and I met in high school, dated, and married while I was studying at Philadelphia College of Art. We've been married twenty-four years. She also has her own business as a silversmith, and decorates hats for fashion shows and limited clientele.

"We have four children. They all draw well, and two of my sons are pursuing art. When my daughter was working as a recreational therapist, she helped patients express themselves through drawing. My youngest son, Myles, whom I thought the most sensitive artist in the family, must have felt that the space was already taken up by his brothers. He wanted his own space. He's a musician and is interested in communications and film.

"I use my children's judgment and listen to their input. Now that they're older we share a dialogue about art. I advise them to 'explore' while they are young and going to school. I do the same by going to museums and shows. It's important to see what other artists are doing. Sometimes another point of view improves my work. I like to try new ideas now. It's a way of growing."

1977. Illustrated the biography, *Mary McLeod Bethune.* "There were no existing photographs of her as a little girl. I had to imagine what she looked like, beginning with her nose structure, working from photographs of her as an older woman. As we grow up, we change, but a certain likeness to our child-self remains."

1979. "*Tonweya and the Eagles, and Other Lakota Indian Tales* is my favorite book. It came at a time when I had gained

(From *Mary McLeod Bethune* by Eloise Greenfield. Illustrated by Jerry Pinkney.)

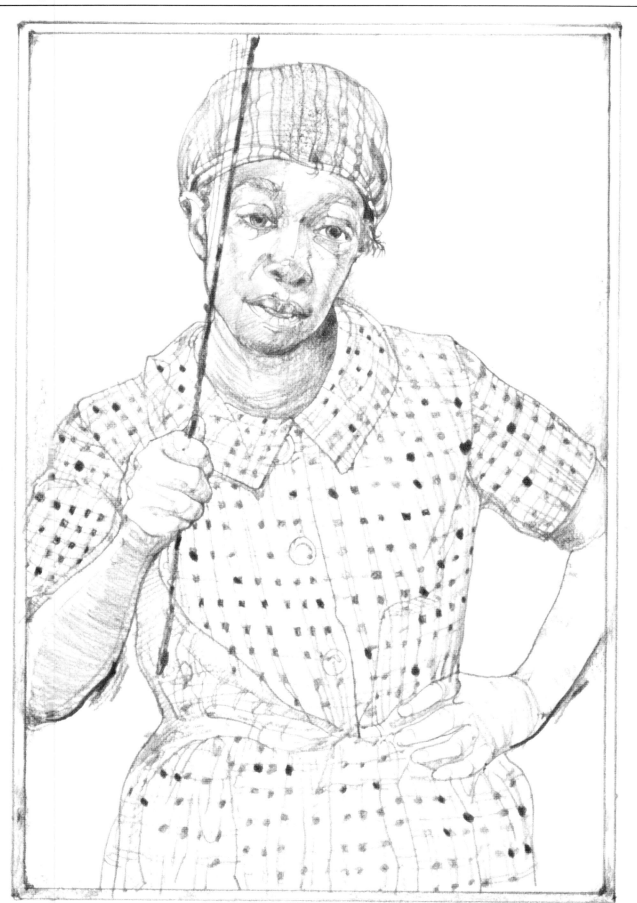

(From *Apples on a Stick: The Folklore of Black Children*, collected and edited by Barbara Michels and Bettye White. Illustrated by Jerry Pinkney.)

Promotional poster for "The Black Heritage Series" of postage stamps designed by Jerry Pinkney. (Copyright © 1983 by the U.S. Postal Service.)

(Jacket illustration by Jerry Pinkney from *Roll of Thunder, Hear My Cry* by Mildred D. Taylor.)

confidence in my drawings. *Tonweya* answers all the questions I was confronting in my work. I was finally able to articulate the animals, the Indians. It was terrific to create real animals—not make-believe animals standing up with little suits on—who communicate with the human characters.

"For *Tonweya* I worked from reference books but I also formed a relationship with the author, Rosebud Yellow Robe. Publishers prefer to keep the author and the illustrator very, very separate, but I initiated the contact, regardless. When I worked with Adjai Robinson, I again asked to be able to work with him, and I even had him review my sketches. It's a risk—an author could change my vision. That didn't happen in either case; both gave me helpful feedback and supplied me with references and photographs.

"Books are my first love because of the union of design and illustration. In working for reproduction, it is really a package. It has a cover, a jacket, an interior. The most exciting thing for me is to get a fresh book in the mail and open it for the first time."

Pinkney enjoys working with children. "A few years ago I did a wonderful project for 'Sesame Street.' The drawings look as fresh today as when I first made them. 'Animal Textures' are drawings with texture, like feathers or stripes on fur. They were blown up giving them an abstract quality, and on another page I drew the actual animals which corresponded to the textures. The kids had to identify which animal went with each texture. For *Contact* magazine, I drew 140 animals for a fea-

ture called 'Pocket Zoo.' The animals were made to be cut out and the kids could then mount them alongside all the information about the animals.

"Recently I took part in a show called 'And Peace Be With Thee,' sponsored by Children's Book Artists for Peace. I used twenty of the animals I designed for 'Pocket Zoo,' (some of which are extinct) and made a sort of animal domino—I started with extinct animals and progressed to real animals, to show how a war would cause all the animals on the planet to become extinct.

"Animals seem to have changed more than anything else in my illustration. Sometimes I humanize them, while at other times, I am much more realistic. Very often, I look back to my whimsical drawings in which animal poses were more like human poses with human gestures. Then I moved away from that and tried to capture the feeling of the animal, as well as its true-to-life characteristics. As with people, my research on animals is done through photographs. I keep a very large swipe file and a library, too.

"I often speak to elementary school children. I show slides, and the kids ask me all kinds of questions. I've also given talks at special schools for kids who have been in trouble, or kids who are struggling with learning disabilities. I try to encourage young people who are interested in becoming artists. I always tell them about the possibilities. When they ask me to look at their drawings after a lecture, I tell them their work looks good. What they are asking from me is the same thing I asked for—someone to pay attention.''

1982. Invited to serve on the United States Postal Stamp Advisory Committee, Pinkney designed the Harriet Tubman, Martin Luther King, Jr., Benjamin Banneker and Whitney Moore Young, Jr. commemorative stamps for the United States Postal Service 'Black Heritage' series. ''I've been making commemorative stamps for seven years now. Ten years ago I became aware that the postal service had decided to use people who were not part of the Department of Engraving to design stamps. I approached the art coordinator at the post office with my portfolio and three years later, the 'Black Heritage' series came out. I was contracted to do three more. I am also one of eighteen civilians serving on the Citizen Stamp Advisory Committee for the Postal Service making recommendations about stamps to be issued.

''The biggest problem in designing a stamp is scale. You can only enlarge the design five times up, and five times up from a postage stamp is not very big. Working in this scale you must always keep in mind that your design will be reduced and reduction changes the final product quite a bit. Negative white areas tend to take on all kinds of different shapes. The 'Black Heritage' series was one of the most difficult projects I've ever worked on. Another problem was finding a symbol that one could identify with. *I* knew who my subject was and knew their contribution, but many of the personalities in the 'Black Heritage' series were unknown to the public.

''I discovered that I couldn't over-research my subjects. I found that if I read biographies and heavily researched, I got lost and came up with things that were too obscure for people to relate to. If, for instance, you want to present Jackie Robinson, you need go no further than the fact that he stole more bases than anyone in baseball. If you try to deal with other elements of his life and career, you are missing the point. While working on commemorative stamps, an artist must also deal with a committee, so there is a lot of compromise involved.''

Pinkney's aspirations are to write and illustrate his own book and to exhibit his drawings. ''The obstacle I have to overcome is accepting that I can develop the conceptual ability of a writer. That will come with time. I have publishers who are willing to look at whatever I do. So it's now a matter of finding the time and the confidence.

''I still take life drawing classes. My fantasy is to be able to do more of my own work and fewer commercial projects. I would like to some day exhibit my drawings. I don't know what the subject matter would be, but I seem to be leaning towards portraiture.''

A recipient of many awards for his illustrations, Pinkney admits that he doesn't think much about awards. ''It's always been exciting to have some of my work in a show, but when I get an award I like to minimize its importance. I don't want the thought of awards to influence my daily work. I don't like to look back. I like to believe I'm always starting out fresh. I do like the idea of getting an award for book illustration simply because an award means more people will read the book. I'd love to get a gold medal from the Society of Illustrators someday—an award which is given by a jury of one's peers—that may change my outlook! But right now, I'd like to think awards roll right off my back.''

About his illustrations for the book *The Patchwork Quilt*, Pinkney commented: ''The book involves a very intimate sharing between two people, a grandmother and her grandchild. It's a

Jerry Pinkney, self-portrait.

very still, yet moving book (I've added a lot of still lifes into the drawings), which deals partly with a grandmother who is ill and bedridden for several months. The editors have allowed me to portray her during her illness when she is pale and weak. I think that is progress, because it is truthful, and it's important for kids to see truthful images. The quilt drove me nuts because it repeats itself. It has to change and yet there should be a consistency as it grows into repeating patterns. I bought an old quilt, hand stitched from the 1890s and that quilt was my model. I changed it in some ways, but that's where I got the feeling. I started with the blue patch, and did one patch at a time. That's the only way I kept my sanity.''

FOR MORE INFORMATION SEE: Lee Kingman and others, compilers, *Illustrators of Children's Books: 1957-1966,* Horn Book, 1968; *Twelve Black Artists from Boston,* Brandeis University, 1969; *Boston Herald Traveler,* May 26, 1970; *Afro-American Artists: A Bibliographical Directory,* Boston Public Library, 1973; *Communication Art Magazine,* May/June, 1975; *American Artist,* January, 1982.

RARICK, Carrie 1911-

PERSONAL: Surname rhymes with ''barrack''; born December 16, 1911, in Somerset, Ohio; daughter of Frank Burrie (a farmer) and Mary (Hoover) Fisher; married Merrill Rarick (a teacher), February 4, 1932 (died, 1969); children: Mrs. Richard R. Gibson. *Education:* Capital University, Two Year Normal degree, 1931, B.A., 1975; Ohio Dominican College, Elderhostel certificate, 1980. *Religion:* Lutheran. *Home:* 723 Montrose Ave., Columbus, Ohio 43209.

CAREER: Hebron (Ohio) public schools, elementary school teacher, 1931-33; Jersey (Ohio) public schools, elementary

When Jeanie went to bed that night, her mom and dad tucked her in. They turned out the light and said good night. Jeanie always smiled when her mom and dad said good night to her. But not tonight. Jeanie didn't feel like smiling tonight.

Jeanie was thinking about moving. She didn't want to move. She didn't want to leave her house. She didn't want to leave her room. She didn't want to leave the tree outside her window. Robins had built a nest in that tree last summer.

16   17

(From *Jeanie's Valentines* by Carrie Rarick. Illustrated by Diana Magnuson.)

school teacher, 1939-56; Beechwood Elementary School, Columbus, Ohio teacher, 1957-79. *Member:* National Retired Teachers Association, Parent Teacher Association (PTA), Society of Children's Book Writers, Verse Writer's Guild of Ohio, Bexley Historical Society. *Awards, honors:* Life Member of PTA Award, 1979.

*WRITINGS—*All juvenile: *The Three Bears Visit Goldilocks* (illustrated by Clare McKinley), Rand McNally, 1950; *Little Penguin* (illustrated by Vivienne Blake Demuth), Rand McNally, 1960; *Mom Says,* North-Side Letter Shop, 1979; *Jeanie's Valentines* (illustrated by Diana Magnuson), Follett, 1982; *Dapper Dan and His Gold Motorcycle,* School Book Fairs, 1984. Also author of articles for the Humane Society of the United States.

WORK IN PROGRESS: A book about events in her school-teaching days; children's books.

SIDELIGHTS: "All my life I have been working with children; I grew up in a family of eight children. I raised one child, had two grandchildren, and taught 39 years of young children. Now I have great-grandchildren who inspire me. My latest book is named after my great-grandchild.

"I lived on a farm—loved it. I retired from teaching in 1979, and have written more since."

CARRIE RARICK

FOR MORE INFORMATION SEE: Columbus Dispatch News, June 8, 1980.

REIGOT, Betty Polisar 1924-

BRIEF ENTRY: Born March 9, 1924, in Brooklyn, N.Y. A full-time writer and lecturer since 1975, Reigot was previously employed as deputy director at the Institute for Research and Evaluation in Hempstead, N.Y. Earlier in her career, she held editorial positions with Harcourt Brace Jovanovich, the *New York Times,* and Ergonomics, Inc. Her career as an author of children's books began with a strong interest in the connection between science and the arts that eventually led to five books dealing with various aspects of the physical world. All published by Scholastic Book Services, the titles include *Wake Up—It's Night: A Science Book about Nocturnal Animals* (1978), *A Book about Planets* (1981), and *Questions and Answers about Bees* (1983). Commenting on her decision to write for children, Reigot observes: "If you are not clear, concrete, and interesting, children will not read what you write. This seemed to me an absorbing challenge. . . ." She is currently researching European history for a biography. *Home and office:* 115 Central Park W., New York, N.Y. 10023.

FOR MORE INFORMATION SEE: Contemporary Authors, Volume 111, Gale, 1984.

REMINGTON, Frederic (Sackrider) 1861-1909

PERSONAL: Born October 4 (some sources cite October 1), 1861, in Canton, N.Y.; died of appendicitis, December 26, 1909, in Ridgefield, Conn.; son of Seth Pierre (a newspaper publisher) and Clara B. (Sackrider) Remington; married Eva Adele Caten, October, 1884. *Education:* Attended Yale University, School of Fine Arts, 1878-80, and Art Students League, 1886. *Residence:* Ridgefield, Conn.

CAREER: American painter, sculptor, illustrator, and writer. After leaving Yale in 1880, Remington traveled West where he lived the life of cowboy, scout, sheep rancher, and stockman, gaining a reputation as an illustrator of frontier scenes; in 1885, returned to New York where he established his career as an illustrator in numerous periodicals and books; served as artist-correspondent during the Indian Wars, 1890-91, in Russia and Algiers, 1892-93, in Cuba during the Spanish-American War, 1898, and elsewhere; began painting in oil and watercolor during the early 1890s; in 1895, created the first of his unique bronze sculptures. Most noted for his depiction of the Old West, Remington produced nearly 3000 paintings, hundreds of magazine and book illustrations, and twenty-five bronze sculptures throughout his lifetime. His work was exhibited in the United States and abroad, including regular showings at the National Academy of Design beginning in 1887, and his first one-man show in New York City, 1893.

COLLECTIONS: Art Institute of Chicago, Chicago, Ill.; Remington Art Memorial, Ogdensburg, N.Y.; Metropolitan Museum of Art, New York City; New York Public Library, New York City; Thomas Gilcrease Institute of American History and Art, Tulsa, Okla.; National Cowboy Hall of Fame, Oklahoma City, Okla.; Amon Carter Museum of Western Art, Fort Worth, Tex.; Stark Museum of Art, Orange, Tex.; Bradford Brinton Memorial, Big Horn, Wyo.; Whitney Gallery of Western Art, Cody, Wyo. *Member:* American Academy of Arts and Letters, National Academy of Design (associate), National Institute of Arts and Letters, Society of Illustrators. *Awards, honors:* Recipient of numerous exhibition honors; silver medal, Paris Exposition, 1889; bronze medal, Chicago World's Fair, 1893.

WRITINGS—Principal works; all self-illustrated: *Pony Tracks* (sketches), Harper & Brothers, 1895, reprinted, American Legacy, 1982; *Drawings by Frederic Remington,* R. H. Russell, 1897, reprinted, B. Franklin, 1971; *Crooked Trails* (short stories), Harper & Brothers, 1898, reprinted, Literature House, 1970; *Remington's Frontier Sketches,* Werner, 1898; *Sundown Leflare* (short stories), Harper & Brothers, 1899; *Stories of Peace and War,* Harper & Brothers, 1899, reprinted, Books for Libraries, 1970; *Men with the Bark On* (short stories), Harper & Brothers, 1900; *A Bunch of Buckskins* (sketches), R. H. Russell, 1901; *John Ermine of the Yellowstone* (novel), Macmillan, 1902; *Done in the Open* (sketches), P. F. Collier & Son, 1902; *The Way of an Indian* (novel), Fox, Duffield, 1906, reprinted, Memento, 1976; *Frederic Remington's Own West,* edited and introduced by Harold McCracken, Dial, 1960; *Frederic Remington's Own Outdoors,* edited by Douglas Allen, introduction by H. McCracken, Dial, 1964; *The Collected Writings of Frederic Remington,* edited by Peggy Samuels and Harold Samuels, Doubleday, 1979.

Remington as a young boy.

FREDERIC REMINGTON

Illustrator; selected works: Theodore Roosevelt, *Ranch Life and the Hunting-Trail* (first serialized in *Century,* 1888), Century, 1888, reprinted, University of Nebraska Press, 1983; Henry Wadsworth Longfellow, *The Song of Hiawatha,* Houghton, 1891, facsimile reprint, Bounty Books, 1982; Francis Parkman, *The Oregon Trail: Sketches of Prairie and Rocky-Mountain Life,* Little, Brown, 1892; Poultney Bigelow, *The Borderland of Czar and Kaiser,* Harper & Brothers, 1894; (with others) Nelson A. Miles, *Personal Recollections and Observations of General Nelson A. Miles, Embracing a Brief View of the Civil War,* Werner, 1896; Owen Wister, *A Journey in Search of Christmas,* Harper & Brothers, 1904. Illustrator of over 135 additional books. Contributor of illustrations, essays, and stories to more than forty periodicals, including *Harper's Weekly, Collier's Weekly, Outing, Century, Critic, Overland,* and *Scribner's Monthly.*

Collections of notebooks and letters are held in the Kansas State Historical Society, the Library of Congress, St. Lawrence University, and the Remington Art Memorial.

SIDELIGHTS: **October 4, 1861.** Born in Canton, New York. From earliest childhood, Remington showed an interest in cowboys, Indians and horses. From the time he could manage to hold a pencil, he was always drawing, and filled scores of notebooks with his early sketches. His father, the founder of a local newspaper, the *St. Lawrence Plaindealer,* encouraged him in his artwork. His mother, however, hoped that Remington would become a businessman, not an artist.

Autumn, 1876. Entered Highland Military Academy in Worcester, Massachusetts. While still at the academy, Remington described himself as a rough character: "I don't amount to anything in particular. I can spoil an immense amount of good grub at any time in the day. . . . I go a good man on muscle. My hair is short and stiff, and I am about five feet eight inches and weigh one hundred and eighty pounds. . . .

"I don't swear much, although it is my weak point, and I have to look my letters over carefully to see if there is any cussing in them. I never smoke—only when I can get treated—and I never condescend to the friendly offer of 'Take something old hoss?' " [Ben Merchant Vorpahl, *My Dear Wister: The Frederic Remington-Owen Wister Letters,* American West Publishing, 1972.[1]]

Remington loved sports, but was less inclined toward studies. His early ambitions included becoming a journalist or an artist. "I have just finished a complete course in book-keeping both single and double entry. I am of quite to [sic] much of a speculative mind to ever make a success at the solemn reality of a book-keeper. No sir, I will never burn any mid-night oil in squaring accounts. The Lord made me, and after a turn of mind which would never permit me to run my life from the point of a pen. . . . I never intend to do any great amount of labor. I have but one short life and do not aspire to wealth nor fame in a degree which could only be obtained by an extraordinary effort on my part.

A tremendous bang roared around the room, and the little group was lost in smoke. ▪ (From *John Ermine of the Yellowstone* by Frederic Remington. Illustrated by the author.)

Yale man Frederic Remington at age sixteen.

A Gendarme in Warsaw. ■ (From *The Borderland of Czar and Kaiser* by Poultney Bigelow. Illustrated by Frederic Remington.)

"No, I am going to try and get into Cornell College this coming June and if I succeed will be a Journalist. I mean to study for an artist any how, whether I ever make a success at it or not." [Peggy Samuels and Harold Samuels, *Frederic Remington: A Biography,* Doubleday, 1982.[2]]

Autumn, 1878. Entered Yale University as one of the first two students to enroll in the new art school. Became a member of the Yale football team.

1880. Father died, leaving Remington a small inheritance. He dropped out of school and tried several different jobs.

August, 1880. Courted Eva Caten. Eighteen-year-old Remington wrote to Caten's father: "For a year I have known your daughter, Eva, and during that time have contracted a deep affection for her. I have received encouragement in all propriety and with her permission and the fact of your countenancing my association, I feel warranted now in asking whether or not you will consent to an engagement between us. If you need time to consider or data on which to formulate I will of course be glad to accede to either."[2]

When Caten's father refused to allow his daughter to marry him, Remington quit his job as a clerk and subsequently held several different jobs.

1881. Went West seeking his fortune. Until he arrived in Montana, the idea of combining his artistic gifts with his Western experiences had not occurred to him. "Evening overtook me one night in Montana and I by good luck made the campfire

of an old wagon freighter who shared his bacon and coffee with me. I was 19 years of age and he was a very old man. Over the pipes it developed that he was born in western New York and had gone West at an early age. His West was Iowa. Thence during his long life he had followed the receding frontiers, always further and further West. . . .

A Study in Sociology in Berlin. ■ (From *The Borderland of Czar and Kaiser* by Poultney Bigelow. Illustrated by Frederic Remington.)

(From *The Song of Hiawatha* by Henry Wadsworth Longfellow. Illustrated by Frederic Remington.)

''I knew the railroad was coming. I saw men already swarming into the land. . . . I knew the wild riders and the vacant land were about to vanish forever—and the more I considered the subject, the bigger the forever loomed.

''Without knowing exactly how to do it, I began to try to record some facts around me, and the more I looked the more the panorama unfolded. . . . I saw the living, breathing end of three American centuries of smoke and dust and sweat. . . .''[1]

Returned to New York with a collection of drawings, of which *Harper's Weekly* accepted one for publication.

1882. Returned to the West. Invested in a sheep ranch in Kansas with the inheritance from his father's estate.

This picture, drawn by Frederic Remington after his visit with the Buffalo Soldiers, first appeared in *Century Magazine*. ■ (From *The Buffalo Soldiers in the Indian Wars* by Fairfax Downey. Illustrated by Frederic Remington.)

Remington in his Mott Street studio in 1885.

1884. Married Eva Caten, with her father's permission. Brought his bride to his ranch in Kansas City. Caten could not adjust to her husband and his unconventional life, however, and returned home to New York after two months.

1885. Having lost his ranch and his wife, Remington traveled West to prove himself as an artist. "Now that I was poor I could gratify my inclination for an artist's career. In art, to be conventional, one must start out penniless."[2]

After nine months of separation from his bride, Remington decided to abort his Western trip and to return East. He convinced his bride to live with him in New York City, where he attempted to establish himself as an illustrator.

January 9, 1886. *Harper's* published the first of Remington's sketches to appear in print under his own name.

May, 1886. *Harper's* sent Remington to Arizona in search of Geronimo, the Indian who had managed to avoid capture by the U.S. Army. "I remembered . . . a Blackfoot upon the Bow River had shown a desire to tomahawk me because I was endeavoring to immortalize him. After a long and tedious course of diplomacy it is at times possible to get one of these people

to gaze in a defiant and fearful way down the mouth of a camera; but to stand still until a man draws his picture on paper or canvas is a proposition which no Apache will entertain for a moment. With the help of two officers, who stood up close to me, I was enabled to make rapid sketches of the scenes and people; but my manner at last aroused suspicion, and my game would vanish like a covey of quail.

"From the parade in front of our tent I could see the long lines of horses, mules, and burros trooping into the agency from all quarters. Here was my feast. Ordinarily the Indians are scattered for forty miles in every direction; but this was ration day, and they all were together. After breakfast we walked down. Hundreds of ponies, caparisoned in all sorts of fantastic ways, were standing around. Young girls of the San Carlos tribe flitted about, attracting my attention by the queer ornaments which, in token of their virginity, they wear in their hair. Tall Yuma bucks galloped past with their long hair flying out behind. The squaws crowded around the exit and received the great chunks of beef which a native butcher threw to them. Indian scouts in military coats and armed with rifles stood about to preserve order. Groups of old women sat on the hot ground and gossiped. An old chief, with a very respectable amount of adipose under his cartridge belt, galloped up to our group and was introduced as Esquimezeu. We shook hands.

Timber-topping in the Rockies. ■ (From *Pony Tracks* by Frederic Remington. Illustrated by the author.)

"These Indians have natural dignity, and it takes very little knowledge of manners for them to appear well. The Apaches have no expression for a good-by or a greeting, and they never shake hands among themselves; but they consider handshaking an important ceremony among white men, and in their intercourse with them, attach great importance to it. I heard an officer say that he had once seen an Apache come home after an absence of months: he simply stepped into the room, sat

We were now out of the smoke. ■ (From an article "The Affair of the --th of July," by Frederic Remington in *Harper's Weekly,* February 2, 1895. Illustrated by the author.)

down without a word, and began rolling a cigarette." [Frederic Remington, *Frederic Remington's Own West,* Dial, 1960.[3]]

In his first year as a commercial artist, twenty-five of Remington's illustrations appeared in newspapers, periodicals, and books.

Autumn, 1887. Moved to the fashionable Marlborough House in New York City, and adopted a metropolitan lifestyle and customs, such as riding in Central Park and attending gala affairs. "That dress coat proposition is one of the most low down tricks which a white man could resort to. Of course it is plain enough . . . that I have outgrown my dress suit which

Watering horses. ■ (From *Pony Tracks* by Frederic Remington. Illustrated by the author.)

is now so tight that I cannot take breath, let alone eat in it. But I patiently take my medicine. Order one French chop and an after dinner coffee—that will be all right if I let out the top button."[2]

Commissioned to do the illustrations for the book, *Ranch Life and the Hunting Trail*, by Theodore Roosevelt, who became a close friend.

1888. Won two prizes at the Annual Exhibition of the National Academy, and exhibited at the American Water Color Society. Remington's fascination with the West compelled him to return there each year, sometimes making as many as four trips a year. "If I sat around the house all the time I couldn't do it. . . . I travel a third or half my time. I can't work steadily more than two or three months. I must go somewhere and see something new. Then when I see what I want I think it over and kind of get my idea of what I am going to do. Then the rest is nothing." [Susan E. Meyer, *America's Great Illustrators*, Abrams, 1978.[4]]

May, 1888. Commissioned by *Century* magazine to illustrate and write a story on the Indian tribes of the Southwest. "'The die is cast,' 'I'll plunge I'll cross,' or in a more prosey diction I will go on and explain that I have beguiled a certain distinguished publisher into sending me on an artistic and litterary [sic] tour through the Indian Territory and into Arizona. I am going to do the 'Black Buffaloes.' . . . I shall then return by

the way of Texas and the Territory. I shall get letters from the Secty of the Interior and can get them from the Secty of War. . . .

"I have yet quires and reams of work to do—I am dead stale and hate to do it but the gods must be propitiated so I will 'sweat' a little yet and by the 1st of June I hope to start on my pilgrimage.

"That reminds me that I am to day undergoing the tortures of the d———, I am doing a penance which would be a theme for Poe. I had 'too many blood of the grape' ensconced in my system last evening. . . . Of course I realize that we are all d——— fools, but the creater should have altered his plans of construction when he made *Man* or he should have designed 'the straight & narrow way' so that it would have covered more ground. . . ."[2]

December, 1889. Purchased an estate in New Rochelle, New York. "I have signed the contract for the purchase of an estate—estate is the proper term—three acres—brick house—large stable—trees—granite gates—everything all hunk [short for hunky dory]—lawn tennis in the front yard—garden—hen house—am going to try and pay $13,000. cold bones for it—located on the 'quality hill' of New Rochelle—30 minutes from 42nd Street—with two horses—both good ones—on the place—duck shooting on the bay in the Fall—good society—sailing & the finest country 'bout you ever saw—what more does one want. I wouldn't trade it for a chance at a Mohamedan paradise."[2]

(From *Ranch Life and the Hunting Trail* by Theodore Roosevelt. Illustrated by Frederic Remington.)

1890. Illustrated Longfellow's *The Song of Hiawatha* which established his reputation as a quality artist and illustrator. When asked by an aspiring young artist for career advice, Remington responded: ''The only advice I could give you is never to take anyone's advice, which is my rule. Most every artist needs 'schooling.' Be always true to yourself—if you imitate any other men ever so little you are 'gone.' Study good pictures and above all draw—draw—draw—and always from nature.''[2]

1892. Invited by *Harper's Weekly* to travel with author Poultney Bigelow. ''I go to Europe and while my plans are not yet matured I hope to be able soon to tell you at what particular point in Europe you can go to and gaze once more upon my classic form. To a man up a tree it looks as though there would be a war in Europe this spring. How is that?. . .

''I am to be in Berlin by the first of June SURE. . . . I am afraid I wont like Europe. I was born in the woods and the higher they get the buildings the worse I like them—I'm afraid those Europeans are too well set up in their minds for me—but you can't tell.''[2]

In Russia, which was close to war with Germany, Remington and his companion Bigelow were under constant surveillance by the political police. ''. . . Bigelow and I have been fired bodily out of Russia. We dodged the police telegrams and got off with our notes and sketches—you talk about Ingins—they aint in it. I have been as lonesome as a toad in a well—cant talk the d——— language. . . .''[2]

January, 1895. Began sculpting. ''. . . My oils will all get old mastery—that is, they will look like *pale molases* in time—my water colors will fade—but I am to endure in bronze—even rust does not touch.—I am modeling—I find I do well—I am doing a cow boy on a bucking broncho and I am going to rattle down through all the ages, unless some Anarchist invades the old mansion and knocks it off the shelf.

He looked on the land of his people and he hated all vehemently. ■ (From an article "The Way of an Indian," by Frederic Remington in *Cosmopolitan Magazine,* November, 1905. Illustrated by the author.)

He shouted his pathos at a wild and lonely wind, but there was no response. ■ (From an article "The Way of an Indian," by Frederic Remington in *Cosmopolitan Magazine*, March, 1906. Illustrated by the author.)

"I have simply been fooling my time away—I can't tell a red blanket from a grey overcoat for color but when you get right down to facts—and thats what you have got to sure establish when you monkey with the plastic clay, I am *there*—there in double leaded type."[2]

1896. Sent by William Randolph Hearst on a "secret" trip to Cuba to cover the conflict between Spain and the Cuban rebels. "... The town is wild with excitement—we have only the Custom House to fear. Two Cuban officers go with us—I am well—and feel that I am to undertake quite the most eventful enterprise of my life—think there will be war with Spain—I leave my effects at the Duval House here...."[2]

1897. Refused the offer of another trip to Germany. "... I shall not try Europe again. I am not built right—I hate parks—collars—cuffs—foreign languages—cut & dried stuff.... Europe is all right for most every body but me—I am going to do America—its new—its to my taste."[2]

April, 1898. Joined the battleship *Iowa* as its only correspon-

dent, following the sinking of the battleship *Maine* when the United States and Spain's relations were cut. Became sorely disillusioned by the Cuban campaign. "... I had been ill during the whole campaign, and had latterly had fever, which, taken together with the heat, sleeping in the mud, marching, and insufficient food, had done for me.

"The sight of that road as I wound my way down it was something I cannot describe. The rear of a battle. All the broken spirits, bloody bodies, hopeless, helpless suffering which drags its weary length to the rear, as so much more appalling than anything else in the world. Men half naked, men sitting down on the road-side utterly spent, men hopping on one foot with a rifle for a crutch, men out of their minds from sunstroke, men dead, and men dying."[2]

1900. Headed West to study and paint the Ute, Navajo, and Apache Indians. "Utes, Navajoes and Apaches are Indians with whom I am not at all familiar. I am going to study them. I don't really know how long I'll be gone. You see, I'm nothing but an artist, and I guess I've got all the peculiarities usually attributed to an artist. I may be gone several weeks; maybe all winter, and then again, I may not be gone very long—but I guess that I'll be gone a good while. I have no plans for disposing of my work and I am, therefore, not hampered by orders."[2]

1902. First novel, *John Ermine of the Yellowstone,* was dramatized for the American stage, with the author in attendance at the Boston tryouts. "The long rehearsals nearly killed me—I was completely done up and now I am in the hands of a doctor. Imagine me, a week without sleep."[2]

March 18, 1905. *Collier* magazine devoted its entire issue to Remington.

A "Famous Artist" stamp honored Frederic Remington in 1940.

December 26, 1909. Died suddenly, at the age of forty-eight, of a ruptured appendix at his home in Ridgefield, Connecticut. After his death, a Remington Memorial Museum was established in his home town of Ogdensburg, New York. His Indian collection, together with his studio effects, were preserved in the Whitney Gallery of Western Art in Cody, Wyoming.

Remington's works are included in the de Grummond Collection at the University of Southern Mississippi.

FOR MORE INFORMATION SEE—Books; juvenile: Robin McKown, *Painter of the Wild West: Frederic Remington,* Messner, 1959; LaVere Anderson, *Frederic Remington: Artist on Horseback,* Garrard, 1971; Clyde B. Moore, *Frederic Remington, Young Artist,* Bobbs-Merrill, 1971; Adeline Peter and Ernest Raboff, *Frederic Remington,* Doubleday, 1973; Donna Baker, *Frederic Remington,* Childrens Press, 1977; Bern Keating, *Famous American Cowboys,* Rand McNally, 1977.

Adult: Harold McCracken, *Frederic Remington: Artist of the Old West,* Lippincott, 1947; Frederic Remington, *Frederic Remington's Own West,* Dial, 1960; H. McCracken, *The Frederic Remington Book: A Pictorial History of the West,* Doubleday, 1966; Marta Jackson, editor and author of biography, *The Illustrations of Frederic Remington,* commentary by Owen Wister, Bounty Books, 1970; Allen Douglas, *Frederic Remington and the Spanish-American War,* Crown, 1971; Henry C. Pitz, editor and author of introduction, *Frederic Remington: One Hundred Seventy-Three Drawings and Illustra-*

tions, Dover, 1972; Ben Merchant Vorpahl, *My Dear Wister: The Frederic Remington-Owen Wister Letters,* American West Publishing, 1972; Peter H. Hassrick, *Frederic Remington,* Abrams, 1973; B. M. Vorpahl, *Frederic Remington and the West: With the Eye of the Mind,* University of Texas Press, 1978; Susan E. Meyer, *America's Great Illustrators,* Abrams, 1978; Peggy Samuels and Harold Samuels, *Frederic Remington: A Biography,* Doubleday, 1982; B. M. Vorpahl, "Frederic Remington," in *Dictionary of Literary Biography,* Volume 12, Gale, 1982; B. W. Dippie, *Remington and Russell,* University of Texas Press, 1984.

Selected periodicals: D. Hedgepeth, "Frederic Remington: Nature in the Old West," *Field and Stream,* March, 1975; B. W. Dippie, "Frederic Remington's Wild West," *American Heritage,* April, 1975; R. Cantwell, "He Went to See the West Die," *Sports Illustrated,* August 11, 1975; "Frederic Remington," *Conservationist,* March, 1977; J. A. Michener, "He Painted the West," *Reader's Digest,* May, 1977; T. H. Watkins, "Remington and the Eli Eleven," *American Heritage,* October/November, 1981.

Motion pictures and filmstrips: "The American Cowboy" (filmstrip, with record and teacher's manual), Bowmar Records, 1969; "Frederic Remington: Artist of the Wild West" (filmstrip, with cassette and program guide), Aids of Cape Cod, 1977; "Frederic Remington: Cowboys, Indians, Cavalry" (motion picture), Sterling Educational Films, 1982.

Football match between Yale and Princeton. ■ (From *Frederic Remington's Own Outdoors* by Frederic Remington. Illustrated by the author.)

ANN RIVKIN

RIVKIN, Ann 1920-

PERSONAL: Born September 17, 1920, in Leeds, England; daughter of Louis (a cabinetmaker) and Sadie (a homemaker; maiden name, Cohen) Simon; married Irvin Rivkin (an accountant), August 29, 1947; children: Shelly, Ken. *Education:* Attended schools in England. *Home:* 771 West 23rd, Vancouver, British Columbia, Canada.

CAREER: Author of books for young people.

WRITINGS: Mystery of Disaster Island (juvenile; illustrated by Affie Mohammed), Scholastic Book Services, 1975; *The Time to Choose* (juvenile; illustrated by A. Mohammed), Scholastic Book Services, 1976. Also author of *Three Day Challenge* (illustrated by Alan Daniel), published by Scholastic-TAB.

ROOS, Stephen (Kelley) 1945-

BRIEF ENTRY: Born February 9, 1945, in New York, N.Y. Author. A 1967 graduate of Yale University, Roos spent twelve years with Harper & Row Publishers where he worked in promotions and as assistant editor. A full-time writer since 1980, he is the author of three companion books that provide an amusing look at life in the fifth and sixth grades. All published by Delacorte, the titles are: *My Horrible Secret* (1983), *The Terrible Truth* (1983), and *My Secret Admirer* (1984). *Publishers Weekly* described Roos as "a fluent, humorous writer, tuned in to the concerns of kids," while *Horn Book* observed that the humor in his writing "stems from the wry character-

izations of a group of typical middle-school students with their not-so-earth shattering concerns and dilemmas." Roos is anticipating the publication of a young adult novel, tentatively titled *Confessions of a Wayward Preppie,* as well as *The Mystery of the Condo Cat.* The latter was written with his parents, authors William Roos and Audrey Kelley (who write under the joint pseudonym Kelley Roos). Currently, he is working on a novel for adults. *Home address:* Canal Rd., High Falls, N.Y. 12440.

FOR MORE INFORMATION SEE: Contemporary Authors, Volume 112, Gale, 1985.

RUFFINS, Reynold 1930-

PERSONAL: Born August 5, 1930, in New York, N.Y.; son of John (a salesman) and Juanita (Dash) Ruffins; married Joan Young (an artist), May 29, 1954; children: Todd, Lynn, Ben, Seth. *Education:* Graduated from Cooper Union, 1951. *Home:* 112-38 178th Place, St. Albans, New York, N.Y. 11434. *Office:* 38 East 21st St., New York, N.Y. 10010.

CAREER: Author and illustrator of children's books, and graphic designer for corporations including IBM, Time-Life, Pfizer, Children's Book Council, MacDonald's, CBS, *New York Times,* and *Family Circle* magazine. Instructor, School of Visual Arts, 1967-70; visiting adjunct professor, Syracuse University, College of Visual and Performing Arts, Department of Visual Communications, 1973, and Parsons School of Design. *Exhibitions:* Bologna Children's Book Fair, 1976; New York Historical Society, "Two Hundred Years of American Illustration." *Awards, honors:* Professional Achievement Award, Cooper Union, 1972; *The Chess Book* was selected for the American Institute of Graphic Arts Children's Books Show, 1973-74; "Children's Choice" Award from Children's Book Council and the International Reading Association, 1976, for *The Code and Cipher Book,* 1978, for *The Monster Riddle Book,* 1980, for *My Brother Never Feeds the Cat,* and 1983, for *Words?! A Book about the Origins of Everyday Words and Phrases;* Silver Medal, from the Society of Illustrators, for "Dragon."

WRITINGS: My Brother Never Feeds the Cat (juvenile; self-illustrated), Scribner, 1979.

All with Jane Sarnoff; all for children; all published by Scribner: *The Chess Book,* 1973; *A Great Bicycle Book* (self-illustrated), 1973, new edition, 1976; *What? A Riddle Book,* 1974; *A Riddle Calendar: 1975,* 1974; *The Code and Cipher Book* (self-illustrated), 1975; *The Monster Riddle Book* (self-illustrated), 1975, revised edition, 1978; *I Know! A Riddle Book,* 1976; *The Nineteen Seventy-Seven Beastly Riddle Calendar,* 1976; *A Great Aquarium Book: The Putting-It-Together Guide for Beginners* (self-illustrated), 1977; *Giants! A Riddle Book and Mr. Bigperson's Side: A Story Book,* 1977; *Take Warning! A Book of Superstitions,* 1978; *Space: A Fact and Riddle Book,* 1978; *The 1979 Out-of-This-World Riddle Calendar,* 1979; *Riddle Calendar, 1980,* 1979; *Light the Candles! Beat the Drums! A Book of Holidays, Occasions, Celebrations, Remembrances, Occurrences, Special Days, Weeks, and Months,* 1979; *If You Were Really Superstitious,* 1980; *That's Not Fair* (self-illustrated), 1980; *Words?! A Book about the Origins of Everyday Words and Phrases* (ALA Notable Book), 1981.

REYNOLD RUFFINS

Illustrator: (With Simms Taback) Harry Hartwick, *The Amazing Maze,* Dutton, 1970; John F. Waters, *Camels: Ships of the Desert,* Crowell, 1974; Franklyn M. Branley, *Light and Darkness,* Crowell, 1975.

ADAPTATIONS: "The Monster Riddle Book" (filmstrip with cassette), Random House, 1981.

SIDELIGHTS: Born August 5, 1930, in New York, N.Y., and reared in Queens. "I played in back yards and empty lots with my only brother. Since he is seven years older, we didn't have much in common but I remember playing soldiers together. He, of course, was always the general and I was always the private. He had some Roosevelt campaign buttons with which he would award me, like a medal, when I did something worthy.

"My father worked for Con Edison and was the first black employee hired by them. He started as a porter, worked his way up to becoming the first black meter reader, and eventually became a salesman. Back then, these were big steps.

"I began drawing at an early age with the encouragement of my father, who would often bring home paper and pencils from work. He also gave me art supplies and on special occasions, like birthdays, at least one of my gifts had something to do with art.

"My mother's side of the family was very musically inclined. My grandmother taught piano, although all of her grandchildren, myself included, rejected music lessons.

"Though we were not big readers, we were always surrounded by lots of magazines and newspapers. My father used to read to me after my ritual Saturday night bath. My most vivid memories are of *The Prince and the Pauper* and one of my father's personal favorites, a short story called 'The Go-Getter' about a man who overcame all odds in spite of his handicaps. I also remember browsing through my mother's illustrated cookbooks.

"I always felt I could draw, and that it was something special. I was often challenged in school by kids who wanted to see if I could draw Superman or Captain Marvel. I didn't particularly like to do it; I hated the idea of copying, preferring instead to draw from my imagination. But there was the class bully who constantly challenged me, so I did it."

(From *The Code and Cipher Book* by Jane Sarnoff and Reynold Ruffins. Illustrated by Reynold Ruffins.)

(From *The Monster Riddle Book* by Jane Sarnoff and Reynold Ruffins. Illustrated by Reynold Ruffins.)

Ruffins attended the High School of Music and Art in Manhattan. "I took the subway every day back and forth from Queens. I don't remember any teachers who particularly influenced me as much as the total atmosphere at the school itself which inspired and affected me even more than my later studies at Cooper Union. I met people I wouldn't have ordinarily met had I attended a local high school, many of whom were children of refugees from Hitler's Germany. These students from different backgrounds and cultures were very mature young people. I still come in contact with many of them; quite a few went on to make names for themselves and have become successful in one way or another.

"During my senior year, an exhibition of student work was held. One of my paintings was so well received by both teachers and students that I was treated like a hero for a week. One of the teachers decided to buy the painting. She presented me with a check for fifty dollars, and invited me to her house in Westchester for dinner. We were served by her maid—I had never been treated so royally before. It was a wonderful feeling to have sold a painting. Fifty dollars was a lot of money in

1948. I can remember getting off the train at Grand Central with the check in my pocket. I strutted up Park and Fifth Avenue, feeling that the city was *mine*."

Attended Cooper Union. "Once you are exposed to an environment in a high school which specializes in art, you begin to wonder what your future will be. There was a lot of discussion going on about art schools and continuing your career. Cooper Union was both competitive and tuition-free, which influenced my decision, since I couldn't afford to go to art school.

"At Cooper Union I studied drawing, painting, mostly fine arts, though later in my training, I took courses in illustration and in advertising. I knew that people made a living at art, but at that time I didn't exactly know how it was done. At Cooper Union, we thought of ourselves as fine artists and easel painters. We came to understand the buying and selling of art, and what we had to do to make money in commercial art, but the thought of leaving a place like Cooper Union and going

door to door with our portfolios under our arms scared all of us to death. Of course we all had naive hopes of impressing people, and making a million dollars.

"While we were still studying at Cooper Union, Milton Glaser, Seymour Chwast, myself and a few other students formed the Push Pin Studios. We rented a small loft on 13th Street in which to work after school and on weekends. We rented one–third of the space and the other two-thirds belonged to a dancer. When the dancer wasn't there at night, we'd hold parties. We picked up a few commercial jobs and my relationship with them continued until I married in 1954. My wife is also an artist and at that time she was doing easel painting. I met her outside of Cooper Union, and later discovered that she was attending my alma mater. After we married, I took a job as an assistant art director at an agency, but later returned to Push Pin.

"Push Pins Studios was always an innovative place. At any one time there were four or five artists there, Milton Glaser, Seymour Chwast, Paul Davis, John Alcorn, Isadore Seltzer, and myself, to name a few. In the 50s and 60s the studio was on the first floor of a brownstone. We had a lovely garden in the back and, because our work space had formerly been a big kitchen, we had both sink and stove in our work area. It was very pleasant and spacious.

"We worked long hours—usually nine in the morning till nine at night. We worked on book jackets, pharmaceutical advertising, projects for CBS- and NBC-TV, and the *Push Pin Almanac*. In the fifties as well as today, Push Pin Studios is a trend setter. We did interesting work for a sophisticated audience."

Ruffins began illustrating children's books in 1973. "I met Jane Sarnoff through a mutual friend at a civil rights' protest march. Jane is a pharmaceutical copywriter and specializes in physician's literature and advertising. We had worked on projects which were unrelated to children's books, became friends,

"Where have you been all day, old cat?" asked Anna. "Playing? I've been working. But Barney hasn't done any work at all today. None. Zero. Zip." ■ (From *My Brother Never Feeds the Cat* by Reynold Ruffins. Illustrated by the author.)

and developed some games together. Scribner approached me with the idea of writing and illustrating a children's book about bicycles. I didn't feel capable as a writer and so asked Jane if she would write the text. As a pharmaceutical writer, she has a knack for making technical things clear. We worked for many years together. She would write a draft, we'd meet and discuss it, we'd fight a bit, we'd talk things out—it was a very good arrangement. If I thought something would make a great visual, she would write around it. My only collaboration in the writing was in terms of discussion. Pen to paper to typewriter is *not* my thing.

"Usually I keep a swipe file for specific projects like *The Chess Book, A Great Bicycle Book,* and the *Great Aquarium Book.* I made up all the fantasy giants in *Giants,* although I used scrap reference and historical background material.

"My monsters have been the most fun and are my favorite characters. Nothing can compare with them. What I like best about creating monsters is that they can't be drawn right or wrong. They just are what they are."

Ruffins' ability to change the pace and style he developed as a commercial artist helped him to develop into a more flexible children's book illustrator. "My advertising illustration ranges from having to make a black and white drawing of a family about to board an airplane to cooking instructions to a full color painting of a horse and rider in London. The demands of my growing children, and of the market made it necessary for me to develop an ability to work in different ways. An extension of that is learning how to apply these acquired skills to book illustration. Whether it's an advantage or a disadvantage, I've never been locked into one way of working. It sounds

immodest, but I have versatility. Presently I enjoy my projects in editorial illustration more than those in advertising.''

Ruffins has four children. "My children have influenced me in the sense that they've kept me at it—working. It's so expensive to raise them! I would have worked a lot less if I didn't have children. They've helped me sustain a certain sense of humor.''

Ruffins, who has taught at the School of Visual Arts in New York City and at Syracuse University, is presently teaching at Parsons School of Design. "I try to make my students comprehend that as illustrators whatever they do must be universally understood. Illustrators have a wide and varied audience. Whatever message one tries to get across through illustration must be absolutely clear. That doesn't mean one has to sac-

rifice individual style. Illustration must be both universal and personal if it is to succeed. The challenge for the illustrator is to create work which reflects his personality, work which can be recognized as the product of his hand and yet appeal to several million people.''

Ruffins' advice to young artists is to "draw all the time. Develop a keen sense of observation. In everything there is something to be learned and remembered. For example, if you study a brick, the brick will change as the sun moves across the sky, it will cast a shadow on one side or another. If you are really interested in art, you should keep your eyes and your mind open.''

Ruffins has won many awards for his illustrations including a

"Better not let Dad or Mom hear you say a D-U-M-B dumb thing like that,"Bert said. ■ (From
That's Not Fair by Jane Sarnoff and Reynold Ruffins. Illustrated by Reynold Ruffins.)

Did sand or dirt ever blow into your eyes? Camels have long heavy eyelashes to help keep sand out of their eyes. ■ (From *Camels: Ships of the Desert* by John F. Waters. Illustrated by Reynold Ruffins.)

(From *Giants! A Riddle Book and Mr. Bigperson's Side: A Story Book* by Jane Sarnoff and Reynold Ruffins. Illustrated by Reynold Ruffins.)

Silver Medal from the Society of Illustrators. ''The Silver Medal which I received for an illustration of a dragon for a large paper company was strictly a commercial job. The company hired me because of the children's books I'd illustrated, and in fact I've landed many commercial jobs because of my book illustrations. The Professional Achievement Award I received from Cooper Union has been the most meaningful award to me.''

For relaxation Ruffins enjoys sailing in Sag Harbor, Long Island and listening to music. ''I like all music, especially classical and jazz which I play in the studio all the time.''

Ruffins is a committed New Yorker. ''I've always considered living elsewhere, but I love New York so much that I'm happy to live here, but enjoy visiting other places.''

FOR MORE INFORMATION SEE: American Artist, September, 1958; *Graphis,* no. 177, 1975; Sally Holmes Holtz, editor, *Fifth Book of Junior Authors and Illustrators,* H. W. Wilson, 1983.

RUSH, Alison 1951-

PERSONAL: Born March 30, 1951, in Birmingham, England; daughter of George Logan (an engineer) and Jean (a nurse; maiden name, Finlayson) Smith; married Malcolm John Rush (a librarian), March 6, 1981. *Education:* University of Durham, B.A. (honors), 1973. *Politics:* Labour. *Home:* 8 Stonebridge, Orton Malborne, Peterborough PE2 ONF, England.

CAREER: Nature Conservancy Council (government agency), Peterborough, England, executive officer, 1979—.

WRITINGS: The Last of Danu's Children (young adult novel), Allen & Unwin, 1981, Houghton, 1982.

WORK IN PROGRESS: A second novel, *Undry;* research for a possible third novel about Morgan Le Fay, a figure in the Arthurian legends.

SIDELIGHTS: "When I want to describe the background to what I write, I cannot approach it in a direct way. I was brought up in a very ordinary part of rural Lancashire, the immediate landscape being a drained marsh, flat, criss-crossed by ditches and hedges, dotted by clumps of trees like islands. There was also an estuary full of migratory birds in winter. This sort of landscape has no ready charm; both the marsh and the estuary are unexpansive and tamed, yet at the same time repellingly bleak—more akin to the nearby industrial landscapes than to the usual idea of the English countryside.

"I never really felt at home in this environment. While you walk on the beach or in the fields, the landscape withdraws into itself, rejects you. It has a very strong character of its own, but that character is without friendliness. It will work for man, but it will not smile on him. I used to read of children whose native countryside was a friend, a welcoming playmate; but my countryside would not anthropomorphize in this way. It was not actively hostile, but it ignored one. I could not relate to the natural environment except when on holiday, in less exacting and more compliant landscapes.

"This did not suit me. It meant always being rootless, unattached. But at last I came to grips with my landscape by reading up on the local folklore and history. Not the very recent history, but more distant accounts of how the area was once a real marsh, inhabited by a tribe called the Setantii. It was an inhospitable district. Time and again the tradition emerges of a disastrous flood which destroyed a forest, engulfed a church, swept away a village. The river goddess survives in local lore as a horrible sprite who claims a human life once every seven years. It became clear that this tamed landscape had once been a grim, dangerous place where people had lived with great difficulty.

"This did not endear my countryside to me, but I now understand it and, magically, with understanding came belonging. I no longer live there, but when I visit it is with a genuine sense of coming home.

"This has been fundamental to the writing I have done so far. My landscape would mean nothing to me without its past, the ghosts, so to speak, of the forest and marshland which no longer exist and the ever-changing coastline. In the same way, human beings mean nothing without their background of thought, history, and mythology. I found that what interested me most in books was the attempt a few authors had made to toe the line between real life and imagination, to examine how fantasy and reality flow into and feed each other. I like pure

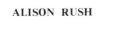

ALISON RUSH

fantasy (such as Tolkien) but I want reality to enter too, in an active way, meaning something in the context of the fantasy—and vice versa. So like many people, I tried to write the kind of story I would like to read.

"I went to the university in Durham, which is a beautiful city. With its castle, cathedral, and river, there was no need to struggle in order to understand its loveliness; most of its history is there on the surface. My time there was spent on Latin and Greek. Thereafter I worked at various office jobs, and joined the Nature Conservancy Council in 1979. This is a government agency charged with the furthering of nature conservation in Great Britain. In 1981 I was married, to the NCC's deputy librarian."

SANDERSON, Ruth (L.) 1951-

PERSONAL: Born November 24, 1951, in Ware, Mass.; daughter of C. Kenneth and Victoria (Sasur) Sanderson; married Kenneth Robinson (a student); children: Morgan. *Education:* Attended Paier School of Art, 1970-74. *Home:* P. O. Box 483, Palmer, Mass. 01069.

CAREER: Illustrator of books for children. *Member:* Western Massachusetts Illustrators Group, Society of Children's Book Writers. *Awards, honors: Five Nests* received the Outstanding Science Book Award from the National Association of Science Teachers; *A Different Kind of Gold* was selected as a notable children's trade book in social studies, 1982; *The Animal, the Vegetable, and John D Jones* was chosen one of *School Library Journal*'s "Best Books 1982."

RUTH SANDERSON

ILLUSTRATOR—All for children, except as indicated; all fiction, except as indicated: Ilka List, *Grandma's Beach Surprise,* Putnam, 1975; Glenn Balch, *Buck, Wild* (Junior Literary Guild selection), Crowell, 1976; Watty Piper (pseudonym of Mabel Caroline Bragg), reteller, *The Little Engine That Could,* Platt & Munk, 1976; Mary Francis Shura, *The Season of Silence,* Atheneum, 1976; Mary Towne, *First Serve* (Junior Literary Guild selection), Atheneum, 1976; Clyde Robert Bulla, *The Beast of Lor,* Crowell, 1977; Charles Mercer, *Jimmy Carter* (biography), Putnam, 1977; Willo Davis Roberts, *Don't Hurt Laurie!,* Atheneum, 1977; Robert Louis Stevenson, *A Child's Garden of Verses,* Platt & Munk, 1977; Charlene Talbot, *The Great Rat Island Adventure* (Junior Literary Guild selection), Atheneum, 1977; Greta Walker, *Walt Disney* (biography), Putnam, 1977; Lynn Hall, *The Mystery of Pony Hollow,* Garrard, 1978; Beverly Renner, *The Hideaway Summer,* Harper, 1978; Miriam Schlein, *On the Track of the Mystery Animal: The Story of the Discovery of the Okapi* (nonfiction), Four Winds, 1978; William Cole, compiler, *The Poetry of Horses,* Scribner, 1979; Susan Farrar, *Samantha on Stage,* Dial, 1979; Norma Simon, *We Remember Philip,* A. Whitman, 1979; William Sleator, *Into the Dream* (Junior Literary Guild selection), Dutton, 1979.

Caroline Arnold, *Five Nests* (nonfiction), Dutton, 1980; Margaret Chittenden, *The Mystery of the Missing Pony,* Garrard, 1980; Nikki Amdur, *One of Us,* Dial, 1981; W. Cole, compiler, *Good Dog Poems,* Scribner, 1981; L. Hall, *The Mysterious Moortown Bridge,* Follett, 1981; L. Hall, *The Mystery of the Caramel Cat,* Garrard, 1981; Cecily Stern, *A Different Kind of Gold,* Harper, 1981; Betsy Byars, *The Animal, the Vegetable, and John D Jones,* Delacorte, 1982; Linda Hayward, *When You Were a Baby,* Golden Press, 1982; Edward

Lear, *The Owl and the Pussycat,* Golden Press, 1982; Peggy Archer, *One of the Family,* Golden Press, 1983; Judith Gorog, *Caught in the Turtle,* Philomel, 1983; Lois Meyer, *The Store-Bought Doll,* Golden Press, 1983; Johanna Spyri, *Heidi,* Knopf, 1984; J.R.R. Tolkien, *The Fellowship of the Ring,* Ariel Books, 1985. Also illustrator of *The Pudgy Bunny Book,* Grosset, 1984, and *Five Little Bunnies,* Golden Press, 1984.

All written by Carolyn Keene (collective pseudonym); "Nancy Drew Mystery Stories" series: *The Triple Hoax,* Wanderer Books, 1979; *The Flying Saucer Mystery,* Wanderer Books, 1980; *The Secret in the Old Lace,* Wanderer Books, 1980; *The Greek Symbol Mystery,* Wanderer Books, 1981 (Sanderson was not associated with other books in the series).

All written by Laura Lee Hope (collective pseudonym); "The Bobbsey Twins" series: *Secret in the Pirate's Cave,* Wanderer Books, 1980; *The Dune Buggy Mystery,* Wanderer Books, 1981; *The Missing Pony Mystery,* Wanderer Books, 1981; *The Rose Parade Mystery,* Wanderer Books, 1981 (Sanderson was not associated with other books in the series).

ADAPTATIONS: "The Little Engine That Could" (filmstrip with cassette or book), 1976.

(From *Don't Hurt Laurie!* by Willo Davis Roberts. Illustrated by Ruth Sanderson.)

She felt Lizinka's eyes boring into her back, and she knew that her own long, blond hair was unkempt. . . . ■ (From *Samantha on Stage* by Susan Clement Farrar. Illustrated by Ruth Sanderson.)

(From *The Season of Silence* by Mary Francis Shura.
Illustrated by Ruth Sanderson.)

SIDELIGHTS: "I grew up in the very small town of Monson,
Massachusetts. It was a magical place for me. Every Saturday
morning I'd ride my bike to the bottom of a mountain and
push it up three miles of winding country road to get to the
top.

"My best friend lived on a farm at the top of that mountain.
Our dream was to someday own horses, and when she was
ten, her parents bought her one. We would gallivant through
the woods on her horse, and then down a dirt road where we
would arrive at our favorite 'secret place,' a pink castle in an
abandoned 'playland.' There were all kinds of buildings to
explore—little stone houses, a frontier saloon, a little chapel
and a ten-foot wooden pumpkin! Unfortunately, as the years
passed, it deteriorated. I often returned there during my art
school years to find a field of abandoned wagons which sank
lower and lower into the ground every year. Now it's been
leveled, there's nothing left. I still love the area and have
moved to Palmer, the next town over from Monson. I'm still
friends with many of the people I grew up with and my parents
still live nearby. I've come back to my roots."

Sanderson began drawing during childhood. "I held an art
class for my second-grade friends and taught them all how to
draw horses. When my mother bought me *How to Draw Horses*
by Walter Foster, I spent hours copying horses, trying to get
them right. I have one older brother and one older sister, neither of whom drew. Though my parents weren't inclined toward art, my mother was creative with her quilting, arranging
flowers, making pine cone wreaths, and every other craft you
can imagine.

"I was born loving horses. I don't know why. My love of
horses is probably the reason I'm an artist today. I have owned
horses on and off since I was thirteen. It was a dream come
true when I was assigned the eighteen paperbacks in the "Black
Stallion" series. They were my favorite books as a child. I
loved the original illustrations, but when I was offered the job
I could see that the illustrations came out of the fifties and
were not stylistically modern. The interiors were nice, but I
thought the covers needed a current look.

"My parents have been supportive of my work, which has
been important for my self-image. Although there are certainly
cases where artists have risen above and in spite of their parents, I think it is very important when one's family is supportive. For me, their encouragement was a real boost."

Sanderson attended Paier School of Art in Hamden, Connecticut. "Paier was recommended to me by an art teacher as a
good all around professional school that teaches the basics of
drawing and painting. I liked the traditional training in anatomy, figure drawing, light and shade. I chose illustration as
my major, although I took courses in figure painting and drawing as well.

"I gravitated towards illustration because I liked having problems to solve. I preferred developing concepts and pictorial
impressions of a manuscript to initiating my own ideas. As an
exercise, we were asked to find a book in the library, read the
story and come up with new ideas for the cover illustration.
During my senior year, I studied with illustrator Michael Eagle. He made us think in new and different ways, stretching
our imagination. Every teacher at Paier contributed something
to our training. Thus our development was a group effort.

"That same year, Mark English, a very successful corporate
editorial illustrator, came to lecture. He liked my work, and
asked me to apprentice for him, which I did for six months in
Redding, Connecticut. During that time, Carol Bancroft, a
children's book agent, was looking for new artists. While I
was apprenticing for English, Carol showed my portfolio to
publishers and within six months she had given me so much
free-lance work that I had to decide whether to follow in English's footsteps and work in commercial adult magazine illustration or strike out on my own and try children's books. I
opted for children's books. I started doing textbook illustration
and then slowly worked my way up to trade books and then
jacket illustration.

"Usually when I'm working on book covers, I juggle five or
six covers at once, but when I take on a big project, I devote
all my time to it. Someday I hope to have time to paint and
do illustration. Right now, I spend over forty hours a week on
illustration."

Sanderson's work is arranged around her family life. "I get
up at 7 a. m., bring my daughter to nursery school and begin
working at about ten. I work all day with breaks for lunch and
supper, then work again at night after my daughter goes to

He was standing at the edge of a large empty field, trying to move toward a glowing object floating over the center of the field. ■ (From *Into the Dream* by William Sleator. Illustrated by Ruth Sanderson.)

bed. Sometimes I spread my work over a seven-day week instead of the usual five. With a studio in my home, it's hard to separate work from leisure time. I always feel I should be in my studio working. Still, illustration is an ideal job. I can make my own hours. If I don't feel inspired one day, I can make it up the next. I tend to be very fast when I'm concentrating. When I have a good mental image of what I want, I can put it down without much of a struggle. With ten years into the business, I know my craft fairly well. Coming up with the idea, or the concept is the hard part. Once I get the mental image, it's just a matter of my hand doing the job!

"Finding the mental image is a different experience for every book. I study the manuscript very closely, carefully reading and re-reading the book until I find the essence of what the author is saying. Then I try to pick the moments that are important and dramatic that really tell the story.

"What inspires me in a text is the descriptive ability of the author. Descriptions are so helpful. Some books are situational and contain a lot more dialogue than environment. It's hard to get a good mental image out of a book of this type. It's not easy to create a pleasing pictorial image for the 'troubled child' stories. For example, stories where the characters are either at home or at school. This type of illustration involves drawing a convincing portrait of an emotional child when all the author has given you is the character's inner turmoil."

A cheer went up as the beast curled its trunk about the spear and held it high. ■ (From *The Beast of Lor* by Clyde Robert Bulla. Illustrated by Ruth Sanderson.)

Sanderson recently completed 100 full-color oil paintings for the new Knopf edition of *Heidi*. "I've always used models, but I work with a camera. It would be outrageous to expect people to pose for hours. I'm not making portraits; I'm working on scenes and actions. I take a roll of film for each scene and then pick the moment that looks right. Many times I will have to take shots of one model one day and another the next. I make sure my lighting is consistent and then I splice the photographs together. In *Heidi* there is a crowd scene in Frankfurt with a horse and carriage, a fountain, kids running in the street, Heidi, the doctor—and all kinds of things going on. I worked from a pile of references an inch thick. I took the horse and carriage from one source, the fountain from another and finally made it work as a whole. It took me a week just to design that scene.

"Sometimes I pin references on my drawing table, or keep them in piles to shuffle through again and again. With a book cover, I usually use two or three pieces of reference, but for *Heidi* I had to have a filing system. For the mountain scenes, I used books on the Alps, on Germany and on Switzerland. I wanted the furniture to look authentic with the period [around 1850], so I used books on antiques as a reference. In one of the illustrations I copied a painting by a German artist from that period. I was really getting into it! It was terrific, I felt as though *I* was back in 1850."

Sanderson has worked in every medium. "The 'Golden Books' are in watercolor. I just did *Five Little Bunnies* for Golden. It was nice after such an intensely emotional book as *Heidi* to paint little bunnies and make them hop around. When you've been involved in a heavier project, the 'Golden Books' are light entertainment, a real breather. For my book covers I use acrylic, air brush, colored pencil and sometimes alkyd. *Heidi* was done in oils, and from now on, I hope to work in oils as much as possible because I love it. I hadn't since art school, mainly because of the time constraint—oils take a long time to dry. After the first coat you must wait two or three days until you can go over it again and then it's another two or three days before the second coat dries. Oils are not conducive to tight deadlines. Because I had a year to do the *Heidi* project, I could wait for some of the paintings to dry, work on others, and then go back.

"Of the books I have illustrated, *Heidi* is without a doubt my favorite. I feel like it was made for me. I loved going back to 1850. Even the clothes in those days were more interesting and elegant than jeans and T-shirts of today! Maybe I was born in the wrong era. I also loved painting the mountains and the landscapes. Some illustrators do figures, and shy away from doing much in the way of backgrounds. In fact, Norman Rockwell hated landscapes. I enjoy landscapes and on *Heidi* I went all out. I enjoyed doing the cover for Anne Turner's *The Way Home* which was set in ninth and tenth century Britain. I painted rolling hills and a castle and marshes. I've been able to go further with my landscapes for jacket illustration than for the majority of my black and white books.

"My favorite illustrators are N. C. Wyeth and Maxfield Parrish. I'm drawn to the fine artists of the pre-Raphaelite period whose work is illustrative and tells a story, as well as to the impressionist painters. Though my own style is fairly representational, I love symbolic art, particularly the work of Magritte.

"I would like to write some day, but I've put it on the back burner for now. I'm not ready to make the commitment. I'm a good illustrator, and if I ever do write, I'll want to be a good

(From *Heidi* by Johanna Spyri. Illustrated by Ruth Sanderson.)

writer, too. Writing is like illustrating, you must practice before you get good at it.''

Sanderson lives ''in a little colonial house right on the main road in Palmer. Out of one of my studio windows I can see a big Catholic Church. My drawing board is next to another window which looks out over the grammar school across the street. I like to watch the kids play at recess while I work. Everything at one time or another inspires me. I like to listen to music while I paint.

''There is a considerable community of authors and illustrators in Massachusetts. I belong to the Western Massachusetts Illustrators Group, which I helped organize. We meet once a month, at which time local artists bring in their work and we help them pick out what would be best to include in their portfolios for the type of jobs they want to pursue. We have some very determined artists and a few who originally concentrated on fine art are now illustrating full time. This year we are producing a promotional calendar featuring the work of thirteen of our artists. We printed it ourselves and are sending it out to publishers to advertise the new illustrators in the group.

''For fun I read, play tennis and go horseback riding, though I don't get to ride as often as I'd like. I play with my little girl, Morgan. Even though she's only four, we already have drawers and drawers of her art work. She goes through more paper a day than I do! We are, of course, very encouraging. She says she wants to be an artist when she grows up, but she's very young, and very much influenced by me.

''I lecture at schools so that kids will have an opportunity to see that it is a real person creating art and not a machine.'' Sanderson's advice to aspiring young artists is to ''practice a lot, on your own. I'm still improving as an artist, as an illustrator; I am better now than when I started ten years ago. Every year you improve, hopefully. You never want to stay in one place.''

FOR MORE INFORMATION SEE: Lee Kingman and others, compilers, *Illustrators of Children's Books: 1967-1976,* Horn Book, 1978.

SARGENT, Sarah 1937-

BRIEF ENTRY: Born March 15, 1937, in Roanoke, Va. Sargent graduated from Randolph-Macon Woman's College and received an M.A. from Yale University. She became an English instructor at the University of North Dakota in 1961. Since then, she has taught English at the universities of Vermont, Minnesota, and Wisconsin—Oshkosh. The author of four juvenile novels, Sargent reveals: ''I am very interested in myth and in the various ways people add dimension to their lives by their participation in myths of one kind or another.''

Weird Henry Berg (Crown, 1980) is the tale of twelve-year-old Henry and a newly-hatched, century-old Welsh dragon named Orm. According to *Publishers Weekly,* it is an ''enthralling novel. . . . [that] owes much of its allure to Sargent's deft mix of reality and fantasy.'' *Horn Book* added, ''The conjunction of fantasy with reality is made believable by the author's narrative skill and by her ability to suggest character through economical description.''

In another fantasy, *Lure of the Dark* (Four Winds, 1984), Sargent combines the contemporary problems of a high school freshman with the chaotic forces behind the Norse god Loki. ''Sargent's fantasy probes good versus evil,'' observed *Booklist,* ''choosing, instead of the medieval setting common to the genre, a contemporary world; this results in an unusual, thought-provoking story. . . .'' The main characters of *Edward Troy and the Witch Cat* (Follett, 1978) and *Secret Lies* (Crown, 1981) are dealt with in more realistic tones as Sargent explores the fantasies children tend to create when abandoned by a parent. She has received several awards for her books, including a first place citation from the Council for Wisconsin Writers in 1979 for *Edward Troy and the Witch Cat* and a notable children's book citation from the American Library Association in 1981 for *Secret Lies.* Her anticipated works are tentatively titled *The Solstice Sun* and *The Seeds of Change.* Home: 627 Ceape Ave., Oshkosh, Wis. 54901.

FOR MORE INFORMATION SEE: Contemporary Authors, Volume 106, Gale, 1982.

SAUNDERS, Susan 1945-

BRIEF ENTRY: Born April 14, 1945, in San Antonio, Tex. Editor and author of books for children. Saunders graduated from Barnard College in 1966 and that same year began her career as a copy editor for John Wiley in New York City. Various editorial positions followed, including those as staff writer for CBS/Columbia House, editor for Visual Information Systems, and editor for Random House's subsidiary, Miller-Brody Productions, Inc. Since 1980 she has been employed as a free-lance writer and editor. Saunders believes ''there is a magic to . . . picture books, that I think doesn't exist anywhere else in literature.'' Her career as an author of children's books began with the publication of *Wales' Tale* (Viking, 1980). Set in an American town during the early 1900s, it is the story of a small girl who goes to market and meets a talking donkey named Wales. *School Library Journal* described it as ''a little magic . . . but more good humor.'' *Publishers Weekly* observed: ''It's a temptation to call Saunders's first book darling. . . . but the author's style doesn't let the fanciful tale dip into soppiness.''

In *Fish Fry* (Viking, 1982), the setting is again the early 1900s (1912, to be exact) as a little girl spends a summer day in East Texas at an old-fashioned event. *Booklist* labeled it ''a blissful re-creation of another place, another time,'' adding that ''young readers will be caught up in the evocative mood of this delightful reminiscence.'' Saunders's other picture books include *A Sniff in Time* (Atheneum, 1982), featuring a hungry wizard named Razzmatazz, and *Charles Rat's Picnic* (Atheneum, 1982), four brief stories that follow the adventures of Charles Rat and his friend, Miranda Armadillo. She also has written three books in Bantam's ''Choose Your Own Adventure'' series: *The Green Slime* (1982), *The Creature from Miller's Pond* (1983), and *The Tower of London* (1984). Saunders's latest book is *Dorothy and the Magic Belt* (Random House, 1985), based on the character created by L. Frank Baum. *Home and office address:* P.O. Box 736, Westhampton, N.Y. 11977.

FOR MORE INFORMATION SEE: Contemporary Authors, Volume 106, Gale, 1982.

SCHELL, Mildred 1922-

PERSONAL: Born October 13, 1922, in Union Furnace, Ohio; daughter of Alfred Michael (a plumber) and Helen (Moomaw) Schell. *Education:* Attended Miami Jacobs Business College, 1941, and Temple University, 1949; graduated from Baptist Institute for Christian Workers (with honors; first in class), 1951; attended University of Maryland Institute for Child Study, summer, 1961. *Politics:* Independent. *Religion:* American Baptist. *Home:* 311 Marathon Ave., Apt. 2, Dayton, Ohio 45406. *Office:* Smith & Schnacke, Mead Tower, Dayton, Ohio 45402.

CAREER: Following high school, Schell worked as a secretary and office manager for eight years; Walnut Hills Baptist Church, Cincinnati, Ohio, director of Christian Education and church secretary, 1951-52; Clarksburg Baptist Church, Clarksburg, W.Va., director of Christian education and recreation, 1952-54; American Baptist Board of Educational Ministries, Valley Forge, Pa., copyeditor and proofreader, 1955-56, assistant editor, 1956-57, editor, 1957-68; Pratt Institute, Brooklyn, N.Y., news editor and assistant director of public relations, 1968-71; Friendship Press, New York, N.Y., promotion assistant, 1971; United Methodist Church, Board of Global Ministries, Women's Division, New York City, executive secretary to the director of Office for Employed Women, 1971-72; Dayton (Ohio) Board of Education, work permit assistant, 1972-73; Smith & Schnacke (law firm), Dayton, executive legal secretary, 1973—; writer, 1948—. Director, St. David's Christian Writers Conference, 1965-74.

MEMBER: American Association of Retired Persons, St. David's Christian Writers' Association, Baptist Institute/Cushing Junior College Alumnae Association (president, 1965-68). *Awards, honors:* Williams Memorial Award, Second Baptist Church of Germantown, 1962, for outstanding service to children; named to the Honor Roll of Christian Education, Ohio Baptist Convention, 1979.

WRITINGS—Juvenile fiction: (Editor) Masahiro Kasuya, *The Way Christmas Came* (translated from the Japanese by Chieko Funakoshi; illustrated by M. Kasuya), Judson, 1973; (editor) Sister Shigeko Yano, *As Jesus Grew* (translated from the Japanese by Valerie Bannert; illustrated by S. Yano), Judson, 1973; (adapter) M. Kasuya, *The Tiniest Christmas Star* (translated from the Japanese; illustrated by M. Kasuya), Judson, 1979; (reteller) M. Kasuya, *A Tower Too Tall* (translated from the Japanese; illustrated by M. Kasuya), Judson, 1979; (adapter) *The Shoemaker's Dream* (illustrated by M. Kasuya), Judson, 1982.

Other: (Editor) *Living as a Christian: Children's Experiences of What Living as a Christian Means to Them*, Friendship, 1965; *The Church's Mission to Persons of Special Need* (teacher's guide), Friendship, 1965; *Mission: The Christian's Calling* (teacher's guide), Friendship, 1966; *A Place for Me* (how-to-use-guide for filmstrip), Friendship, 1968; *The Americas: How Many Worlds?* (teacher's guide/course plan; includes resource kit, "Look, Listen, and Learn"), Friendship, 1969; (with Phoebe Hathaway Foster) *Everyone Is Special* (vacation church school course; illustrated by Sidney A. Quinn), Judson, 1970; *Sing the Glory of Africa* (how-to-use guide for filmstrip), Friendship, 1971; (editor) Faye DeBeck Flynt, Norma McPhee, and Rosabelle Thangiah, *Points of Entry: Discussion Starters on Mission and Development*, Friendship, 1973; (editor) Elliott Wright, *Go Free* (study book), Friendship, 1973; *Teaching Children about the Mission of the Church Today* (teacher's guide), Friendship, 1973.

MILDRED SCHELL

Acts: How the Church Began (quarter lessons), American Baptist Board of Education and Publication, 1974; (contributing editor) *The Churches at Work in Europe*, Friendship, 1974; *Wanted: Writers for the Christian Market*, Judson, 1975; *Hebrews: Counsels of Faith and Courage* (quarter lessons), American Baptist Board of Education and Publication, 1975; *All God's Children Belong!* (vacation church school course; illustrated by Charles Shaw), Abingdon, 1976; *Journey toward Christmas*, privately printed, 1980; *Latin America* (curriculum unit), Board of International Ministries, American Baptist Churches, U.S.A., 1980; *Baptists in Europe* (curriculum unit), Board of International Ministries, American Baptist Churches, U.S.A., 1981; (contributor) Elizabeth W. Gale, editor, *Children Together 2*, Judson, 1982.

Also author of filmstrip scripts with how-to-use guides, including "The Bible around the World," 1960, "Trip to Brasilia," 1964, and "New Neighbors from Cuba," 1964, all published by Friendship; "Q & A: Toward a Better Church School" and "Teaching for Decision," both published by American Baptist Division of Church Education, 1978.

Contributor of poetry to *Moon Age Poets*, edited by Jaye Giammarino, Prairie Press, 1970. Contributor of stories, articles, and poetry to various publications, including *Baptist Leader, Christian Herald, Time of Singing, Young People*, and *Story World*. Member of editorial board of *Encore*, 1955-64.

WORK IN PROGRESS: Teaching plans for a Uniform Series unit, for adults and resources, pupil material and teaching plans for a unit in Uniform Series of Sunday Church school curriculum for adults.

SIDELIGHTS: ''I was privileged to grow up in what is suddenly being called the 'Great Depression.' Those of us who lived through it never thought of it as 'great,' and I suppose, though I really don't remember, we did not even use the term 'depression.' I am among the fortunate ones who never faced actual hunger or real privation—though we certainly knew we were poor. But then, so was everyone else, and to a young person it didn't really matter a lot. My parents, like most parents, evidently felt it was their role to face the problems and protect the young from any feeling of insecurity. And so,

I and my friends had the privilege of making our own fun, developing creativity that might have lain dormant had there been money for 'store bought' forms of fun. From those times, I have often recalled ways to do things that could become tools for teaching children. And, from those times, too, I have recalled many persons who had character and personality to become models for story people.

"One day, many years ago, I was standing in a long church corridor. People of all ages and sizes and shapes were passing

Outside Martin's window the snow fell softly.
Inside, Martin worked on his shoes.
As he worked, he thought, "It was such a lovely dream.
How I wish it might come true! How happy
I would be to have Jesus as my guest."
He sighed and went on with his work.

"You naughty boy! How dare you steal my apple!"
Martin dropped the shoe he was working on.
Outside his window an old woman held a boy by the arm.
In the boy's hand was an apple he had taken from
her basket. The boy tried to run away, but the old woman
held his arm tightly.

(From *The Shoemaker's Dream*, English text by Mildred Schell. Illustrated by Masahiro Kasuya.)

by on their way to the activities offered. It must have been at holiday time, for there was an air of excitement and happiness. But I noticed something strange. Adults greeted every other adult they passed, but for the most part the children might have been invisible to adults. I was startled enough to wonder whether this were always true. Research from the sidelines of many church corridors since has demonstrated that it is. Adults will greet children they know—but they do not see the children they do not know, though they always greet adults, known or unknown. From that experience and similar ones, I became an advocate for children as real, living, moving, breathing, important parts of society wherever they are. This eventually sent me scurrying off to learn how to minister for children and to a number of years spent in writing and editing for children and their teachers and parents.

"My years as an editor in elementary publications for our denominational publishing house opened the doors through which have come invitations to continue my ministry on behalf of children through writing.

"I have taught in church school situations for children and/or adults for some part of every year since I was fifteen—now nearly forty-seven years. My 'retirement' from curriculum writing doesn't seem to 'stick.' These days, I write for adults, however; and as long as assignments come and time permits, I likely will continue to do so. I continue to be an observer of persons and watch for those adventures which might one day be words on pages to enrich the lives of others.

"Because I worked with writers and would-be writers as an editor, I saw a need for places and ways in which those who wanted to write might hone their skills and develop their techniques, have contact with others of similar interests, and gain guidance in how to write in ways that would be marketable. This interest led me to participation in writers' conferences, especially in the St. David's Christian Writers' Conference (Pa.) over a long period of years. That association has brought opportunites to critique, to counsel and to encourage writers. It is almost more exciting to see a piece published which a conferee-student has done than to see my own writings in print. It is eminently sad to know that many who could write and be published never will, because they do not choose to pay the price of hard work and careful craftsmanship.

"Curricular writing presented me with challenges to try my hand at a variety of kinds of writing—poetry, filmstrip scripts, record content, drama, stories, articles, how-to's. It was a difficult school in some ways, but it was rewarding in its variety.

"My very first published piece was a poem for which Lord Tennyson should have received some credit, so closely was its modeling on one of his. That was when I was an eighth-grader who had an English teacher so perceptive that she insisted the poem be submitted to the school paper; then volunteered to spend a couple of hours a week after school teaching me form and meter. I hope that she might be pleased to know that nearly 50 years later, I still find my greatest enjoyment as a writer in the field of poetry and it still gets published from time to time—now without need to apologize for plagiarism.

"My first published short story was the result of badgering from a professor in English composition in college. Only through his interest did I realize that the ability to write is a trust which one is called to handle faithfully and as well as one can. Until then, I assumed everyone could write. When he set me to

reading the compositions of my classmates, I discovered the error of my thinking!

"Because I had the great good fortune to encounter two highly concerned teachers, I have tried to be that kind of teacher to others—and it has been and continues to be a rewarding and satisfying kind of life."

SCHWARTZ, Amy   1954-

BRIEF ENTRY: Born April 2, 1954, in San Diego, Calif. Author and illustrator of books for children. A free-lance illustrator since 1976 when she graduated from the California College of Arts and Crafts, Schwartz has also been employed as an elementary school art teacher and as a production assistant for Simon & Schuster. She is both author and illustrator of three picture books, beginning with *Bea and Mr. Jones* (Bradbury, 1982). It is the amusing story of little Bea, tired of kindergarten, who changes places with her advertising executive father who is, likewise, fed up with his business environment. *School Library Journal* called the book "visual caricature all the way," with drawings that portray "human figures . . . [as] rounded rather than angular, more symbolic of kindly peoplehood than naturalistic actors in life's drama."

In *Begin at the Beginning* (Harper, 1983), Schwartz provides a lesson in procrastination when second-grader Sara can't decide what to paint for her school art project. After several postponements her mother advises, "you can only begin at the beginning," sending Sara back to her original idea. *School Library Journal* again took note of Schwartz's illustrations, labeling them as "sort of a surreal Lois Lenski Family Small for the '80s . . . a refreshingly unique style." Schwartz's third picture book, *Mrs. Moskowitz and the Sabbath Candlesticks* (Jewish Publication Society, 1984) was described by *Booklist* as a "warm, loving story" in which elderly Mrs. Moskowitz finally accepts her new apartment as home after polishing two tarnished Sabbath candlesticks, an act that eventually leads to a family Shabbat dinner. "[The] pencil drawings are full of emotion and humor," *Booklist* added. "Even more than the text, they show that when one door is closed, another can be opened." In addition to her own books, Schwartz has provided the illustrations for Amy Hest's *The Crack-of-Dawn Walkers* (Macmillan, 1984) and Eve Bunting's *Jane Martin, Dog Detective* (Harcourt, 1984). *Residence:* Brooklyn, N.Y.

FOR MORE INFORMATION SEE: Contemporary Authors, Volume 110, Gale, 1984.

SELTZER, Richard (Warren, Jr.)   1946-

PERSONAL: Born February 23, 1946, in Clarksville, Tenn.; son of Richard Warren (an educator) and Helen (a writer; maiden name, Estes) Seltzer; married Barbara Hartley (a writer and publisher), July 28, 1973; children: Robert Richard Hartley, Heather Katherine Hartley, Michael Richard Hartley. *Education:* Yale University, B.A., 1969, graduate study, 1969-70; University of Massachusetts, M.A., 1973. *Home:* 33 Gould

St., West Roxbury, Mass. 02132. *Agent:* Ashley Darlington Grayson, 1342 18th St., San Pedro, Calif. 90732. *Office:* B & R Samizdat Express, P.O. Box 161, West Roxbury, Mass. 02132.

CAREER: University of Massachusetts, Amherst, Mass., instructor, 1973; Benwill Publishing, Boston, Mass., editor of *Electronics Test* and *Circuits Manufacturing* magazines, 1973-79; B & R Samizdat Express, West Roxbury, Mass., publisher, 1974—; *Word Guild* magazine, Cambridge, Mass., editor, 1977; Digital Equipment Corp., Maynard, Mass., editor of employee newspaper, 1979—. Free-lance translator of Russian. *Military service:* U.S. Army Reserve, 1969-75; became specialist, fifth class.

WRITINGS: *The Lizard of Oz* (fiction; illustrated by Christin Couture), B & R Samizdat Express, 1974; *Now and Then and Other Tales from Ome* (juvenile; self-illustrated), B & R Samizdat Express, 1976; *Rights Crossing* (two-act play; first produced in Columbia, Pa., 1977), Lancaster Historical Society, 1979; *The Name of Hero* (novel; first volume of trilogy), J. P. Tarcher, 1981. Also author of plays "Amythos" (three-act) and "Mercy" (two-act).

ADAPTATIONS: "The Lizard of Oz" (radio play), broadcast on WOMR-Radio (Provincetown, Mass.), spring, 1984.

WORK IN PROGRESS: The second and third volumes of a trilogy of historical novels based on the life of Russian cavalry officer, explorer, and monk, Alexander Bulatovich; *The Name of Man* and *The Name of God;* a collection of children's stories, *The Monsters at Our House.*

RICHARD SELTZER

Miss Morgan decided to take him to the river because she felt she owed him something. . . . ■ (From *The Lizard of Oz* by Richard Seltzer. Illustrated by Christin Couture.)

SIDELIGHTS: "Although I'm now immersed in writing historical novels for adults and in my regular job, writing a newspaper for a computer company, I still get the greatest satisfaction from writing children's stories and seeing the reactions of kids as they hear or read them."

FOR MORE INFORMATION SEE: The Self-Publishing Writer, spring, 1976.

SHREVE, Susan Richards   1939-

BRIEF ENTRY: Born May 2, 1939, in Toledo, Ohio. Educator and novelist. Shreve graduated magna cum laude from the University of Pennsylvania in 1961 and received her M.A. from the University of Virginia in 1969. During the late 1960s and early 1970s, she taught English in private schools at various locations in Pennsylvania and Washington, D.C. as well as Cheshire, England. Since 1976 she has been an associate professor of literature at George Mason University in Fairfax, Va. Shreve had already gained a reputation as an adult novelist (*A Fortunate Madness* and *A Woman Like That*) when she began writing novels for young adults. Many critics have focused on her ability to realistically portray familial relationships in her writings for both age groups.

Shreve is the author of six novels for older teens and two for younger readers, all published by Knopf. Falling into the first category are *The Nightmares of Geranium Street* (1977), *Loveletters* (1978), *Family Secrets: Five Very Important Stories* (1979), *The Masquerade* (1980), and *The Revolution of Mary Leary* (1982). The protagonists are adolescents, sometimes humorous, often-times not, faced with problems ranging from drugs, to an out-of-wedlock pregnancy, to a well-meaning but smothering mother. *School Library Journal* described Shreve's writing as "heavy on substance yet marked by simplicity which now and then comes very close to being elegant," also noting her "fine ear for the way kids talk." *Horn Book* agreed, commenting on her "terse style and her uncompromising perception of character" which, combined together, can "create a story that is deeply disturbing and sensitively told." She displays the same perceptiveness in her two novels for younger readers, *The Bad Dreams of a Good Girl* (1982) and *The Flunking of Joshua T. Bates* (1984). Shreve also continues to write for her original reading audience. Her fifth adult novel is entitled *Dreaming of Heroes* (Morrow, 1984). *Home:* 3201 36th St. N.W., Washington, D.C. 20016.

FOR MORE INFORMATION SEE: Contemporary Authors, New Revision Series, Volume 5, Gale, 1982; *Publishers Weekly,* July 23, 1982; *Contemporary Literary Criticism,* Volume 23, Gale, 1983.

SIMONS, Barbara B(rooks)   1934-
   (Barbara Brooks)

PERSONAL: Born December 4, 1934, in Rockford, Ill.; daughter of Ralph Raymond and Ruth Laura (Freed) Brooks; children: Elizabeth. *Education:* Northwestern University, B.S., 1955. *Home:* 511 West Aldine Ave., Chicago, Ill. 60657. *Office:* 154 East Erie St., Chicago, Ill. 60611.

CAREER: Encyclopaedia Britannica, Inc., Chicago, Ill., subeditor, 1957-60; Science Research Associates, Chicago, staff editor, 1960-64; Systems for Education, Chicago, editor, 1964-68; free-lance editor and writer, 1965-71; Times-Mirror Magazines, Inc., Chicago, managing editor of *Contemporary Publishers* and *Volume Library,* 1971—. *Member:* Women in Communications, Alpha Omicron Pi.

WRITINGS—For children: (Under name Barbara Brooks; with Richard Whittingham) *The Earth and the Stars* (illustrated by George Suyeoka), Southwestern, 1973; (compiler with Ruth Rooney) *Treasured Tales of Childhood,* Southwestern, 1974, Volume I: *Fables and Nursery Rhymes,* Volume II: *Stories about Animals,* Volume III: *Stories about People,* Volume IV: *All-Time Favorites; Volcanoes: Mountains of Fire,* Raintree, 1976.

"Adventure in Nature" series; all illustrated by Al Lowenheim; all published by Oak Tree: *A Visit to the Forest,* 1978; *. . .Ocean,* 1978; *. . .Prairies,* 1978; *. . .Mountains,* 1980.

Contributor under name Barbara Brooks to anthology, *Great Stories from World Literature,* compiled by Doris Heitkotler, Southwestern, 1973. Managing editor, *Illustrated Home Reference: A Quick and Useful Guide for Home and School Use* and *Webster's New World Dictionary with Student Handbook,* both published by Southwestern, 1973.

SKOLD, Betty Westrom   1923-

PERSONAL: Born August 27, 1923, in Braham, Minn.; daughter of Anshelm Theodore (a banker) and Marie (a nurse; maiden name, Hedlund) Westrom; married William Skold (a dental technician), December 29, 1956; children: Thomas;

BETTY WESTROM SKOLD

adopted children: Carol Skold Uecker, William, Jeffrey. *Education:* Gustavus Adolphus College, B.A., 1949. *Politics:* Democrat. *Religion:* Lutheran. *Home:* 4816 Diane Dr., Hopkins, Minn. 55343.

CAREER: Faribault Daily News, Faribault, Minn., editor of women's page, 1949-53; National Lutheran Council, Division of American Missions, Chicago, Ill., staff writer, 1953-56. Member of alumni board of Gustavas Adolphus College, late 1960s; member of Library Associates; president of Chapel View Nursing Home Auxiliary, 1979-81. Public speaker and leader of spiritual retreats. *Member:* American Swedish Institute. *Awards, honors:* Woman of Achievement award from West Suburban Chamber of Commerce, 1981.

WRITINGS—For children, except as noted: *Sacagawea: The Story of an American Indian,* Dillon, 1977; *Lord, I Have a Question: Story Devotions for Girls,* Augsburg, 1979; *The Kids Are Gone, Lord, But I'm Still Here* (adult), Augsburg, 1981; *Lord, I Need an Answer: Story Devotions for Girls,* Augsburg, 1982; *I'm Glad You're Open Weekdays* (adult prayer conversations), Augsburg, 1985. Contributor of articles to religious periodicals, including *Lutheran.*

SIDELIGHTS: "Why has most of my writing, both for children and for adults, gravitated toward issues of faith? Perhaps because I grew up in a home in which contact with God was as natural as breathing. My parents introduced me to a loving God who created the gift of laughter as surely as he created moral correctness and wisdom and honor.

"At a Lutheran college, Gustavus Aldolphus, I was encouraged to express my faith through the things I do best. While my principal 'showcase writing' in college was in humorous features for the campus weekly, I was at the same time jotting down my private experiences in a makeshift journal.

"A four-and-one-half year episode of tuberculosis at age twenty contributed to my development as a writer. On a practical level, it shut one door, a contemplated teaching career, and set me to looking for an alternate way of making a living. Tuberculosis also presented me with a block of quiet time with few interruptions in which to read books and to practice the craft of writing.

"Following college graduation I served a four-year hitch as a writer on a small town paper, the *Faribault Daily News,* a priceless setting for gaining experience. I was given a wide range of assignments—straight news, features, social notes, weddings, obituaries. There were even occasional forays into the sports pages and the editorial columns. I learned how to turn out a large volume of copy in a short time without agonizing over detail.

"When I felt that I had served a satisfactory apprenticeship at the *Daily News,* it seemed right to look to the church for new opportunities, since I view all of life in terms of discipleship. I found an interesting challenge as staff writer for the rural church program of the National Lutheran Council.

"This work sent me out from Chicago into the countryside in many directions, gathering facts and impressions for pamphlet materials, news releases, and magazine features. It also broadened my experience by giving me a taste of big city living.

"In my early thirties, I returned to Minnesota to marry a widower with three children. This meant a quickie course in a multitude of new skills. I legally adopted Bill's three children and submerged myself in a life of cookie baking and laundry and P.T.A. A year and a half later I gave birth to a baby boy and learned to rear a child 'from scratch.' During those years the writing lay fallow except for some 'freebie' publicity work for my local church and some 'closet' poetry writing.

"When the children outgrew their need for my hourly vigilance, I began to cast about for some work to do. Keeping books for my husband's dental laboratory was a part of the answer, but the writer in me refused to be denied. I investigated some journalistic possibilities, but nothing jelled. Then I enrolled in a night class in writing for children. Through this class I made contact with an educational publisher who assigned me to do a child's biography of Sacagawea. In that first book I learned the discipline of research and learned to handle the ego-shattering experience of being edited.

"My joy in writing has persisted because I have been willing to try new things, to write for a variety of age groups, to move from journalism to poetry and from essays to biography and fiction.

"Writing should spring from what you know best. It is more important that the reader can identify with the material than that she or he should be intrigued by its novelty. The material for my children's books has been mined from memories of my own childhood as well as memories from the lives of my children. For my women's books, I reach back into every experience I have had as a wife, as a mother, and as a woman.

"In regard to style, I use the same approach for children as I do for adults. I am in love with plain, strong words and simple expression. These are the basic raw materials for good writing of any kind. My writing mentor from earlier days challenged me to peel away the adjectives and get down to 'meat-and-potatoes' writing. To me, this kind of writing is not only clear, but it is also beautiful.

"I should like my young readers to understand their parents' point of view, but the parents are always depicted as somewhat imperfect. They are flawed human beings who make mistakes, real people who are sometimes dead wrong.

"In *Lord, I Have a Question* and *Lord, I Need an Answer,* I made no secret of the fact that I wanted the young reader to shape up in a moral and ethical sense. In a day when even children are seen as targets for raw 'realism' and books about ugliness and seamy morality, I insist that this is only one side of reality, that goodness and nobility and happiness are fully as 'real.'"

SMALLWOOD, Norah (Evelyn) 1910(?)-1984

OBITUARY NOTICE: Born about 1910; died October 11, 1984. Publishing executive. Smallwood began her career in publishing as a secretary to the chairman of Chatto & Windus in 1936. Her responsibilities with the company were enlarged during World War II, and she became increasingly involved with book design. In 1945 she earned a partnership in the firm. Smallwood was appointed chairman and managing director in 1975. She is credited with building a strong children's department and acquiring British rights to the works of leading American authors. For her services to literature Smallwood was named an officer of the Order of the British Empire and awarded an honorary doctorate by the University of Leeds.

FOR MORE INFORMATION SEE—Obituaries: *Times* (London), October 12, 1984; *AB Bookman's Weekly,* November 26, 1984.

SMITH, Anne Warren 1938-

PERSONAL: Born July 3, 1938, in Ticonderoga, N.Y.; daughter of Thurman Clifford (vice-president of International Paper Co.) and Laura (Myers) Warren; married Frederick J. Smith (a marine economist), August 22, 1959; children: Amy Katherine, Rebecca Louise. *Education:* Cornell University, B.S., 1960; graduate study at Oklahoma State University, 1960-62. *Home:* 3720 North West Fillmore Ave., Corvallis, Ore. 97330.

CAREER: Author of books for young people. Also worked as assistant to a behavioral psychologist, 1962-64. *Member:* Society of Children's Book Writers, Camp Fire, Inc., Pi Beta Phi, Corvallis Folklore Society, Corvallis Singers. *Awards, honors:* Juvenile novel and juvenile short fiction awards, Pacific Northwest Writers Conference, 1977, for "The Westward Wish," and "I Don't Know You Anymore."

WRITINGS: Blue Denim Blues (juvenile novel), Atheneum, 1982; *Sister in the Shadow,* Atheneum, 1985.

WORK IN PROGRESS: Suspended Summer, a juvenile novel; young adult novel about a young woman who suffers from manic depressive illness; short stories and articles.

SIDELIGHTS: ''People are fascinating to me. I watch them in stores, eavesdrop on their conversations in restaurants, and cry at airports as I watch them say good-bye. Each person is unique, but each has the same need, the need to feel worthwhile. People have to feel good about themselves before they can make all of society happier and healthier. It has to start *inside* each person.

''There's a lot of me in *Blue Denim Blues:* my feelings about Oregon and small college towns, my enjoyment in playing Blue Grass music in a group, my own shortcomings as a parent. There are many children in the book—the one's I've known as I baby-sat, taught preschool, and mothered, and the one's I've guided in and out of the woods as a Camp Fire leader.

''It's my opinion that the finest professions are those that involve work with small children. In a good preschool, with a good teacher, a child thrives emotionally—and what a fine investment that is in the life of a future adult. So when my main character admits sadly that the only thing she's good at is working with children, I say: You are important! Go to it!

''The character of Janet reminds me of myself as a youngster, afraid to speak out, and certain that a gathering of more than

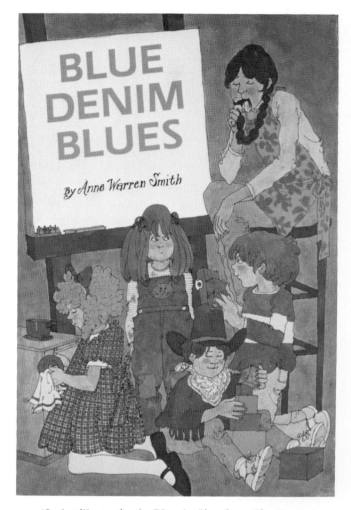

(Jacket illustration by Blanche Sims from *Blue Denim Blues* by Anne Warren Smith.)

two people constituted a hostile crowd. I wasn't as courageous as Janet; I could never have applied for the teaching job as she did. But she did apply, and those two great equalizers, music and children, propelled her into accomplishments she'd never imagined for herself.''

ANNE WARREN SMITH

SORLEY WALKER, Kathrine

PERSONAL: Born in Aberdeen, Scotland; daughter of James (an editor and journalist) and Edith Jane (Robertson) Sorley Walker. *Education:* Attended Crouch End College, King's College, London, University of Besancon, and Trinity College of Music. *Religion:* Church of Scotland. *Home:* 60 Eaton Mews W., London SW1W 9ET, England.

CAREER: Geographical Magazine, London, England, editorial assistant, 1951-57; free-lance writer and editor, 1960—. *Member:* Critics' Circle (London).

WRITINGS: Brief for Ballet, Pitfield Press, 1947; *Beauty Is Built Anew* (verse), Maclellan, 1948; *Robert Helpmann* (monograph), Rockliff, 1958; (translator) *Haydn,* J. Calder, 1960;

The Heart's Variety (verse), Mitre Press, 1960; (editor with Dorothy Gardiner) *Raymond Chandler Speaking,* Houghton, 1962; *Eyes on the Ballet,* Methuen, 1963, revised edition, John Day, 1965; *Joan of Arc,* J. Cape, 1965; *Eyes on Mime,* John Day, 1969; *Saladin: Sultan of the Holy Sword,* Dobson, 1971; *Dance and Its Creators,* John Day, 1972; (editor) A. V. Coton, *Writings on Dance, 1938-1968,* Dance Books, 1975; (with Joan Butler) *Ballet for Boys and Girls,* Prentice-Hall, 1979; *Emotions and Atmosphere* (verse), Beacon Press, 1979; *The Royal Ballet: A Picture History,* Threshold Books, 1981, DaCapo, 1982; *De Basil's Ballets Russes,* Hutchinson, 1982, Atheneum, 1983. Also author of short stories and children's serial plays for BBC Scottish Radio.

London editor, *Dance Encyclopedia,* Simon & Schuster. Contributor to *Encyclopaedia Britannica, Encyclopedia of Dance and Ballet, Enciclopedia dello Spettacolo* and *International Encyclopedia of Dance.* Ballet critic, *Playgoer,* 1946-51, and *Daily Telegraph,* 1962—. Contributor to *Dancing Times, Ballet Review, Dance Chronicle, Stage, Lady, Theatre Notebook, Hemisphere, Dance Gazette, Dance and Dancers,* and other publications.

WORK IN PROGRESS: Book on ballet and related arts in Britain between World War I and World War II; book on the background of the major ballet companies for students and teachers.

SIDELIGHTS: "I spent the first three years in India (Bombay) as my father was *Reuter's* editor there. Tragically, he died at

KATHRINE SORLEY WALKER

the age of twenty-eight of amoebic dysentery and my mother and I returned to Scotland.

Lynn Seymour is working on her ballet *The Court of Love* with dancers of the Sadler's Wells Royal Ballet. ■ (From *Ballet for Boys and Girls* by Kathrine Sorley Walker and Joan Butler. Photograph courtesy of Nobby Clark.)

"A delicate child, I had a serious illness (myocarditis) when I was ten, and the family moved a year later to the south of England where the climate was less rigorous. I have, therefore, grown up a Londoner, but inevitably proud of my Scots heritage. As an adult I have travelled widely, returning to India more than once on visits and spending considerable time in Australia, Northeastern United States, and Italy.

"I never envisaged any other career than that of a writer. My family background on both sides inclined heavily to the arts. Although much of the emphasis was on teaching and education, various members of the family wrote prose and verse or practised as journalists, while others (including my mother) drew and painted. I had a flair for writing from my earliest days, and also had the closest and wisest encouragement from my mother, who was both sympathetic and critical of my work.

"From the first I shared my mother's passionate interest in the theatre and all forms of performing arts were dominant elements in my life. My love of ballet led me into the field of dance criticism, but I never intended to specialize so strictly, and would still like to reach out into other fields—adult and juvenile fiction, history or drama."

HOBBIES AND OTHER INTERESTS: Theater; history, particularly Europe in the seventeenth and eighteenth centuries; geography, natural history, and botany, particularly in reference to Australia.

DONALD D. SPENCER

SPENCER, Donald D(ean)   1931-

PERSONAL: Born March 28, 1931, in Louisa, Ky.; son of Jefferson Burns (a cabinetmaker) and Gladys (Oharu) Spencer; married Rae Brinlee; children: Sandra, Susan, Sherrie, Steven, Laura, Michael. *Education:* San Diego State College (now University), B.A., 1960; Southeastern University, Ph.D., 1982. *Office:* Camelot Publishing Co., P.O. Box 1357, Ormond Beach, Fla. 32074.

CAREER: Ryan Aeronautical Co., San Diego, Calif., engineer, 1957-60; Sperry Univac, San Diego, systems analyst, 1960-62; General Electric Co., Daytona Beach, Fla., computer scientist, 1962-71; Abacus Computer Corp., Ormond Beach, Fla., president, 1967-75; Camelot Publishing Co., Ormond Beach, president, 1975—. College teacher; lecturer. *Military service:* U.S. Marine Corps, 1950-54; became sergeant; received Purple Heart. *Member:* World Future Society, Association for Computing Machinery, National Council of Teachers of Mathematics, Association for Educational Data Systems, Institute of Electrical and Electronics Engineers, Robotics International of the Society of Manufacturing Engineers, Data Processing Management Association.

WRITINGS: The Computer Programmer's Dictionary and Handbook, Blaisdell, 1968; *Game Playing with Computers,* Spartan, 1968, 2nd edition, Hayden, 1976; *Programming with USA Standard FORTRAN and FORTRAN IV,* Blaisdell, 1969; *Fundamentals of Digital Computers,* Sams, 1969, 2nd edition, 1978.

Simpletran, Abacus Computer Corp., 1970; *A Thesaurus of Computer Names,* Abacus Computer Corp., 1970; *A Guide to BASIC Programming: A Time-Sharing Language,* Addison-Wesley, 1970, 2nd edition, 1975; *Computers,* Abacus Computer Corp., 1973; *Computers and Programming Guide for Engineers,* Sams, 1973, 2nd edition published as *Computers and Programming Guide for Scientists and Engineers,* 1980; *The Story of Computers,* Abacus Computer Corp., 1973, 2nd edition, Camelot, 1977; *A Guide to Teaching about Computers in Secondary Schools,* Abacus Computer Corp., 1973; *Computers in Society,* Hayden, 1974; *Computer Acronym Handbook,* Prentice-Hall, 1974; *Computers in Action: How Computers Work,* Hayden, 1974, 2nd edition, 1978; *Introduction to Information Processing,* C. E. Merrill, 1974, 3rd edition, 1981; *Sixty Challenging Problems,* Hayden, 1974, 2nd edition, 1979.

Computer Dictionary, Camelot, 1975, 2nd edition, 1979; *Computer Science Mathematics,* C. E. Merrill, 1976; *FORTRAN Programming,* Camelot, 1977, 2nd edition, 1980; *Problem Solving with FORTRAN,* Prentice-Hall, 1977; *Game Playing with BASIC,* Hayden, 1977; *Accent on BASIC,* Camelot, 1977; *A Quick Look at BASIC,* Camelot, 1977; *Microcomputers at a Glance,* Camelot, 1977; *Problems for Computer Solution,* Hayden, 1977, 2nd edition, 1979; *Fun with Microcomputers and BASIC,* Reston, 1977, 2nd edition, 1981; *BASIC: A Unit for Secondary Schools,* Camelot, 1977, 2nd edition, Sterling Swift, 1980; *Visual Masters for Teaching FORTRAN Programming,* Sterling Swift, 1978; *Fun with Computers and BASIC,* Camelot, 1978; *Computer Awareness Book,* Camelot, 1978, 2nd edition, Sterling Swift, 1982; *Using BASIC in the Classroom,* Camelot, 1978; *Data Processing: An Introduction,* C. E. Merrill, 1978, 2nd edition published as *Data Processing: An Introduction with BASIC,* 1982; *The Computer Quiz Book,* Camelot, 1978; *Some People Just Won't Believe a Computer,* Camelot, 1978; *Computer Dictionary for Everyone,* Scribner, 1979, 3rd edition, 1985; *Visual Masters:*

BASIC Programming, Camelot, 1979, 2nd edition, Sterling Swift, 1982; *Visual Masters: Teaching about Computers,* Camelot, 1979, 2nd edition, Sterling Swift, 1982.

What Computers Can Do, Camelot, 1980 (educational edition), Sterling Swift, 1982, new edition, Scribner, 1984; *Computers for Kids,* Camelot, 1980; *The Illustrated Computer Dictionary,* C. E. Merrill, 1980, 2nd edition, 1983; *BASIC Programming Concepts,* C. E. Merrill, 1981; *Student Guide: Introduction to Information Processing,* C. E. Merrill, 1981 (see above); *Exploring the World of Computers,* Sterling Swift, 1982; *Programming the TRS-80 Pocket Computer,* Prentice-Hall, 1982; *Computers in Number Theory,* Computer Science Press, 1982; *BASIC Workbook for Microcomputers,* Sterling Swift, 1982; *Computer Poster Book,* Sterling Swift, 1982; *Microcomputer Coloring Book,* Sterling Swift, 1982; *Illustrated Computer Dictionary for Young People,* Sterling Swift, 1982; *Famous People of Computers,* Sterling Swift, 1982; *Pocket Guide of Computer Terminology,* Sterling Swift, 1982; *BASIC Programming* (educational edition), Sterling Swift, 1982, (trade edition), Scribner, 1984; *Problem Solving with BASIC* (educational edition), Sterling Swift, 1982, (trade edition), Scribner, 1984; *Basic Quiz Book,* Sterling Swift, 1982; *Computer Literacy Test Questions,* Sterling Swift, 1982; *Student Guide: Data Processing* (see above), C. E. Merrill, 1982; *An Introduction to Computers,* C. E. Merrill, 1983; *Understanding Computers* (educational edition), Sterling Swift, 1984, (trade edition), Scribner, 1984; *Student Guide: Understanding Computers* (see above), Sterling Swift, 1984.

SORRY, OUR PRESIDENT IS OUT OF TOWN, OUR FIRST VICE—PRESIDENT IS OUT SICK, AND OUR SECOND VICE—PRESIDENT IS A COMPUTER.

(From *Some People Just Won't Believe a Computer* by Donald D. Spencer.)

Computers and Information Processing, C. E. Merrill, 1985; *Student Guide: Computers and Information Processing* (see above), C. E. Merrill, 1985; *A Guide to Computer Careers,* Macmillan, 1985; *Principles of Information Processing,* C. E. Merrill, 1985; *Learning BASIC for Micros: A Worktext,* C. E. Merrill, 1985; *Learning BASIC for Micros: A Worktext for the IBM PC,* C. E. Merrill, 1985; *Learning BASIC for Micros: A Worktext for the Apple II,* C. E. Merrill, 1985; *Learning BASIC for Micros: A Worktext for the TRS-80,* C. E. Merrill, 1985.

WORK IN PROGRESS: Several books in computer science and robotics.

SIDELIGHTS: With his G.I. bill benefits and several part-time jobs, Spencer earned his degree in mathematics. His course of study included one computer course, the only one offered at the university. Most of his training in the field of computers was sponsored by private industry in the form of company-held seminars. " . . . It interested me. I would sit in the computer room alone at night, just me . . . alone with millions of dollars of equipment at my disposal. I would still be there when the morning shift would come in and I would have to stop." [John Carter, "In Computer's Dark Ages, He Took the Byte," *Evening News* (Florida), August 28, 1984.[1]]

After receiving his B.A. from San Diego State College, Spencer was hired to work with the pioneering group of computer elites at Univac. The atmosphere at Univac was charged with the excitement of discovery. However, Spencer considers himself a forward thinker far more excited about the future trends of computers. Computers, he envisions, will become "a part of everyone's life as soon as we get rid of the keyboard."[1] The next innovation will be a voice recognition system.

Some of Spencer's books have been translated into Japanese, German, Swedish, and Spanish. "Work is my play. I'm always thinking about another book."[1]

STRAND, Mark 1934-

PERSONAL: Born April 11, 1934, in Summerside, Prince Edward Island, Canada; son of Robert Joseph and Sonia (Apter) Strand; married Antonia Ratensky, September 14, 1961 (divorced, 1974); married Julia Garretson, March 15, 1976; children: Jessica. *Education:* Antioch College, B.A., 1957; Yale University, B.F.A., 1959; State University of Iowa, M.A., 1962. *Home:* 475 Third Ave., Salt Lake City, Utah 84103.

CAREER: University of Iowa, Iowa City, instructor in English, 1962-65; University of Brazil, Rio de Janeiro, Fulbright lecturer, 1965-66; Mount Holyoke College, South Hadley, Mass., assistant professor, 1967; visiting professor at University of Washington, Seattle, 1968, 1970, Columbia University, New York, N.Y., 1969, and Yale University, New Haven, Conn., 1969-70; Brooklyn College of the City University of New York, associate professor, 1970-72; Princeton University, Princeton, N.J., Bain-Swiggett Lecturer, 1973—. Hurst Professor of Poetry, Brandeis University, University of Virginia, Wesleyan University, Harvard University, and University of Utah. *Awards, honors:* Fulbright scholarship for study in Italy, 1960-61; Ingram Merrill fellowship, 1966; National Council for the Humanities grant, 1967-68; Rockefeller fellowship, 1968-69; Edgar Allan Poe award, 1974; National In-

At that moment Luke heard a moaning, whistling wind at his back. ■ (From *The Planet of Lost Things* by Mark Strand. Illustrated by William Pène du Bois.)

MARK STRAND

stitute of Arts and Letters award, 1975; Guggenheim fellowship, 1975-76; National Endowment for the Arts, 1977; fellowship of the Academy of American Poets, 1979.

WRITINGS: Sleeping with One Eye Open (poems), Stone Wall Press, 1964; *Reasons for Moving* (poems), Atheneum, 1968; (editor) *The Contemporary American Poets*, New American Library, 1968; *Darker* (poems), Atheneum, 1970; (editor) *New Poetry of Mexico* (anthology), Dutton, 1970; (translator) *18 Poems from the Quechua,* Halty Ferguson, 1971; *The Story of Our Lives* (poems), Atheneum, 1973; (translator and editor) Rafael Alberti, *The Owl's Insomnia,* Atheneum, 1973; *The Sargeantville Notebook* (poems), Burning Deck, 1974; (editor with Charles Simic) *Another Republic: Seventeen European and South American Writers,* Ecco Press, 1976; *The Monument,* Ecco Press, 1978; *The Late Hour* (poems), Atheneum, 1978; *Selected Poems,* Atheneum, 1980; *The Planet of Lost Things* (juvenile; illustrated by William Pène du Bois), Potter, 1983; *Art of the Real: Nine American Figurative Painters,* Potter, 1983; *The Selected Poems of Carlos Drummond de Andrade,* Random House, 1984.

WORK IN PROGRESS: More poems.

SIDELIGHTS: "I have no idea how I came to write books, and I have no definable audience in mind when I write. My poems, stories, even essays, are versions of what I've read—misrememberings, misunderstandings. The process by which they are shaped is a mystery to me and I would just as soon keep it that way. I know that reading is important to me, that if I didn't do it, I wouldn't write.''

FOR MORE INFORMATION SEE: Yale Review, autumn, 1968; *Contemporary Literature,* Volume X, number 2, 1969; *Virginia Quarterly Review,* summer, 1969; *Antioch Review,* fall/winter, 1970-71; Carolyn Riley, editor, *Contemporary Literary Criticism,* Volume VI, Gale, 1976.

STRASSER, Todd 1950(?)- (Morton Rhue)

BRIEF ENTRY: Born about 1950. Author of novels for young adults. Strasser spent his childhood on Long Island where his father owned a dressmaker factory. During the 1960s he became an active participant in the drug culture, a lifestyle that changed abruptly in 1972 when his cousin died from an overdose. Returning to Beloit College, Strasser subsequently earned a degree in English and later held positions with the *Record* (Middletown, N.Y.), a Madison Avenue advertising agency, and *Esquire* magazine. Now the author of young adult novels like *Angel Dust Blues* (Coward, 1979), *Friends Til the End* (Delacorte, 1981), *Rock n' Roll Nights* (Delacorte, 1982), and *Workin' for Peanuts* (Delacorte, 1983), Strasser is particularly concerned with the lack of quality reading material for young males. It is this gap he strives to fill through his novels, although the topics covered—drugs, death, sex, rock music—and sensitivity of his characters ensure popularity with teenage members of both sexes. Among his latest works are *Turn It Up!, The Complete Computer Popularity Program* (both Delacorte, 1984), and *A Very Touchy Subject* (Delacorte, 1985). Under the pseudonym Morton Rhue, Strasser is the author of *The Wave* (Delacorte, 1981), the novelization of a television drama based on a true incident when a history high school teacher re-enacted Hitler's youth movement with alarming results. *Residence:* New York, N.Y.

FOR MORE INFORMATION SEE: People Weekly, April 16, 1979; *Media and Methods,* February, 1983; Alleen Pace Nilson and Kenneth L. Donelson, *Literature for Today's Youth,* 2nd edition, Scott, Foresman, 1985.

STREN, Patti 1949-

BRIEF ENTRY: Born in 1949. Canadian author and illustrator of books for children. Prior to her writing career, Stren studied to be a Montessori teacher and worked with autistic children in Israel; as an art student, she studied under cartoonist R. O. Blechman and author/illustrator Maurice Sendak. Stren is known for her simple, unpretentious stories and broken-lined, cartoon-like drawings. The binding theme amongst her books is very basic, namely, the universal need for love and understanding. Many critics have found her witty and whimsical style equally appealing to children and adults. In her first book, *Hug Me* (Harper, 1977), the hero is a likeable porcupine named Elliot Kravitz who yearns to be hugged. Not surprisingly, he has a difficult time finding a recipient for his affections. The book became a children's best-seller and also acquired a large reading audience on college campuses. ''It's the kind of bright picture book,'' observed *Publishers Weekly,* ''that finds its way into college bookstores and is offered as a love token by yearning swains.''

In *Sloan and Philamina; or, How to Make Friends with Your Lunch* (Dutton, 1979), Stren creates an endearing anteater who would rather make friends with an ant than eat her for lunch. ''Once again Patti Stren champions the nonconformist. . . ,'' noted *Maclean's.* ''Her tender-hearted humor make[s] this book a wonderful encore. . . .'' She continues to explore the need for love and acceptance in her first novel for children, *There's a Rainbow in My Closet* (Harper, 1979). It is the story of Emma, a highly imaginative child, who feels unappreciated at school but finds comfort in the relationship that she develops with her visiting grandmother. A reviewer for *Canadian Children's Literature* called it ''a funny book, a tender, wistful story, a tough, lively, endearing novel full of shifts in tone and mood, full of colour. . . .'' Stren's other picture books are *Bo, the Constrictor That Couldn't* (Green Tree, 1978), *Mountain Rose* (Dutton, 1982), and *I'm Only Afraid of the Dark (at Night!!)* (Harper, 1982). She is also the illustrator of Rosemary Allison's *Yaaay Crickets!!!* and Phyllis Green's *Eating Ice Cream with a Werewolf.*

FOR MORE INFORMATION SEE: Children's Literature Review, Volume 5, Gale, 1983.

TARSKY, Sue 1946-

PERSONAL: Born July 26, 1946, in New York, N.Y.; daughter of George and Virginia Krawchick. *Education:* Cedar Crest College, B.A., 1968. *Residence:* London, England.

CAREER: Simon & Schuster, Inc., New York, N.Y., editorial assistant of adult books, 1968-71; Random House, Inc., New York City, editorial assistant of adult books, 1971-73, assistant editor of children's books, 1973-75; Usborne Publishing Ltd., London, England, editor of children's books, 1976-77; Marshall Cavendish Children's Books Ltd., London, editor, 1977-78; Walker Books Ltd., London, editor of children's books, 1978-84; Creative Bytes Ltd., London, co-founder and director, 1984—. *Awards, honors: The Prickly Plant Book* was selected as one of the outstanding science books for children, 1981, by the National Teachers Association/Children's Book Council Joint Committee.

WRITINGS—All juvenile: *The NatureTrail Book of Wild Flowers* (illustrated by David Ashby and others), edited by Sue Jacquemier and others, Usborne, 1977; (with Malcolm Hart and Ingrid Selberg) *The Children's Book of the Countryside* (illustrated by D. Ashby and others), Usborne, 1978; (with Michael Raine) *The Spectrum Book of Subroutines,* Grisewood & Dempsey, 1985.

''Taking a Walk'' series; all published by Marshall Cavendish: *Taking a Walk in the Town* (illustrated by Grahame Corbett), 1978; *. . . in the Park* (illustrated by G. Corbett), 1978; *. . . at the Seashore* (illustrated by Jane Walton), 1978; *. . . in the Countryside* (illustrated by J. Walton), 1978.

''How Does Your Garden Grow?'' series: *The Prickly Plant Book* (illustrated by G. Corbett and Will Giles), Walker Books, 1980, Little, Brown, 1981; *The Window Box Book* (illustrated by G. Corbett and Amanda Severne), Walker Books, 1980; *The Potted Plant Book* (illustrated by W. Giles, Barbara Firth, and Jane Wolsak), Walker Books, 1980, Little, Brown, 1981.

''Look and Say'' series; all illustrated by Clive Scruton; all published by Simon & Schuster: *Apple and Pear,* 1983; *Cup*

Opuntias are useful plants for grafting. The way shown here is called wedge grafting (see p. 35).

(From *The Prickly Plant Book* by Sue Tarsky. Illustrated by Will Giles.)

and Bowl, 1983; *Doll and Drum,* 1983; *Table and Chair,* 1983.

"Time to Talk" series; all illustrated by David Bennett; all published by Simon & Schuster: *Playtime,* 1983; *Shopping,* 1983.

"Chatterbox" series; all published by Random House: *Who Goes Moo?* (illustrated by Deborah Ward), 1985; *Open the Door* (illustrated by D. Ward), 1985; *I Can* (illustrated by Katy Sleight), 1985; *Who Goes Splash?* (illustrated by K. Sleight), 1985.

Computer software; all for children under the age of five; all published by Griffin Software, 1985, except where indicated: (With M. Raine) *Bathtime; Shapes; Odd One Out;* (with M. Raine) *Windsurfer* (for all ages), Entersoft Ltd., 1985.

Editor; all juvenile: (With S. Jacquemier) Peter Holden, *Spotter's Guide to Birds* (illustrated by Trevor Boyer), Usborne, 1977; Alfred Leutscher, *A Walk through the Season* (illustrated by Graham Allen and others), Walker Books, 1981; *Never a Dull Moment* (illustrated by C. Scruton and others), Schocken, 1983.

ADAPTATIONS—Computer software; all for children under the age of five; all published by Griffin Software, 1985: *Shopping; Doll and Drum; Cup and Bowl.*

WORK IN PROGRESS: A picture book for William Collins & Sons Ltd.; four picture-story books for Carousel Books/Corgi Books.

SIDELIGHT: "I was lucky; my parents and primary school teachers sparked a love of books and reading in me, and I have always felt that words hold a bit of magic. Add to this an active imagination and a firm belief in the power of illustration and art, and I don't see how I could have ended up doing anything but writing and editing children's books. I especially enjoy creating books for children under the age of five, probably because it lets me experiment with all the things I like best, to make books that are pure fun.

"The transition from books to software was a natural progression for me. Software takes books one stage further; it lets me animate the static pictures in a book, quickly. Software also encourages children to respond to the words and pictures on the screen, letting them cause certain things to happen in a way that's impossible in a book. With good programs, just as with good books, children's imaginations are the only limits to their experiences.

"Computers and children's books now share my time. I am now very involved with interactive video. Computers will never replace books for me, but I enjoy both and each seems to create new ideas for the other."

Children, you are very little,
And your bones are very brittle;
If you would grow great and stately,
You must try to walk sedately.
—Robert Louis Stevenson

TAYLOR, Ann 1782-1866
(Ann Gilbert; A Lady, Juvenilia, pseudonyms)

PERSONAL: Born January 30, 1782, in Islington, London, England; died December 20, 1866, in Nottingham, England; daughter of Isaac II (an engraver, author, and minister) and Ann (an author; maiden name, Martin) Taylor; married Joseph Gilbert (a clergyman), December 24, 1813 (died, 1852); children: eight. *Education:* Educated at home, mostly by her father, primarily in the arts of sketching and engraving. *Residence:* Nottingham, England.

CAREER: Poet and author of books for adults and children. At the age of sixteen won first prize with a poetical solution of a riddle in the *Minor's Pocket Book;* beginning that same year, 1798, became a regular contributor to the publication, under the pseudonym "Juvenilia"; produced first book of verse, *Original Poems for Infant Minds,* in collaboration with sister, Jane Taylor, and others, 1804; coauthor of other books for children with sister, 1804-13; produced works on her own, beginning 1813.

WRITINGS: (Under pseudonym, A Lady) *My Mother* (poem; engraved by P. W. Tomkins), P. W. Tomkins (London), 1807, William Charles (Philadelphia), 1816; *The Wedding among the Flowers* (in verse), Darton & Harvey (London), 1808 [another edition illustrated by her brother, Isaac Taylor III, with preface by Henry Taylor, 1914]; *The Mother's Fables in Verse Designed through the Amusement to Correct Some of the Faults and Follies of Children,* revised edition, Darton, Harvey & Darton, 1812 (Taylor was not associated with the original edition); *Hymns for Infant Schools,* B. J. Holdsworth (London), 1827; *Original Anniversary Hymns, Adapted to the Public Services of Sunday Schools and Sunday School Unions,* B. J. Holdsworth, 1827; (under name Ann Gilbert) *Sketches from a Youthful Circle,* [London], 1834; (under name Ann Gilbert) *The Convalescent: Twelve Letters on Recovery from Sickness,* Jackson & Walford (London), 1839; (under name Ann Gilbert) *Seven Blessings for Little Children,* Jackson & Walford, 1844; (under name Ann Gilbert) *A Biographical Sketch of the Rev. Joseph Gilbert,* assisted by son, Josiah Gilbert, Jackson & Walford, 1853; (under name Ann Gilbert) *Autobiography and Other Memorials of Mrs. Gilbert,* two volumes, edited by Josiah Gilbert, H. S. King (London), 1874.

All with sister, Jane Taylor; all for children: (With Adelaide O'Keeffe and others) *Original Poems for Infant Minds,* Darton & Harvey, Volume I, 1804, Volume II, 1805, Kimber, Conrad (Philadelphia), 1806, published as *Original Poems for Infant Minds, Two Volumes* [and] *Rhymes for the Nursery,* preface by Christina Duff Stewart, Garland Publishing, 1976 [other editions include those illustrated by Henry Anelay, Virtue (London), 1865; R. Barnes, T. Kennedy, and others, George Routledge & Sons (London), 1868]; (with others) *Rhymes for the Nursery,* Darton & Harvey, 1806, [Hartford], 1813, published as *Original Poems for Infant Minds, Two Volumes* [and] *Rhymes for the Nursery,* preface by C. D. Stewart, Garland Publishing, 1976 [another edition illustrated by John Gilbert, D. Appleton (New York), 1851].

Rural Scenes; or, A Peep into the Country, Darton & Harvey, 1806, Samuel Wood & Sons (New York), 1823; *City Scenes; or, A Peep into London* (illustrated by brother, I. Taylor III), [publisher unknown], 1806, James P. Parke (Philadelphia), 1809; *Limed Twigs to Catch Young Birds,* Darton & Harvey, 1808, Johnson & Warner (Philadelphia), 1811; *Hymns for Infant Minds,* Thomas Conder (London), 1808, S. T. Armstrong

Ann Taylor, from a sketch by her father.

(Boston), circa 1810 [another edition illustrated by Josiah Gilbert, Hodder & Stoughton, 1876]; *Signor Topsy-Turvy's Wonderful Magic Lantern; or, The World Turned Upside Down* (poems), Tabart & Co. (London), 1810, William Charles, 1811; (with others) *The Associate Minstrels,* Thomas Conder, 1810; *Original Hymns for the Use of Children,* [publisher unknown], circa 1810; *Original Hymns for Sunday Schools,* Josiah Conder, 1812, published in America as *Original Hymns for Sabbath Schools,* S. T. Armstrong, 1820.

Collections; all with J. Taylor: *Select Rhymes for the Nursery,* Darton & Harvey, 1806, Johnson & Warner, 1810; *The Poetic Garland: A Collection of Nursery Rhymes* (contains selected poems from *Rhymes for the Nursery*), compiled by Thomas Teller, S. Babcock (New Haven), 1845; *The Snow-Drop: A Collection of Rhymes for the Nursery,* S. Babcock, circa 1849; *The Original Ongar Poems for Children,* compiled by Samuel O. Beeton, Ward, Lock & Tyler (London), 1872; *The Poetical Works of Ann and Jane Taylor* (illustrated by Birdet Foster; contains *Hymns for Infant Minds, Original Poems,* and *Rhymes for the Nursery*), Ward, Lock & Tyler, 1877; *Little Ann, and Other Poems* (illustrated by Kate Greenaway), George Routledge & Sons, 1883; *Tales, Essays, and Poems,* Roberts Brothers, 1884; (with A. O'Keeffe and others) *Sundry Rhymes from the Days of Our Grandmothers,* compiled and illustrated by George W. Edwards, A. D. F. Randolph (New York), 1888.

Greedy Dick, and Other Stories in Verse (illustrated by Edmund Smyth), Hodder & Stoughton, 1903; (with A. O'Keeffe) *The "Original Poems" and Others* (illustrated by F. D. Bedford), edited by E. V. Lucas, Wells Gardner (London), 1903, Frederick A. Stokes, 1904; *Rhymes for Children,* compiled by Melvin Hix, Educational Publishing, 1907; (with A. O'Keeffe) *Meddlesome Matty and Other Poems for Infant Minds* (illustrated by Wyndham Payne), introduction by Edith Sitwell, John Lane, 1925, Viking, 1926; *Ann Taylor Gilbert's Album,* Garland Publishing, 1978.

Taylor's works are included in numerous anthologies. Also contributor under names Clara, Maria, Anna, and A. to periodicals including *Minor's Pocket Book, Literary Magazine and American Register, Eclectic Review, Sheffield Iris, London University College Magazine,* and *Sunday School Magazine.*

SIDELIGHTS: **January 30, 1782.** Born in Islington, London into a family of writers known as "The Taylors of Ongar." Her father was an engraver, author, and minister, and her mother, an author.

June, 1786. Moved to the countryside of Lavenham. "But now the rapidly increasing family, and its consequent expenses, suggested the desirableness of removing to the country, and my dear parents, young, poor, loving, simple-minded, with

(From *The "Original Poems" and Others* by Ann and Jane Taylor. Edited by E. V. Lucas. Illustrated by F. D. Bedford.)

I can eat everyday while the rest are at play. ■ (From "The Plum Cake" by Ann Taylor in *The "Original Poems" and Others* by Ann and Jane Taylor. Edited by E. V. Lucas. Illustrated by F. D. Bedford.)

My father and mother are dead,
Nor friend, nor relation I know;
And now the cold earth is their bed,
And daisies will over them grow.

■ (From "The Orphan," in *Little Ann, and Other Poems* by Jane and Ann Taylor. Illustrated by Kate Greenaway.)

nothing to call experience, resolved to transplant their household to what then appeared a remote and dreary distance from every relative or friend. They had neither of them been more than twenty miles from London in their lives. . . .

"The house which a cottager described as 'the first grand house in Shilling Street' was indeed so, compared with former residences.

"It was the property of, and had been inhabited by a clergyman. On the ground floor were three parlours, two kitchens, and a dairy, together with three other rooms never inhabited; and above them were six large bedrooms. An extensive garden, well planted, lay behind. . . . There was also a large yard, with a pig-stye, uninhabited, till my sister Jane and I cleared it out for the purpose of dwelling in it ourselves. It was a substantial little building of brick, but, having no windows, and the door swinging from the top, it was somewhat incommodious, yet there, after lessons, we passed many a delighted hour." [Ann Gilbert, *Autobiography and Other Memorials of Mrs. Gilbert* edited by Josiah Gilbert, C. Kegan Paul, 1878.[1]]

With her sister Jane, who was a year younger, Taylor was educated at home by her father. ". . . We were taught the formal rudiments, and in the garden and elsewhere, constantly under the eye of our parents, we fell in with more than is always included in the catalogue of school learning at so much per quarter. Books were a staple commodity in the house. From my mother's habit of reading aloud at breakfast and at tea, we were always picking up something; to every conversation we were auditors, and, I think, quiet ones, for, having no nursery, the parlour would have been intolerable otherwise.

"There was a large room adjoining, having a glass door into it, and there, or in the garden, we were at liberty to romp. A closet in this room was allowed us as a babyhouse, round the walls of which were arranged our toys, but I must acknowledge that here we were not the aborigines, an interminable race of black ants had taken previous possession, and we could only share and share alike with them.

"I do not know how far children so completely invent little histories for themselves as we did. We most frequently personated two poor women making a hard shift to live; or we were 'aunt and niece,' Jane the latter and I the former; or we acted a fiction entitled 'the twin sisters,' or another, the 'two Miss Parks.' And we had, too, a great taste for royalty, and were not a little intimate with various members of the royal family. Even the two poor women, 'Moll and Bet,' were so exemplary in their management and industry as to attract the notice of their Royal Highnesses the Princesses ('when George the Third was King.') . . . These were simple, healthy, inexpensive toys and pleasures, and, having such resources always at hand at home, and without excitements from abroad, we were never burdensome with the teazing enquiry, 'What shall we play at? What shall we do?' Yet we had always assistance at hand if needed. Both father and mother were accessible, and many a choice entertainment did we owe to their patient contrivances. My father, especially, was never weary of inventing, for our amusement or instruction.

"Of course my dear mother, with health never strong, and all the needlework of the household on her hands, could not undertake our entire instruction. Reading, the Needle, and the Catechism, we were taught by her, and as my father was constantly engraving at the high desk in the same room, it was easy for him to superintend the rest. We were never severely treated, though both my parents were systematic disciplinarians. But I record one instance of mistaken punishment only

to show how possible it is, when a child is confused or alarmed, for parents to fall into that error. It must have been when I was very young, for it was owing to a supposed obstinacy in not spelling the word *thy*. I had been told it repeatedly, t-h-y, in the same lesson, still at the moment it every time unaccountably slipped from the memory. My mother could only attribute it to wilful perverseness, though I believe that was a disposition I could not be charged with. She felt, however, so fully persuaded that I knew, and would not say, that she proceeded to corporal punishment, very rarely administered, but not so entirely abandoned as is the fashion now. . . ."[1]

1792. Began to write verses at the age of ten. "The time at which I began to string my thoughts (if thoughts) into measure I cannot correctly ascertain. It could not be after I was ten years old, and I think when only seven or eight, and arising from a feeling of anxiety respecting my mother's safety during illness. Not wishing (I conclude) to betray myself by asking for paper at home, I purchased a sheet of foolscap from my friend, Mr Meeking, and *filled* it with verses in metre imitated from Dr Watts, at that time the only poet on my shelves. What became of this effusion I do not know, but I should be glad to exchange for it, if I could, any of my later ones,—

> 'Not for its worth, we all agree,
> But merely for its oddity,'

as Swift says of learning in ladies.

"The earliest stanza that dwells in my memory, whether belonging to this production or not I cannot tell, is the following

> 'Dark and dismal was the weather,
> Winter into horror grew;
> Rain and snow came down together,
> Everything was lost to view.'

"Certain it is, anyway, that from about this date it became my perpetual amusement to scribble, and some large literary projects occupied my reveries. A poetic rendering of the fine moral history of Master Headstrong; a poem intended as antecedent to the Iliad; a new version of the Psalms; and an argumentative reply to Winchester on Future Punishment, were among these early projects, and more or less executed.

"Though from the result in substantial pecuniary benefit to ourselves (as much needed as unexpected), together with, I venture to hope, some good to others, I have great reason to be thankful for the habit thus contracted, yet I have certainly suffered by allowing the small disposable time of my youth to expend itself in writing rather than in reading. My mind was in this way stinted by scanty food. Of that I am fully sensible, and leave it as a warning to whomsoever it may concern. If I had not breathed a tolerably healthy atmosphere it would have been lean indeed. But there was always something to be imbibed; either from my mother's reading at meals, or that in which we afterwards all took turn in the workroom; from my father's untiring aptness to teach, his regular habit of settling all questions by reference to authorities, and the books that were always passing through the family.

"Wherever my father moved there soon arose a book society, if there had not been one before. One word, however, about the reading aloud at meals. I believe my mother fostered thereby a habit of despatching hers too quickly, by which her digestion was permanently injured; and, again, it hindered our acquiring readiness in conversation. To listen, not to talk, became so much a habit with us, as rather to impair fluency of expression—at least in speech."[1]

1795. Family moved to the town of Colchester. "It surprises me to remember that, although now at the womanly age of fourteen, one of my first cares, in conjunction with Jane, was to fit up a closet in our bed-room as a doll's house. That this was a pleasure shortly to wane we did not foresee. The closet was duly furnished, but it did not do; and I remember the pang of regret and disappointment with which the discovery broke upon me that dolls and doll's houses did not maintain their interest for ever. The closet was arranged, but, that done, we could never enjoy it afterwards. The new interests of Colchester consigned the doll regime to oblivion. Yet I never could sympathize with the philosophy which proscribes the doll. What harm does it do? Certainly in our own case it did not interfere with or curtail the processes of an assiduous education. No more time was expended in the doll house than formed a reasonable relaxation, and many were the good results, with, as far as my convictions reach, no bad ones. A cheerful use of the needle is acquired in dressing these innocents; much thought, contrivance, arrangement, and prelusive affection are brought into play; and the natural avidity with which a little girl, left to her own choice, seizes, caresses, loves a doll, seems to indicate the suitableness of the amusement."[1]

The entire family joined in the work of engraving, which helped to sustain them financially. "We had, as before, a large room designated the 'Workroom.' . . . Here, at his high desk at one end, stood my father, and long tables ran from thence the length of the room, where the eldest of us were soon practising the engraver's art. Nearest to him sat my brother Isaac, then Martin, then myself, and next to me Jane. Behind us a second range of tables was occupied, two or three days a–week, by pupils. Happy days,—mornings, evenings,—Happy years!— have I spent in that shabby old room!"[1]

1797. First poem was printed. "Writing, as a mere manual exercise, was always agreeable to me, independently of the pleasing necessity of giving expression to the emotions, new and innumerable, of the young bosom, though in truth as old, and as often repeated as the moonlights and spring days, the hopes and affections by which, in every age, they have been elicited. . . . I made my first poetical appearance in print on the occasion of a contested election, when Robert Thornton being the Tory candidate, and a Mr Shipley the Whig, I ventured an election song for home-reading solely. But it happened to be seen, and was speedily printed, a distinction that no doubt I felt as somewhat dazzling. The production, I am constrained to say, exhibits sadly little wit, and much more than was appropriate of the moral lectures."[1]

1798-1799. Entered a magazine literary contest under the pen-name "Juvenilia." "I had made the purchase of a *Minor's Pocket Book,* and on reading the solutions of enigmas, and other poetic contributions to which prizes were adjudged, it struck me that, without great presumption, I might aim at as much literary distinction as these prizes conferred.

"With lively interest, therefore, I possessed myself of the prescribed conditions, unravelled enigma, charade, and rebus, and forwarded the results under the signature of 'Juvenilia,' as directed, to 55 Gracechurch Street. I little thought that it was bread I thus cast on the waters, or rather that it would return as bread after many days. I had, indeed, to wait long, and as the interesting season approached for the new pocket books to make their appearance in the window of old Mr Gibbs the bookseller, frequent and anxious were my glances in passing by. At last they arrived, and on turning them over on his counter with as much indifference as could be assumed, I ascertained that the first prize—six pocket books—had been awarded to 'Juvenilia.' Besides the general poetical solution,

I find six charades with the same signature, some of which might not be worse for a little correction, but I must regard them gratefully, as productive of long continued advantages. From this time I was a regular contributor for twelve or fourteen years, and latterly became the editor, resigning only on my marriage. From this early connection with Darton and Harvey arose our regular, and as it proved profitable employment.

"In the *Minor's Pocket Book* for **1800,** I appeared under the signature of 'Clara' and we were now so far known to Darton and Harvey as to be frequently employed on small plates for their juvenile works. Writing was as yet only the amusement of my limited leisure, and a visit to London with my father, with which he indulged me in May of this year, greatly stimulated my zeal as an artist, and for a time rendered art almost the favourite pursuit."[1]

1804. *Original Poems for Infant Minds,* a collection of poems for children by Ann and Jane Taylor, was published. "We were now regularly placing small sums at interest; but it was not till we began to publish for ourselves that we felt the solid advantage that literature might bring to us. The *Hymns for Infant Minds* were [sic] the first venture we thus made. In the first year of their publication we realized £150. But an un-looked-for disappointment awaited us in the failure of our publisher, an old friend, who was, I daresay, as sorry for us as we were for him. All our little savings were now floated off to meet expenses, and we had to make a fresh start. Valuable as money had always been to us, and still was, we yet could not feel the loss, as it was supposed among our friends that we must—almost ought to have done. The pleasures of writing, and the credit we were gaining by it, so over–balanced the simple money misfortune that we bore it with admired equanimity. Before the 1st of January 1811 the third edition of *Hymns for Infant Minds* had made their appearance, and we enjoyed the entire profit.

"The confinement inseparable from years of engraving had long appeared to our friends too much to continue; though, indeed, I did not feel it. But the suggestion was perpetually made to us, 'Do take pupils; you know your father's methods, you have now a name yourselves, and we feel sure you would succeed.' Such was the advice continually given, and in time it worked its way, though never into my affections. But it mingled with the prospect now opening to us of remove and change, and tinged everything with the feeling of an uncertain future."[1]

1810. *The Associate Minstrels,* written with her brother and sister, was published.

1811. Family moved to Ongar. ". . . We closed, as it proved, our many years of work-room work. The Castle House, a quaint and very pleasant country residence, was engaged for us at Ongar, whither my father repaired to receive the furniture, &c., and, when all was ready, to welcome us—my mother, self, Jane, Jefferys, and Jemima, to the new home. . . .

"The important change had now been effected. At last we had done with things behind, but the future was still looming on us from an unexplored distance. We had given up engraving, so far as it implied daily employment, though it was arranged that if occasionally my father required assistance, I should render it when at home. . . ."[1]

December 24, 1813. Married the Rev. Joseph Gilbert, a thirty-three-year-old widower, and a classical tutor at Rotherham College. Taylor settled into married life at Rotherham, where she devoted herself to domestic duties rather than to literary

Shilling Street, Lavenham showing the two Taylor homes. ▪ (From *The Taylors of Ongar* by Doris Mary Armitage.)

ones. "The first week I came I experienced a real sick qualm by a present of a wild duck, before the cookery-book had arrived!. . . All that I could remember was put into requisition, and I did right in all respects,—did not stuff it, did not cook the giblets, did truss it right,—did rejoice when it was all over! I was told, too, that when the students came to tea there must be a plum-cake—cookery-book a month on the road! was obliged to postpone the visit till it arrived,—managed extremely well when it did. Professedly Yorkshire customs, I do not mind learning. . . . Whenever I can,—but there is always 'some bed or some border to mend, or something to tie or to stick,'—I endeavour to get to writing about eleven, and write during the morning, more or less, as I am able.'"[1]

October, 1814. First child, a son, born. "I cannot describe to you the flood of tenderness which the dear little boy has opened in my heart, but surely of the pleasures attending this time of peril the one-half was not told me. As we both for the first time looked at the child together, every one left the room, aware that they were happy moments and for about a minute my husband returned our joint and fervent thanks to the kind Hand which had dealt with us in peculiar favour. Nothing delights me more than to witness the spring of fatherly affection, and the solicitude which it occasions. He has discovered that it is a good thing and a pleasant, for a man to be a father."[1]

The family increased in size to include eight children.

1824. Sister and literary collaborator, Jane Taylor, died.

1827. First child died after an illness. His death left Taylor with a morbid anxiety over the eternal welfare of her other children. "I should be grieved that such a stroke should pass off without making a deep and solemn impression on every one of us, especially on our dear surviving children. . . . Nothing is like a *sight* of death and the grave, to impress the familiar neglected lesson, that *we* must give an account of ourselves at the bar of God. We see how wholly unexpected such a summons may come, and then, if ever, we feel the importance of being also, and always ready. Ah! if you had been awakened from your sleep to see your dear, tender brother die; if you had stood for hours at his bedside, unable to render the slightest assistance in that awful conflict, and uncertain whether the soothing words addressed to him could find their way to his departing spirit, I think your impressions of the awfulness of dying, would have been far deeper than they can be now; and you would feel that to be habitually prepared for such an hour, is greater happiness than anything or everything beside. . . .

"During his illness nothing could exceed his patience, submission, and clear collectedness. His memory was most distinct and accurate, and his fear of occasioning either expense or trouble very engaging. . . .

"On Tuesday morning your papa and I drest his coffin with snowdrops and evergreens, and at half-past two, with many kisses, and tears, we all took our last leave of him. Dear, dear child! His memory is like a sweet heavenly flower to us. We all sung round his coffin, 'Peace, 'tis the Lord Jehovah's hand,'

and at three *he was taken away from his father's house*. Mr Cecil prayed over his grave, a deep one, in the solid rock, and there we left our dear, sweet, tender, beloved child.'''[1]

December, 1829. Father died, followed by the death of her mother five months later.

1838. Wrote articles for anti-slavery literature. Demands from her household duties left her with little time for writing. ''I have scarcely more *command* of my own time or faculties than I have of yours, so that I seldom engage for such services. Sometimes a thought will flow, all without my care or payment, so that it is no trouble, and loses no time, to gather as it drops. At others, when, perhaps, much occupied, or bound to a fixed period for its completion, I may spend a day over a single verse, and that without success. I am sadly disabled by the pressure of more than I have time for. This has been my lot through life—always yesterday eating out the comfort of today!'''[1]

January 30, 1852. Turned seventy years old. To her children, she wrote: ''Dear children, I wish you, in return for all your kindness, a life as long as mine, as happy as mine in all outward circumstances, and, dear friends, as true and warm as mine. . . . O seek till you find the right sort of happiness, and let the thought of future regrets be ever at hand, to aid and corroborate present duty, whether in the outward world, the home circle, or the little theatre within, where all the great battles have to be fought.'''[1]

December 12, 1852. Husband died. ''About three o'clock on Sunday morning, . . . the audible breathing gradually subsided, and sank at last into the quietest calm. We were all assembled round his bed, and at about twenty minutes before four, we concluded that he had left us, though so gently, that for nearly half an hour we remained uncertain whether he were indeed gone. None but those who witnessed, could conceive the beautiful expression which for some time rested on his countenance. Not a movement had passed over his features— not a gasp, not a sigh was drawn—and from that which he had always dreaded, 'the unknown pang of dying,' he was, we feel sure, entirely saved.'''[1]

January, 1853. Began making arrangements to move, to dispose of her husband's library, and to settle herself and her daughters in another house. ''It is indeed a strange, incongruous mixture, which the world, as it moves on irrespective of our sorrows, introduces into our hearts and hands. But such are the terms on which we survive even the dearest. We *must* go on! We are permitted to weep only for a time, and even that with interruptions, which may be salutary, but which we should not have chosen for ourselves. The interval since my dear husband's death has been one of unresting business— coming and going of my children—and only a few quiet hours in which to look at either the past or the future with its *continued* bereavement! It seems so strange that this will not alter—cannot improve, except by a gradual 'reviving of the spirits,' which, though kindly aimed at by our friends, it seems cruel to wish for. How often do I long to see him, as even lately, coming down from the study in his gown, his candle lighted, and his white hair almost on his shoulders! But it will never be again! That word *never* we do not at first realize. Continually the thought crosses me for the moment, 'Oh, I will tell him!' as things occur that would once have interested him. How far he knows now, without telling, who shall say?

''We are obliged to plan and act for ourselves, and *that* I do feel. His children come and go, and we arrange for future comfort without his advice, or a kind look or word of acquiescence. For some length of time he had desired that we should do so; but we always felt that we could ask an opinion if we would. Now we have just to make ourselves comfortable, and *please ourselves!* A sad change to get used to!'''[1]

During the year of **1853** Taylor attended to household charges and to the writing of a memoir of her husband.

1854. Moved to a new home, called ''College Hill.'' ''It *is* a pleasant spot to call *home*. I do so enjoy it daily and hourly, often opening a door, or looking out of my window, for the simple pleasure of seeing how pleasant it is! Certainly the one half was not told me of the addition which the kind thought, so beautifully executed, has made to my regular enjoyment. Really the children think I am getting gay.'''[1]

1865. Suffered from lameness, but still managed to travel with a friend to Scotland. ''My knee does not in the least improve, and now that spring says, 'just step out and shake hands with me,' I feel it the more trying. . . . But what right have I, in my eighty-third year, to wonder at anything, or to expect much improvement? The earthly house of this tabernacle must dissolve, and at present it is doing it gently.

''One thing I am, or ought to be, very thankful for, that the rheumatism does not trouble me in the night. Very generally when a chronic rheumatism attacks old people, it makes its headquarters between the blankets.'''[1]

December 20, 1866. Died at her home at the age of eighty-four. In her last will, she wrote to her children: ''May you share largely, and for ever, in an enduring inheritance. See that ye fail not of the grace of God; to His everlasting love I commend you.''

Engraving by Ann Taylor. ■ (From *The Taylors of Ongar* by Doris Mary Armitage.)

Taylor's works have been translated into German and Russian.

FOR MORE INFORMATION SEE: Athenoeum (obituary), December 29, 1866; Ann Gilbert, *Autobiography and Other Memorials of Mrs. Gilbert,* edited by Josiah Gilbert, C. Kegan Paul, 1878; Doris M. Armitage, *The Taylors of Ongar,* W. Heffer & Sons (Cambridge, England), 1939; Laura Benet, *Famous Poets for Young People,* Dodd, 1964; G. Edward Harris, *Contributions toward a Bibliography of the Taylors of Ongar and Stanford Rivers,* Archon Books, 1965; Roger Lancelyn Green, *Tellers of Tales,* F. Watts, 1965; Brian Doyle, *The Who's Who of Children's Literature,* Schocken Books, 1968; Christina D. Stewart, *The Taylors of Ongar: An Analytical Bio-Biograpay,* two volumes, Garland Publishing, 1975.

TAYLOR, Jane 1783-1824

PERSONAL: Born September 23, 1783, in Holborn, London, England; died April 12 (some sources cite April 13), 1824, in Ongar, Essex, England; daughter of Isaac II (an engraver, author, and minister) and Ann (an author; maiden name, Martin) Taylor. *Education:* Educated at home, mostly by her father, chiefly in the arts of sketching and engraving. *Residence:* Ongar, Essex, England.

CAREER: Poet and author of books for children. Began writing poems and planning books as early as age eight; first published poem "The Beggar Boy," appeared in the *Minor's Pocket Book,* 1804; produced first book of poems, *Original Poems for Infant Minds,* in collaboration with sister, Ann Taylor, and others, 1804; created the well-known poem "Twinkle, Twinkle, Little Star" (originally "The Star"); wrote other children's books with A. Taylor, 1804-13; continued writing on her own, until about 1823.

WRITINGS: Display: A Tale for Young People (juvenile), J. Eliot (Boston), 1815; *Essays in Rhyme; or, Morals and Manners,* Wells & Lilly (Boston), 1816 (published in England as *Essays in Rhyme, on Morals and Manners,* Taylor & Hessey, 1816; (with mother, Ann Martin Taylor) *Correspondence between a Mother and Her Daughter at School,* Taylor and Hessey, 1817, W. B. Gilley (New York), 1818, another American edition published as *Familiar Letters between a Mother and Her Daughter at School,* J. Loring, 1827; (author of preface) written by brother, Jefferys Taylor, *Harry's Holiday,* [London], 1818; (author of preface) E. Whitty, *A Mother's Journal during the Last Illness of Her Daughter, Sarah Chisman,* B. J. Holdsworth (London), 1820, S. T. Armstrong (Boston), 1821; *A Day's Pleasure: To Which Are Added Reflections on a Day's Pleasure* (originally published in *Youth's Magazine*), M. Day (New York), 1833; *The Discontented Pendulum* (religious tract), J. Groom (London), 1855; *Personal Religion: A Letter to Some Young Friends,* Hodder & Stoughton, 1868; *How It Strikes a Stranger,* Houghton, 1882.

All with sister, Ann Taylor; all for children: (With Adelaide O'Keeffe and others) *Original Poems for Infant Minds,* Darton & Harvey (London), Volume I, 1804, Volume II, 1805, Kimber, Conrad (Philadelphia), 1806, published as *Original Poems for Infant Minds, Two Volumes* [and] *Rhymes for the Nursery,* preface by Christina Duff Stewart, Garland Publishing, 1976 [other editions include those illustrated by Henry Anelay, Virtue & Co. (London), 1865; R. Barnes, T. Kennedy, and others, George Routledge & Sons, 1868]; (with others) *Rhymes for the Nursery,* Darton & Harvey, 1806, [Hartford], 1813, published as *Original Poems for Infant Minds, Two Volumes* [and] *Rhymes for the Nursery,* preface by C. D. Stewart, Garland Publishing, 1976 [another edition illustrated by John Gilbert, D. Appleton (New York), 1851].

Rural Scenes; or, A Peep into the Country, Darton & Harvey, 1806, Samuel Woods & Sons (New York), 1823; *City Scenes; or, A Peep into London* (illustrated by brother, Isaac Taylor III), [publisher unknown], 1806, James P. Parke (Philadelphia), 1809; *Limed Twigs to Catch Young Birds,* Darton & Harvey, 1808, Johnson & Warner (Philadelphia), 1811; *Hymns for Infant Minds,* Thomas Conder (London), 1808, S. T. Armstrong, circa 1810 [another edition illustrated by nephew, Josiah Gilbert, Hodder & Stoughton, 1876]; *Signor Topsy-Turvy's Wonderful Magic Lantern; or, The World Turned Upside Down* (poems), Tabart & Co. (London), 1810, William Charles (Philadelphia), 1811; (with others) *The Associate Minstrels,* Thomas Conder (London), 1810; *Original Hymns for the Use of Children,* [publisher unknown], circa 1810; *Original Hymns for Sunday Schools,* Josiah Conder, 1812, published in America as *Original Hymns for Sabbath Schools,* Samuel T. Armstrong, 1820.

Collections: (With A. Taylor) *Select Rhymes for the Nursery,* Darton & Harvey, 1806, Johnson & Warner, 1810; *The Contributions of Q. Q. to a Periodical Work* (some contents originally published in *Youth's Magazine,* 1816-22), two volumes, edited by I. Taylor III, B. J. Holdsworth (London), 1824, G. & C. Carvill, E. Bliss, & John P. Haven (New York), 1827, another edition published as *A Day's Pleasure, and Other Contributions of Q. Q.,* Robert Carter & Brothers, 1882; *Memoirs and Poetical Remains of the Late Jane Taylor: With Extracts from Her Correspondence,* two volumes, edited by I. Taylor III, B. J. Holdsworth, 1825, Crocker & Brewster (Boston), 1826, also published as *Poetical Remains and Correspondence of the Late Jane Taylor,* five volumes, Perkins & Marvin (Boston), 1832; *The Writings of Jane Taylor,* three volumes, edited by I. Taylor III, Saxton & Peirce (Boston), 1835; *The Pleasures of Taste, and Other Stories,* edited by Sarah J. Hale, Marsh, Capen, Lyon, & Webb (Boston), 1839.

(With A. Taylor) *The Poetic Garland: A Collection of Nursery Rhymes* (contains selected poems from *Rhymes for the Nursery*), compiled by Thomas Teller, S. Babcock (New Haven), 1845; (with A. Taylor) *The Snow-Drop: A Collection of Rhymes for the Nursery,* S. Babcock, circa 1849; *Original Poems, by Jane Taylor: 1783-1824,* Hall & Co., (London), 1870; (with A. Taylor) *The Original Ongar Poems for Children,* compiled by Samuel O. Beeton, Ward, Lock & Tyler, 1872; (with A. Taylor) *The Poetical Works of Ann and Jane Taylor* (illustrated by Birdet Foster; contains *Hymns for Infant Minds, Original Poems,* and *Rhymes for the Nursery*), Ward, Lock & Tyler, 1877; Helen Cross Knight, *Jane Taylor: Her Life and Letters,* Thomas Nelson & Sons, circa 1880; (with A. Taylor) *Little Ann, and Other Poems* (illustrated by Kate Greenaway), George Routledge & Sons, 1883; (with A. Taylor) *Tales, Essays, and Poems,* Roberts Brothers (Boston), 1884; (with A. Taylor, A. O'Keeffe, and others) *Sundry Rhymes from the Days of Our Grandmothers,* compiled and illustrated by George W. Edwards, A. D. F. Randolph (New York), 1888.

(With A. Taylor) *Greedy Dick, and Other Stories in Verse* (illustrated by Edmund Smyth), Hodder & Stoughton, 1903; (with A. Taylor and A. O'Keeffe) *The "Original Poems" and Others* (illustrated by F. D. Bedford), edited by E. V. Lucas, Wells Gardner (London), 1903, Frederick A. Stokes, 1904; (with A. Taylor) *Rhymes for Children,* compiled by Melvin

Jane and Ann Taylor. Portrait by their father, Isaac.

Hix, Educational Publishing, 1907; *Jane Taylor: Prose and Poetry*, introduction by F. V. Barry, Humphrey Milford (London), 1925; (with A. Taylor and A. O'Keeffe) *Meddlesome Matty and Other Poems for Infant Minds* (illustrated by Wyndham Payne), introduction by Edith Sitwell, John Lane, 1925, Viking, 1926.

Taylor's works are included in numerous anthologies. Contributor, under own name as well as names Eliza, J.T., J. and Q.Q., to periodicals including *Minor's Pocket Book, Youth's Magazine,* and *Sheffield Iris.*

SIDELIGHTS: **September 23, 1783.** Born in Holborn, London, England. The members of the Taylor family were noted writers—both parents were published authors, as were two brothers and sister Ann. Jane was the second child born to the Taylors—her sister preceded her by a year. For the first years of her life, Jane was considered a frail and sickly child.

1786. Family moved to the country where the rural lifestyle improved Taylor's health. Her brother Isaac recalled this change many years later in a memoir of his sister: "Accustomed as she had been to the narrow bounds, and to the many restraints of a London house, Jane's spirits broke forth with unusual emotions of pleasure amid the ample space, and the agreeable objects that now surrounded her.

"Very soon after her removal to the country, Jane displayed, not merely a healthy vivacity and childlike eagerness in the amusements provided for her by her fond parents, but an uncommon fertility of invention in creating pleasures for herself:—It was evident to those who observed her, that, even from her third or fourth year, the little girl inhabited a fairy land, and was perpetually occupied with the imaginary interests of her teeming fancy." [Issac Taylor III, editor, *Memoirs and Poetical Remains of the Late Jane Taylor: With Extracts from Her Correspondence,* Crocker & Brewster, 1826. [1]]

Ann echoed brother Isaac's observation when she recalled Jane's early propensity for writing. "I can remember that Jane was always the saucy, lively, entertaining little thing—the amusement and the favorite of all that knew her. At the baker's shop she used to be placed on the kneading board, in order to recite, preach, narrate, &c. to the great entertainment of his many visitors. And at Mr. Blackadder's she was the life and fun of the farmer's hearth. Her plays, from the earliest that I can recollect, were deeply imaginative; and I think that in 'Moll and Bet'—'The Miss Parks'—'The Miss Sisters'—'The Miss Bandboxes,' and 'Aunt and Niece,' which I believe is the entire catalogue of them, she lived in a world wholly of her own creation, with as deep a feeling of reality as life itself could afford. These lasted from the age of three or four, till ten or twelve. About the latter time her favorite employment, in play time, was whipping a top; during the successful spinning of which she composed tales and dramas, some of which she afterwards committed to paper. She would spend hours in this kind of reverie, in the large unfurnished parlour, at our own house at Lavenham. . . ."[1]

From an early age, Taylor showed a precocious writing ability. As soon as she began to write, she decided to write a book. "I do believe that this habit of *castle-building* is very injurious to the mind. I know I have sometimes lived so much in a *castle,* as almost to forget that I lived in a *house;* and while I have been carefully arranging aërial matters *there,* have left all my solid business in disorder *here.* To be perpetually fancying what *might be,* makes us forget what we really are; and while conjuring up what we might have, we are negligent of what we really possess." [Isaac Taylor, "Memoir of Jane Taylor," in *The Family Pen: Memorials, Biographical and Literary of the Taylor Family, of Ongar,* edited by Rev. Isaac Taylor, Volume I, Jackson, Walford, and Hodder, 1867.[2]]

Jane and Ann were educated at home by their father and mother. Their education was unstructured, but stimulating. From their father they learned geography, history, chemistry, astronomy, and the family trade of engraving. From their mother, the two Taylor sisters learned domestic duties. During mealtime it was a family practice for their mother to read aloud.

The two sisters managed to write during spare moments squeezed from a busy day of doing housework and helping their father with engraving. "We find it is employment that gives recreation its greatest charm; and we enjoy with a double relish little pleasures which, to those who are already fatigued with doing nothing, appear tiresome or uninteresting. When I see people perpetually tormented with *ennui*—satiated with amusement—indifferent to every object of interest, I indeed congratulate myself that I have not one spare moment, in which these demons can assail me.

". . Ann and I often remark to each other that, whatever agreeable recreations we may occasionally indulge in, and much as we really enjoy them, we are never so happy as when steadily engaged in the room where we engrave; that is our paradise:—you may smile at the comparison, and we know the inconveniences connected with our engagements there; but use reconciles us to them; and experience teaches us that comfort and happiness are compatible with these apparent inconveniences:—we have every inducement to industry, and we are thankful that that which is necessary, is also agreeable to us. We want nothing but a little more society:—one congenial family within our reach would be a treasure: for though we do love each other, and enjoy each other's society greatly; yet there are times when we long to recreate our wearied spirits with an intelligent friend."[2]

When her sister Ann began to submit poems regularly to a children's magazine called the *Minor's Pocket Book,* Jane quickly followed suit and sent in a poem called "The Beggar Boy," her first published work.

1804. First book of easy-reading poetry, written with Ann and entitled *Original Poems for Infant Minds,* was published. Volume one was quickly followed by a second volume.

1806. *Rhymes for the Nursery* was published. This book, which was more popular than the sisters' first book, included Jane's most famous poem, "The Star." It began, "Twinkle, twinkle little star. . . ." "In truth, Jane Taylor of the morning and Jane Taylor of the evening are as different people, in their feelings and sentiments, as two such *intimate* friends can possibly be. The former is an active handy little body, who can make beds or do plain work, and now and then takes a fancy for drawing, &c. But the last mentioned lady never troubles her head with these menial affairs;—nothing will suit her but the *pen;*—and though she does nothing very extraordinary in this way, yet she so far surpasses the first-named gentlewoman, that any one who had ever received a letter from both, would immediately distinguish between the two, by the difference of the style. But to drop this ingenious allegory, I assure you it represents the truth, and I am pretty well determined not again to attempt letter-writing before breakfast. For really I am a mere machine—the most stupid and dronish creature you can imagine, at this time. The unsentimental realities of breakfast may claim some merit in restoring my mental faculties; but its effects are far surpassed by the evening's tea: after that comfortable, social, invigorating meal, I am myself, and begin to

Young Thomas was an idle lad. ■ (From "Evening" by Jane Taylor in *The "Original Poems" and Others* by Ann and Jane Taylor. Edited by E. V. Lucas. Illustrated by F. D. Bedford.)

think the world a pleasanter place, and my friends more agreeable people, and *entre nous,* myself a much more respectable personage, than they have seemed during the day; so that by eight o'clock I am just worked up to a proper state of mind for writing.'²

After the literary success of the Taylors' first volumes of poetry, the sisters were given more time for writing. Jane set up her own study in the Taylor house so that she could write with greater ease. "My verses have certainly one advantage to boast, beyond any that ever escaped from my pen heretofore—that of being composed in my own study.... One of my first engagements ... was to fit up an unoccupied attic, hitherto devoted only to household lumber; this I removed by the most spirited exertions, and supplied its place by all the apparatus necessary for a poet, which, you know, is not of a very extensive nature: a few book-shelves, a table for my writing-desk, one chair for myself, and another for my muse, is a pretty accurate inventory of my furniture.... It possesses one advantage which, as a poet,... surpasses them all—it commands a view of the country—the only room in the house, except one, which is thus favoured; and to me this is invaluable. You may now expect me to do wonders! But even if others should derive no advantages from this new arrangement, to me I am sure, they will be numerous. For years I have been longing for such a luxury, and never before had wit enough to think of this convenient place. It will add so much to the comfort of my life, that I can do nothing but congratulate myself upon the happy thought.... Although it is morning, and, I must tell you, but little past six, I have half filled this sheet, which capability I attribute chiefly to the sweet fields that are now smiling in vernal beauty before me."²

1808. *Hymns for Infant Minds,* written with Ann, was printed. By 1860 this book had gone through forty-five editions. "I think I have some idea of what a child's hymn ought to be; and when I commenced the task, it was with the presumptuous determination that none of them should fall short of the standard I had formed in my mind. In order to this, my method was to shut my eyes, and imagine the presence of some pretty little mortal; and then endeavor to catch, as it were, the very language it would use on the subject before me. If, in any instances, I have succeeded, to this little imaginary being I should attribute my success. And I have failed so frequently, because so frequently I was compelled to say,—'Now you may go, my dear, I shall finish the hymn myself.'"¹

Concerning her literary success and the public approval that she and Ann had received, Jane wrote: "I do not deny, it would be ungrateful to do so—that the approbation we have met with, and the applause, especially of some whose opinion was particularly precious, have been sources of constant satisfaction: and perhaps, occasionally, my weak mind has been partly overset by them. Yet, I think I may say, my humiliations have usually counterbalanced such feelings.

"Well, I hope I can say I have different views of life, and a higher ambition than formerly. I dare not trust my treacherous heart a moment. But yet, upon examination, I think I may say, I should feel at least contented to pass silently and soberly through the world, with a humble hope of reaching heaven at the end of my pilgrimage. I have many, many difficulties in my way; and when I compare the state of my mind with that which is required of those who follow Jesus, and see how much must be done ere I can attain it, I have no other comfort than this—'With God all things are possible'...."²

1810. *The Associate Minstrels* was published. "They were

written to gratify my own feelings, and not for the 'Wreath;' (such was then proposed to be the title of the volume) yet you have pressed them into the service; and what shall I say? I feel that, in permitting them to be published, I make some sacrifice;—as indeed all do who once begin to express their feelings in rhyme; for sentiments and feelings that, in plain prose, would only be whispered in secret to a chosen friend, in this form gain courage, and court the gaze, and bear the ridicule of the vulgar and unfeeling. Since I have had time to think soberly about the 'Wreath'—for this must always be its title, I have felt far less anxious about the share I am to have in it. Now I am not going to tease you with any of my 'morbid humility;' for I am as weary of it, and as angry with it, as you are; but I must just tell you how it affects me. I think I know pretty well how to estimate my poetical talent; at least, I am perfectly persuaded I do not *underrate* it; and, in comparison with my blooming companions in this garland, I allow my pieces to rank as the leaves; which are, you know, always reckoned a necessary, and even pleasing part of a bouquet: and I may add that I am not only contented, but pleased with this station;—it is safe, and snug; and my chief anxiety is not to suffer any thing ridiculous, or very lame to appear:—with these views I consent. The opinion of the little hallowed circle of my own private friends is more to me than the applauses of a world of strangers. To them my pieces are already known; by them their merits and their faults are already determined; and if they continue to smile kindly upon my simple muse, she will not,... be put in ill-humor.''

1811. Family moved to Ongar where Taylor's father became pastor of a congregation. "It is a strange sensation to survey the map of England without an idea of what part of it we are to occupy. Yet perhaps we feel less anxiety about it than you may suppose. Not to be further removed from London than we now are, is our chief solicitude; and to be nearer would be very desirable; more especially on account of being able to see our dear brothers more frequently. For my own part, might I choose a situation, it should be a very retired one, among plain good people, whom we could love:—a village, not a town. My love of quiet and retirement daily increases; and I wish to cultivate this taste:—it suits me, and does me good. To part with our house here—the high woods, and the springs, will cost me a struggle; and more especially my dear quiet attic. Might I hope to find such another in our next encampment, I should be less uneasy.''¹

1813. Ann Taylor married the Rev. Joseph Gilbert, thus terminating the sisters literary collaboration and their constant companionship. "From the early days of 'Moll and Bett,' down to these last times, we have been more inseparable companions than sisters usually are, and our pursuits and interests have been the same. My thoughts of late have often wandered back to those distant years, and passed over the varied scenes which chequered our childhood and youth:—there is scarcely a recollection, in all that long period, in which we are not mutually concerned, and equally interested. If this separation had taken place ten years ago, we might, by this time, have been in some degree estranged from each other; but having passed so large and important a portion of life in such intimate union, I think we may confidently say it never will be so. For brothers and sisters to separate is the common lot;—for their affection and interest to remain unabated is not common, but I am sure it is possible, and I think the experience we have already had, proves that we may expect its continuance...."²

1815. After the marriage of sister, Taylor continued writing on her own. A book for children, *Display: A Tale for Young People,* was published.

1816. *Essays in Rhyme, on Morals and Manners* was published.

1817. Became seriously ill. A tumor was discovered, which undermined her health throughout the remaining years of her life. Doctors in London confirmed that the tumor was fatal. "I heard it with great composure; and my spirits did not at all sink till after I returned home. Since then I have had many desponding hours, from the fear of death. The happiness I enjoyed for a short time has given place to a hope, which, though faint, secures me from distress."[2]

Believing that her last years would be spent at her home in Ongar, Taylor engaged in charity work in the community. She originated a Ladies' Working Society for the benefit of the poor, and became a teacher in the church's Sunday school. "After all, a little, or perhaps a great deal of Christian humility is the best antidote to the uncomfortable feelings generated by mixing with society either above or beneath one; and the simple desire to do good to others will dissipate in a moment a thousand unfavourable feelings."[2]

1818. "I have still occasional pain, which keeps alive anxiety; but on the whole my spirits are pretty good. I endeavour to cast *this* care upon God: and especially to impress my mind with the consideration that, even if my most sanguine hopes of recovery should be realized, it would make no *essential* difference in my prospects. There is no cure for *mortality*. Attention and supreme regard to my eternal interests is abso-

Ah, Mary! what, do you for dolly not care?
And why is she left on the floor?
Forsaken, and cover'd with dust, I declare;
With you I must trust her no more.

■ (From "Negligent Mary," in *Little Ann and Other Poems* by Jane and Ann Taylor. Illustrated by Kate Greenaway.)

Sporting on the village green. ■ (From "The English Girl" by Jane Taylor in *The "Original Poems" and Others* by Ann and Jane Taylor. Edited by E. V. Lucas. Illustrated by F. D. Bedford.)

lutely necessary, independent of all immediate considerations. . . ."[2]

Autumn, 1821. Underwent new medical treatment at Margate. During the winter months she lived near London where she had the advantage of constant medical advice. Two London surgeons whom she consulted at this time gave her little hope for recovery. "It requires *much* utterly to extinguish the hope of recovery; with God nothing is impossible. Besides, it is really difficult, while occupied with the usual pursuits of life, and while able to go in and out much as usual—it is difficult to realize the probability of death at hand. But it comes strangely across me at times when, forgetting it, I have been planning as usual for the future. Then a dark cloud overshadows me, and hides all earthly concerns from my sight, and I hear the murmuring of the deep waters. I expect I shall have deep waters to pass through—already I feel the sting of death, but am not without hope that it may be taken away."[2]

January, 1824. "I have been very much indisposed for many weeks past, with a severe attack of rheumatism, which has greatly confined me to the house, and affected my general health. From this, I am thankful to say, I am slowly recovering; but in other respects, I cannot boast of improvement; yet the chastisements with which I am visited are still lighter than my expectations; and how much lighter than my deserts! I am endeavouring, but with small success, 'to forget the things that are behind, and to press forward.' But oh, how little can

affliction in *itself* do to produce spiritual affections! I feel this; and that, without the grace of God to help me, all these rendings from life and earthly happiness will be in vain."[2]

The cancer progressed during the winter months. Taylor experienced shortness of breath with such severity that she was unable to join in conversation or walk unaided. "The weather for some weeks past has been very unfavourable to me. I think there is still a hope that my strength and appetite may be restored, at least to what they were, when I am able to take the air, and perhaps to change it. But I more often think that a gradual decline has commenced; and if you were to see how much I am reduced, you would not wonder at my forming such an opinion. My bones indeed 'look and stare upon me;' my strength, too, fails me, so that I cannot walk more than once or twice across the room at a time, and whenever I do, I feel as if all within me were hanging in heavy rags. Whenever the weather permits, I am drawn round the garden, which is a great refreshment.

"I need not tell you how kindly I am nursed, and how tenderly all is done that can be done for my relief and comfort. I have also to be thankful for being so free from pain: my suffering now is almost entirely from debility, and weariness, and difficulty of breathing; but what I am most of all thankful for, is that the prospect of death is less formidable to me, owing to my having more 'peace in believing;' and an increase of this is all I want in order to reconcile me to it entirely. I often think, too, that if I am taken off by a gradual decay I ought to rejoice, as being thereby rescued probably from far greater suffering; but I desire to leave it all with God.''[2]

April 12, 1824. Died at her home in Ongar. ''I fear I cannot finish. Oh, my dear friends, if you knew what thoughts I have now, you would see as I do, that the whole business of life is preparation for death! Let it be so with you.''[2]

Taylor was buried in the burial ground of the Chapel at Ongar.

Her works have been translated into Dutch, French, German and Russian.

FOR MORE INFORMATION SEE: Isaac Taylor III, editor, *Memoirs and Poetical Remains of the Late Jane Taylor: With Extracts from Her Correspondence,* Crocker & Brewster, 1826; Isaac Taylor, editor, *The Family Pen: Memorials Biographical and Literary, of the Taylor Family, of Ongar,* two volumes, Jackson, Walford, and Hodder, 1867; Doris M. Armitage, *The Taylors of Ongar,* W. Heffer & Sons (England), 1939; Laura Benet, *Famous Poets for Young People,* Dodd, 1964; G. Edward Harris, *Contributions toward a Bibliography of the Taylors of Ongar and Stanford Rivers,* Archon Books, 1965; Roger L. Green, *Tellers of Tales,* F. Watts, 1965; Brian Doyle, *The Who's Who of Children's Literature,* Schocken Books, 1968; Christina D. Stewart, *The Taylors of Ongar: An Analytical Bio-Biography,* two volumes, Garland Publishing, 1975; C. D. Stewart, ''Another Jane,'' *Book Collector,* spring, 1977; Joseph Kastner, ''Everyone Knows Her Rhyme, but Who Remembers Jane?,'' *Smithsonian,* October, 1983.

MADONNA ELAINE TILTON

TILTON, Madonna Elaine 1929-
(Rafael Tilton)

PERSONAL: Born October 4, 1929, in Laurin, Mont.; daughter of Charles Lester (a miner and rancher) and Clara (a tailor; maiden name, Nickol) Tilton Hansen. *Education:* College of St. Teresa, B.A., 1959; Fordham University, M.A., 1963. *Religion:* Catholic. *Residence:* Minneapolis, Minn. *Agent:* Nick Ellison, 55 5th Ave., New York, N. Y. 10003. *Office:* Academy of Our Lady of Lourdes, Box 4900, Rochester, Minn. 55903; and 310 East 38th St., Minneapolis, Minn. 55409.

CAREER: Member of Roman Catholic women's religious community, Third Order Regular of Saint Francis, 1949—; grade school teacher, 1951-59; high school English teacher, 1959-77; Cotter High School, Winona, Minn., teacher of English, 1971-77; Winona State University, Winona, instructor in English, 1980-81; User Services, Minnesota Educational Computing Consortium, editor, 1982-83; full-time writer, 1982—. Counselor, Minnesota High School Press Association, 1971-79; publications advisor, College of St. Teresa, 1980-81. Member, Cable Television Commission, City of Winona, 1978-82, precinct chairwoman, 1981-82; member, Family Affairs Commission, St. Mary's Council of Catholic Women, 1978-82. *Member:* International Registry of Women Religious Artists, The Delta Kappa Gamma Society International, London Club, Pax Christi. *Awards, honors:* Stephen K. Maynard Award, Kentucky State Poetry Society, 1981; second place, Catholic Press Association of the U. S. and Canada, and UNICEF International listing, both 1983, both for *The Immortal Dragon of Sylene, and Other Faith Tales;* first prize, Fifth Annual Poetry Contest of the American Association of University Women, 1984.

WRITINGS: Transformational Grammar: Units for Grades 7-9, Project English/ERIC, University of Minnesota, 1966; ''The Fountain Is for You'' (three-act play), first produced in Delano, Minn. at St. Peter's Grade School, February 11, 1967; ''An Equal and Opposite Reaction'' (one-act play), first produced in Rochester, Minn., at Academy of Our Lady of Lourdes at Assisi Heights, July 6, 1978; (editor with Lois Welshons, Miriam Hansen, and others) *Joy 6 Teacher Manual,* Winston Press, 1979; *Isidore Finds Time to Care: A Story about St. Isidore* (juvenile; illustrated by Dagmar Frinta), Winston Press, 1980; (under name Rafael Tilton) *The Immortal Dragon of Sylene, and Other Faith Tales* (young adult; illustrated by Troy Howell), Winston Press, 1982.

Also journalism and editoral advisor of Minnesota *Communicator,* 1971-73, and the *Minneapolis Spokesman.* Contributor of poetry to *Listen, Loonfeather, Pig Iron, Satori, The Cord, Inkling,* and *Pegasus,* and short story to *Epiphany.* Contributor of articles to *Teacher's Journal, Modern Ministries,* and *Armchair Detective.*

WORK IN PROGRESS: Biography of Phoebe Atwood Taylor; a second book of ''faith tales.''

SIDELIGHTS: ''Born and raised in depression-rich western Montana, I began experiencing fascinating people and freedom of spirit almost immediately. My aunt came to 'sit' with each of us five children in turn. I, in particular, led her a merry chase, and she still regales me with stories of the day the hornet crawled up the tent pole to meet my bare bottom, the day I sat in the middle of the road and dared the cars to run over me before she could 'tum and det me,' the day the cracked wooded butter bowl became my rocking chair.

"My self-educated aunt Anna Nickol was my idol. She started her first book on brown paper sacks. She gave me my first limited edition—typed and handpainted on 8½x11 paper, 'The Fairies' House Cleaning.' She is family historian and favorite story teller of fifty-eight nieces and nephews, and one of my most treasured books is her *More Damn Kids,* written about her adventures as a babysitter.

"When we moved from our country school district into a more populated area, Montana ethics apparently required parents to answer very few questions. I started in the fourth grade, my mother having determined that the building housing the first three grades was deficient. I credit my success to the teacher who helped me learn the alphabet when I was five, and the one who was midwife to my breakthrough realization that 'addition' meant 'five and two are seven.' I had finished my first novel that previous summer as I was nearing eight years old and was well on my way to a record-time polishing off of all the books in the school and public libraries.

"I did, however, favor mythology, westerns, mysteries, and romance until my college English teacher, Sister Bernetta Quinn, herself an author, began to encourage my writing and more serious reading. I loved the book club and any kind of research or study. When I joined the Franciscans, I still had had only eleven consecutive years of school. This may account for the sympathy I had for seniors who thought they had been going to school forever.

"Saint Francis inspired my most ardent dreams. After learning to share with a family in financial difficulty, earning shoes by picking beans, giving up savings to buy hay for the cow, and sending home money my first Christmas in college, Francis's joy in poverty seemed a natural next step. I am still convinced that his imitation of Christ is the answer to consumerism and the arms race, and I am active in several peace organizations as well as continuing in the prayer and ministry to which I was called when I was eighteen.

"During my twenty-five years of teaching I kept a journal and developed a file of about two hundred poems. I did considerable professional writing during the sixties. Two of my plays have been produced in schools: 'The Fountain Is for You' (St. Bernadette and the Lady of Lourdes) and 'An Equal and Opposite Reaction,' but neither has been published.

"In *The Immortal Dragon of Sylene* everything came together for me—my background in mythology and religion, my love of research, my interminable hours with student creative writing, my education in language, linguistics and medieval lore, my openness to adventures with newness, my introspective preference for living inside.

"I want to write stories that slow children down, give them a deep experience, set the psychological stage for a moment of silence. At the same time, I want parents to read the stories to the little ones and to find satisfaction. I want the stories memorable enough to call the children back for later rereadings. Imagery, poetry, suggestions of the timeless world of the unconscious, intriguing allusions to real times and places to be met in history, geography, social studies, and the biological sciences. I try to validate everything so as not to disillusion the latest scholar or the TV documentary viewer.

"I handled each legend in *The Immortal Dragon* from the point of view of today's problems. Nuclear threats, death, and violence are real, but they aren't dead ends. My stories are faith tales in the deepest sense. They express my faith in God

(From "Siegfried, Child of the Forest," in *The Immortal Dragon of Sylene and Other Faith Tales* by Rafael Tilton. Illustrated by Troy Howell.)

and in the power of the spirit to meet and accept the saint that struggles to be born in each of us, the saint who is revealed when we acknowledge the disenchanted macho, the nurturing aunt, the lost child, the loyal companion, the sick physician, the unregenerate adversary that speaks within.

"I don't worry too much if a bit of the plot gets lost in fantasy or detail or flashback. The book is a catalyst. I count on that primary story teller, the parent, the grandparent, to clear up the difficulty and in the interchange to strike a new balance of understanding with the child. Then that person will take up the recounting of his or her own personal odyssey.

"The stories I write are very honestly my own stories. They are the history of the place I am coming from while I write them. Onto the past of my emotions and feelings I weave the present of a new time of day and year, a new character who calls forth something better in me.

"And the teacher in me wants everyone to read every one of them! I love to read them aloud, and I love to look at the artist's drawings, to wonder what echoes still speak to him, what stories will appeal the most to each person I hand them to. Now the reading is energizing me as I launch my new series.

"When I'm not writing, I like to pray and meditate, or sew, read, paint, cook, walk, ride the buses and plan fantastic futures for myself and the whole human race."

TOLLIVER, Ruby C(hangos) 1922-

BRIEF ENTRY: Born May 29, 1922, in Fort Worth, Tex. Tolliver received her diploma from the Port Arthur Business College in 1942 and, through the years, has held various clerical positions in Texas. As the author of five novels for young adults, she believes "good kids can have exciting adventures, too." Tolliver reveals that her books "are Christian-oriented without being preachy," with characters who are caught at pivotal points in their lives when decisions must be made concerning both job and spiritual goals. All published by Broadman, the titles are: *Summer of Decision* (1979), *Decision at Sea* (1980), *More Than One Decision* (1981), *Decision at Brushy Creek* (1981), and *A Matter of Doors* (1984). Tolliver is currently working on *The Survivors,* a novel about five young adults faced with a terminally ill parent. *Office:* Route 20, Box 1212, Conroe, Tex. 77301.

FOR MORE INFORMATION SEE: Contemporary Authors, Volume 111, Gale, 1984.

TORGERSEN, Don Arthur 1934-

BRIEF ENTRY: Born September 27, 1934, in Chicago, Ill. A 1961 graduate of the University of Illinois, Torgersen began his career as editor and contributor for the Science & Mechanics Publishing Co. in Chicago. During the 1960s he was employed as an editor for Chicago International Manuscripts and the Allied News Co.; from 1971 to 1975 he held the position of manager of producers for Society for Visual Education. In 1976 he founded his own publishing, advertising, and audiovisual firm—Don Arthur Torgersen Productions—located in Palatine, Ill. A prolific writer, Torgersen is the author of over thirty books for children. A dozen of these deal with the magical world of gnomes, trolls, witches, and dragons, books he describes as "similar in genre to the German *Maerchen*—tales that move through fabulous, somewhat unreal worlds filled with marvelous, terrifying, and delightful events."

In 1978 Torgersen received an award from the Norwegian-American Literary Society for *The Troll's Three Christmas Wishes;* in 1980 and 1983, he was the recipient of awards from Children's Reading Round Table for, respectively, *The Scariest Night in Troll Forest* and *The Last Days of Gorlock the Dragon.* He is also the author of fourteen animal nature books published by Encyclopaedia Britannica Educational Corp., as well as the "Animal Safari Nature Library" series published by Childrens Press. The latter contains eight titles like *Elephant Herds and Rhino Horns* (1982), *Killer Whales and Dolphin Play* (1982), and *Wolf Fangs and Fox Dens* (1984). In 1983 Torgersen was awarded for his contributions to children's literature at the Illinois Young Authors Conference.

In addition to his books, Torgersen has written and produced over forty educational documentary films through Society for Visual Education, including the series "Documentary on Canada," "The New Japan," "The American Experience in Democracy," and "Wildlife Stories." Included among his current projects are *Ten Little Indian Tales,* a book on native American folktales; *Arinbjorn,* a Viking novel; *King of the Hill,* memoirs of his own childhood; and additional gnome and troll books. *Home and office:* 1062 Old Mill Dr., Palatine, Ill. 60067.

FOR MORE INFORMATION SEE: Contemporary Authors, Volume 111, Gale, 1984.

VINCENT, Félix 1946-
(Félix)

PERSONAL: Born June 18, 1946, in Miribel, France; son of Jacques (a salesman) and Yvette (Faure) Vincent; married Cecilia Bazante (an artist and painter), September 22, 1977; children: Natasha, Julie. *Education:* Earned baccalauréat in experimental sciences, Lyon, 1966; Ecole des Beaux-Arts, Lyon, certificate, 1970, additional study, 1972; Ecole Nationale des Beaux-Arts, Toulouse, diploma, 1971; Ecole Nationale Supérieure des Arts Décoratifs, Paris, diploma, 1972; also attended Ecole Nationale d'Architecture, Lyon, 1972; and University of Montreal, 1973-76. *Home and office:* Mas de la Mer, 13 Bis Bd. de la Plage, 83 270 St. Cyr/Mer, France.

CAREER: Painter and illustrator. College d'Enseignement Secondaire des Tilleuls, St. Maur, France, and College d'Enseignement Secondaire, St. Exupéry, Villiers Lebel, France, teacher, 1972; University of Montreal, Montreal, Quebec, Canada, assistant teacher, 1973-74; Ecole Nationale Supérieure d'Agronomie, Dijon, France, and Institut National de Promotion Supérieure Agricole, assistant teacher, 1974-75; Keystone Press Agency, Montreal, photographer, 1976-78. Has taught courses in painting and animation in Quebec, 1980-82.

FÉLIX VINCENT

(From *Les Saisons* by Raoul Duguay. Illustrated by Félix Vincent.)

EXHIBITIONS—One-man shows: Galerie "Jacquie," Montreal, 1975; Galerie "Libre," Montreal, 1976-80; Galerie "Altamira," Quito, 1977-79; Sterling Library, Baytown, Texas, 1978; Galerie Alliance, Montreal, 1983; House of Culture, Bandol, France, 1985.

Group shows: Galerie St. Jean, Quebec, 1976; Salon de Lyon, 1978-80; Musée d'Art Contemporain de Montreal, 1979; Place des Arts, Montreal, 1979; Musée de St. Quentin, Aisne, 1981; Mairie du 15 éme, Paris, 1981; Musée de Ville St. Laurent, Quebec, 1982; Pavillon du Québec, "Man and His World," Montreal, 1982; Galerie Crescent, Montreal, 1982.

Collections: Glenbow Institute, Calgary, Canada; Musée d'Art Naïf de l'Ile de France; Musée des Beaux-Arts de Joliette, Quebec; Ville de Lyon, France; Musée d'Art Contemporain de Montreal; and oil companies, including Esso-Standard Oil, Shell, B. P. *Awards, Honors:* "Critici en Erba" and "Caractère de l'année," Children's Book Fair, Bologna, Italy, 1978, and "Ehrende Anerkennung," Leipzig, Germany, 1979, both for *Pays des chats/Catlands;* honorable mention, Salon de Lyon, 1978, for an oil painting.

WRITINGS—All self-illustrated: *Pays des chats/Catlands,* Tundra (Canada), 1977; *Emilie, la baignoire à pattes* (title means "The Walking Bathtub"), Heritage (Canada), 1978; *La Chaise à Sébastien,* (title means "Sebastian's Chair"), Fides (Canada), 1982; *L'Enfant lumière* (title means "The Child of Light"), Meridien (Canada), 1982. Contributor to *Montreal Scene, Montreal Star* and *Video Presse.*

Illustrator: Louis Pauwels, *L'Arche de Noé et les naïfs* (title means "Noah's Ark and the Naive"), Max Fourny (France), 1977; Jean-Claude Lauret, *La Fête et les naïfs* (title means "The Feast and the Naive"), Max Fourny, 1979; Helen Renard, *Le Rêve et les naïfs* (title means "The Dream and the Naive), Max Fourny, 1981; Raôul Duguay, *Les Saisons* (title means "The Seasons"), La courte échelle (Canada), 1981; Max Fourny, *Album mondial de la peinture naïve* (title means "World Book of Naive Painting"), Hervas (France), 1981; Philippe Camby, *Le Paradis et les naïfs,* Max Fourny, 1983.

SIDELIGHTS: "I spent most of my childhood in the country, by a big river in France. There I explored islands, beaches, birds, snakes, frogs, fish and loved them all." Originally Vincent intended to be an architect, but turned to painting as a vocation.

"For me illustration (not so much writing because it is impossible to do everything) is a branch of painting. I use the same techniques. It's a way of showing the same painting to thousands of people and sharing it with them. The content of the images, in my illustrations comes from my memory, observation, imagination and fantasy. . . ."

Vincent has also taught drawing and photography in France and in Canada. "I don't believe in gifts of talent. I don't believe that myth. If you like something, work a lot at it, have a passion for it, you can learn.

"I am always learning. That's why I always think my last

painting is always the best. I look a lot, too, in museums in every city I visit, and I sketch all the time. *That* is the best way to study.'' [Doris Giller, ''The Purrfect Catalyst,'' *Montreal Scene,* October 22, 1977.]

HOBBIES AND OTHER INTERESTS: Guitar playing, gardening (ornamental plants, fruit trees, etc.), traveling.

FOR MORE INFORMATION SEE: Gazette (Montreal), October 15, 1977; *Montreal Scene,* October 22, 1977; *Baytown Sun* (Texas), February 3, 1978, February 26, 1978; *Vient de Paraître* (Montreal), May, 1978; *The World of Children's Books,* University of Alberta (Canada), fall, 1978; *Marie-France* (Paris), February, 1980; *Montreal Ce Mois-ci,* August, 1981.

WALLACE-BRODEUR, Ruth 1941-

BRIEF ENTRY: Born August 25, 1941, in Springfield, Mass. After graduating from the University of Massachusetts in 1962, Wallace-Brodeur joined the psychology staff of Pineland Hospital and Training Center in Pownal, Maine. She has been employed as a full-time writer since 1975 and is the author of three juvenile novels. An absurd premise is the basis of *One April Vacation* (Atheneum, 1981) in which Kate thinks she may only have one week to live. When she loses a nasal hair at the beginning of her spring vacation, she remembers what a junior high school student told her: anyone who loses a nasal hair will die within a week. In the days remaining she follows the advice of her friend Aunt Melindy to do only the things that please her most.

School Library Journal found that ''Kate's relationships with her sister and Melindy are realistically and warmly developed, and Kate's vigil through the final moments of her week's term is wrenching.'' *Horn Book* observed, ''The episodic accounts of her refreshingly relaxed, ordinary family life contribute a halcyon air and humor which counterbalance Kate's apprehension of death.'' *Booklist* added, ''The subject of a child's confrontation with her own mortality is treated with compassionate humor.'' In another story about death, *The Kenton Year* (Atheneum, 1980), Mandy learns to adjust to the loss of her father after she and her mother move to Vermont. Wallace-Brodeur's third book, *Callie's Way* (Atheneum, 1984), focuses on the friendship between Callie, a girl with personal problems, and Megal, a bedridden stroke patient. *Booklist* stated, ''This well-told story gets high marks for believability.'' Wallace-Brodeur is also a contributor to magazines and newspapers. *Residence:* Montpelier, Vt.

FOR MORE INFORMATION SEE: Rutland Herald and Times Argus, July 13, 1980; *Burlington Free Press,* January 28, 1981; *Contemporary Authors,* Volume 107, Gale, 1983.

WALLNER, Alexandra 1946-

BRIEF ENTRY: Born February 28, 1946, in Germany. A freelance illustrator and writer, Wallner received bachelor's and master's degrees from Pratt Institute. She has been an assistant art director for *American Home* and an associate art director for *New Ingenue.* An author and illustrator of her own books

for children, she also has illustrated books by other authors. Her picturebook *Munch* (Crown, 1976) shows pigs, elephants, and hippos indulging on food. *Booklist* noted its ''many humorous concoctions whipped up and served poetry-style.'' She also produced *Ghoulish Giggles and Monster Riddles* (Albert Whitman, 1982) which *Booklist* called an ''effective joke collection.'' Among Wallner's other works are two books featuring ''Strawberry Shortcake,'' both illustrated by Mercedes Llimona. They are *The Adventures of Strawberry Shortcake and Her Friends* (Random House, 1980) and *Strawberry Shortcake and the Winter That Would Not End* (Random House, 1982). She has provided illustrations for *Trudy's Straw Hat* by Martha Gamerman, *The Friends of Charlie Ant Bear* by Malcolm Hall, and *Un-Frog-get-table Riddles* by Joanne E. Bernstein and Paul Cohen. Wallner is currently working on a book entitled *The Changing Neighborhood. Home and office:* 82 Broadview Rd., Woodstock, N.Y. 12498.

FOR MORE INFORMATION SEE: Contemporary Authors, New Revision Series, Volume 13, Gale, 1984.

WATSON TAYLOR, Elizabeth 1915-

PERSONAL: Born January 4, 1915, in Berkshire, England; daughter of Felix John (an artist) and Lilian Elizabeth (Tennant) Watson Taylor. *Education:* Mothercraft Training Society, nursery nurse certificate, 1934. *Politics:* Conservative. *Religion:* Church of England. *Home:* Ashley Hill Cottage, Honey Lane, Hurley-near-Maidenhead, Berkshire, SL6 6RB, England.

CAREER: British Broadcasting Corp., London, England, monitoring supervisor, 1939-46; employed as a nanny in California, 1947-52; British Overseas Airways Corp., London Airport, London, interpreter and passenger attendant, 1954-66; linguist, retired, 1966; translator of children's books,

ELIZABETH WATSON TAYLOR

They rode through fields where the most exquisite fruits and vegetables grew, all of which were made of marzipan, icing sugar or chocolates with soft centres . . . . ■ (From "The Christmas Country," in *The Magic Inkstand and Other Stories* by Heinrich Seidel. Translated by Elizabeth Watson Taylor. Illustrated by Wayne Anderson.)

1976—. *Awards, honors:* The Adventures of Maya the Bee was selected as one of the children's books of the year, 1980, by the National Book League; *The Magic Inkstand, and Other Stories* was selected by the National Book League as one of the children's books of the year, 1983, named to the International Board of Books for Young People honor list, 1984, and awarded an honors diploma at the Leipzig International Book Fair, 1984.

WRITINGS—Translator; all for children: (From the German) Werner Schmidmaier and Hans Manz, *Tim and Tilly and the Time Machine* (illustrated by Philippe Fix), J. Cape, 1977; (from the German) Robert Gernhardt, *One More Makes Four* (poems; illustrated by Almut Gernhardt), J. Cape, 1978; (from the French) Pascale Allamand, *The Animals Who Changed Their Colors* (illustrated by P. Allamand), Lothrop, 1979; (from the German) Waldemar Bonsels, *The Adventures of Maya the Bee* (illustrated by L. R. Brightwell), Hutchinson, 1980; (from the German) Heinrich Seidel, *The Magic Inkstand, and Other Stories* (illustrated by Wayne Anderson), Merrimack, 1982.

SIDELIGHTS: "I speak perfect German, good French and Italian, and some Spanish. I have travelled extensively (during my work as a nanny for Joan Crawford, I did not experience anything her daughter Tina describes in *Mommie Dearest*). Unfortunately, I did not start my free-lance translating until I was over fifty. It is what I am best at."

WAUGH, Carol-Lynn Rössel 1947-
(C. C. Rössel-Waugh, joint pseudonym)

PERSONAL: Surname rhymes with "law"; maiden name rhymes with "muscle"; born January 5, 1947, in Staten Island, N.Y.; daughter of Carl Frederick (a retired stock examiner) and Muriel (a poet, maiden name, Kiefer) Rössel; married Charles Gordon Waugh (a professor and editor), November 11, 1967; children: Jenny-Lynn, Eric-Jon Rössel. *Education:* State University of New York at Binghamton, B.A., 1968; Kent State University, M.A., 1979. *Politics:* Democrat. *Home and office:* 5 Morrill St., Winthrop, Me. 04364. *Agent:* Andrea Brown, 240 East 48th St., New York, N.Y. 10017.

CAREER: Singer Co., Augusta, Me., sewing instructor, 1971-72; doll and teddy bear artist, 1973—; writer, 1978—; painter and photographer. Art history instructor, University of Maine, 1976-77; adult education teacher in Winthrop, Me., autumn, 1978; public speaker. *Member:* Society of Children's Book Writers, Original Doll Artist Council of America (ODACA), Good Bears of the World, Maine Association of Women in the Fine and Performing Arts. *Awards, honors:* More than thirty awards for original dolls and paintings.

WRITINGS: (Contributor of short story with husband, Charles G. Waugh, under pseudonym C. C. Rössel-Waugh) Isaac Asimov, Martin H. Greenberg, and C. G. Waugh, editors, *Flying Saucers*, Fawcett, 1982; *Petite Portraits: Miniature Dolls by Contemporary American Doll Artists*, Hobby House, 1982; *My Friend Bear* (juvenile; illustrated by Susan Meddaugh), Little, Brown, 1982; *The Octagon Houses of Maine*, Mosaic Press, 1982; *Teddy Bear Artists: Romance of Making and Collecting Bears*, Hobby House, 1984; (with Susanna Droyan) *The Contemporary Artist Doll: A Guide for Collectors*, Hobby House, 1985. Also author and photographer of video entitled "The Gorham-Bear Story," Gorham-Textron, 1984-85.

Editor with I. Asimov and M. H. Greenberg: *The Twelve Crimes of Christmas*, Avon, 1981; *The Big Apple Mysteries*, Avon, 1982; *Show Business Is Murder*, Avon, 1983; *Thirteen Horrors of Hallowe'en*, Avon, 1983; *Murder on the Menu*, Avon, 1984.

Contributor to *Doll Catalog*, and to magazines, including *Miniature Gazette, Doll Reader, Ladies' Home Journal Needle and Craft, Maine Antique Digest, Miniature World, Dollmaker, Nutshell News, International Doll Revue*, and *Teddy Bear and Friends*. Reviewer of books on bears for *Bear Tracks*, and reviewer of juvenile books for the *Sunday Sun-Journal* (Lewiston-Auburn, Maine).

SIDELIGHTS: "Most of my work involves children: the books, the dolls, the teddy bears, the painting, and photography. I've never grown up, so I'm still on their level. I *remember*. Children are very special, complex individuals and I'll spend my life trying to understand them. Fortunately, we have a small ambassador from the world of children in our house—Eric-Jon. He has brought me back again to the world of imaginary bears who make midnight calls on plastic telephones. With his help, I'll never have to be serious and stodgy and (heaven forbid!) grown up. He's immortalized now, in *My Friend Bear*. And is he ever proud of it—a biography at age three-and-one-half!

"When I was in high school, I had a chemistry teacher who used to write plays about the things that were happening in our little town (Tottenville, Staten Island, N.Y.). He judged our senior play contest one year, and I won. In my senior yearbook he wrote that someday I would become a famous

CAROL-LYNN RÖSSEL WAUGH

Bear and I are big. ■ (From *My Friend Bear* by Carol-Lynn Rössel Waugh. Illustrated by Susan Meddaugh.)

writer. I thought it was most peculiar, because I intended to become a French teacher. Well, he went on to win a Pulitzer Prize for one of his plays about Tottenville High. I always look back at that as an important influence, because it showed me that it could be done, even if one came from a provincial backwater like Tottenville. Most of all, it told me that one can do well if he writes about what he knows, because it's really alien (and maybe even intriguing) to almost everyone else. So I write about what I know. And now I'm working on a young adult novel about Tottenville. I hope to do a tenth as well. Oh, yes. My teacher's name was Paul Zindel.

"About *My Friend Bear*, I feel strongly that teddy bears are important friends for children. This book grew out of the strong relationship between Eric-Jon and his friend, My Friend Bear. We share our house with around 200 bears, all of whom we know by name—some better than others. For a wedding gift, Charles gave me a stuffed koala bear. Teddy bears, to us, are symbols of love.''

HOBBIES AND OTHER INTERESTS: ''I speak French, and some Spanish and Russian. My avocations are photography and watercolor painting.''

FOR MORE INFORMATION SEE: Staten Island Advance, July 5, 1976, February 10, 1980, December 13, 1981, July 11, 1982; *Kennebec Journal,* August 27, 1976, October 8, 1976, September 8, 1979, July 18, 1982; Kathryn Falk, *Miniature Needle Point and Sewing Projects for Dollhouses,* Hawthorn, 1977; *Doll Castle News,* June/July, 1977, November/December, 1979; *Small Talk,* July, 1977; *Antique Trader,* September 21, 1977; Helen Ruthberg, *Miniature Room Settings,* Chilton, 1978; *National Doll World,* January/February, 1978; *Miniature and Dollhouse Crafts,* February, 1978; *Miniature Gazette,* winter, 1979; Peggy Bialosky and Alan Bialosky, *Teddy Bear Catalog,* Workman Publishing, 1980; Mae Shafter Rockland, *The New Jewish Yellow Pages,* SBS, 1980; Donna Felger, editor, *The Doll Catalog,* Hobby House, 1980; *Miniature Collector,* August, 1980; *Bear Tracks,* spring, 1981, summer, 1982, fall, 1982; *Los Angeles Times Book Review,* August 1, 1982.

WEBB, Sharon   1936-

PERSONAL: Born February 29, 1936, in Tampa, Fla.; daughter of William Wesley (a meteorologist) and Eunice (a teacher; maiden name, Tillman) Talbott; married W. Bryan Webb (a real estate agent), February 6, 1956; children: Wendy Webb Nesheim, Jerri Webb Thompson, Tracey. *Education:* Florida Southern College, 1953-56; Miami-Dade Community College, A.D.N., 1972. *Politics:* Democrat. *Religion:* Protestant. *Home address:* Route 2, P.O. Box 2600, Blairsville, Ga. 30512. *Agent:* Adele Leone, Adele Leone Agency, Inc., 52 Riverside Dr., New York, N.Y. 10024.

CAREER: South Miami Hospital, Miami, Fla., registered nurse, 1972-73; Union General Hospital, Blairsville, Ga., registered nurse, 1973-75; Towns County Hospital, Hiawassee, Ga., registered nurse, 1975-79; Murphy Medical Center, Murphy, N.C., registered nurse, 1979-80; full-time writer, 1980—. *Member:* Authors League of America, Authors Guild, Science Fiction Writers of America (South/Central regional director, 1983).

WRITINGS: RN (nonfiction), Zebra, 1982; *The Adventures of Terra Tarkington* (science fiction), Bantam, 1985.

''Earthsong Triad''; science fiction for young adults: *Earthchild,* Atheneum, 1982; *Earth Song,* Atheneum, 1983; *Ram Song,* Atheneum, 1984. Also contributor of over thirty short stories to numerous periodicals, including *Isaac Asimov's Science Fiction Magazine, Amazing,* and *Parsec.*

WORK IN PROGRESS: Pestis 18, a medical-suspense novel set in Atlanta and the Georgia Sea Islands, to be published by TOR Books.

SIDELIGHTS: ''I was born on the twenty-ninth of February in Tampa, Florida. Although I began to read at three, my

(Jacket illustration by Neil Feigeles from *Earth Song* by Sharon Webb.)

writing career didn't begin until I was seven when I wrote a murder mystery. Unfortunately, that document is lost forever. I do recall one character in it, a little girl—the heroine, of course—who found a dead body in bed with her. For some reason, my story shocked my mother.

''I was not published immediately. In fact, I wasn't published until eight years later when I simultaneously became feature editor of the Plant High School newspaper, and Florida's youngest (and perhaps only) female disc jockey on WFLA, the NBC radio affiliate for the Tampa Bay area.

''I have always read fantasy; I first read science fiction when I was a sixth grader and it opened delicious ways of thinking. Like most readers of science fiction, I wanted to write it. Unfortunately, a college creative writing course stood in my way. 'Style,' quoted the professor. And plot was a four-letter word. Nevertheless, I continued to major in English until I left Florida Southern College to marry Bryan Webb.

''By the time I was twenty-three, I had three babies and no professional publishing credits. I was going a little nuts. . . . That's when I started writing in earnest and began to publish all sorts of things: nasty little greeting cards, short stories, light verse, heavier verse, a newspaper column, humor features, nonfiction articles, and book reviews for the *Miami News.*

At this time, I began a serious collection of rejection slips—which I still own and add to occasionally.

"My first professional sale was to *Alfred Hitchcock's Mystery Magazine,* shortly followed by *Fantasy and Science Fiction*—and in those days I wrote under a male pen name (No, I'm not going to tell you what it is, but if you want to look through old copies of *The Best from Fantasy and Science Fiction,* you might be able to figure it out.) Even the editors thought I was a man. I eventually passed out of my George Sand emulation mode and for a time, gave up writing.

"When I was a child I decided there were several career options open to me: I could be a chemist, a geologist, an opera star, a professional roller-skater, a writer, or a nurse. So, having temporarily abandoned writing, I picked up another option and went to nursing school, graduating in 1972.

"Nursing school was extremely stressful. I used to mutter under my breath, 'I'm going to write a book about this someday.' And I did. It was called *RN,* published in 1982 by Zebra Books.

"In June of 1973 we moved from Miami to the Blue Ridge Mountains of northern Georgia, and came to rest on the site of an old Cherokee battlefield, in the shade of Blood and Slaughter Mountains. In spite of the sanguine names, it is a gentle place—a holy place to the Indians, and to me.

"And I started to write science fiction again, short stories at first. My novelette 'Variation on a Theme from Beethoven,' published in *Isaac Asimov's Science Fiction Magazine* and Donald A. Wollheim's *1981 Annual World's Best SF,* led to first one book, then a trilogy. My third book *Earth Song* came out in 1983 from Atheneum, followed by a Bantam reprint of the first book of the Earthsong Triad, *Earthchild. Ram Song* is the final book of the trilogy."

WERNER, Herma 1926-
(Eve Cowen, Joma Pinner)

BRIEF ENTRY: Born November 12, 1926, in New York, N.Y. Werner is the author of a number of adventure, sports, and mystery stories aimed at young adults with low reading levels. In a genre where the writing is too often mediocre, reviewers of *High/Low Report* took special note of Werner's adept characterizations and interesting storylines. Among her titles are *Going for the Win* (Scholastic Book Services, 1978), written with John Piniat, and *The Dragster* (Scholastic Book Services, 1979). She coauthored *The Magic Arm* (Educational Challenges, Inc., 1978) under the pseudonym Joma Pinner, and as Eve Cowen produced *Jungle Jenny* (Fearon-Pitman, 1979), *Catch the Sun, High Escape,* and *Race to Win* (all Childrens Press, 1981). Werner considers her writing "work of redeeming social value, and more than enough reason for getting up in the morning." An artist as well as a writer, she received her B.F.A. from Cooper Union in 1976. Her paintings have been exhibited at galleries and libraries throughout New York City, and she has completed some unpublished illustrations for children's books. *Home:* 4818 43rd St., Woodside, N.Y. 11377.

FOR MORE INFORMATION SEE: Contemporary Authors, Volumes 85-88, Gale, 1980.

WILLIAMS, Jay 1914-1978
(Michael Delving)

PERSONAL: Born May 31, 1914, in Buffalo, N.Y.; died of a heart attack, July 12, 1978, in London, England; son of Max (a vaudeville show producer) and Lillian (Weinstein) Jacobson; married Barbara Girdansky, June 3, 1941; children: Christopher, Victoria. *Education:* Attended University of Pennsylvania, 1932-33, and Columbia University, 1934; also attended Art Students' League. *Residence:* West Redding, Conn. *Agent:* Candida Donadio & Associates, 111 West 57th St., New York, N.Y. 10019.

CAREER: Appeared in vaudeville shows and night clubs, acting as master of ceremonies or as a comedian, 1935-37; assistant social director in adult summer camps, 1935-37; press agent for Dwight Deere Wiman, Jed Harris, and Hollywood Theater Alliance, 1936-41; full-time writer, 1945-78. *Military service:* U.S. Infantry, 1941-45; awarded the Purple Heart. *Member:* Society of Authors (Great Britain), Authors Guild. *Awards, honors:* Guggenheim Fellowship, 1949; Boys' Club of America Award, 1949, for *The Roman Moon Mystery;* Young Readers Choice Award, 1961, for *Danny Dunn and the Homework Machine,* and 1963, for *Danny Dunn on the Ocean Floor; The Practical Princess* was chosen one of *School Library Journal*'s Best books, 1969 and received a Golden Apple Award at the Biennale of Illustrators, Bratislava, Czechoslovakia; *The Silver Whistle* was selected one of the "Fifty Best Books of the Year" by the American Institute of Graphic Arts, 1972; Lewis Carroll Shelf Award, 1972, for *The Hawkstone; Petronella* was a Children's Book Showcase Title, 1974; *Everyone Knows What a Dragon Looks Like* was chosen one of *New York Times*'s Best Illustrated Books of the Year, 1976, was included in the American Institute of Graphic Arts Book Show,

JAY WILLIAMS

The little boy, Conn, stuck out his tongue and licked chocolate off his lips. ■ (From *The Cookie Tree* by Jay Williams. Illustrated by Blake Hampton.)

1977, and received the Irma Simonton Black Award, Bank Street College of Education, 1977.

WRITINGS—Juvenile fiction; published by Oxford University Press, except as indicated: *The Stolen Oracle* (illustrated by Frederick Chapman), 1943; *The Counterfeit African*, 1944; *The Sword and the Scythe* (illustrated by Edouard Sandoz), 1946; *Eagle Jake and Indian Pete* (illustrated by John Brimer), Rinehart, 1947; *The Roman Moon Mystery*, 1948; *The Magic Gate* (illustrated by J. Brimer), 1949.

Puppy Pie (illustrated by Wayne Blickenstaff), Crowell, 1962; *I Wish I Had Another Name* (verse; illustrated by Winifred Lubell), Atheneum, 1962; *The Question Box* (illustrated by Margot Zemach), Norton, 1965; *Philbert the Fearful* (illustrated by Ib Ohlsson; also see below), Norton, 1966; *What Can You Do with a Word?* (illustrated by Leslie Goldstein), Macmillan, 1966; *The Cookie Tree* (illustrated by Blake Hampton), Parents Magazine Press, 1967; *The Sword of King Arthur* (illustrated by Louis Glanzman), Crowell, 1968; *The Horn of Roland* (illustrated by Sean Morrison), Crowell, 1968; *To Catch a Bird* (illustrated by J. Polseno), Crowell, 1968; *The King with Six Friends* (illustrated by Imero Gobbato), Parents Magazine Press, 1968; *The Good-for-Nothing Prince* (illustrated by I. Gobbato), Norton, 1969; *The Practical Princess* (illustrated by Friso Henstra; also see below), Parents Magazine Press, 1969; *School for Sillies* (illustrated by F. Henstra), Parents Magazine Press, 1969.

Published by Parents Magazine Press, except as indicated: *A Box Full of Infinity* (illustrated by Robin Lawrie), Norton, 1970; *Stupid Marco* (illustrated by F. Henstra; also see below), 1970; *The Silver Whistle* (illustrated by F. Henstra; also see below), 1971; *A Present from a Bird* (illustrated by Jacqueline Chwast), 1971; *The Hawkstone*, Walck, 1971; *Seven at One Blow* (illustrated by F. Henstra), 1972; *The Youngest Captain* (illustrated by F. Henstra), 1972; *Magical Storybook* (illustrated by Edward Sorel), American Heritage, 1972; *The Hero from Otherwhere*, Walck, 1972; *Petronella* (illustrated by F. Henstra; Junior Literary Guild selection; also see below), 1973; *Forgetful Fred* (illustrated by F. Henstra; also see below), 1974; *A Bag Full of Nothing* (illustrated by Tom O'Sullivan), 1974; *The People of the Ax*, Walck, 1974.

Moon Journey (adapted from *From the Earth to the Moon* by Jules Verne; illustrated by Daniel le Noury), MacDonald & Jane's, 1976, published in America as *Voyage to the Moon*, Crown, 1977; *Everyone Knows What a Dragon Looks Like* (illustrated by Mercer Mayer; Junior Literary Guild selection), Four Winds Press, 1976; *The Burglar Next Door* (illustrated by DeAnne Hollinger), Four Winds Press, 1976 (published in England as *Daylight Robbery*, Penguin, 1977); *The Reward Worth Having* (illustrated by M. Mayer), Four Winds Press, 1977; *The Time of the Kraken*, Four Winds Press, 1977; *Pettifur* (illustrated by Hilary Knight), Four Winds Press, 1977; *The Wicked Tricks of Tyl Uilenspiegel* (illustrated by F. Henstra), Four Winds Press, 1978; *The Practical Princess and Other Liberating Fairy Tales* (illustrated by Rick Schreiter; includes *The Practical Princess, Stupid Marco, The Silver Whistle, Forgetful Fred, Petronella* and *Philbert the Fearful*), 1978; *The Magic Grandfather* (illustrated by Gail Owens), Four Winds Press, 1979 (British edition illustrated by A. Mieke, MacDonald & Jane's, 1979); *The City Witch and the Country Witch* (illustrated by Ed Renfro), Macmillan, 1979; *The Surprising Things Maui Did* (illustrated by Charles Mikolaycak), Four Winds Press, 1979; *One Big Wish* (illustrated by John O'Brien), Macmillan, 1980; *The Water of Life* (illustrated by Lucinda McQueen), Four Winds Press, 1980.

"The kestrel isn't there now," he said. ■ (From *To Catch a Bird* by Jay Williams. Illustrated by Jo Polseno.)

"Danny Dunn" series; with Raymond Abrashkin; all science fiction; all published by McGraw: *Danny Dunn and the Anti-Gravity Paint* (illustrated by Ezra Jack Keats), 1956; *. . . on a Desert Island* (illustrated by E. J. Keats), 1957; *. . . and the Homework Machine* (illustrated by E. J. Keats), 1958; *. . . and the Weather Machine* (illustrated by E. J. Keats), 1959; *. . . on the Ocean Floor* (illustrated by Brinton Turkle), 1960; *. . . and the Fossil Cave* (illustrated by B. Turkle), 1961; *. . . and the Heat Ray* (illustrated by Owen Kampen), 1962; *. . ., Time Traveler* (illustrated by O. Kampen), 1963; *. . . and the Automatic House* (illustrated by O. Kampen), 1965; *. . . and the Voice from Space* (illustrated by Leo Summers), 1967; *. . . and the Smallifying Machine* (illustrated by Paul Sagsoorian), 1969; *. . . and the Swamp Monster* (illustrated by P. Sagsoorian), 1971; *. . ., Invisible Boy* (illustrated by P. Sagsoorian), 1974; *. . ., Scientific Detective* (illustrated by P. Sagsoorian; Junior Literary Guild selection), 1975; *. . . and the Universal Glue* (illustrated by P. Sagsoorian), 1977.

Juvenile nonfiction: *Augustus Caesar*, Row, 1951; *The Battle for the Atlantic*, Random House, 1959; *The Tournament of the Lions* (illustrated by E. J. Keats), Walck, 1960; *Medusa's Head* (illustrated by Steele Savage), Random House, 1961; (with Margaret B. Freeman) *Knights of the Crusades*, Horizon, 1962; (with Charles W. Lightbody) *Joan of Arc*, Horizon, 1963; (with Bates Lowry) *Leonardo da Vinci*, American Heritage, 1965; *Life in the Middle Ages* (illustrated by R. Tor and H. Shekerjian), Chanticleer, 1966; (with Lacey B. Smith) *The Spanish Armada*, American Heritage, 1966.

Adult fiction: *The Good Yeoman*, Appleton, 1948; *The Rogue from Padua*, Little, Brown, 1952; *The Siege*, Little, Brown, 1953; *The Witches*, Random House, 1957; *Solomon and Sheba*, Random House, 1959; *The Forger*, Atheneum, 1961; *Tomorrow's Fire*, Atheneum, 1964; *UNIAD*, Scribner, 1968.

Under pseudonym Michael Delving; all mysteries: *Smiling, the Boy Fell Dead*, Scribner, 1966; *The Devil Finds Work*, Scribner, 1969; *Die Like a Man*, Collins, 1970, Scribner, 1971; *A Shadow of Himself*, Scribner, 1972; *Bored to Death*, Scribner, 1975 (published in England as *Wave of Fatalities*, Collins, 1975); *The China Expert*, Collins, 1976, Scribner, 1977; *No Sign of Life*, Doubleday, 1979.

Adult nonfiction: *Fall of the Sparrow* (illustrated by Richard Taylor), Oxford University Press, 1951; *A Change of Climate*, Random House, 1956; *The World of Titian*, Time-Life, 1968; *Stage Left*, Scribner, 1974.

Contributor: Edwin Seaver, editor, *Cross Section: A Collection of New American Writing*, Fischer, 1945; *Adventures Now and Then*, 1957; *The Best from Fantasy and Science Fiction*, Doubleday, 6th series, 1957, 11th series, 1962; *Trails to Treasure*, Ginn, 1961; Orville Prescott, editor, *The Undying Past*, Doubleday, 1961; Thomas Boardman, editor, *The Hostile Future*, 1965; *Bright Horizons: Book 3*, Scott Foresman, 1969; *The World of Language: Book 6*, Follett, 1970. Contributor of stories to *Saturday Evening Post, Esquire, True, American Scholar, Red-book*, and other magazines.

ADAPTATIONS: ''Danny Dunn and the Homework Machine'' (play), produced by Metromedia-On-Stage, 1969; ''Danny Dunn and the Swamp Monster'' (cassette with book and teacher's guide), Listening Library, 1985.

SIDELIGHTS: **May 31, 1914.** Born in Buffalo, New York, and raised in Rochester, Williams's earliest memories were of imaginative games he played in the woods. ''At the age of 12 I won a prize (it was a book) for the best original ghost story told round the campfire in a boys' camp. The experience went to my head and I have been telling stories to children ever since. I don't think of myself as anything but a spinner of tales; I have no pretensions to being educator, moralist, or propagandist, although inevitably, unless a writer has perfect insulation between himself and his writing, into every work one's beliefs, enjoyments, and sense of morality will find their way like mice into a country kitchen. Even my non-fiction has grown out of subjects which attracted me because they were good stories. And what is a good story? I have no universal definition, but for me it is one which binds teller as much as

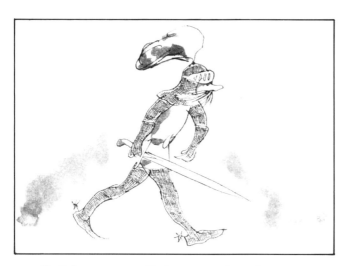

Sir Brian was gone. He had gone with a firm stride, sword in hand, into the castle. ■ (From *Philbert the Fearful* by Jay Williams. Illustrated by Ib Ohlsson.)

reader in a web of surprise, tension, and wonderment. To all intents and purposes, I'm still back at that campfire.'' [D. L. Kirkpatrick, *Twentieth Century Children's Writers*, St. Martin's Press, 1978.[1]]

Williams went to a high school in New York City before entering the University of Pennsylvania. After two years, he transferred to Columbia University where he majored in English and took part in amateur theatricals. After college, Williams studied art briefly at the Art Students League. ''I had many occasions to bless the year I once spent at the Art Students' League, a year up to now distinguished only for the fact that the great Kuniyoshi himself said to me, 'You would do better to give up trying to be an artist.' '' [Jay Williams, *A Change of Climate*, Random House, 1956.[2]]

1936-1941. Following in his father's footsteps, Williams worked in the theater as a comedian, stage manager, and press agent.

1941. Married Barbara Girdansky. ''. . . We have done a great deal of traveling, alone together, then with our son, Christopher, and then with the addition of our daughter, Victoria. Almost every trip has had entangled in it some noteworthy piece of confusion, or many such items, from the time I rewrote a novel while driving across the United States, to the time we arrived in the city of Oxford without hotel reservations, and carrying four large suitcases, and discovered that it was graduation week as well as the day of the Oxford boat races.''[2]

1943. First book was published, a historical-mystery novel entitled *The Stolen Oracle*, for boys from twelve to fourteen. Writing was not easy for Williams—he rewrote the first chapter seven times. At the time of publication Williams was serving in the army. ''I enjoy telling stories. I start out with a story; in the course of writing, it begins to tell me what I think of life. All kinds of questions arise which the story forces me to answer.

''. . . And the theme that seems to run through every story I've ever written is this: the mystery of what lies beneath the surfaces of things. The stories are all about appearances of things. In my books everyone is asking questions.'' [Aidan Chambers, ''Letter from England: The Magic of the Mask,'' *Horn Book*, February, 1977.[3]]

1945. Awarded a Purple Heart at the close of World War II. After his return from military service, Williams devoted himself to full-time writing.

1949. Financed by a Guggenheim fellowship, Williams made a trip to Europe with his wife and son to gather material for new historical novels. ''. . . We were living in London and we were offered a lift by some friends who were driving from Holland to Switzerland; we decided to go along with them as far as Paris and to stay there a week or so. Christopher was then six years old and we knew we would have difficulty sightseeing. Also, we suffered from a chronic disability common to the families of authors: anemia of the pocketbook. We cabled a good friend of ours, a painter named Jack Keats who was then studying in Paris, and asked him to book us into some modest but pleasant pension. He wrote back saying that the one where he was living was about as good as any, that it had the virtue of being a step away from the Boulevard Montparnasse, and that it was certainly cheap, so he had reserved a room for us there.

''At first glance, the Pension Dagobert seemed ideal. There was an elevator. Our room was large and light, it had two tall

The house turned round to face her, and out came an old witch. ■ (From *The Practical Princess and Other Liberating Fairy Tales* by Jay Williams. Illustrated by Rick Schreiter.)

Felix had a small room in the attic where he hung the cage with the small gray bird in it. ■ (From
The Reward Worth Having by Jay Williams. Illustrated by Mercer Mayer.)

He lived in a snug cottage beside the river and spent his days fishing or working in his garden. . . .
■ (From *The Water of Life* by Jay Williams. Illustrated by Lucinda McQueen.)

windows opening on a balcony that overlooked the Rue Stan-islas, it had a washstand and a little gas-ring, and the toilet was just outside the door. The street itself was quiet and rather pretty, with a church on one corner and a good bakery on the other, and just as Jack had said, the gay life of the Boulevard Montparnasse was only a step away: cafés famous in hundreds of stories—the Dôme and the Rotonde—with their crowds of cosmopolitan artists, international spies, and rug sellers.

"Disillusionment, however, was no further away. To begin with, a glance at the prices of the Dôme and the Rotonde convinced us that we would have to be satisfied with less illustrious cafés. Two or three evenings were enough to dem-onstrate that the cosmopolitan artists were, for the most part, Americans concealed beneath odd whiskers and dirndls; their command of the language of Balzac and Proust was restricted to ordering beer and asking for the bill. We had several spirited conversations with the lady who owned the grocery store across the street and with the baker around the corner, but never about Art. And the balconies of the Rue Stanislas, instead of being the scene of Murger's bohemian revels, held small boys who flew paper airplanes, weary workmen with their pipes, and a very fat woman who never seemed to eat or sleep but rested

motionless staring at the street, her chin pillowed on arms that resembled large, creaseless, bologna sausages. There was, it is true, that elevator, and we lived on the third floor, but we never summoned up courage enough to ride in it after the first time: it groaned and staggered, its cage creaked ominously, and from time to time it stopped to gather strength, usually between floors. But the greatest shock was the cooking.

"Barbara, who had gone to school in Paris when she was eleven or twelve, had reminisced about the good bourgeois cuisine of France until my chin was chapped from irrestrain-able drooling. One of my relatively few vices is eating, and where others might dream of the dim, blue shadows of Parisian streets, or the smell of mimosa, or the bridges of the Seine, I dreamed of *coq au vin* and Strasbourg *pâtés*, of truffles, stews, soufflés, and sauces.

"At our first meal in the pension, a strange, grayish-brown object was served; it sat aloof and chill on a white plate in a small puddle of congealed gravy. This, we were told, was a *rôti* of beef. There were also, as I recall, some potatoes, and a collection of cuttings from an old, wet piece of cardboard. To finish, we were given what M. Dagobert, the owner of the

"I am Prince Ferdinand of Firebright," he replied. "Would you mind stepping aside? I'm trying to get a suntan and you're standing in the way." ■ (From *Petronella* by Jay Williams. Illustrated by Friso Henstra.)

pension, amused himself by calling *petit suisse*; this was a crumbling portion of cottage cheese—attempting by its smell and color to pass itself off as roquefort although it was supposed to be cream cheese—decorated with two or three chips of sugar so aged that they did not dissolve in the mouth but kept their shape, like glass. They may have been glass.

"We left the table feeling hungry and cold and cheerless, and told ourselves that things were bound to be better at the next meal. Perhaps the cook was frightened by the unexpected arrival of three more boarders, or perhaps this was her day off and one of the chambermaids was cooking. The only thing that disturbed us privately was that Jack appeared to eat with a good appetite as if nothing out of the ordinary were taking place.

"That was lunch. Dinner was, if possible, even more disheartening. This time there was grease soup, filet of grease, and, although this may seem improbable, a kind of greasy fruit salad. After dinner I found that my tongue had a tendency to snap against the roof of my mouth.

"We walked a little through the crowded streets, but it was hard to savor Paris under the leaden weight of that dinner. We went to bed early. I was just dozing off, when I was jolted wide awake by a grinding, racking noise that set the bones of my head vibrating; then there was a deep-toned shuddering boom, seemingly from the room next door. It was the bell of the church on the corner. I have forgotten the name of that church but I have never forgotten its bells. For the next three weeks we were to live with them, awaking regularly every hour of the night, bathed in sweat, our heads splitting, furniture grating along the floor, the windows rattling, the soap dish falling with a crash, the endless violent explosions of each hour rocketing about the room like a trapped thunderstorm.

"The next few weeks were, of course, not wholly black although they were overcast by hunger and sleeplessness. We had many pleasant walks and some bus rides, although once Christopher fell off the back of a bus. We went to the Louvre and got lost immediately in the Egyptian wing and never did find our way to the Mona Lisa, which was, perhaps, not a catastrophe. We met an amiable young American who was working for UNESCO and who had a daughter a little older than Christopher. This child spoke French like a native, and she and Christopher used to play in the Luxembourg Gardens, where they were always watched by dozens of clean little French children in rompers and bobby-pins, whose admiration and envy of our tree-climbing and fence-shinnying rowdies was matched only by the horror of their nursemaids. There were a few memorable days."[2]

1953. Wrote the historical novel, *The Siege,* a well-researched book about medieval life. His aim in the book, Williams wrote, was to create "a more comprehensible picture of the true mind of the Middle Ages.

"That is an era associated with romance, although in fact it was thoroughly unromantic and thoroughly practical; it is thought of as an Age of Faith, although it was, in fact, an age of bitter religious conflict, of doubt, of disputation, a time in which priests were bitterly hated and the major part of the people were far from Christian; it is, above all, called the Dark Ages although it was a long way from being as dark as almost any

of the ages that followed it, including our own frightened atomic age. Although a tremendous body of information exists concerning these years, say, roughly, between the eleventh and the fifteenth centuries, ignorance about them is general, and begins in school textbooks which piously rehash the misconceptions of the nineteenth century and serve them up hot as a brand-new dish to students whose impressions are concocted out of Hollywood chivalry and the balderdash of historical novels.

"In school, for instance, I was always taught that Europe in the thirteenth century was unquestionably Christian, that all

It was not absolutely true to say that Prince Palagon was doing nothing. He was, as a matter of fact, counting butterflies. ■ (From *The Good-for-Nothing Prince* by Jay Williams. Illustrated by Imero Gobbato.)

princes owed allegiance to the Pope, that all men accepted obediently and humbly the authority of priests—for was this not the Age of Faith and of Authority? But a cursory glance at the annals of history shows that the case was far otherwise. In the south of France alone, at least half the population belonged to a religion which called itself Christian—the Albigensian faith—but which considered the Pope to be the Antichrist in person. Paganism, particularly among the peasantry, was widespread, and as for the kings, one ruler after another turned a cold shoulder to papal commands, and even after promising obedience to the Pope, broke their promises whenever it was expedient to do so. Even excommunication was often ignored.''[2]

1956. First ''Danny Dunn'' book published. The science fiction series for young people was conceived by Raymond Abrashkin. Abrashkin, almost completely paralyzed from a desperate illness, was the idea man and Williams was the writer. Abrashkin couldn't speak and would point to letters on a drawing of a typewriter keyboard. The coauthors developed a shorthand in which a letter or two stood for a whole word. ''Although the series is science-fiction, its stories are firmly based on scientific fact. For instance, the Lamont Geological Laboratories furnished information for *The Ocean Floor* and I.B.M.

contributed greatly to *The Homework Machine*. For *The Heat Ray*, I was shown one of the first lasers in use. An attempt has always been made to keep the science in the stories ahead of actual scientific developments. Many of the inventions suggested in *The Automatic House*, then purely hypothetical—such as the video-telephone, the rotating house, and the door responding to voice control—actually appeared in public use within a year after the book was published. And many more suggestions come from the children themselves.

''Danny has managed to keep ahead of the news in other than technological matters. The Danny Dunn books have, almost from the beginning, featured a girl named Irene who wants to become a physicist and who demonstrates a knowledge of science equal to Danny's. Irene was around long before it was popular for girls to take their places as full-fledged people in children's books. And the fan mail which comes in shows clearly that quite as many girls as boys read and enjoy the books.''

Response to the series was enormous—fan mail averaged a thousand letters a year. Abrashkin died after the fifth ''Danny Dunn'' book had been published. Before his death, he had the satisfaction of knowing that the series was firmly established

Everyone who went in or out of the city had a merry word from him, for that was all he had to give. ■ (From *Everyone Knows What a Dragon Looks Like* by Jay Williams. Illustrated by Mercer Mayer.)

Fred did a jig, he was so happy. But then he began to wonder what to do with all the money. ■
(From *One Big Wish* by Jay Williams. Illustrated by John O'Brien.)

and popular. "'. . . In the Danny Dunn books . . . the stories look as though they are pretty simple—about a kid who gets mixed up in scientific adventures—but they really deal with the necessity of thinking for yourself, of asking certain key questions about the universe, of trying all the time to get at the truth.'"[3]

1960. Wrote a children's nonfiction story of the medieval age. The book, entitled *The Tournament of the Lions*, was illustrated by Ezra Jack Keats. "As a boy, I read the *Chanson de Roland*—'Song of Roland'—in a translation by Scott-Moncrieff; I was thrilled by it, but I must confess it puzzled me, too. How could Roland be so pigheaded, and Charlemagne so blind? It wasn't until I had studied something about the Middle Ages, many years later, that I began to understand why these people did not behave as moderns would. For the 'Song of Roland' is not a tale about real people, but a kind of mirror of the ideas that governed chivalry: honor, vassalage, brotherhood, piety and prowess.

"It is possible there was a real Roland, but the facts of history

are quite different from the legend. Charlemagne was a young man when he invaded Spain. He took Pamplona but was defeated before Saragossa, and returned to France. During his retreat, his rear guard was ambushed by the wild Basque mountaineers, and among others a captain named Hruodland was slain. The 'Song of Roland' is not history, however. It is a heroic ballad, and dates from the middle of the eleventh century—more than two hundred years after the time of Charlemagne." [Jay Williams, "Author's Note," *The Tournament of the Lions*, Walck, 1960.[4]]

1966. First book written under the pseudonym Michael Delving was published. Williams wrote a total of seven books, all mysteries, using his pseudonym. "I seem to have several compartments. I was long known as a historical novelist, I have another following as a mystery-story writer under the name of Michael Delving, and I have written books for older children, such as *The Hawkstone* and *The Horn of Roland*. I get about a thousand letters a year from children for my science-fiction books: the Danny Dunn series, of which there are twelve. And I have written seventeen books for younger children. . . .

"Children often ask me whether any of the adventures in my books are 'real.' Some of them are: cave exploration with my son when he was younger resulted in *Danny Dunn and the Fossil Cave*; my long interest in archery produced one of my earliest novels. Having children and grandchildren makes for a built-in audience on which to test ideas, and my daughter always wanted books in which girls played an important part. . . .

"For younger children I've done any number of books in which girls are the tough and capable central characters. I've always loved magical tales and fairy tales. . . ."

1975. *Petronella*, one of Williams's numerous children's books was illustrated by the award-winning artist Friso Henstra. Williams commented on the artistic superiority of the illustrator: ". . . Friso did a wonderful job with that book. He did with all my stories he's illustrated. . . . There are people who adore him. . . . The ones who dislike him usually say he's too grotesque. Maybe . . . it's because Friso is really an artist—a sculptor primarily—who is well known and admired in his native Holland, where they realize he's working in the tradition that includes painters like Bosch and Dürer. They weren't realists or impressionists; they were painters of good and evil.

"If you look carefully at his pictures in my books, you'll see that his people aren't conventionally attractive. They're not pretty in any way, not cute. Friso is unrestrained with his giants and monsters. There's nothing quaint about them. They come from his own private store of images, and some adults find his images disturbing. I don't think many children do, not in the same way. They aren't threatened by them as some adults seem to be.

"Besides that, Friso designs the page as a work of art, decoratively rather than narratively. Remove the text and it's hard to follow the story and the details of the plot. You see that very well in *Petronella*. And you also see how brilliantly he works out the essential ideas behind the story: the outward appearances and inner realities. Look at the way he handles the Enchanter. He's holding a mask, and he's wearing a huge-brimmed hat that shades his face and hides his head, just as the enormous black cloak hides his body. You're not sure about this character. And Friso transforms him into an axe and a fish, and he's seen chasing Petronella almost menacingly. Then, right at the end, look, the Enchanter takes off the hat and throws away the mask, and he's revealed, the man beneath the surface, young, handsome. That's pure technical genius."[3]

Williams, a prolific writer, spent much of his time in England. He wrote many different kinds of books—historical novels, mysteries, nonfiction books for adults and young people, science-fiction stories, and books for young children. "Many of the children who write to me ask, 'Is it hard work being a writer?' The answer is yes—and no.

"It is very hard work thinking up ideas and getting a story to sound real. It is also hard work imagining just how people talk, and making them talk and move just the way you want them to, inside your head and then on paper. But it isn't hard work when you take pleasure in what you're doing—and I do. . . .

"I have been earning my living by writing books for thirty-three years. I have written sixty-six books of all kinds, for children of all ages and for grownups. I love reading, and I read a great deal, both adult books and children's books. Some of my favorites are *The Hobbit, Julie of the Wolves,* and *The Wind in the Willows.*

"I have been married for thirty-four years, and my wife and I enjoy traveling to other countries and living there. We have lived in a village in Connecticut since 1946, although nine of those years were spent living in a village in England, where our children went to school when they were young. I have built model trains and sailing ships, been a Cubmaster and director of an American Indian dance team, collected Chinese and Japanese paintings, and helped found a field archery club.

"But most of all, I like writing stories for children, who seem to have as much fun reading them as I have writing them." ["Meet Your Author: Jay Williams," *Cricket*, December, 1975.[5]]

July 12, 1978. Died of a heart attack in London, England. "For painters and writers and photographers alike, the essential problems are the same: first, to search for some statement that may be made about life, and then to find means to communicate it to someone else. Because this search cannot really be satisfied, restlessness is bound to be one of the characteristics of the artist."[2]

HOBBIES AND OTHER INTERESTS: Archery, fencing, Oriental art, traveling and living in other countries, building model ships.

FOR MORE INFORMATION SEE: Current Biography, H. W. Wilson, 1955; Jay Williams, *A Change of Climate,* Random House, 1956; *Christian Science Monitor,* April 22, 1965, November 3, 1976; *Saturday Review,* August 21, 1965, October 18, 1969; *Times Literary Supplement,* September 23, 1965, November 3, 1972; *New York Times Book Review,* November 7, 1965, November 5, 1972, March 10, 1974, October 24, 1976; *Book Week,* October 30, 1966; *America,* November 5, 1966; *New Yorker,* December 17, 1966; *Books & Bookmen,* December, 1967, January, 1977; *Observer,* December 3, 1967, December 7, 1975; *Antiquarian Bookman,* September 16, 1968; *Library Journal,* September, 1968, March 15, 1970; *Wall Street Journal,* November 12, 1968; *Social Education,* May, 1969; *Instructor,* December, 1969.

Horn Book, April, 1970, February, 1977; *Parents' Magazine,* June, 1970; *Booklist,* October 1, 1971; *Grade Teacher,* November, 1971; *McCall's,* January, 1973; *Apollo,* July, 1973; *Book World,* April 21, 1974, May 14, 1978, March 11, 1979; *Cricket,* December, 1975; John Wakeman, editor, *World Authors: 1950-1970,* H. W. Wilson, 1975; *The Writers Directory: 1976-1978,* St. Martin's Press, 1976; *Growing Point,* April, 1976; *Teacher,* April, 1976; *New York Times,* December 20, 1976; *Language Arts,* March, 1977; *Newsweek,* July 18, 1977; *Top of the News,* spring, 1978; *Times Educational Supplement,* August 11, 1978; *Reading Teacher,* October, 1978; D. L. Kirkpatrick, *Twentieth-Century Children's Writers,* St. Martin's Press, 1978; Doris de Montreville and Elizabeth D. Crawford, editors, *Fourth Book of Junior Authors and Illustrators,* H. W. Wilson, 1978.

Obituaries: *New York Times,* July 16, 1978; *Publishers Weekly,* July 24, 1978; *School Library Journal,* September, 1978; *Current Biography,* September, 1978; *Horn Book,* October, 1978; *AB Bookman's Weekly,* November 6, 1978.

WILLIAMS-ELLIS, (Mary) Amabel (Nassau Strachey) 1894-1984

OBITUARY NOTICE—See sketch in *SATA* Volume 29: Born May 10, 1894, in Newlands, near Guildford, England; died August 27, 1984. Editor and author of books for children and adults. Williams-Ellis served as the literary editor of *Spectator* from 1922 to 1923. A writer of varied interests, she was the author of over a dozen books for children, including *But We Know Better* Men Who Found Out: Stories of Great Scientific Discoverers, *How You Are Made,* and the six-volume history *Life in England.* She also retold numerous fairy and folk tales in more than ten books like *Fairies and Enchanters, Dragons and Princes. Fairy Tales from Round the World, Gypsy Folk Tales,* and *The Rain-God's Daughter, and Other African Fairy Tales.* Williams-Ellis wrote many adult books, including novels, short stories, biographies, and histories. She completed her memoirs, *All Stracheys Are Cousins,* the year before her death.

FOR MORE INFORMATION SEE: Contemporary Authors, Volume 105 Gale, 1982. *Obituaries: Times* (London), August 29, 1984; *AB Bookman's Weekly,* November 26, 1984.

WOHLBERG, Meg 1905-

PERSONAL Born February 6, 1905, in New York, N.Y.; daughter of Charles (a foreman) and Rose Wohlberg; married Jerome C. Eisenberg (a lawyer), June 14, 1974. *Education:* Attended Rochester/Eastman School of Art. *Home:* New York City.

CAREER: Illustrator.

WRITINGS: Little Bimbo and the Lion (self-illustrated), Holt, 1942; *Jody's Wonderful Day* (self-illustrated), Crown, 1945; (with M. Horn) *Toby's Trip* (self-illustrated), Macmillan, 1943. Also author of *Baby's Diary* published by Chilton.

MEG WOHLBERG

He hated being little. When the children painted pictures, he always drew the biggest ones. ▪ (From *The Smallest Boy in the Class* by Jerrold Beim. Illustrated by Meg Wohlberg.)

Illustrator: Helen Hoke and Miriam Teichner, *Fuzzy Kitten,* Messner, 1941; Clement C. Moore, *The Night Before Christmas,* Crown, 1944; Elizabeth De Huff, *Toodle's Baby Brother,* University of New Mexico Press, 1946; Jerrold Beim, *The Smallest Boy in the Class,* Morrow, 1949.

Marguerite Walters, *The Real Santa Claus,* Lothrop, 1950; Leon Harris, *Night Before Christmas—in Texas, That Is,* Lothrop, 1952; Catherine Wooley, *Lunch for Lennie,* Morrow, 1952; Alice E. Goudey, *Smokey, the Well Loved Kitten,* Lothrop, 1952; Jane Thayer (pseudonym of Catherine Wooley), *Where's Andy?,* Morrow, 1954; J. Thayer, *Sandy and the Seventeen Balloons,* Morrow, 1955; Marion Belden Cook, *Five Cents to See the Monkey,* Knopf, 1956; Adele DeLeeuw, *Donny, the Boy Who Made a Home for Animals,* Little, Brown, 1957; J. Thayer, *Andy Wouldn't Talk,* Morrow, 1958; Carolyn Wolcott, *God Gave Us Seasons,* Abingdon, 1958; Esphyr Slobodkina, *Billie,* Lothrop, 1959.

C. Wolcott, *God Made Me to Grow,* Abingdon, 1960; J. Thayer, *Andy and His Fine Friends,* Morrow, 1960; Dorry Van Den Honert, *Demi the Baby Sitter,* Morrow, 1961; Joseph Schrank, *Puppy in the Pet Shop,* Lothrop, 1961; C. Wolcott, *I Can Talk with God,* Abingdon, 1962; Paula Hendrich, *Baby in the Schoolroom,* Lothrop, 1962; J. Thayer, *Andy's Square Blue Animal,* Morrow, 1962; J. Thayer, *Andy and the Runaway Horse,* Morrow, 1963; Harry T. Peck, *Adventures of Mabel,* New York Graphic Society, 1963; Charlotte Pomerantz, *The*

Bear Who Couldn't Sleep, Morrow, 1965; Janice M. Udry, *Next Door to Laura Linda,* A. Whitman, 1965; J. Thayer, *Rockets Don't Go to Chicago, Andy,* Morrow, 1967; Bernice Hogan, *A Small Green Tree and a Square Brick Church,* Abingdon, 1967; Miriam E. Mason, *Matilda and Her Family,* Macmillan, 1967; J. Thayer, *A Contrary Little Quail,* Morrow, 1968; J. Thayer, *Andy and Mr. Cunningham,* Morrow, 1969.

"Getting to Know" series; all published by Coward: Jim Breetveld, *Getting to Know the United Nations Crusaders; How UNICEF Saves Children,* 1961, revised edition, 1970; Carl Taylor, . . . *Burma,* 1962; Ella Griffin, . . . *UNESCO: How U.N. Crusaders Fight Ignorance,* 1962; Grace Halsell, . . . *Peru,* 1964.

SIDELIGHTS: Although a love of books gave Wohlberg a strong desire to enter the field of book illustrating, her first job after art school was in advertising. "It seemed awful at the time but I have often been grateful for what I learned about basic problems of production, about working under direction, etc. Somewhere along the line the urge to become a children's book illustrator could no longer be suppressed. For a while my careers as advertising and book illustrator overlapped." [Lee Kingman and others, compilers, *Illustrators of Children's Books: 1957-1966,* Horn Book, 1968.[1]]

Wohlberg eventually was able to devote all her time to book illustration. She works in a studio in "a small . . . four-story New York City house with a garden. I live here with my husband, and always there is a pet or two. The house is one I remodelled myself."[1]

Wohlberg's works are included in the Kerlan Collection at the University of Minnesota.

FOR MORE INFORMATION SEE: Lee Kingman and others, compilers, *Illustrators of Children's Books: 1957-1966,* Horn Book, 1968.

WYETH, Betsy James 1921-

PERSONAL: Born September 26, 1921, in East Aurora, N.Y.; daughter of Merle Davis (a newspaper editor) and Amy Elizabeth (Browning) James; married Andrew Wyeth (an artist), May 15, 1940; children: Nicholas, James Browning. *Education:* Attended Colby Junior College. *Religion:* Protestant. *Home and office address:* Chadds Ford, Pa. 19317. *Agent:* Robert Lescher, 155 East 71st St., New York, N. Y. 10021.

WRITINGS: (Editor) *The Wyeths: The Letters of N. C. Wyeth, 1901-1945,* Gambit, 1971; *Wyeth at Kuerners,* Houghton, 1976; *The Stray* (juvenile; illustrated by Jamie Wyeth), Farrar, Straus, 1979; *The Art of Jamie Wyeth,* Houghton, 1980; *Christina's World,* Houghton, 1982.

SIDELIGHTS: Wyeth's books have drawn upon her family and her surroundings. Her first book, *The Wyeths: The Letters of N. C. Wyeth, 1901-1945,* was a collection of letters written by her father-in-law, Newell Convers Wyeth, the American illustrator and mural painter best known for his illustrations of numerous American classics such as *Treasure Island, Kidnapped,* and *Robin Hood.* "I was very young when I first met N. C. Wyeth, only seventeen. He seemed to me then a force to be challenged and overcome. I married his youngest son when I was eighteen, and together we lived under my father-in-law's shadow. 'The old days' were continually referred to: golden years, when the five Wyeth children were growing up together. And as I overheard these reminiscences, it was as if life itself had come to a finish, all excitement in living had gone, nothing new remained but the horror of World War II—and memories of past Christmases, past intimacies, past voices. I rebelled with all my being. The little schoolhouse my husband and I lived in, owned by my father-in-law, I repainted in the brightest colors I could dream up. And when 'Pa,' as we called him, came by each morning to deliver the mail, I could sense his disapproval. I knew that he and I would never really come to know each other, and between us stood his son,

Betsy James Wyeth with artist son, Jamie.

In a few minutes he had fallen again into a drunken sleep. ■ (From *The Stray* by Betsy James Wyeth. Illustrated by Jamie Wyeth.)

deeply devoted to his father and stimulated by the vitality of his young bride. Ever so gradually we built our life together. 'Pa' was left out. I was almost pleased when he failed to understand some of my husband's early attempts at tempera. Indeed, he could hardly, I felt, be expected to; he was bogged down in the *past*. Then one bright morning in Maine a neighbor came knocking at our door with a telephone message: 'Call home immediately!' I can even now hear the calm voice on the other end of the line from a million miles away: 'Pa was killed an hour ago.' If I could just once say to him, 'I'm sorry!' Perhaps this was my motivation while I worked on the manuscript.'' [Betsy James Wyeth, editor, *The Wyeths: The Letters of N. C. Wyeth, 1900-1945,* Gambit, 1971.]

Wyeth has also written books about her husband, Andrew, and son, Jamie, also famous American artists. Her children's book, *The Stray,* is set in the Wyeth family town of Chadds Ford, Pa. The characters in her story, however, are all animals, neatly humanized in a text that is accompanied with illustrations by Jamie Wyeth.

FOR MORE INFORMATION SEE: Atlantic, December, 1971, December, 1976; *Saturday Review,* December 11, 1971; Betsy James Wyeth, editor, *The Wyeths: The Letters of N. C. Wyeth, 1900-1945,* Gambit, 1971; *Nation,* January 24, 1972; *New York Review of Books,* December 9, 1976; *Washington Post Book World,* December 12, 1976.

CUMULATIVE INDEX TO
ILLUSTRATIONS AND AUTHORS

Illustrations Index

(In the following index, the number of the volume in which an illustrator's work appears is given *before* the colon, and the page on which it appears is given *after* the colon. For example, a drawing by Adams, Adrienne appears in Volume 2 on page 6, another drawing by her appears in Volume 3 on page 80, another drawing in Volume 8 on page 1, and another drawing in Volume 15 on page 107.)

YABC

Index citations including this abbreviation refer to listings appearing in *Yesterday's Authors of Books for Children,* also published by the Gale Research Company, which covers authors who died prior to 1960.

Author Index

The following index gives the number of the volume in which an author's biographical sketch, Brief Entry, or Obituary appears.

This index includes references to all entries in the following series, which are also published by Gale Research Company.

YABC—*Yesterday's Authors of Books for Children: Facts and Pictures about Authors and Illustrators of Books for Young People from Early Times to 1960*, Volumes 1-2

CLR—*Children's Literature Review: Excerpts from Reviews, Criticism, and Commentary on Books for Children*, Volumes 1-8

Author Index

Author Index

Y

Z